Summer Employment Directory of the United States 1992

Summer Employment Directory of the United States 1992

41st Edition

**Distributed in the U.K. and Europe
by Vacation Work
9 Park End Street, Oxford OX1 1HJ, England**

Peterson's Guides

Princeton, New Jersey

ISSN 0081-9352
ISBN 1-56079-119-5

Printed in the United States of America

10 9 8 7 6 5 4 3 2 1

Contents

How to Use This Book   7

Abbreviation Chart   9

How to Conduct a Successful Summer Job Search
by Sandra Schocket   11

Working for the Federal Government   19

**Foreign Applications for U.S. and Canadian
Summer Employment and Training**
by Robert M. Sprinkle   21

National Listings   25

State-by-State Listings   29

Category Index   239

Employer Index   248

How to Use This Book

What are you going to do to make this summer special? You already have a good start. *The Summer Employment Directory of the United States 1992* is an indispensable catalog of interesting and enriching summer work experiences for students, teachers, and anyone looking for summer employment. You'll find detailed, up-to-date information on approximately 15,000 jobs across the country—from counselors, instructors, and lifeguards to theater stage hands, wildlife guides, and office clerical workers—the list is endless. And many of these jobs require little or no previous experience.

There are many different ways you can use the *Summer Employment Directory* to find the right work opportunity. If your primary consideration is the geographic location of a job (for instance, you would like to spend the summer working near your hometown or in a particular area of the country), you can turn directly to the **State-By-State Listings,** where employers are listed alphabetically by state. Those employers with locations in more than one state are featured in the **National** section; be sure to check there for additional job openings throughout the country.

Another way you can put the *Summer Employment Directory* to work for you is by looking for jobs according to the kinds of services they provide. The opportunities in this book are divided into fourteen main areas as listed in the **Category Index** at the back of the book. If you know, for instance, that you want to work at a summer camp that specializes in physical disability programs, turn to the **Category Index** for a listing of all such camps that are featured in the book. Use the following list as your guide:

Business/Industry
Camps (academic, behavioral problems, development disabilities, general activities, horsemanship, learning disabilities, outdoor adventure/travel, performing arts, physical disabilities, religious, special needs, sports, visual impairment)
Conference Centers
Conservation/Environmental Programs
Expeditions, Guide Trips, Tours
Government
Hotels/Motels
National Parks
Ranches
Resorts
Restaurants
Summer Schools
Summer Theaters
Theme/Amusement Parks

Of course, if you already know the name of the employer you want to contact, you can simply turn to the **Employer Index** for a page reference to the description of that employer's jobs.

Once you have found an employer that interests you, you can read about the opportunities they provide. The **General Information** section of each profile provides you with details about the location, size, focus, and special features of the facility. You can check the **Profile of Summer Employees** to see if you fit the profile of the average employee and get an idea of who your coworkers might be. **Employment Information** includes descriptions of the jobs that are available from the employer as well as the important details of when openings are available, salaries, and special requirements for a particular position. Any **Benefits** of the workplace, such as gratuities, laundry facilities, health insurance, or the possibility of college credit, are also noted. The **Contact** paragraph provides you with helpful information on how the employer wants you to apply for a position and the application deadline. Finally, most of the employers have chosen to write an additional narrative description of the kinds of employees they are looking for; you can get a good "feel" for many of the facilities from these statements.

The data in this book were collected in the spring and summer of 1991 from employers anxious to fill staff vacancies with high-quality, motivated workers. A representative of each employer completed a survey in which they described the job opportunities they will offer in the summer of 1992. Although Peterson's does not assume responsibility for the hiring policies or actions of these employers, we believe the information listed is accurate and up-to-date.

The *Summer Employment Directory* also features three essays that will provide additional help in your search for a summer job. If you are just learning how to apply for a summer job, be sure to read "How to Conduct a Successful Summer Job Search" on page 11. You may also want to learn more about "Working for the Federal Government" on page 19. Foreign job hunters are urged to read "Foreign Applications for U.S. and Canadian Summer Employment and Training" on page 21.

Remember, even in these days of high unemployment, all the employers listed in this book are actively looking for help—they are waiting for your application. We hope this book will help make your summer a fun, interesting, and profitable experience.

Abbreviation Chart

The following are abbreviations commonly used in the book.

ACA	American Camping Association
ALS	Advanced Life Saving
ARC	American Red Cross
BUNAC	British University North American Club
CAA	Camp Archery Association
CHA	Camp Horsemanship Association
CIT	Counselor-in-training
CPR	Cardiopulmonary Resuscitation
EMR	Educationally Mentally Retarded
EMT	Emergency Medical Technician
EOE	Equal Opportunity Employer
HSA	Horsemanship Safety Association
ICCP	International Camp Counselors Program
IDC	Instructor Development Center
LD	Learning Disabled
LPN	Licensed Practical Nurse
NAUI	National Association of Underwater Instructors
NRA	National Rifle Association
PADI	Professional Association of Diving Instructors
RN	Registered Nurse
SASE	Self-addressed, stamped envelope
SCI	Small Craft Instructor
SLS	Senior Life Saving
WSI	Water Safety Instructor

How to Conduct a Successful Summer Job Search

by Sandra Schocket

July 2, 1992

Dear Bill,

> *The campers have gone off to their tennis lessons, so I finally have some time to write. My job search really paid off. This camp is beautiful! Jenny, my co-counselor, is from St. Louis, and so far we get along fine. We have 8 really cute ten-year-olds in our cabin. I'm a general counselor, which means I go with the kids to all their activities—except for tennis, because the instructor doesn't want me around. Even the food here is good, or maybe it's all this outdoor activity that's making me extra hungry. Well, have to go. Would you believe I am pitching a softball game?*
> *Hope you have found a job by now.*

Love,
Suzy

Next summer, will you be Suzy or Bill? Will you conduct an organized job search or go out at the last minute to find what's left? For most students, a summer job is a necessity. Students by the thousands head to camps, resorts, stores, restaurants, and offices. They babysit, mow lawns, pump gas, paint houses, and run their own businesses.

Whether your goal is to earn career-related credentials or next year's tuition, your summer job search should be serious business. Conducting a well-planned job campaign can make the difference between getting the job you want and settling for what's available.

Job hunting may seem to be a bewildering process to people who don't do it very often or haven't done it before. Following a simple plan can help you to organize your effort and gain valuable job-hunting skills.

The first step

Start by asking yourself some questions:

1. *What do I want to do and where do I want to do it?*
   If ideas don't come immediately to mind, seek some help.
   * Visit your college or school placement office—summer job listings are posted

---

Sandra Schocket is a career consultant and freelance writer whose articles have appeared in major magazines and newspapers. She is the author of the book Summer Jobs: Finding Them, Getting Them, Enjoying Them.

as early as January. Make an appointment with a counselor to discuss your summer job plans.
- Go to the library. Your college library and large public libraries have newspapers on file. Look at summer help-wanted advertisements for this summer and also for last year. Many places have the same openings each year. Ask the librarian to point out helpful reference materials as well as summer job guidebooks such as this one.
- Ask your teachers for recommendations. They often know of openings in their field.
- Talk to friends, relatives, and neighbors. Ask them to refer you to people they know.

Once you have an idea of what you want to do, deciding where is the next step. Do you want to live away from home or find a job in your hometown? Do you have a car, or will you need to use public transportation? Defining your geographic limits may rule out some of your job choices and add others.

2. *How much will I need to earn?*

By now you are beginning to learn that these considerations are all related. A job away from home might be fun but will enough money be left after paying the rent? A solution may be to look for a job that includes room and board. Jobs at resorts, on cruise ships, at camps, and as mothers' helpers offer opportunities for living away from home. Finding a well-paying career-related job may be your goal. Many students are able to get such experience each summer. Fields most likely to offer well-paying jobs are engineering, computer science, accounting, general business, math, and science. If you cannot find a paying job in your field, consider working as an unpaid intern. Jobs in the media are frequently unpaid but are also much sought after. Students who take these jobs often earn money working in stores and restaurants. Combining paid and unpaid jobs will help you to gain experience in your field as well as income for college expenses.

3. *What are my skills?*

The next step is to identify your marketable skills. Most people have many more skills than they realize. Skills can be specific, such as knowing a particular word-processing system, or general, such as planning, organizing, and managing. Perhaps your skills include music, sports, or writing. To analyze your skills, think of some jobs you have done or projects you have completed. List the skills that you used to accomplish these tasks. As an example, your skills analysis might look something like this:

SUZY CLARK

Intramural sports coordinator
Managed intramural sports program for three dormitories that involved five sports and over 150 participants.

Skills used
management
organization

ability to get along with different types of people
working well under pressure
creativity
administrative: making room arrangements, hiring
     officials (umpires, referees)
financial: working within a budget, arranging for
     payments for workers and equipment
ability to meet deadlines
listening
leadership
persuading
ability to work with students and administrators

Repeat this exercise, choosing one or two more jobs and the skills you used to complete each one. Your "jobs" could include volunteer work and college activities.

To match your skills to potential summer jobs, analyze want-ads, look at job listings, ask people about what they do, and read career guides in the library. Look at job descriptions in this directory. You will gain an understanding of skills needed for various jobs. Go through your skills list and circle the skills that will qualify you for jobs that you would like to do. These are the skills you can promote in your resume and cover letter and talk about in your interview.

Suzy Clark's job objective is to be a senior camp counselor. By analyzing her previous experience, she was able to identify skills important for that position.

Job objective: senior counselor/group leader

Skills
   management
   ability to get along with different types of people
   working well under pressure
   creativity
   listening
   leadership
   persuading
   ability to work with students and administrators
   sports abilities: field hockey, basketball, swimming

Other skills
   experience working with children
   customer service experience
   supervisory experience in a camp

The Resume

After you have done your research and have identified some job interests, you are ready to write a resume. You might wonder if a resume is always necessary for a summer job. For some jobs, a resume will be a requirement. For many others, an application will do. Even when a resume is not necessary, attaching one offers you the opportunity to tell employers what you want them to know about you, not just what the application asks for.

WRITING YOUR RESUME

Remember, your resume is not your autobiography. It is a brief advertisement of your experience and abilities. Its purpose is to get you an interview. Include only information that will stimulate an employer's interest.

Your resume should include:

1. *Name, address, and telephone number.* If you live away from home, include both your temporary and permanent addresses.
2. *Job objective.* Tell an employer what job you are applying for; do not expect someone to figure this out for you. If you have several different jobs in mind, make up different resumes with a separate job objective for each one.
3. *Education.* Include the name and location of your college, your major, and your GPA if it is at least 3.0. Include honors, awards, and scholarships.
4. *Experience.* List previous summer and part-time positions and the year in which you held them. Include the name and city of the employer, your job title, and a few brief phrases about what you did. Of course, the best experience is a job related to your job objective, but don't worry if you don't have it. Employers also look for experience that shows you are mature, hardworking, and responsible.
5. *Activities.* This category is very important. Include teams, clubs, and civic involvement. List any offices you have held. If you have few or no activities because you work, indicate this under *Personal.* (For example, "Work 30 hours a week while attending school full-time.")
6. *Skills.* Include foreign languages, computer skills, and any other skills that are relevant to the job you are seeking. Include certifications and licenses. List only skills that you do very well and can discuss in an interview.
7. *Personal.* Information such as health, age, religion, race, and national origin are normally omitted from resumes. Employers may ask for them only if they are valid job requirements. For example, a bartender must be over 21. Only members of a minority group may be eligible for certain affirmative action programs. Include such information only if it will help you to get the job.

Do not include the names and addresses of references on your resume. Make a separate list, and offer them if they are requested.

PRODUCING YOUR RESUME

Typing and printing a resume used to be time-consuming and expensive. The word-processor has changed all that. By writing your resume on a word-processor and storing it on a computer disk, you can do a professional job quickly and easily. You can even design different resumes and change them to meet your needs.

Whether produced on a computer or typewriter, your resume should be neat, attractive, and preferably one page long. Use white, beige, or gray 8½" x 11" paper. Make your resume visually interesting by varying the size of the type and using capital letters for your name and category headings. Bold type and underlining will highlight areas you want to emphasize, such as your previous job titles. Use broad margins at the top, bottom, and sides so that your information will stand out on the page. If you are in a field such as art or architecture, you can incorporate drawings or a design into your resume. For most jobs, however, gimmicks are not appropriate and will not help you obtain an interview.

SUZANNE CLARK

123 Elm Street   39 Lakeside Hall
Concord, MA 02217   State University
508-555-1234   Oak Hill, MA 02718
                                                           315-777-2222

OBJECTIVE: Summer job as senior counselor or group director

EDUCATION: State University, Oak Hill, MA—B.A. 1993
                             Major: Psychology, GPA 3.1

HONORS: Dean's List, 3 semesters
                             President's Scholarship

EXPERIENCE: Intramural athletic coordinator, 1991–1992
                             State University, Oak Hill, MA
                             Planned and administered athletic program for
                             three dormitories and five sports.
                             Managed publicity, recruited players, worked
                             with students and administrators.
                             Arranged for room space, hired and paid
                             officials, kept budget.

                             Hostess, Summer 1991
                             Grand Lake Lodge, Adirondack, NY
                             Greeted guests, made reservations, coordinated
                             schedules of servers.
                             Position involved steady contact with customers
                             in a high-volume tourist setting.

                             Counselor, Summer 1990
                             Woodlands YMCA Day Camp, Concord, MA
                             Supervised group activities for campers in 9–12
                             age group.
                             Taught volleyball and basketball to girls.
                             Participated in production of camp play.
                             Led nature hikes, assisted in overnight trips.

ACTIVITIES: Varsity field hockey, 1989–1991
                             Freshman senate representative, 1989
                             Downtown soup kitchen volunteer, 1989–1992
                             Big Sister/Little Sister volunteer, 1992

SKILLS: Fluent French; ability to coach field hockey and
                             volleyball.
                             Computer skills: IBM, MS-DOS, Wordperfect.
                             CPR and first aid certificates.

The cover letter

You will need a cover letter to accompany your resume when you answer a help-wanted advertisement, write to a referral, or respond to the jobs listed in this book. Your cover letter is your opportunity to sell yourself to an employer. Be enthusiastic. Tell the employer how you heard about the job and how your skills and experience will fit. Say when you will be available for an interview.

Type your cover letter on 8½" x 11" stationery or plain white paper. When possible, address it to an individual. You can find out the name of the person you should write to by calling the employer and asking for the name and title of the person who does the hiring. This book provides that information for you. Double check for typing and spelling errors. In resumes and cover letters, accuracy and neatness are essential.

SUZANNE CLARK

123 Elm Street
Concord, MA 02217
508-555-1234

39 Lakeside Hall
State University
Oak Hill, MA 02718
315-777-2222

March 1, 1992

Janet Tyler, Camp Director
Camp Tippecanoe
Country Lane
Tippecanoe, ME 02123

Dear Ms. Tyler:

While seeking out summer job opportunities in the State University job placement office, I saw your listing for a group activity leader. My part-time job as intramural athletics coordinator and my previous camping experience make me a qualified candidate for such a position.

All of my previous jobs have included administrative duties and customer service. My supervisors have praised me for my ability to combine both functions. I would love to continue to use and improve these skills at Camp Tippecanoe this summer.

The camp as described in your advertisement sounds like a place where children can learn and grow. I know that I have the ability to make a contribution to your program, and I am especially looking forward to spending a summer in Maine. In two weeks I will be on spring break and would love to have the opportunity to discuss the job with you. I will call you to arrange a time.

Thank you, and I look forward to meeting you soon.

Sincerely,

Suzanne Clark

Applying for jobs

With your resume complete, you are ready to apply. Use this directory to find employers looking for your talents. Answer help-wanted advertisements in the newspaper. Get referrals from your college placement office. Go to local businesses. Call any sources that you spoke with earlier. Speak to teachers, friends, relatives, and neighbors. Develop a network of people who can help you to identify leads and find a job.

Interviewing

If your resume, application, or telephone appeal impresses an employer, you will be invited for an interview. The purpose of the interview is to see if there is a match between your abilities and the employer's needs. If you have time, prepare for the interview by getting some information about what the employer wants. You may be able to find information in the library or from someone who works there.

Remember, first impressions are lasting impressions. Whether applying to a neighborhood store or a major corporation, dress neatly and appropriately (no sneakers, T-shirts, or jeans, even if they may be standard attire once you get the job).

QUICK TIPS FOR INTERVIEWING
- Greet the interviewer with a smile and a firm handshake.
- Maintain eye contact with the interviewer throughout the interview.
- Even if you are nervous, try to appear eager and enthusiastic.
- Answer questions honestly and don't be afraid to admit you don't know something.
- Ask questions. "Who will I report to?" "What will a typical day be like?"
- At the end of the interview, ask what the next step will be and when you will hear from them.

Following through

Follow up your interview with a thank-you note, repeating your interest in the job. Don't wait to hear from one employer before applying to others. Until you have a firm offer, keep applying.

Summer Employment Directory 1992 is your guide to openings in camps, theme parks, resorts, government agencies, and many other settings throughout the country. Write or call to let them know you are interested. Be persistent and don't get discouraged. A productive summer will be your reward.

Working for the Federal Government

The federal government offers summer jobs requiring education and skills ranging from none to a Ph.D. However, the first page of a booklet published annually by the U.S. Office of Personnel Management—"Summer Jobs: Opportunities in the Federal Government," hereafter called Announcement No. 414—carries this stern warning: "Opportunities are **extremely limited.** The number of summer jobs available is relatively small in comparison to the large number of applicants. Therefore, you should not limit your efforts to obtain summer work solely with the Federal Government."

If you are employed by the government, you can have the opportunity to gain valuable professional experience in your summer months as well as earn a salary. You could be a biological or engineering aid for the Department of Agriculture; a computer assistant with the National Science Foundation; or a management analyst with the Department of Labor.

Other positions offer outdoor work. The National Park Service, for example, has openings for park rangers as well as for technicians in such areas as wildlife management and recreation. Other government departments have openings for legal interns, veterinary trainees, and writers/editors.

To obtain information—deadline dates, forms needed, positions open—get a copy of Announcement No. 414 from any Federal Job Information Center (FJIC). (Note: Each FJIC area center also includes with Announcement No. 414 a supplement of additional jobs in its jurisdiction that are not listed in the general announcement, so contact the FJIC office nearest the location where you would like to work. Copies of No. 414 for summer 1992 will be available in January 1992.)

Most summer jobs with the federal government require United States citizenship, and applicants must file the appropriate forms with each agency where they wish to be considered for summer employment. Standard Form SF-171, Personal Qualifications Statement and OPM Form 1170/17, List of College Courses and Certificate of Scholastic Achievement (to be completed when applying for jobs based on education), may be obtained from the FJIC Centers or any OPM area office.

Some federal jobs require applicants to apply as early as January. Late applications are never accepted. You may apply directly for jobs in some government agencies, and you can find a list of these in booklet No. 414.

The Office of Personnel Management has classified government summer jobs into five groups. Jobs in Group I are mostly clerical positions on the level GS-1 through GS-4. Jobs in Group II, which are also in grades GS-1 through GS-4, involve technical or nonclerical work. Most of these jobs require some related education and/or experience.

Jobs in Group III are in grades GS-5 and above and involve technical, professional, and administrative work. To be considered for these positions, you must be a college graduate, a graduate student or be planning to attend graduate school, or a faculty member or possess the equivalent in experience or a combination of education and experience related to the position for which you are applying.

Group IV positions are for trades and labor jobs. This group includes such jobs as printing plant worker, animal caretaker, and carpenter's helper.

Group V covers the Summer Employment Program for Needy Youth (Summer Aid Program), which provides summer jobs for young people from low-income families and for youths who need income from summer jobs in order to return to school in the fall. To apply, contact your local State Employment Service. If there is no State Employment Service office in your area, contact any Federal Job Information Center for information on referral procedures.

Persons with disabilities should investigate special application procedures by contacting the selective placement coordinator of the agency where they desire work.

Foreign Applications for U.S. and Canadian Summer Employment and Training

by Robert M. Sprinkle

In an effort to be as accurate as possible on job information for students from outside the United States, we have specifically asked each employer whether he or she is interested in receiving applications from foreign students coming to the United States for the summer and is willing to fill out *and* submit all the required government forms to enable the student to obtain the proper visa. If an employer in the United States does offer you a job, make certain that he or she has obtained and filed the correct forms *before* you come to the U.S. Working with an improper visa (including work while waiting for a change to be granted one) can be cause for arrest and detention by the U.S. Immigration and Naturalization Service. A student *cannot* arrange a proper visa alone—there must be an American sponsor to take care of the necessary paperwork on behalf of the individual. Also, you are responsible for obtaining your passport before leaving for the United States.

Visas

As a *general rule,* there are only three U.S. visas that are suitable for students coming to the United States for summer employment/training:

H-2 "Temporary Worker"
   The procedures for this visa require a 2-step process to be followed by the employer. First, a "labor certification" must be secured through the state employment service of the area where the individual will work. Following rules established by the U.S. Department of Labor, the employer must submit evidence to demonstrate that: (a) a real job exists (i.e., not a job made up to suit the background of the foreign national); (b) that substantial efforts have been made to fill the job with a U.S. citizen; and (c) that no qualified U.S. citizens have applied for the job. Once the "labor certification" has been granted, the employer must then file an application with the U.S. Immigration and Naturalization Service District Office covering the area where the person will work.

H-3 "Industrial Trainee"
   This visa does not require a "labor certification." The employer must submit the H-3 application to the Immigration Service District Office covering the area where

Robert M. Sprinkle is the Executive Director, Association for International Practical Training, Inc., and has written numerous articles on international practical training, overseas employment, and student travel.

the person will work. The application must include a detailed training plan to show what the trainee will do in the United States, including how much time will be spent in "classroom and other instruction" and how much time will be devoted to "on-the-job" work. The application must also provide information to show why the individual cannot receive suitable or similar training in his or her own country.

J-1 "Exchange Visitor"

The J-1 visa may be used only by individuals who are participants in educational programs that have been specifically approved by the U.S. Information Agency. There are eight different J-1 categories, each with its own specific rules and regulations. Approved "Exchange Visitor Programs" are granted only to U.S. sponsoring organizations such as government agencies, schools, hospitals, and private educational exchange organizations. Each sponsor is granted a specific "program description"—a short statement that specifically mentions those activities permitted for participants in the sponsor's specific program.

Of the eight J-1 categories, *only* the "trainee" category is suitable for foreign students coming to the United States for paid practical training. The number of sponsors having J-1 programs that permit practical training employment is extremely limited. The International Association of Students in Economics and Business Management (AIESEC), 841 Broadway, Suite 608, New York, NY 10003; and the IAESTE Trainee Program (The International Association for the Exchange of Students for Technical Experience), c/o Association for International Practical Training, 10400 Little Patuxent Parkway, Suite 250, Columbia, MD 21044-3510, are the two principal trainee exchange organizations for students. The maximum length of practical training time permitted any one person (regardless of the number of sponsors or employers) is 18 months.

There are also a small number of J-1 authorizations for summer "work-travel" programs. An example is the authorization granted to the Council on International Educational Exchange (205 East 42nd Street, New York, NY 10017), which is the cooperating organization for the BUNAC (British Universities North American Club) summer work program. The summer work-travel programs do permit students to work at any job they may find. However, the J-1 authorizations are not for practical training or for summer camp positions. There are important restrictions: (a) the work experience must occur during the "summer" (November–February, for students from the Southern Hemisphere) with no extensions permitted; and (b) changes to either another J-1 sponsor or to some other type of visa are not permitted.

A third type of J-1 authorization covers placement in summer camps for camp-counselor experience. An example is the authorization granted to the International Camp Counselor Program of the YMCA (356 West 34th Street, 3rd Floor, New York, NY 10001). Such placements are limited to approximately eight weeks and must be for genuine counseling/teaching assignments. Placement in office, kitchen, or custodial jobs is not permitted.

If an employer's applications for either an H-2 or H-3 visa are successful, the District Office of the Immigration and Naturalization Service will advise the U.S. Embassy in the student's country. The student can then secure the visa and travel to the U.S. In the case of the J-1 visa, the sponsoring organization that has agreed to include the student issues a U.S. government document called an IAP-66 (a "Certificate of Eligibility"). The IAP-66 is sent to the student to use to apply for the J-1 visa in his or her country. Upon entering the U.S., the admitting Immigration Inspector issues a Form I-94 (Arrival/Departure Record) on which is noted the specific visa granted and the date when the "Permit-to-Stay" expires. Admission to the United States in the H-2, H-3, or Trainee category of the J-1 visa with such status being noted on the Form I-94 is the only documentation needed for the student to proceed to the work place and take up the assignment.

Employment eligibility verification

A law was passed in 1986 that requires all U.S. employers to examine documentation proving that persons hired after November 6, 1986 (the date the law came into effect) are either citizens of the United States or non-citizens legally authorized for employment during their stay in the United States.

Essentially, the law requires that within three business days after a person is hired, the employer must *physically examine* documentation that (1) establishes proof of the new employee's identify; and (2) establishes that the person is either a U.S. citizen or is a non-citizen who has the legal right to be employed in the United States. The law and the related regulations, administered by the U.S. Immigration and Naturalization Service (INS), require that a record of the verification process be maintained in the employer's files for a period of three years after the date of hiring. For this purpose, the INS has developed the I-9 Form, which the Service began distributing in May 1987.

Virtually all kinds of employment are covered, from a full-time job with a large employer such as IBM to mowing grass on a regular basis for your next door neighbor. Certainly, *all* of the jobs listed in the *Summer Employment Directory 1992* will require you and your employer to complete the I-9 form. The I-9 form is in two parts. The top half must be filled out by the employee—you. You then present the form, together with your documentation, to your employer, who will complete the bottom half of the form.

Full-time foreign students

Individuals enrolled at U.S. colleges and universities for full-time academic study are usually admitted on the basis of the F-1 (Student), M-1 (Student), or Student category of the J-1 visa. In each case, practical training *after* completion of the study program and award of a certificate or degree is possible—up to twelve months for the F-1 student, up to six months for the M-1 student, and up to eighteen months for the student category of the J-1 visa. Under certain circumstances—such as enrollment in a "cooperative education" program—employment *before* graduation is also possible for the F-1 and J-1 students, but *not* for the M-1 students. In *all* cases, whether before or after graduation and whether on the F-1, M-1, or student category of the J-1 visa, the student remains under the legal sponsorship of the U.S. college or university concerned. Thus, assistance with proper arrangements for periods of employment *must* be sought from the foreign-student adviser of the student's school.

Canadian citizens

SED also lists jobs in Canada. As in the United States, foreign workers are permitted to enter Canada to take seasonal jobs only when the jobs cannot be filled by Canadian citizens or legal residents. The number of aliens given authorization to work varies somewhat from province to province.

A job offer from a Canadian employer must be presented by the employer to the nearest Canada Employment Center (CEC) office. If the CEC agrees that no qualified Canadian resident is available to fill the job, the Canadian office nearest your home will be notified. That office will contact you and ask you to come in to be interviewed and to apply for Employment Authorization. The interview will determine if you are qualified for the job and if you may enter Canada temporarily under Canada's immigration laws. You will be required to pass a medical examination should the job be in the food services area.

If you application is approved, you will receive a visa and an Employment Authorization to cover the particular job for a predetermined amount of time. The Employment Authorization must be issued before you enter Canada; you will not be allowed to enter Canada to look for a job. In all but a few exceptional cases, persons who have entered Canada already on a visitor's visa will not be able to obtain authorization to work. For more information, contact the nearest Canadian consulate.

In conclusion

Most countries of the world have very strict regulations regarding employment for noncitizens in order to protect job opportunities for their own citizens. The United States is no different from other countries, especially in periods of high unemployment. What is different, however, is the U.S. system of visas and the rules and regulations that apply to each type (and subtype) of visa. The process of securing a proper visa takes a good deal of time (sometimes as long as four to six months) and can often be frustrating. Thus, it is wise to contact prospective employers as early as possible so that the employer has sufficient time to undertake the paperwork involved. If you have applied to or have been accepted by an organization such as AIESEC or IAESTE, make that fact known to the employer as each sponsoring organization has its own internal procedures that must be followed. With careful advance preparation, the complexities of the U.S. visa system can be handled.

National Listings

FOCUS EDUCATIONAL PROGRAMS

General Information Precollege programs (credit/noncredit courses) and full recreation/ sightseeing on college campuses in the United States. Campuses visited are Tufts, Emory, Pepperdine, and American University. Established 1983. Operated by Focus Educational Services, Inc. Affiliated with American Camping Association, Independent Counselors' Association, Better Business Bureau. Features include location near major cultural centers in diverse parts of the nation–Boston, Atlanta, Malibu, Washington, D.C.

Profile of Summer Employees Total number 90; average age 26. Employees are 50% female, 10% minorities, 10% college students, 10% international.

Employment Information Openings are from June 23 to August 12. Year-round positions also offered. College credit possible. Jobs available: 20 *academic instructors* with teacher certification at $600–$2400 per season; 20 *residence counselors* with a minimum age of 21 at $600–$1200 per season. International students encouraged to apply.

Benefits Preemployment training, on-the-job training, formal ongoing training, on-site room and board at no charge, laundry facilities, ample time off to explore, nearby cultural center.

Contact Applicant should send resume or write for application by April 30 to Carole Rydell, Administrative Assistant, Focus Educational Programs, Department SED, P.O. Box 120, Short Hills, New Jersey 07078; 201-467-1770, fax 201-376-5793.

This is an opportunity to begin the task of learning the craft of teaching in a boarding-school atmosphere. It allows veteran teachers to create their own course and to teach in their own manner. Students are entering grades 9–12.

STRAW HAT AUDITIONS

General Information Provides casting and staff-hiring sessions for several dozen non-Equity summer theaters and theme parks across the United States. Established 1979. Owned by Strut and Fret, Inc. Features include auditions held in New York City in March and Los Angeles in April.

Profile of Summer Employees Total number 300. Employees are 50% female, 1% minorities, 5% high school students, 25% college students, 20% local residents.

Employment Information Openings are from June 1 to August 31. Year-round positions also offered. Jobs available: *professional designers (sets, lights, costumes); stage technicians; lighting crew; costume crew; carpenters; box office staff; publicity directors; non-Equity stage managers and assistants; sound or lighting board operators; musical directors.* International students encouraged to apply.

Contact Applicant should write for application by March 1 to Straw Hat Auditions, Department SED, P.O. Box 1226, Port Chester, New York 10573-8226.

Auditions are competitive, and only a limited number of applicants are accepted. Requirements for performers include substantial performing experience in school, college, and local or professional theaters. Recommendation by a faculty member is required for *student applications. There is $40 application fee if an applicant is accepted for an audition. The interview fee for staff technicians is only $15. Send a business-size, self-addressed, stamped envelope to receive an application for an audition or interview. Please note on the outside of the envelope whether a "Performer Interview" or "Staff Interview" is requested. Do not pay the fee or send any materials until you have received your official application form. No application will be sent without the required SASE. Telephone requests cannot be honored.*

SUPERCAMP

General Information   Residential ten-day program for teens that includes life skills and academic courses designed to build self-confidence and lifelong learning skills. Established 1981. Owned by Bobbi DePorter. Affiliated with American Camping Association. Features include ropes course; dining hall; dorm rooms; sessions held on beautiful college campuses in six states (Florida, Massachusetts, Illinois, Texas, Washington, California).
Profile of Summer Employees   Total number 250; average age 25. Employees are 50% female, 65% college students. Requires nonsmokers.
Employment Information   Openings are from June to August. Jobs available: 20 *instructors* with teaching experience and college graduate status at $750–$2250 per season; 20 *directors* with presentation skills and college graduate status at $1500–$4500 per season; 10 *counselors* with counseling degree at $1000–$3000 per season; 10 *nurses* with RN license at $1000–$3000 per season; 150 *team leaders* with high school graduate status and an age between 18–25 at $500–$1000 per season; 125 *classroom coordinators* with high school graduate status (minimum age 18) at $500–$1000 per season.
Benefits   Preemployment training, on-the-job training, on-site room and board at no charge, laundry facilities, travel reimbursement.
Contact   Applicant should call for information by April 15 to Human Resources Director, SuperCamp, Department SED, 1725 South Hill Street, Oceanside, California 92054; 800-527-5321, fax 619-722-3507.

   SuperCamp employees have the opportunity to work with fun and exciting new friends from across the country while gaining outstanding communication and leadership skills. Staff members have the chance to support teens through powerful, life-changing experiences, and to become familiar with new accelerated-learning techniques.

WILDLIFE CAMPS

General Information   Coeducational, residential camp offering environmental education programs for youngsters ages 9–17. Established 1971. Owned by National Wildlife Federation. Affiliated with American Camping Association. Features include two locations: Hendersonville, North Carolina, and Jamestown, Colorado; views of the Blue Ridge Mountains or Rocky Mountains; miles of hiking trails; rock-climbing and rapelling wall; volleyball and recreation field; waterfront; comfortable cabins.
Profile of Summer Employees   Total number 45; average age 23. Employees are 40% female, 1% minorities, 95% college students, 1% international, 3% local residents. Prefers nonsmokers.
Employment Information   Openings are from June 1 to August 25. College credit possible. Jobs available: 30 *counselors/instructors* with outdoor education experience and first

aid certification at $1200–$1600 per season; 12 *backpacking leaders* with trip-leading experience and first aid certification at $1200 per season; 1 *waterfront supervisor* with WSI certification at $1100 per season; 2 *nurses* with RN license at $3000 per season.

Benefits On-the-job training, on-site room and board at no charge, laundry facilities, health insurance.

Contact Applicant should write for application or call for information by February 15 to Susan Johnson, Manager, Youth Programs, Wildlife Camps, 1400 16th Street, NW, Washington, D.C. 20036; 800-432-6564, fax 703-442-7332.

Staff members at Wildlife Camps gain professional experience working at the nation's largest conservation/education organization. The summer camp program received presidential recognition for its distinctive emphasis on environmental education.

State-by-State Listings

Alabama

NATIONAL PARK SERVICE

Contact Applicant should write for application (must be 18 by May 13; U.S. citizenship required) to Regional Office of the National Park Service, Southeast Region, National Park Service, 75 Spring Street, SW, Atlanta, Georgia 30303.

Jobs are located in Alabama at the following facilities: Horseshoe Bend National Military Park, Natchez Trace Parkway, Russell Cave National Monument, Tuskegee Institute National Historic Site. Also see District of Columbia listing.

Alaska

ALASKAN WILDERNESS OUTFITTING COMPANY, INC.
P.O. Box 1516
Cordova, Alaska 99574

General Information Fishing lodges and floatplane tours of Alaska. Established 1984. Owned by Pat Magie, Tom and Katie Prijatel. Affiliated with Alaska Visitors' Association. Located 150 miles southeast of Anchorage. Features include fishing; beautiful scenery; wilderness; wildlife.

Profile of Summer Employees Total number 15; average age 22. Employees are 25% female, 75% college students. Prefers nonsmokers.

Employment Information Openings are from May 1 to October 15. Jobs available: 8 *fishing guides* with knowledge of sport fishing at $1200–$1600 per month; 4 *camp cooks* at $1200–$1600 per month; 2 *general laborers* at $800–$1200 per month; 2 *assistant cooks* at $800–$1200 per month.

Benefits On-the-job training, on-site room and board at no charge, laundry facilities.

Contact Applicant should send resume by April 15 to Pat Magie, President, Alaskan Wilderness Outfitting Company, Inc., P.O. Box 1516, Cordova, Alaska 99574; 907-424-5552.

AMERICAN & PACIFIC TOURS, INC. (A&P)
West Fifth Avenue and K Street, Suite 434
Anchorage, Alaska 99510

General Information Japanese land operator for Japanese tourists that provides planned, individualized, and special guided trips. Established 1972. Owned by Keizo Sugimoto. Affiliated with Alaska Visitors' Association, Anchorage Convention and Visitors' Bureau,

Alaska Sportfishing Association. Features include endless hours of daylight; good employers; opportunity to see and learn new things about Alaska; opportunity to practice Japanese; beautiful scenery and wildlife.

Profile of Summer Employees   Total number 8; average age 23. Employees are 50% female, 50% minorities.

Employment Information   Openings are from May 20 to September 15. Spring break, Christmas break positions also offered. Jobs available: 8 *tour guides* with current driver's license and fluency in Japanese at $1300 per month. International students encouraged to apply.

Benefits   On-the-job training, travel reimbursement.

Contact   Applicant should send resume by April 30 to Keizo Sugimoto, President, American & Pacific Tours, Inc. (A&P), P.O. Box 10-1068, Anchorage, Alaska 99510; 907-272-9401, fax 907-272-0251.

BRISTOL BAY LODGE
P.O. Box 1509
Dillingham, Alaska 99576

General Information   Wilderness sportfishing lodge catering to 20 anglers per week. Established 1972. Owned by Ron and Maggie McMillan. Affiliated with Trout Unlimited, Federation of Fly Fishermen, Audubon Society, Nature Conservancy. Located 350 miles west of Anchorage on 5 acres. Features include remote location (accessible by float plane); scenic area (mountain, lakes, rivers); wilderness lodge; great sportfishing; hot tub and sauna; fly-tying bench; game room and library.

Profile of Summer Employees   Total number 20; average age 21. Employees are 25% female, 50% college students.

Employment Information   Openings are from June 5 to September 20. Jobs available: 1 *chef* with experience at $2000–$2400 per month; 4 *household workers* at $900 per month; 2 *pilots* with communication, instrumentation, and seaplane ratings (over 1,500 hours); 1 *pilot/mechanic* with communication, instrumentation, and seaplane ratings (P or A and I); 10 *fishing guides* with CPR and standard first aid certificates at $800–$1200 per month.

Benefits   On-the-job training, on-site room and board at no charge, laundry facilities, travel reimbursement, sharing of gratuities.

Contact   Applicant should send resume by April 1 to Ron McMillan, President/General Manager, Bristol Bay Lodge, Route 1, Box 580, Ellensburg, Washington 98926; 509-964-2094, fax 509-964-2269.

NATIONAL PARK SERVICE

Contact   Applicant should write for application (must be 18 by May 13; U.S. citizenship required) to Regional Office of the National Park Service, Alaska Region, National Park Service, 2525 Gambell Street, Room 107, Anchorage, Alaska 99503.

Jobs located in Alaska at the following facilities: Anchorage Interagency Visitor Center, Aniakchak/Katmai, Bering Land Bridge, Denali, Fairbanks Interagency Visitor Center, Gates of the Arctic, Glacier Bay, Kenai Fjords, Klondike Gold Rush, Lake Clark,

Northwest Alaska Areas, Sitka, Wrangell/St. Elias, Yukon-Charley Rivers National Park. Also see District of Columbia listing.

RAINBOW KING LODGE
P.O. Box 106
Dliamna, Alaska 99606

General Information   Deluxe fishing lodge offering weekly guest packages for the upper-end income market. Established 1974. Owned by Parker J. Woods. Located 190 miles southwest of Anchorage on 4 acres. Features include remote Alaskan "bush" experience; scenic beauty; great fishing; exposure to new ideas and culture; opportunity to save money; friendly family staff environment.

Profile of Summer Employees   Total number 45; average age 22. Employees are 35% female.

Employment Information   Openings are from June 1 to October 1. Jobs available: 14 *fishing guides* with first aid/CPR certificate and fly-fishing experience at $1050–$1850 per month; 10 *lodge workers* with waitress experience (preferred) at $1050–$1700 per month; 4 *maintenance personnel* at $1050–$1850 per month.

Benefits   On-the-job training, on-site room and board at no charge, laundry facilities.

Contact   Applicant should send resume or write for application by April 1 to Karen Maurice, Manager, Rainbow King Lodge, P.O. Box 2409, Lake Oswego, Oregon 97035; 800-458-6539, fax 503-638-3630.

No alcohol or drug use is permitted during employment.

TIKCHIK NARROWS LODGE
Box 220248
Anchorage, Alaska 99522

General Information   Lodge specializing in sportfishing and fly-out trips catering to high-profile people. Established 1969. Owned by Fredrick and Holly Hodson. Affiliated with Anchorage Convention and Visitors' Bureau. Located 350 miles west of Anchorage on 7 acres. Features include location in 1.7 million-acre state park; accessibility by floatplane only; beautiful scenery; world's best freshwater sportfishing.

Profile of Summer Employees   Total number 25; average age 25. Employees are 33% female, 5% minorities, 20% college students, 10% retirees, 5% local residents. Prefers nonsmokers.

Employment Information   Openings are from June 7 to September 30. Jobs available: 1 *kitchen assistant* at $900 per month; 1 *cabin cleaner* at $900 per month; 1 *nanny/kitchen helper* at $800 per month; 2 *lodge-help personnel* at $900 per month; 1 *bartender/groundskeeper* at $900 per month; 1 *tackle and fish manager* at $900 per month.

Benefits   On-the-job training, on-site room and board, laundry facilities, very large gratuities.

Contact   Applicant should send resume by May 1 to Holly Hodson, Owner, Tikchik Narrows Lodge, Department SED, Box 220248, Anchorage, Alaska 99522.

Arizona

GRAND CANYON NATIONAL PARK LODGES
P.O. Box 699
Grand Canyon, Arizona 86023

General Information   National park concessioner providing all hotel, restaurant, retail, and transportation services on the south rim of the Grand Canyon. Established 1901. Owned by AMFAC Resorts Inc. Located 80 miles south of Flagstaff.

Profile of Summer Employees   Total number 1,100. Employees are 30% minorities, 20% college students, 20% retirees, 30% local residents.

Employment Information   Openings are from February 15 to January 3. Year-round positions also offered. College credit possible. Jobs available: *guest-room attendant; kitchen/utility staff; retail clerk; cashier; busperson; hosts/hostesses; cooks; cook's helpers.*

Benefits   On-the-job training, on-site room and board at $16 per week, laundry facilities, health insurance, food in employee cafeterias at cost.

Contact   Applicant should write for application or call for information to Personnel Department, Grand Canyon National Park Lodges, Department SED, P.O. Box 699, Grand Canyon, Arizona 86023; 602-638-2343.

This is the chance of a lifetime to live within a national park. Our hotels, restaurants, and retail shops have openings for experienced workers as well as those beginning their careers. Wages range from $4.25 to $5.65 per hour depending on position and experience. Employment opportunities other than the ones detailed in this listing may exist.

NATIONAL PARK SERVICE

Contact   Applicant should write for application (must be 18 by May 13; U.S. citizenship required) to Regional Office of the National Park Service, Western Region, National Park Service, 450 Golden Gate Avenue, Box 36063, San Francisco, California 94102.

Jobs located in Arizona at the following facilities: Canyon de Cheny, Casa Grande Ruins, Chiricahua, Coronado, Glen Canyon, Grand Canyon, Hubbell Trading Post, Montezuma Castle, Navajo, Organ Pipe Cactus, Petrified Forest, Pipe Spring, Saguaro, Southern Arizona Group Office, Tonto, Tumacacori, Walnut Canyon, Wupatki/Sunset Crater. Also see District of Columbia listing.

Arkansas

NATIONAL PARK SERVICE

Contact   Applicant should write for application (must be 18 by May 13; U.S. citizenship required) to Regional Office of the National Park Service, Southwest Region, National Park Service, P.O. Box 728, Santa Fe, New Mexico 87501.

Jobs located in Arkansas at the following facilities: Buffalo National River, Fort Smith, Hot Springs, Pea Ridge. Also see District of Columbia listing.

NOARK GIRL SCOUT CAMP
Route 3, Box 22
Huntsville, Arkansas 72740

General Information   Residential camp serving approximately 450 girls ages 7–17 over a seven-week period. Established 1967. Owned by Noark Girl Scout Council. Located 40 miles east of Fayetteville on 1,039 acres. Features include location near Ozark Mountains; primitive outdoor living.

Profile of Summer Employees   Total number 20; average age 20. Employees are 95% female, 95% college students, 75% local residents.

Employment Information   Openings are from June 1 to July 30. Jobs available: 6 *unit leaders* with a minimum age of 21 at $100–$150 per week; 12 *unit counselors* with a minimum age of 18 at $80–$120 per week; 1 *waterfront director* with WSI and lifeguard certificates (minimum age 21) at $100–$150 per week; 1 *health supervisor* with RN, LPN, or paramedic status (minimum age 21) at $120–$180 per week. International students encouraged to apply.

Benefits   On-the-job training, formal ongoing training, on-site room and board at no charge, laundry facilities, health insurance.

Contact   Applicant should write for application or call for information by April 15 to Camp Director, Noark Girl Scout Camp, Department SED, P.O. Box 6353, Springdale, Arkansas 72766; 501-750-2442.

California

CAMP JCA SHOLOM
34342 Mulholland Highway
Malibu, California 90265

General Information   Residential Jewish camp offering a warm, supportive atmosphere for campers ages 7–17. Established 1951. Owned by Jewish Community Centers Association. Affiliated with American Camping Association, United Way. Located 25 miles north of Los Angeles on 135 acres. Features include new Olympic-size swimming pool; expanded ropes course; location in beautiful Malibu Mountains; human development training.

Profile of Summer Employees   Total number 75; average age 20. Employees are 50% female, 10% minorities, 20% high school students, 78% college students, 10% international, 70% local residents. Prefers nonsmokers.

Employment Information   Openings are from June to August. Winter break positions also offered. Jobs available: 40 *counselors* with high school senior status at $1000–$3000 per season; 8 *swimming and water safety instructors* with CPR, ALS, and WSI certification at $1000–$3000 per season; 1 *ropes-course leader* with ability to lead groups through high and low elements at $1000–$3000 per season; 1 *song leader* with ability to lead camp-wide singing of American and Hebrew folk songs, highly spirited nature, and guitar playing skills at $1000–$3000 per season; 1 *Jewish education instructor* with knowledge of Jewish traditions, culture, history, and fun, plus the ability to develop and lead camp-wide programs, including all-day Shabbat programs, at $1000–$3000 per season; 3 *unit heads* with college graduate status and three years of camping experience plus good Jewish program skills (graduate training or social work experience helpful) at $1000–$3000 per season; 2 *teen travel leaders* with college graduate status, knowledge of out-of-doors (experience with children essential), plus current first aid and CPR certification (minimum age 21) at $1000–$3000 per season; 1 *registered nurse* with ability to run the infirmary, supervise nurse's aide, and interact well with parents, plus pediatric experience in a camp setting at $1000–$3000 per season; 1 *bus driver* with current Class II California driver's license and a clean driving record (knowledge of mountain driving extremely helpful) at $1000–$3000 per season. International students encouraged to apply.

Benefits   On-the-job training, on-site room and board at no charge, laundry facilities.

Contact   Applicant should send resume, write for application, or call for information by March 31 to Tamara Kupetz, Program Director, Camp JCA Sholom, Department SED, 5870 West Olympic Boulevard, Los Angeles, California 90036; 213-857-0036.

Camp JCA Sholom is filled with Jewish culture. Our staff members form memories that will last a lifetime.

CAMP LAKOTA
Star Route, Box 9999
Frazier Park, California 93225

General Information   Residential camp serving 140 girls ages 7–17 weekly and emphasizing activities, horsemanship, and Girl Scout programs. Established 1949. Owned by San Fernando Valley Girl Scout Council. Affiliated with Girl Scouts of the United States of America, American Camping Association. Located 75 miles north of Los Angeles on 54 acres. Features include backpacking, swimming, and horse programs; international staff members; proximity to mountains and Los Padres National Forest; clean, fresh air.

Profile of Summer Employees   Total number 45; average age 20. Employees are 95% female, 30% minorities, 95% college students, 20% international, 2% local residents. Prefers nonsmokers.

Employment Information   Openings are from June 20 to August 26. Spring break, winter break, Christmas break positions also offered. Jobs available: 1 *business manager* at $160–$200 per week; 1 *arts and crafts director* at $150–$190 per week; 1 *nature specialist* at $150–$190 per week; 1 *health supervisor (nurse)* with RN license (preferred) at $225–$285 per week; 1 *riding director* with AHA certificate or equivalent (preferred) at $200–$275 per week; 4 *wranglers* with horse experience at $150–$190 per week; 2 *pool directors* with WSI and lifeguarding certificates at $155–$200 per week; 30 *counselors* at $150–$190 per week; 1 *maintenance person* at $150–$180 per week. International students encouraged to apply.

Benefits   Preemployment training, on-the-job training, on-site room and board at no charge, laundry facilities, health insurance.

Contact   Applicant should write for application or call for information by May 31 to Linda A. Lagoy, Outdoor Administrator, Camp Lakota, Department SED, 9421 Winnetka Avenue, Chatsworth, California 91311; 818-886-1801, fax 818-407-5001.

Come experience the fun and great environment at Camp Lakota.

CAMP MOUNTAIN MEADOWS
Sequoia National Forest
California

General Information   Residential Girl Scout camp serving 75–100 campers weekly with high adventure activities including backpacking, mountain biking, and horseback riding. Established 1954. Owned by Girl Scouts Joshua Tree Council. Affiliated with American Camping Association. Located 60 miles south of Bakersfield on 15 acres. Features include location in the southern Sierra Nevadas (Greenhorn Mountain); small friendly camp; primitive sites (sleeping under the stars).

Profile of Summer Employees   Total number 20. Prefers nonsmokers.

Employment Information   Spring break positions offered. College credit possible. Jobs available: 3 *unit leaders* with a minimum age of 21 at $1400 per season; 10 *assistant unit leaders* with a minimum age of 18 at $1200 per season; 3 *specialists* with backpacking, counselor-in-training, and rock-climbing experience at $1500 per season; 1 *nurse* with RN, LVN, or EMT license at $2100 per season.

Benefits   Preemployment training, on-the-job training, on-site room and board at no charge, health insurance.

Contact   Applicant should send resume, write for application, call for information, or apply in person by May 15 to Pam Kerney, Facilities Manager, Camp Mountain Meadows, P.O. Box 2164, Bakersfield, California 93303; 805-327-1409, fax 805-327-3837.

Salaries are in accordance with California minimum wage laws. Pre-camp training includes leadership skills, team building, and problem solving.

CAMP SCHERMAN
Mountain Center, California

General Information   Residential Girl Scout camp serving over 2,000 girls per season. Established 1968. Owned by Girl Scout Council of Orange County. Affiliated with Girl Scouts of the United States of America, American Camping Association. Located 50 miles west of Palm Springs on 700 acres. Features include high desert chaparral; 2 lakes and a pool; miles of trails; modern cabins and facilities; mainstreaming of campers with special needs; large, diverse staff; programs such as archery, arts and crafts, backpacking, swimming, canoeing, sailing, riding, singing, and cooking.

Profile of Summer Employees   Total number 90; average age 21. Employees are 95% female, 10% minorities, 90% college students, 5% international, 5% local residents. Prefers nonsmokers.

Employment Information   Openings are from June 14 to August 25. Jobs available: 30 *unit staff* at $1750 per season; 10 *staff supervisors* at $1980 per season; 1 *counselor-in-training director* at $2050 per season; 1 *counselor-in-training assistant director* at $1800 per season; 1 *boating director* with lifeguard training, first aid, and CPR certification at $2100 per season; 1 *waterfront director* with lifeguard training, first aid, and CPR certification at $2100 per season; 5 *waterfront staff* with lifeguard training, first aid, and CPR certification at $1860 per season; 5 *boating staff* with lifeguard training, first aid, and CPR certification at $1860 per season; 5 *program assistants* with skills in nature, arts and crafts, archery, and rock-climbing at $1750 per season; 5 *riding assistants* with horseback-riding and teaching experience at $1750 per season; 4 *program directors* with skills and experience in nature, arts and crafts, archery, or rock-climbing at $1980 per season; 2 *awareness aide staff* with experience working with disabled campers at $1750 per season; 5 *kitchen* *staff* at $2200 per season; 2 *packout cooks* at $2200–$2300 per season; 4 *maintenance personnel* at $2480 per season.

Benefits Preemployment training, on-the-job training, on-site room and board at no charge.

Contact Applicant should send resume, write for application, or call for information by May 1 to Maria Genovese, Assistant Outdoor Program Director, Camp Scherman, Department SED, P.O. Box 3739, Costa Mesa, California 92628-3739; 714-979-7900.

EMANDAL–A FARM ON A RIVER
16500 Hearst Road
Willits, California 95490

General Information Coeducational residential camp for 45 youngsters ages 7–15 for half the summer and a family vacation farm for 45–55 people of all ages for the second half. Established 1965. Owned by Clive and Tamara Adams. Affiliated with American Camping Association, Western Association of Independent Camps. Located 140 miles north of San Francisco on 1,000 acres. Features include close proximity to a river and national forest; an organic farm; diverse backgrounds of people; location 16 miles from town; opportunity to view birds and other wildlife.

Profile of Summer Employees Total number 20; average age 25. Employees are 60% female, 1% minorities, 15% high school students, 50% college students, 1% retirees, 10% international, 20% local residents. Requires nonsmokers.

Employment Information Openings are from May 15 to December 15. College credit possible. Jobs available: 15 *camp counselors* with ability to work for six weeks at $700 per season; 8 *family camp workers* with ability to work for six weeks at $150 per week; 2 *gardeners* with ability to work for the entire summer at $150 per week; 1 *pickle maker* with ability to work for the entire summer at $150 per week; 1 *office person* with ability to work until Christmas at $150 per week. International students encouraged to apply.

Benefits Preemployment training, on-the-job training, on-site room and board at no charge, laundry facilities, health insurance.

Contact Applicant should send resume, write for application, or call for information by April 15 to Tamara Adams, Director, Emandal–A Farm on A River, Department SED, 16500 Hearst Road, Willits, California 95490; 707-459-5439, fax 707-459-1808.

We also feature a mail-order business offering such products as jam, jelly, salsa, and pickles.

FOUNDATION FOR THE JUNIOR BLIND
5300 Angeles Vista Boulevard
Los Angeles, California 90043

General Information Residential camp serving blind and visually impaired children and their families. Established 1955. Affiliated with American Camping Association. Located 10 miles north of Malibu on 50 acres. Features include location near Malibu and the Santa Monica Mountains.

Profile of Summer Employees Total number 60; average age 20. Employees are 50% female, 25% minorities, 4% high school students, 50% college students, 8% international, 5% local residents. Prefers nonsmokers.

Employment Information Openings are from June 15 to August 21. Spring break, winter break, Christmas break, year-round positions also offered. College credit possible. International students encouraged to apply.

Benefits Preemployment training, on-the-job training, formal ongoing training, on-site room and board at no charge, laundry facilities, health insurance, honorarium/stipend.

Contact Applicant should send resume, write for application, or call for information by April 15 to Mark Lucas, Director of Recreation, Foundation for the Junior Blind, Department SED, 5300 Angeles Vista Boulevard, Los Angeles, California 90043; 213-295-4555, fax 213-296-0424.

Staff members have the opportunity to gain valuable leadership experience and to work with the visually impaired.

FURNACE CREEK INN AND RANCH
P.O. Box 187
Death Valley, California 92328

General Information Resort in Death Valley National Monument Park. Established 1931. Located 140 miles east of Las Vegas, Nevada on 10 acres. Features include desert location; unusual geological formations; hot and dry climate; hiking; elevation below sea level; beautiful area.

Profile of Summer Employees Total number 180. Employees are 50% female.

Employment Information Year-round positions offered. International students encouraged to apply.

Benefits On-the-job training, formal ongoing training, on-site room and board at $66 per month, laundry facilities, health insurance, tuition reimbursement, free golf, tennis, and swimming.

Contact Applicant should send resume or call for information to Marie Litte, Personnel Director, Furnace Creek Inn and Ranch, Department SED, P.O. Box 187, Death Valley, California 92328; 619-786-2311, fax 619-786-2511.

HUNEWILL GUEST RANCH
Twin Lakes Road
Bridgeport, California 93517

General Information Guest ranch accommodating 45–55 guests weekly. Established 1930. Owned by Hunewill Family. Operated by Hunewill Land and Livestock. Affiliated with Dude Ranchers' Association. Located 120 miles south of Reno, Nevada on 4,800 acres. Features include lush meadows; great horses; view of Sierra Nevada Mountains; working cattle ranch; individual cottages; Victorian ranch house with kitchen and dining room.

Profile of Summer Employees Total number 19; average age 21. Employees are 75% female, 5% high school students, 85% college students, 10% local residents. Prefers nonsmokers.

Employment Information Openings are from May 20 to September 21. Jobs available: 4 *waiters/waitresses* with waiter/waitress skills (preferred) at $185 per week; 3 *cabin staff* with an eye for neatness and ability to work quickly at $175 per week; 1 *maintenance* *person* with previous experience performing ranch chores or similiar duties and/or strong mechanical aptitude at $190 per week; 1 *cook* with previous experience at $1400 per month; 1 *breakfast/pastry chef* with experience at $1200 per month; 3 *wranglers* with extensive horse experience and good people skills at $775 per month.

Benefits   On-the-job training, on-site room and board at $128 per month, laundry facilities, free horseback riding during time off, tips which range from $30–$80 weekly.

Contact   Applicant should send resume and attach photo by January 15 to Betsy Hunewill Elliott, Assistant Manager, Hunewill Guest Ranch, Department SED, 101 Hunewill Lane, Wellington, Nevada 89444; 702-465-2238.

Located in one of the finest vacation areas in California, Hunewill Guest Ranch provides staff members the opportunity to meet successful doctors, lawyers, and other professionals and their families.

IDYLLWILD SCHOOL OF MUSIC AND THE ARTS
P.O. Box 38
Idyllwild, California 92349

General Information   Residential program serving 100–300 children, teenagers, and adults weekly in intensive performing and visual arts courses. Established 1950. Owned by Idyllwild Arts Foundation. Affiliated with National Association of Independent Schools, California Association of Independent Schools, Network of Visual and Performing Arts Schools, Music Educators' National Conference, California Music Educators' Association. Located 110 miles southeast of Los Angeles on 205 acres. Features include outstanding professional faculty of artists/educators; pristine mountain environment; arts courses for the entire family; availability of on-campus accommodations; wide range of courses.

Profile of Summer Employees   Total number 45; average age 21. Employees are 60% female, 15% minorities, 95% college students, 5% international. Prefers nonsmokers.

Employment Information   Openings are from June 15 to August 25. Jobs available: 1 *deans of students–children's center* with extensive supervisory experience with children ages 9–12 in a residential setting (minimum age 25) at $300–$500 per week; 2 *dean of students–youth programs* with extensive experience working with children in a residential setting (minimum age 23) at $300 per week; 10 *resident counselors–children's center* with experience working with children ages 9–12 in a residential setting (minimum age 21) at $150 per week; 18 *resident counselors–youth program* with at least a year of college completed (minimum age 18, camp experience helpful) at $125–$150 per week; 1 *pool manager/lifeguard* with advanced lifesaving, first aid, and CPR certification plus extensive experience working in public pools at $250–$300 per week; 3 *lifeguards* with advanced lifesaving, first aid, and CPR certification plus completion of at least a year of college at $150 per week; 1 *technical director* with three or more years of experience in a summer arts program and extensive technical theater background (minimum age 25) at $350–$400 per week; 2 *technical assistants* with at least a year of college completed and technical theater experience (minimum age 18) at $150 per week; 8 *art studio assistants (work/study)* with at least a year of college completed (minimum age 18). International students encouraged to apply.

Benefits   Preemployment training, on-the-job training, on-site room and board at no charge, laundry facilities, free arts classes as schedule permits.

Contact   Applicant should write for application or call for information by February 1 to Steven Fraider, Director, Summer Program, Idyllwild School of Music and the Arts,

Department SED, 315 West Ninth Street, Suite 306, Los Angeles, California 90015; 213-622-0355, fax 213-622-6185.

Idyllwild is looking for high-energy people who can work well both in groups and independently. They must be committed to the arts and to the needs of children and teenagers. The summer program is fast-paced, intensive, and great fun.

JAMESON RANCH CAMP
Glennville, California 93226

General Information Private, residential camp involving children in a mountain ranch lifestyle. Established 1934. Owned by Ross and Debby Jameson. Affiliated with American Camping Association, Western Association of Independent Camps. Located 40 miles east of Bakersfield on 520 acres. Features include outdoor sleeping; food for camp produced on-site; family camp with a strong feeling of community; property bordered on two sides by Sequoia National Forest; elevation of 4,600 feet.

Profile of Summer Employees Total number 22; average age 20. Employees are 50% female, 20% minorities, 90% college students, 5% retirees, 10% international, 5% local residents. Requires nonsmokers.

Employment Information Openings are from June 16 to September 2. College credit possible. Jobs available: 2 *swimming instructors* with WSI certificate at $1800 per season; 4 *lifeguards* with ALS certificate at $1800 per season; 1 *rock-climbing instructor* at $1800 per season; 2 *horse instructors* at $1800 per season; 1 *crafts instructor* at $1800 per season; 1 *mountain-biking instructor* at $1800 per season; 1 *drama instructor* at $1800 per season; 1 *horse-vaulting instructor* at $1800 per season; 1 *archery instructor* at $1800 per season; 1 *riflery instructor* at $1800 per season; 2 *kitchen persons* at $1800 per season; 1 *head cook* at $2600 per season. International students encouraged to apply.

Benefits Preemployment training, on-the-job training, formal ongoing training, on-site room and board at no charge, laundry facilities.

Contact Applicant should send resume, write for application, call for information, or apply in person by June 15 to Ross Jameson, Owner/Director, Jameson Ranch Camp, Department SED, Glennville, California 93226; 805-536-8888.

We are a family run business in which everyone—staff and campers— participates in ranch activities and experiences. Our counselors are great role models for children. Counselors also teach outdoor skills and help with ranch activities such as gardening, cow milking, animal care, and building projects.

KENNOLYN CAMPS
8205 Glen Haven Road
Soquel, California 95073

General Information Three related camps—residential camp serves 245 campers ages 6–13; Hi-Camp has 135 teenagers ages 13–16; Day Camp is for ages 5–13. Established 1946. Owned by Max and Marion Caldwell. Affiliated with American Camping Association, Western Association of Independent Camps, Camp Horsemans' Association, American Vaulting Association, Camp Archery Association, National Rifle Association. Located 8 miles northeast of Santa Cruz on 300 acres. Features include over thirty daily activities; ocean and mountain activities; location in coastal redwoods; an old logging town atmosphere; Hi-Camp situated on hill overlooking bay; in operation over 45 years with the same owner and director.

Profile of Summer Employees   Total number 150; average age 28. Employees are 50% female, 10% minorities, 70% college students, 30% international. Requires nonsmokers.

Employment Information   Openings are from June 15 to September 1. Year-round positions also offered. International students encouraged to apply.

Benefits   Preemployment training, on-the-job training, formal ongoing training, on-site room and board at $50 per month, health insurance.

Contact   Applicant should send resume, write for application, call for information, or apply in person by May 1 to Max Caldwell, Owner, Kennolyn Camps, Department SED, 8205 Glen Haven Road, Soquel, California 95073; 408-479-6714, fax 408-479-6718.

LAWRENCE WELK RESORT
8860 Lawrence Welk Drive
Escondido, California 92026

General Information   Provides high-quality service to vacationers. The resort has 132 hotel rooms and 300 time-shares available. Established 1964. Owned by Lawrence Welk. Affiliated with United Way. Located 80 miles north of San Diego on 325 acres. Features include live theater; conference center; golf courses; restaurant; commercial center; excellent climate, tranquil mountainous setting; close to beaches, zoo, wild animal park, Los Angeles; friendly staff.

Profile of Summer Employees   Employees are 60% minorities, 2% high school students, 2% college students, 22% retirees, 95% local residents. Prefers nonsmokers.

Employment Information   Openings are from May 15 to September 30. Year-round positions also offered. Jobs available: 2 *pool attendants* with people-oriented personality at $700 per month. International students encouraged to apply.

Benefits   On-the-job training, free theater tickets per performance, use of golf courses, discount cards to attractions in San Diego and Los Angeles.

Contact   Applicant should send resume or write for application to Carmen Monje, Human Resources Representative, Lawrence Welk Resort, 8860 Lawrence Welk Drive, Escondido, California 92026; 619-749-3000, fax 619-749-6182.

LOS ANGELES DESIGNERS' THEATRE
Box 1883
Studio City, California 91614-0883

General Information   Produces stage productions and teaches theatrical producing including the legal aspects of production. Established 1970. Owned by Los Angeles Designers' Theatre. Affiliated with United States Institute for Theatre Technology.

Profile of Summer Employees   Total number 72; average age 25. Employees are 50% female, 20% minorities, 50% college students, 5% international. Prefers nonsmokers.

Employment Information   Year-round positions offered. College credit possible. Jobs available: 6 *directors;* 15 *actors and actresses;* 15 *singers and dancers;* 1 *set designer;* 1 *lighting designer;* 1 *property designer;* 1 *sound designer;* 1 *costume designer;* 1 *program/*

graphics designer; 12 crew members; 2 cutters/drapers; 2 electricians; 2 carpenters; 1 musical director; 1 choreographer. International students encouraged to apply.

Benefits Preemployment training, on-the-job training, formal ongoing training.

Contact Applicant should send resume and portfolio (slides okay), reviews, or video tape of prior work to Richard Niederberg, Artistic Director, Los Angeles Designers' Theatre, Department SED, P.O. Box 1883, Studio City, California 91614-0883; 213-650-9600, fax 818-766-6437.

We have a very successful, hands-on program that teaches commercial theatrical production of theater, dance, music, ballet, music video, film, video tape, and other forms of live and recorded entertainment. Staff members have the opportunity to demonstrate their talent to the Los Angeles entertainment industry and can add valuable experience to their resumes.

NATIONAL PARK SERVICE

Contact Applicant should write for application (must be 18 by May 13; U.S. citizenship required) to Regional Office of the National Park Service, Western Region, National Park Service, 450 Golden Gate Avenue, Box 36063, San Francisco, California 94102.

Jobs located in California at the following facilities: Cabrillo, Channel Islands, Death Valley, Golden Gate, Joshua Tree, Lassen Volcanic, Lava Beds, Pinnacles, Point Reyes, Redwood, San Francisco Maritime, Santa Monica Mountains, Sequoia and King's Canyon, Whiskeytown, Yosemite. Also see District of Columbia listing.

OFFENSE-DEFENSE FOOTBALL CAMP

General Information Teaches boys ages 8–18 to play football. Established 1970. Owned by Mike Meshken. Features include locations at Menlo College, Atherton and the University of California, Riverside; proximity to Los Angeles or San Francisco; pools and weight rooms; football atmosphere with "live contact" in full pads; 60 college coaches and 19 NFL professionals.

Profile of Summer Employees Total number 100; average age 23. Employees are 10% female, 30% college students, 10% retirees. Requires nonsmokers.

Employment Information Openings are from June 15 to July 15. College credit possible. Jobs available: 1 *swimming instructor/lifeguard* with WSI or Red Cross certificate at $200 per week; 20 *counselors* at $100–$150 per week; 50 *college or high school football coaches* with ongoing involvement in coaching at $200–$300 per week; 6 *athletics trainers (student)* at $175 per week; 6 *athletics trainers* with certification at $300–$450 per week.

Benefits Preemployment training, on-the-job training, formal ongoing training, on-site room and board, laundry facilities, travel reimbursement.

Contact Applicant should send resume or call for information by April 10 to Mike Meshken, President, Offense-Defense Football Camp, Department SED, California Division, P.O. Box 317, Trumbull, Connecticut 06611; 800-243-4296.

SANTA CATALINA SCHOOL SUMMER CAMP
1500 Mark Thomas Drive
Monterey, California 93940

General Information   Residential day camp for girls ages 8–14 with an emphasis on performing and fine arts and athletics. Established 1953. Owned by Santa Catalina School. Affiliated with American Camping Association, Western Association of Independent Camps, National Association of Independent Schools. Located 75 miles south of San Jose on 35 acres. Features include location on Monterey Bay near Carmel; beautiful campus with gardens and Spanish architecture; gymnasium (built 1990); 500-seat theater; dormitories (single and double rooms); 6 tennis courts.

Profile of Summer Employees   Total number 40; average age 35. Employees are 80% female, 5% minorities, 40% college students, 5% retirees, 5% international, 60% local residents. Prefers nonsmokers.

Employment Information   Openings are from June 15 to July 31. Jobs available: 10 *counselors* with a year of college completed at $750–$1000 per season; 5 *head counselors* with three years of college completed and prior experience at $850–$1100 per season. International students encouraged to apply.

Benefits   Preemployment training, on-the-job training, on-site room and board at no charge, laundry facilities.

Contact   Applicant should send resume, write for application, or call for information by April 1 to Mrs. Katie M. Aimé, Director of Summer Programs, Santa Catalina School Summer Camp, 1500 Mark Thomas Drive, Monterey, California 93940; 408-655-9386, fax 408-649-3056.

Santa Catalina School Summer Camp gives people the opportunity to form friendships with campers and counselors from around the world. International students who wish to be considered for employment should submit all pertinent application information prior to February.

SANTA CRUZ SEASIDE COMPANY/SANTA CRUZ BEACH BOARDWALK
400 Beach Street
Santa Cruz, California 95060

General Information   West Coast's only beachside amusement park serving visitors year-round. Established 1907. Owned by Charles Canfield. Affiliated with Northern California Attractions Association, International Association of Amusement Parks and Attractions, Greater San Francisco Bay Area Vacation Council. Located 90 miles south of San Francisco. Features include over 20 major rides; two National Historical Landmarks; state landmark designation for entire park; a mile-long beach; proximity to state parks in Santa Cruz Mountains; location 40 miles north of Monterey.

Profile of Summer Employees   Total number 800; average age 20. Employees are 50% female, 40% minorities, 60% high school students, 30% college students, 5% retirees, 8% international, 70% local residents. Prefers nonsmokers.

Employment Information   Openings are from May 24 to September 2. Jobs available: 150 *ride operators* with a minimum age of 17; 100 *food-service operators* with a minimum age of 16. International students encouraged to apply.

Benefits On-the-job training, formal ongoing training, on-site room and board at $60 per week, laundry facilities, bus passes, free rides, discounts on food and merchandise. **Contact** Applicant should write for application, call for information, or apply in person to Keith Johnstone, Employment Manager, Santa Cruz Seaside Company/Santa Cruz Beach Boardwalk, Department SED, 400 Beach Street, Santa Cruz, California 95060-5491; 408-427-1777, fax 408-423-2438.

Wages for employees are $4.60 per hour.

SKY MOUNTAIN CHRISTIAN CAMP
P.O. Box 79
Emigrant Gap, California 95715

General Information Camp conference center serving nondenominational church groups. Established 1976. Affiliated with American Camping Association, Christian Camping International. Located 65 miles east of Sacramento on 40 acres. Features include location on the shore of Lake Valley Reservoir in Tahoe National Forest, just 40 miles from Lake Tahoe; ski resorts only 20 minutes away; year-round operation; elevation of 6,000 feet.

Profile of Summer Employees Total number 30; average age 20. Employees are 50% female, 40% high school students, 40% college students, 20% local residents. Requires nonsmokers.

Employment Information Openings are from June 15 to August 25. Jobs available: 3 *kitchen assistants* with experience performing food preparation (minimum age 18) at $100 per week; 4 *dishwashers* with a minimum age of 16 at $100–$200 per week; 1 *head cook* with two years experience in large quantity cooking (minimum age 21) at $200–$250 per week; 2 *carpenters* with two years experience (minimum age 20) at $250 per week; 4 *laborers* with a minimum age of 17 at $100–$150 per week; 1 *groundskeeper* with fix-it ability (minimum age 21) at $100–$150 per week; 1 *mechanic* with two years experience (minimum age 20) at $150–$200 per week; 1 *housekeeper* with a minimum age of 16 at $150–$200 per week; 8 *counselors* with experience in children's ministry and completion of a year of college (minimum age 18) at $150 per week; 2 *assistant counselors* with ability to work well with children (minimum age 16) at $100 per week; 1 *nurse* with advanced first aid certification or better (minimum age 18) at $150 per week; 1 *secretary* with a year of office experience (minimum age 21) at $150 per week; 2 *lifeguards* with senior lifeguard certificate (minimum age 18) at $100–$125 per week; 1 *sailing instructor* with senior lifeguard certificate and sailing experience (minimum age 18) at $100–$125 per week; 1 *waterfront coordinator* with senior lifeguard certificate (minimum age 21) at $150–$175 per week.

Benefits Preemployment training, on-site room and board at no charge, laundry facilities, travel reimbursement.

Contact Applicant should write for application, call for information, or apply in person by April 30 to Dezra Saunders, Camp Coordinator, Sky Mountain Christian Camp, P.O. Box 79, Emigrant Gap, California 95715; 916-389-2118.

Numerous recreational and sightseeing opportunities. Fun and fellowship with Christian emphasis.

WHITING'S FOODS
817 Beach Street
Santa Cruz, California 95060

General Information   Offers food service counter sales to patrons at a coastal amusement park. Established 1951. Affiliated with British Universities North America Club, Council on International Educational Exchange. Located 75 miles south of San Francisco. Features include proximity to beach and Monterey Bay; location near San Francisco, 5 miles from the Redwoods and 15 minutes from Silicon Valley and Monterey.

Profile of Summer Employees   Total number 200; average age 21. Employees are 50% female, 10% minorities, 30% high school students, 30% college students, 10% retirees, 20% international. Requires nonsmokers.

Employment Information   Openings are from March 1 to October 1. Spring break positions also offered. Jobs available: 25 *food-service counter salespersons* at $600–$700 per month. International students encouraged to apply.

Benefits   On-the-job training, discount on meals, opportunity for advancement, flexible schedules.

Contact   Applicant should send resume by May 30 to Margie Whiting Sisk, Personnel, Whiting's Foods, Department SED, 817 Beach Street, Santa Cruz, California 95060; 408-423-1890, fax 408-423-0569.

Foreign applicants may only apply with a work visa. Applicants must enjoy working with the public. (No beards allowed.) We offer excellent crew member incentives, and teamwork is highly promoted. It's a great place to meet peers and to work in a fun atmosphere for a company that cares.

YMCA CAMP OAKES
P.O. Box 452
Big Bear City, California 92314

General Information   Residential summer camp serving children from around the world in a traditional summer camp program. Established 1905. Owned by YMCA of Greater Long Beach. Affiliated with American Camping Association. Located 110 miles east of Long Beach on 230 acres. Features include fully equipped observatory; international clientele and staff; academic programs; specialty camps; progressive programming; elevation of 7,300 feet in the San Bernardino Mountains.

Profile of Summer Employees   Total number 60; average age 23. Employees are 50% female, 10% minorities, 5% high school students, 95% college students, 10% international, 80% local residents.

Employment Information   Openings are from June 18 to September 4. Jobs available: 3 *program directors* with three years previous experience (minimum age 21) at $230–$280 per week; 1 *aquatic director* with WSI and first aid/CPR certification (minimum age 21) at $225–$255 per week; 1 *wilderness director* with experience and first aid/CPR certification (minimum age 21) at $250–$283 per week; 4 *lifeguards* with lifeguard certification (minimum age 18) at $150–$200 per week; 8 *cabin counselors* with a year of college completed (minimum age 18) at $140–$190 per week; 4 *junior counselors* with a minimum age of 17 at $110–$150 per week; 7 *program specialists* with experience in riflery, crafts, wrangling, nature, archery, ropes-challenge course, and astronomy (minimum age 18) at $140–$190 per week; 1 *health-care coordinator* with RN or EMT training (minimum age

21) at $175–$250 per week; 4 *cooks* with previous experience (minimum age 18) at $120–$225 per week. International students encouraged to apply.

Benefits Preemployment training, on-the-job training, on-site room and board at no charge, laundry facilities.

Contact Applicant should write for application or call for information by May 31 to Frank P. McRae, Program Director, YMCA Camp Oakes, Department SED, P.O. Box 90995, Long Beach, California 90809-0995; 213-496-2756, fax 213-425-1169.

We offer two separate programs throughout the summer. Our branch camping allows children from the local area to attend a one-week program. Our Ranger program allows children from around the world to attend a multi-week progressive camping program with traditional YMCA values.

YOSEMITE PARK & CURRY CO.
Yosemite National Park, California 95389

General Information The main concessionaire for Yosemite National Park. Owned by Yosemite Park & Curry Co. Located 280 miles west of San Francisco. Features include location in the great outdoors; waterfalls; high mountains; scenic views (photographer's paradise); excellent hiking and rock-climbing.

Profile of Summer Employees Total number 1,100; average age 33.

Employment Information Openings are from April 1 to September 5. Spring break, winter break, Christmas break, year-round positions also offered. Jobs available: 50 *food-service persons;* 50 *roomkeepers;* 50 *custodians;* 50 *fast food attendants* with cash handling experience; 50 *sales clerks* with cash handling experience; 50 *front-desk personnel* with computer experience; 50 *hosts/hostesses* with restaurant experience; 50 *cooks* with cooking experience; 50 *auditors* with accounting experience; 50 *stable persons* with experience caring for horses; 50 *tour guides* with ability to foster good guest relations and a familiarity with Yosemite National Park. International students encouraged to apply.

Benefits On-the-job training, on-site room and board at $51 per week, laundry facilities, health insurance, recreation discounts, retail discounts, restaurant discounts.

Contact Applicant should write for application or call for information to Dorothy Richards, Manager of Employment Personnel Department, Yosemite Park & Curry Co., Department SED, Yosemite National Park, California 95389; 209-372-1236.

Good working conditions, opportunities to meet interesting people, and enjoyable outdoor activities make this a wonderful opportunity to live and work in one of America's most beautiful national parks. (Hourly wages are $4.50 and up.)

Colorado

ASPEN LODGE RANCH RESORT
6120 Highway 7
Estes Park, Colorado 80517

General Information Ranch resort catering to families, conferences, and special functions. Established 1940. Affiliated with Colorado Dude and Guest Ranch Association,

American Automobile Association, Mobil Travel Guide. Located 65 miles northwest of Denver on 82 acres. Features include location bordering Rocky Mountain National Park; full recreation and sports facilities, including livery stables, tennis courts, racquet ball, swimming, hot tub, sauna, and weight room.

Profile of Summer Employees   Total number 35; average age 18. Employees are 50% female.

Employment Information   Openings are from May 1 to October 1. Year-round positions also offered. Jobs available: *sports center attendant; children's counselor; wait staff; housekeepers; wranglers* with extensive horse experience; *bartenders; groundskeepers; conference attendants; guest-service attendants.*

Benefits   On-the-job training, on-site room and board at $175 per month, laundry facilities, free use of all recreational facilities.

Contact   Applicant should write for application or call for information by March 31 to Patty Lyons, Assistant Manager, Aspen Lodge Ranch Resort, Department SED, 6120 Highway 7, Estes Park, Colorado 80517; 303-586-8133.

BAR LAZY J GUEST RANCH
447 County Road 3, Box N
Parshall, Colorado 80468

General Information   Guest ranch with a capacity of 40 people. Established 1912. Owned by Lawrence and Barbara Harmon. Affiliated with Colorado Dude and Guest Ranch Association, Dude Ranchers' Association, Granby Chamber of Commerce. Located 105 miles northwest of Denver on 40 acres. Features include horseback riding; great food; Colorado River fishing; children's program.

Profile of Summer Employees   Total number 16; average age 21. Employees are 50% female, 82% college students, 18% retirees. Requires nonsmokers.

Employment Information   Openings are from May 1 to September 30. Jobs available: 1 *head wrangler* with horse experience at $700 per month; 4 *wranglers* with horse experience at $400 per month; 2 *counselors* with experience working with children at $350 per month; 2 *waitresses/waiters* at $350 per month; 2 *housekeepers* at $350 per month; 1 *kitchen helper* at $400 per month; 1 *assistant cook* at $500 per month.

Benefits   On-the-job training, formal ongoing training, on-site room and board at no charge, laundry facilities.

Contact   Applicant should write for application or call for information by May to Larry Harmon, Owner, Bar Lazy J Guest Ranch, Box N, Department 1 (SED), Parshall, Colorado 80468; 303-725-3437.

Bar Lazy J Guest Ranch staff members have the opportunity to work with people from all over the United States.

CHELEY COLORADO CAMPS
P.O. Box 1170
Estes Park, Colorado 80517

General Information   Residential camp serving 475 campers ages 9–17 for four-week sessions. Established 1921. Owned by Don and Carole Cheley. Affiliated with American Camping Association, Western Association of Independent Camps. Features include view of 14,000-foot snow-capped peaks; proximity to Rocky Mountain National Park; 500 miles of hiking trails; 8,000-foot elevation; 140 horses; log/stone lodges and cabins; international clientele.

Profile of Summer Employees Total number 180; average age 21. Employees are 50% female. Requires nonsmokers.

Employment Information Openings are from June 10 to August 15. Spring break positions also offered. College credit possible. Jobs available: *nurses; cooks; drivers; counselors; office staff.* International students encouraged to apply.

Benefits Preemployment training, on-the-job training, formal ongoing training, on-site room and board at no charge, travel reimbursement, health insurance.

Contact Applicant should write for application by March 30 to Don Cheley, Director, Cheley Colorado Camps, Department SED, P.O. Box 6525, Denver, Colorado 80206; 303-377-3616, fax 303-377-3605.

COFFEE BAR CAFE
167 East Elkhorn Avenue, P.O. Box 2210
Estes Park, Colorado 80517

General Information Family restaurant seating 58 persons and serving breakfast, lunch, and dinner. Established 1940. Owned by Robert Akins. Affiliated with National Restaurant Association, Colorado Restaurant Association, Estes Park Chamber of Commerce. Located 75 miles northwest of Denver. Features include location near Rocky Mountain National Park; outdoor activities in the area; busy restaurant; opportunities to meet guests and other students from throughout the country; elevation of 7,500 feet.

Profile of Summer Employees Total number 16; average age 19. Employees are 60% female, 10% minorities, 80% college students, 10% local residents.

Employment Information Openings are from May 1 to October 15. Year-round positions also offered. College credit possible. Jobs available: 5 *servers* with previous serving experience; 2 *hosts;* 4 *dishwashers;* 3 *line cooks* with previous cooking experience; 2 *kitchen assistants.* International students encouraged to apply.

Benefits On-the-job training, meal furnished with work shift, eligibility for end-of-season bonus.

Contact Applicant should write for application by May 15 to Robert Akins, Owner, Coffee Bar Cafe, Department SED, P.O. Box 2210, Estes Park, Colorado 80517; 303-586-3589.

Individuals interested in positions should write for complete employment and wage information. Enclose a large self-addressed, stamped envelope when writing. We can assist in arranging housing at an employee's request at a cost of $25 to $45 weekly. Other housing is available in the area at a cost of $250 to $400 monthly. International students are welcome to apply if they can obtain work permits in their country of origin through organizations such as BUNAC and CIEE. All applicants should be a minimum age of 18 and be able to stay at least through Labor Day. Compensation consists of hourly wages plus tips for certain positions.

COLORADO MOUNTAIN RANCH, TROJAN SUMMER CAMP
P.O. Box 711
Boulder, Colorado 80306

General Information   Residential and day camps each serving approximately 80 campers, boys and girls ages 6–16. Offers both one- and two-week sessions that can be combined to extend three, four, five weeks or more. Owned by The Walker Family. Located 10 miles west of Boulder on 200 acres. Features include family-owned operation since 1947; great camp spirit; elevation of 8,500 feet in the Colorado Rockies.

Profile of Summer Employees   Total number 55; average age 22. Employees are 50% female, 98% college students, 2% international. Prefers nonsmokers.

Employment Information   Openings are from June 1 to August 25. Jobs available: 3 *swimming instructors* with WSI certificate at $900 per season; 8 *wranglers* at $900 per season; 2 *archery instructors* at $900 per season; 2 *riflery instructors* at $900 per season; 2 *arts and crafts instructors* at $900 per season; 3 *gymnastics instructors* at $900 per season; 1 *head cook/kitchen manager* at $1500 per season; 8 *kitchen workers* at $900 per season; 3 *maintenance persons* at $900 per season; 3 *bus drivers* at $900 per season; 8 *cabin counselors* at $900 per season; 10 *day-camp counselors* at $900 per season; 1 *drama instructor* at $900 per season; 1 *Indian lore instructor* at $900 per season; 1 *movie-making instructor* at $900 per season; 3 *backpacking instructors* at $900 per season; 1 *sports and games instructor* at $900 per season. International students encouraged to apply.

Contact   Applicant should write for application or call for information by May 31 to Colorado Mountain Ranch, Trojan Summer Camp, P.O. Box 711, Boulder, Colorado 80306; 303-442-4557.

   Colorado Mountain Ranch attracts children from all over the United States as well as from foreign countries. It is a small summer camp run as a community where everyone, staff and campers alike, has the opportunity to grow in a safe, warm environment.

CROSS BAR X YOUTH RANCH
2111 County Road 222
Durango, Colorado 81301

General Information   A Christian camp serving 20 low-income youths. Established 1977. Owned by Cross Bar X Youth Ranch Inc. Affiliated with Christian Camping International. Located 12 miles east of Durango on 35 acres. Features include Bible lessons; horseback riding; a lake for swimming and fishing; backpacking; specialized care; concerned, personalized atmosphere.

Profile of Summer Employees   Total number 9; average age 22. Employees are 50% female, 100% college students. Requires nonsmokers.

Employment Information   Openings are from June 1 to August 15. College credit possible. Jobs available: 8 *counselors* at $50 per week; 1 *cook* at $50 per week.

Benefits   Preemployment training, on-site room and board at no charge, laundry facilities.

Contact   Applicant should write for application by May 1 to Nick Brothers, Director, Cross Bar X Youth Ranch, Department SED, 2111 County Road 222, Durango, Colorado 81301; 303-259-2716.

DROWSY WATER RANCH
P.O. Box 147 J
Granby, Colorado 80446

General Information Mountain dude ranch serving 60 guests weekly. Established 1929. Owned by Ken and Randy Sue Fosha. Affiliated with Colorado Dude and Guest Ranch Association, Dude Ranchers' Association, Colorado Hotel and Motel Association. Located 95 miles west of Denver on 600 acres. Features include horseback riding; children's programs; evening entertainment; location near Colorado mountains.

Profile of Summer Employees Total number 25; average age 21. Employees are 52% female, 15% high school students, 75% college students, 5% local residents. Requires nonsmokers.

Employment Information Openings are from May 15 to September 15. College credit possible. Jobs available: 7 *horse wranglers/guides* with experience and first aid certificate at $500 per month; 3 *maintenance staff* at $500 per month; 3 *assistant cooks* at $500 per month; 1 *head chef* with experience at $800 per month; 2 *dishwashers* at $500 per month; 2 *counselors* with experience or education at $500 per month; 6 *housekeeping staff/wait persons* at $500 per month; 1 *office person* with experience at $500 per month. International students encouraged to apply.

Benefits On-the-job training, on-site room and board at no charge, laundry facilities, tips.

Contact Applicant should send resume, write for application, or call for information by June 15 to Randy Sue Fosha, Owner, Drowsy Water Ranch, P.O. Box 147 J, Granby, Colorado 80446; 303-725-3456.

Excellent opportunity to meet and entertain people from all over the world. Staff can participate in all ranch activities. We encourage staff interaction with guests.

ELK MOUNTAIN RANCH
Buena Vista, Colorado 80111

General Information Guest ranch serving 35 guests on a weekly basis, June to mid-September. Established 1981. Owned by C. LaRue and Susan Boyd. Affiliated with Colorado Dude and Guest Ranch Association, Dude Ranchers' Association, Colorado Hotel and Motel Association. Located 120 miles southwest of Denver on 5 acres. Features include an exceptional wilderness setting and activity program; elevation at 9,600 feet; small size; highly personalized service and staff; horseback riding through exceptional terrain with panoramic vistas; a true mountain getaway surrounded by the San Isabel National Forest.

Profile of Summer Employees Total number 12; average age 20. Employees are 50% female, 100% college students. Requires nonsmokers.

Employment Information Openings are from May to September. College credit possible. Jobs available: 1 *cook* with high-quality service and love of great food at $500 per month; 6 *wranglers* with prior experience riding and/or instructing horsemanship plus basic knowledge of horses (care, feeding, grooming) at $375 per month; 1 *children's counselor* with prior experience with children of all ages at $375 per month; 5 *wait staff/housekeeping personnel/dishwashers* with service and quality orientation at $375 per month; 1 *assistant cook* with love of cooking at $375 per month; 1 *general maintenance person* with general knowledge and experience of minor repairs, groundskeeping, and vehicle maintenance at $375 per month. International students encouraged to apply.

Benefits On-the-job training, on-site room and board at no charge, laundry facilities, employees spend days off as if they were guests, tips average $600 per person per month of employment.

Contact Applicant should send resume, write for application, call for information, or apply in person by April 15 to Susan Boyd, Owner, Elk Mountain Ranch, Department SED, 7075 East Euclid Drive, Englewood, Colorado 80111; 303-694-2818.

Our staff members are known for their great service and high standards. Employees have the chance to form friendships and memories that will last a lifetime.

FLYING G RANCH, TOMAHAWK RANCH
400 South Broadway
Denver, Colorado 80209

General Information Residential camps for girls ages 7–14 serving approximately 1,500 girls throughout the summer. Established 1945. Owned by Girl Scouts–Mile Hi-Council. Affiliated with American Camping Association. Located 65 miles southwest of Denver on 320 acres. Features include horseback riding; hiking and backpacking in Colorado Rocky Mountains; rock-climbing; archery; ropes course.

Profile of Summer Employees Total number 60; average age 20. Employees are 99% female, 5% minorities, 1% high school students, 90% college students, 1% retirees, 1% international, 75% local residents.

Employment Information Openings are from June 6 to August 14. Jobs available: 2 *assistant camp directors/program directors* with administrative and supervisory experience at $150–$250 per week; 2 *health supervisors* with RN or LPN license at $250–$290 per week; 11 *troop leaders* with supervisory skills and experience working with children at $130–$175 per week; 27 *assistant troop leaders* with experience working with children at $95–$130 per week; 1 *riding director* with ability to teach, train, and supervise campers and staff in horsemanship at $135–$180 per week; 6 *riding counselors* with training and experience in Western riding at $95–$130 per week; 2 *arts and crafts specialists* with ability to teach craft activities at $95–$155 per week; 2 *nature specialists* with nature and ecology awareness at $95–$155 per week; 1 *sports/archery instructor* with ability to teach games, sports, and archery at $95–$155 per week; 1 *farm specialist* with experience in feeding and caring for farm animals at $95–$155 per week; 1 *rock-climbing/ropes-course instructor* with training in different levels of rock-climbing and ability to teach ropes course at $95–$155 per week; 1 *arts/drama specialist* with ability to teach music, dance, puppetry, or theater to groups of children at $95–$155 per week; 2 *campcraft specialists* with knowledge of hiking, backpacking, compass, and cooking at $95–$155 per week.

Benefits Preemployment training, on-the-job training, on-site room and board at no charge, laundry facilities, time off during camp.

Contact Applicant should write for application or call for information by May 1 to Debora A. Speicher, Camp Administrator, Flying G Ranch, Tomahawk Ranch, Department SED, 400 South Broadway, Denver, Colorado 80209; 303-778-8774.

HARMEL'S RANCH RESORT
6748 County Road 742
Almont, Colorado 81210

General Information   Family-oriented guest ranch with 38 lodging units, stables, dining room, lounge, heated pool, and general store. Established 1959. Owned by Bill and Jody Roberts. Affiliated with Colorado Dude and Guest Ranch Association, American Automobile Association. Located 150 miles west of Colorado Springs on 300 acres. Features include location in Taylor Canyon at the confluence of Taylor River and Spring Creek, surrounded by the Gunnison National Forest; excellent fishing; horseback riding, whitewater rafting, mountain biking, hay rides, cookouts, and square dances.

Profile of Summer Employees   Total number 45; average age 21. Employees are 50% female, 75% college students, 2% international, 20% local residents. Prefers nonsmokers.

Employment Information   Openings are from May 15 to September 30. College credit possible. Jobs available: 7 *wranglers* with first aid and CPR certificate at $400 per month; 15 *housekeepers/wait persons* at $325 per month; 2 *children's program director* at $400 per month; 3 *store personnel* at $325 per month; 3 *ranch hands* at $325 per month; 3 *kitchen workers* at $350–$450 per month.

Benefits   On-the-job training, on-site room and board at no charge, laundry facilities, free use of ranch amenities (rafting, horseback riding, pool), uniform (shirts) provided, end-of-season tip pool.

Contact   Applicant should send resume, write for application, or call for information by February 15 to Brad Milner, Manager, Harmel's Ranch Resort, P.O. Box 944, Gunnison, Colorado 81230; 303-641-1740.

HOLIDAY INN RESORT AND CONFERENCE CENTER OF ESTES PARK
101 South St. Vrain, P.O. Box 1468
Estes Park, Colorado 80517

General Information   Resort offering guests 155 rooms in an exceptional setting. Located 65 miles south of Denver. Features include new conference center; restaurant, lounge, and banquet facility; modern, spacious housing available; proximity to Rocky Mountain National Park; nestled in high mountain valley at an elevation of 7,500 feet.

Profile of Summer Employees   Total number 40.

Employment Information   Openings are from June 1 to October 1. Year-round positions also offered. College credit possible. Jobs available: *buspersons; wait staff; host; cooks; kitchen help (pantry, dishwashing);* 2 *housemen* with ability to perform custodial duties, luggage handling, and conference set-ups; 10 *room attendants (housekeeping);* 3 *front-desk personnel* with ability to check-in guests and take reservations; *clerks* with switchboard and cash handling ability; *banquet staff.* International students encouraged to apply.

Benefits   On-the-job training, on-site room and board at $21 per week, 50% off all meals in the restaurant.

Contact   Applicant should send resume, write for application, call for information, or apply in person by July 1 to Deborah J. Marshall, Personnel Director, Holiday Inn Resort and Conference Center of Estes Park, Department SED, P.O. Box 1468, Estes Park, Colorado 80517; 303-586-2332, fax 303-586-2332 Ext. 299.

First consideration is given to those who can work longest, preferably from early June *to October. Wages range from $2.13 to $5 an hour depending upon an individual's position. (Please note that room attendants are paid per room.)*

THE HOME RANCH
54880 Routt County Road 129
Clark, Colorado 80428

General Information   Ranch resort accommodating 36 guests per week. Established 1978. Owned by L. Kendrick Jones. Affiliated with Relais and Chateaux, American Automobile Association, Colorado Dude and Guest Ranch Association. Located 172 miles west of Denver on 750 acres. Features include Rocky Mountain setting; excellent food; horseback riding; hiking in the wilderness; fishing; ranch music and entertainment.

Profile of Summer Employees   Total number 34; average age 30. Employees are 50% female, 5% minorities, 5% high school students, 50% college students, 5% retirees, 5% international, 30% local residents. Prefers nonsmokers.

Employment Information   Openings are from June 1 to September 30. Winter break positions also offered. Jobs available: 3 *children's counselors* at $775 per month; 2 *kitchen helpers* at $775 per month; 6 *waiters* at $775 per month; 6 *housekeepers* at $775 per month; 4 *maintenance personnel* at $775 per month; 2 *hiking guides* at $775 per month; 6 *wranglers* with first aid certificate at $775 per month; 2 *dishwashers* at $775 per month; 3 *cooks* at $775 per month. International students encouraged to apply.

Benefits   On-the-job training, on-site room and board at no charge, laundry facilities, limited use of facility.

Contact   Applicant should write for application by May 30 to Jodee Richison, Manager, The Home Ranch, Department SED, Box 822, Clark, Colorado 80428; 303-879-1780, fax 303-879-1795.

The Home Ranch provides excellent exposure to the hospitality industry.

IMPERIAL HOTEL
123 North Third Street
Cripple Creek, Colorado 80813

General Information   The only original gold camp hotel still in existence, serving guests in an atmosphere of elegance and hospitality. Established 1896. Owned by Wayne and Dorothy Mackin. Located 42 miles southwest of Colorado Springs. Features include beautiful mountain scenery; historic gold-mining town; guest rooms furnished with antiques; gourmet buffet dining; classic melodrama theater (has been a feature for the last forty-four seasons); location behind Pikes Peak at an elevation of 9,500 feet.

Profile of Summer Employees   Total number 70; average age 20. Employees are 50% female, 10% minorities, 75% college students, 15% local residents.

Employment Information   Openings are from May 15 to September 5. Jobs available: 4 *pantry persons;* 5 *kitchen persons;* 4 *housekeepers;* 8 *waiters/waitresses;* 4 *buspersons;* 4 *bartenders;* 2 *hosts/hostesses; reservations staff;* 4 *secretaries;* 4 *desk clerks;* 1 *night desk clerk;* 1 *campground assistant.*

Benefits   On-the-job training, formal ongoing training, on-site room and board at no charge, laundry facilities, end-of-season bonus.

Contact   Applicant should write for application by June 1 to Stephen or Bonnie Mackin, Managers, Imperial Hotel, P.O. Box 957, Cripple Creek, Colorado 80813; 719-689-2922, fax 719-689-2307.

LONGS PEAK INN GUEST RANCH
6925 Colorado Highway 7, Longs Peak Route
Estes Park, Colorado 80517

General Information   Guest ranch accommodating 75 persons (summer only). Established 1902. Owned by Virginia and Bob Akins. Affiliated with Colorado Dude and Guest Ranch Association, Colorado Hotel and Motel Association, Estes Park Accommodations Association. Located 75 miles northwest of Denver on 100 acres. Features include location near Rocky Mountain National Park; small size; scenic location; close staff-guest relationship; good weather; elevation of 9,000 feet.

Profile of Summer Employees   Total number 40; average age 20. Employees are 55% female, 80% college students, 10% international, 10% local residents.

Employment Information   Openings are from May 15 to September 30. College credit possible. Jobs available: 5 *servers;* 2 *desk clerks;* 3 *hosts;* 2 *dishwashers;* 3 *cooks* with previous restaurant experience; 3 *kitchen helpers;* 3 *maintenance persons;* 6 *housekeepers;* 4 *children's counselors;* 1 *bartender* with a minimum age of 21; 5 *wranglers* with extensive horse experience; 1 *truck driver* with experience with medium trucks; 2 *recreation staff.*

Benefits   On-the-job training, on-site room and board at no charge, activities, use of facilities, eligibility for end-of-season bonus.

Contact   Applicant should write for application by May 15 to Virginia Akins, Owner, Longs Peak Inn Guest Ranch, Department SED, Longs Peak Route, Estes Park, Colorado 80517; 303-586-2110.

Individuals interested in positions should write for complete employment and wage information. Enclose a large self-addressed, stamped envelope when writing. International students are welcome to apply if they can obtain work permits in their country of origin through organizations such as BUNAC and CIEE. All applicants should be a minimum age of 18 and able to stay at least through Labor Day. Compensation includes a monthly salary.

NATIONAL PARK SERVICE

Contact   Applicant should write for application (must be 18 by May 13; U.S. citizenship required) to Regional Office of the National Park Service, Rocky Mountain Region, National Park Service, P.O. Box 25287, Denver, Colorado 80225-0287.

Jobs located in Colorado at the following facilities: Bent's Old Fort, Black Canyon of the Gunnison, Colorado National Monument, Curecanti, Dinosaur, Florissant Fossil Beds, Great Sand Dunes, Mesa Verde, Rocky Mountain National Park. Also see District of Columbia listing.

NORTH FORK GUEST RANCH
55395 Highway 285, P.O. Box B
Shawnee, Colorado 80475

General Information A ranch providing an all-inclusive package (meals, activities, and lodging) accommodating 35–40 guests weekly. Established 1985. Owned by Dean May. Affiliated with Colorado Dude and Guest Ranch Association, Dude Ranchers' Association, American Automobile Association. Located 50 miles southwest of Denver on 520 acres. Features include horseback riding; white-water rafting; hiking; swimming; overnight pack trip; trap shooting.

Profile of Summer Employees Total number 16; average age 20. Employees are 60% female, 90% college students, 10% local residents. Requires nonsmokers.

Employment Information Openings are from April 1 to December 1. College credit possible. Jobs available: 2 *cooks* at $400–$500 per month; 5 *waitresses/cabin girls* at $300–$400 per month; 5 *wranglers* with horse-care and handling experience at $400–$500 per month; 1 *kids' counselor* with WSI certificate (preferred) at $300–$400 per month; 2 *maintenance persons* at $300–$400 per month.

Benefits On-the-job training, on-site room and board at no charge, laundry facilities, one 24-hour period off per week, tip pool, ability to take part in all activities offered.

Contact Applicant should write for application or call for information by June 1 to Dean and Karen May, Owners/Managers, North Fork Guest Ranch, Department SED, P.O. Box B, Shawnee, Colorado 80475; 800-843-7895, fax 303-674-1432.

PEACEFUL VALLEY LODGE AND RANCH RESORT
Box 2811, Star Route
Lyons, Colorado 80540

General Information Dude ranch serving 100–150 people in a week-long program. Established 1953. Owned by Karl and Mabel Boehm. Affiliated with Colorado Dude and Guest Ranch Association, Dude Ranchers' Association, American Automobile Association. Located 60 miles northwest of Denver on 320 acres. Features include horseback riding; four-wheel drive trips; swimming pool; tennis court; llama treks; breakfast and dinner rides.

Profile of Summer Employees Total number 55; average age 20. Employees are 50% female. Prefers nonsmokers.

Employment Information Openings are from May to September. Year-round positions also offered. Jobs available: 8 *waiters/waitresses;* 3 *dishwashers;* 4 *assistant cooks;* 12 *wranglers* with first aid certification; 4 *counselors* with first aid certification; 7 *housekeepers;* 2 *drivers/mechanical personnel;* 2 *gardeners/grounds crew;* 4 *maintenance staff;* 1 *office person.* International students encouraged to apply.

Benefits On-the-job training, on-site room and board at no charge, laundry facilities, use of facilities, opportunities for staff to use their talents (church choir, evening programs, talent show, melodrama, etc.).

Contact Applicant should send resume, write for application, or call for information by March 1 to Karl E. Boehm, President, Peaceful Valley Lodge and Ranch Resort, Department SED, Star Route, Lyons, Colorado 80540; 303-747-2881, fax 303-747-2167.

ROCKY MOUNTAIN PARK COMPANY (THE TRAIL RIDGE STORE)
Rocky Mountain National Park
Estes Park, Colorado 80517

General Information   Provides high-quality gifts and food service to national park visitors. Only vistor services operation inside Rocky Mountain National Park. Established 1937. Owned by Forever Resorts. Affiliated with Tourist Industry Retail Merchants' Association, Indian Arts and Crafts Association, National Parks Conference of Concessioners. Located 22 miles west of Estes Park on 1 acre. Features include rock-climbing and backcountry hiking; situated in area above timberline in Alpine tundra; 355 miles of incredible hiking trails; 71 peaks over 12,000 feet high; located at 12,000 foot elevation (spectacular).

Profile of Summer Employees   Total number 55; average age 23. Employees are 67% female, 4% minorities, 40% college students, 8% retirees, 5% international, 2% local residents. Prefers nonsmokers.

Employment Information   Openings are from May 31 to October 15. College credit possible. Jobs available: 20 *gift shop sales clerks* with outgoing, energetic personality at $195–$202 per week; 14 *snack bar assistants* with outgoing, energetic personality at $195–$202 per week; 4 *stockroom assistants* with physical ability to perform heavy lifting at $195–$202 per week; 4 *parking attendants* with outgoing, patient personality at $195–$202 per week; 3 *sales supervisors* with three months prior retail and supervisory experience at $260–$270 per week; 2 *foods supervisors* with three months prior food and supervisory experience at $260–$270 per week; 3 *merchandising assistants* with three months prior merchandising experience or six credit hours in color and design at $198–$215 per week.

Benefits   Preemployment training, on-the-job training, on-site room and board at $60 per week, transportation to and from work daily, subsidized activities program, personalized employee meal program.

Contact   Applicant should write for application, call for information, or apply in person by May 29 to William K. Almond, General Manager, Rocky Mountain Park Company (The Trail Ridge Store), P.O. Box 2680, Estes Park, Colorado 80517; 303-586-9319, fax 303-586-2332.

The Trail Ridge Store is located high atop Rocky Mountain National Park in northern Colorado. We offer a personalized summer experience in a spectacular location. Applicants must be able to work at a 12,000-foot elevation and enjoy a fast-paced work atmosphere. Our dormitory is in Estes Park, a resort community on the eastern boundary of the national park, 35 miles north of Boulder, Colorado. We have a full activities program for summer employees. (Please note that international students who wish to apply for employment must provide their own work visas.)

ROCKY MOUNTAIN VILLAGE–HOME OF THE EASTER SEAL HANDICAMP
2644 County Road 306, Empire Junction
Empire, Colorado 80438

General Information   Residential camp serving children and adults with physical and mental disabilities. Established 1951. Owned by Colorado Easter Seal Society. Located

40 miles west of Denver on 95 acres. Features include location in the front range of the Rocky Mountains; close proximity to Vail, Breckenridge, etc.; mountain trails for biking and hiking; swimming, tennis courts, camping, horseback riding, and fishing; computers. **Profile of Summer Employees** Total number 45; average age 20. Employees are 55% female, 20% high school students, 75% college students, 5% local residents. Prefers nonsmokers.

Employment Information Openings are from May 20 to August 31. College credit possible. Jobs available: 1 *program director* at $1600 per season; 1 *assistant cook* at $2000–$2100 per season; 1 *head nurse* with RN license at $3000 per season; 1 *trip specialist* with outdoor camping experience at $1200–$1500 per season; 1 *arts and crafts instructor* at $1200 per season; 1 *computer specialist* at $1200 per season; 1 *animal specialist* at $1200 per season; 1 *pool specialist* with WSI/lifesaving certification at $1200 per season; 1 *athletics specialist* at $1200 per season; 8 *female counselors* at $1000–$1100 per season; 8 *male counselors* at $1000–$1100 per season; 4 *female counselors-in-training* at $500–$700 per season; 4 *male counselors-in-training* at $500–$700 per season; 3 *maintenance helpers* at $1000–$1100 per season; 3 *kitchen helpers* at $1000–$1100 per season; 1 *secretary* at $1000–$1200 per season. International students encouraged to apply.

Benefits Preemployment training, on-the-job training, on-site room and board at no charge, laundry facilities.

Contact Applicant should write for application or call for information by March 15 to Director of Personnel, Rocky Mountain Village–Home of the Easter Seal Handicamp, P.O. Box 115, Empire, Colorado 80438; 303-892-6063.

Our camp offers a unique camping experience for people with disabilities and provides a "boot camp" experience for those wanting to work with physically challenged individuals.

SANBORN WESTERN CAMPS
Florissant, Colorado 80816

General Information Boys' and girls' camps serving ages 7–17 in two- to five-week sessions. Established 1949. Owned by Sanborn Western Camps. Affiliated with American Camping Association. Located 35 miles west of Colorado Springs on 6,000 acres. Features include mountain climbing; Western riding; rafting; natural science activities; trips.

Profile of Summer Employees Total number 120; average age 23. Employees are 50% female, 20% minorities, 10% high school students, 90% college students, 5% international. Prefers nonsmokers.

Employment Information Openings are from June 6 to August 22. Year-round positions also offered. College credit possible. Jobs available: 8 *riding instructors* at $900 per season; 8 *canoeing instructors* at $900 per season; 8 *rock-climbing instructors* at $900 per season; 20 *backpacking instructors* at $900 per season; 10 *ecology instructors* at $900 per season; 8 *tennis instructors* at $900 per season; 4 *drama instructors* at $900 per season; 4 *geology instructors* at $900 per season; 8 *swimming instructors* at $900 per season; 8 *arts and crafts instructors* at $900 per season; 8 *campcraft instructors* at $900 per season; 8 *rafting instructors* at $900 per season; 8 *sports instructors* at $900 per season; 8 *caving instructors* at $900 per season; 10 *mountaineering instructors* at $900 per season; *cooks; nurses; interpreters.* International students encouraged to apply.

Benefits Preemployment training, on-the-job training, on-site room and board at no charge, laundry facilities, health insurance.

Contact   Applicant should send resume, write for application, or call for information by May 10 to Rick Sanborn, Director, Sanborn Western Camps, Florissant, Colorado 80816; 719-748-3341.

SCANTICON DENVER
200 Inverness Drive West
Englewood, Colorado 80112

General Information   Hotel and resort catering to Fortune 500 businesses for conferences of up to 275 people. Established 1989. Owned by Scanticon Corporation. Affiliated with Denver Chamber of Commerce, South Metro Chamber. Located 12 miles south of Denver on 200 acres. Features include conference facilities; golf course; restaurants; audiovisual setup; beautiful views.

Profile of Summer Employees   Total number 30; average age 21. Employees are 40% female, 25% high school students, 25% college students, 50% local residents.

Employment Information   Openings are from May 1 to September 30. Year-round positions also offered. College credit possible. International students encouraged to apply.

Benefits   Preemployment training, on-the-job training, formal ongoing training, free food for meals and breaks, uniforms and cleaning.

Contact   Applicant should apply in person by June 1 to Susan Kerner, Director of Personnel, Scanticon Denver, 200 Inverness Drive West, Englewood, Colorado 80112; 303-397-7051.

SKY HIGH RANCH
30924 North Highway 67
Woodland Park, Colorado 80863

General Information   Residential camp for girls in grades 2–12. Weekly capacity is 130 campers. Established 1951. Owned by Girl Scouts–Wagon Wheel Council. Affiliated with American Camping Association. Located 25 miles west of Colorado Springs on 880 acres. Features include location bordering national forest land; 2 ponds; equestrian center; diverse program; camper planning of activities; nature/environmental programs.

Profile of Summer Employees   Total number 34; average age 22. Employees are 100% female, 8% minorities, 5% high school students, 60% college students, 50% local residents. Prefers nonsmokers.

Employment Information   Openings are from June 6 to August 6. College credit possible. Jobs available: 1 *camp director* at $275 per week; 1 *assistant camp director* at $220 per week; 1 *program specialist* at $140 per week; 1 *health supervisor* with RN license at $200 per week; 6 *unit leaders* at $120 per week; 14 *unit counselors* at $90 per week; 1 *head cook* at $200 per week; 1 *assistant cook* at $110 per week; 2 *kitchen aides* with a minimum age of 16 at $80 per week; 1 *riding director* with CHA certification (preferred) at $120 per week; 2 *riding assistants* at $90 per week; 1 *waterfront director* with WSI and lifeguard certification at $120 per week; 1 *waterfront assistant* with lifeguard certification at $90 per week.

Benefits   Preemployment training, on-the-job training, on-site room and board at no charge, laundry facilities, health insurance.

Contact   Applicant should write for application or call for information by May 15 to Wynne Whyman, Program Director, Sky High Ranch, Department SED, 3535 Parkmoor Village Drive, Colorado Springs, Colorado 80917; 719-597-8603, fax 719-597-8606.

Girl Scouts–Wagon Wheel Council is looking for staff members who have an ability to work with children and enjoy the outdoors. The diverse program at our rustic camp includes pioneers, horsemanship, Native American culture, photography, backpacking, canoeing, science, counselors-in-training, swimming, and arts. Salaries listed are base salaries and increase depending on experience. All positions require a minimum age of 18 or graduation from high school.

TUMBLING RIVER RANCH
P.O. Box 30
Grant, Colorado 80448

General Information   Guest ranch serving families. Established 1940. Owned by Jim and Mary Dale Gordon. Affiliated with Colorado Dude and Guest Ranch Association, Dude Ranchers' Association. Located 62 miles southwest of Denver on 200 acres. Features include log cabins (all rooms have fireplaces) and 2 lovely rock lodges.

Profile of Summer Employees   Total number 30; average age 20. Employees are 50% female. Prefers nonsmokers.

Employment Information   Openings are from May 15 to October 1. Winter break positions also offered. College credit possible. Jobs available: *waitresses; cabin girls; cooks; assistant cooks; secretary; children's counselors; drivers; mechanics; wranglers; general maintenance persons; groundskeepers.*

Benefits   On-the-job training, formal ongoing training, on-site room and board, laundry facilities, end-of-summer bonus.

Contact   Applicant should write for application or call for information by April 1 to Mary Dale Gordon, Owner, Tumbling River Ranch, P.O. Box 30, Grant, Colorado 80448; 303-838-5981.

Tumbling River Ranch offers a family atmosphere with a close-knit staff, the opportunity to learn many different jobs, and good working conditions. Please note that there are openings for 30 college students (minimum age 19 with sophomore standing or above) and teachers, from mid-May through September. Payment for employees is monthly and tips are additional.

VAIL ASSOCIATES, INC.
P.O. Box 7
Vail, Colorado 81658

General Information   Owners and operators of Vail and Beaver Creek ski resorts. Established 1962. Affiliated with Colorado Ski Country USA. Located 100 miles west of Denver. Features include location in the heart of the Rocky Mountains; year-round recreation facilities; family-oriented resort area.

Profile of Summer Employees   Total number 300.

Employment Information   Openings are from May 31 to September 1. Winter break, Christmas break, year-round positions also offered. Jobs available: *hospitality positions; food-service personnel; golf course staff; grounds/maintenance persons; child-care staff;*

summer day-camp attendants; lift-operations personnel; wranglers. International students encouraged to apply.

Benefits On-the-job training, formal ongoing training, on-site room and board at $300 per month, laundry facilities, health insurance, free season ski pass (winter employees), living in the beautiful Rocky Mountains, employee day care.

Contact Applicant should write for application, call for information, or apply in person to Personnel Office, Vail Associates, Inc., P.O. Box 7, Vail, Colorado 81658; 303-476-5601 Ext. 3300.

We have a variety of summer and winter seasonal positions available as well as year-round career opportunities. The number one ski area in North America, Vail, and its sister mountain, Beaver Creek Resort, are always interested in hardworking, dedicated, and enthusiastic people to staff our resorts and provide high-quality service to our guests. (Please note that a $200 room deposit is required of employees.)

VILLAGE AT BRECKENRIDGE RESORT
655 Park Street, P.O. Box 8329
Breckenridge, Colorado 80424

General Information Hosts individuals, families, groups, and conventions in 7 hotel/lodge buildings. Established 1988. Owned by Mr. Ron Tuchschmidt. Affiliated with Colorado Restaurant Association, Breckenridge Resort Chamber, Summit County Resort Chamber. Located 80 miles west of Denver on 37 acres. Features include location at the base of mountains in a town listed on the National Register of Historic Places; health club facilities, hot tub, and pools; hiking and biking trails; pond for fishing and paddle boating; close proximity to chair lifts, Alpine Slide, a human maze, and horseback riding; all types of music throughout the summer; mall and plaza for convenient shopping (craft fair held at these locations in summer).

Profile of Summer Employees Total number 275; average age 25. Employees are 50% female, 10% minorities, 60% college students, 5% international, 35% local residents.

Employment Information Openings are from May 30 to August 30. Winter break positions also offered. Jobs available: *front-desk clerks* with congenial, people-oriented personality; *reservationists* with excellent phone and computer skills; *PBX operators* with excellent phone skills; *cooks (all types); kitchen stewards; wait staff* with pleasant, service-oriented attitude; *buspersons* with pleasant, service-oriented attitude; *cashiers/hosts/hostesses* with pleasant and friendly personality, detail orientation, and money-handling experience; *housekeepers* with friendly, thorough, and efficient work habits; *laundry personnel; parking lot attendants* with friendly personality and knowledge of, or ability to learn about, town activities.

Benefits On-site room and board at $625 per month, free employee meal per shift worked, uniforms (if required), 10% employee discount in our restaurants.

Contact Applicant should send resume, write for application, or call for information and apply in person after May 30 to Keith Schmotzer, Human Resource Director, Village at Breckenridge Resort, Department SED, P.O. Box 8329, Breckenridge, Colorado 80424; 303-453-2000, fax 303-453-1878.

Compensation levels for jobs detailed in this listing range from $2.13 to $9.00 per hour depending on position, skill level, and experience. (Wages for certain positions are supplemented with tips.)

THE WHITEMAN COLORADO CAMPS
42605 Routt County Road 36
Steamboat Springs, Colorado 80487

General Information   Residential camp serving 60 campers ages 7–18 per session. Strong group dynamics and outdoor-education emphasis. Established 1957. Owned by The Whiteman School, Inc. Affiliated with American Camping Association. Located 150 miles northwest of Denver on 180 acres. Features include well-maintained indoor gymnasium; athletics field; outdoor sand volleyball court; riding trails through the woods; spacious dormitory cabins; easy access to private hot springs.

Profile of Summer Employees   Total number 28; average age 21. Employees are 57% female, 14% high school students, 86% college students. Requires nonsmokers.

Employment Information   Openings are from June 6 to August 17. Year-round positions also offered. Jobs available: 1 *nurse* with RN license at $1500 per season; 3 *cooks* with previous experience at $600–$2000 per season; 3 *wranglers* with strong horsemanship and teaching skills at $600–$1000 per season; 1 *program coordinator* with leadership experience and strong organizational skills at $950 per season; 4 *wilderness instructors* with previous teaching experience and technical skills (minimum age 21) at $950 per season; 1 *arts and crafts counselor* at $825 per season; 10 *senior counselors* with camping or teaching experience, lifeguard training, and first aid certificate (preferred) at $825 per season; 4 *assistant counselors* at $550 per season; 1 *office manager* with previous experience (minimum age 21) at $200 per week. International students encouraged to apply.

Benefits   Preemployment training, on-the-job training, on-site room and board at no charge, local discounts.

Contact   Applicant should send resume, write for application, call for information, or apply in person by April 1 to Jay B. Poulter, Director, The Whiteman Colorado Camps, 42605 Routt County Road 36, Steamboat Springs, Colorado 80487; 303-879-4816, fax 303-879-1307.

   The key to our success is our experienced, sensitive, and caring staff/team. They encourage campers to meet and overcome challenges, to develop group living skills, and to appreciate the world around them. Our common goal is to increase each individual's self-confidence and positive feelings of self-worth.

WILDERNESS TRAILS RANCH
23486 County Road 501
Bayfield, Colorado 81122

General Information   An American-plan ranch accommodating 50 guests weekly. Established 1950. Owned by Gene and Jan Roberts. Affiliated with Mobil Travel Guide, American Automobile Association, Colorado Dude and Guest Ranch Association. Located 230 miles north of Albuquerque, New Mexico on 160 acres. Features include excellent horseback riding with instruction and hay rides; spectacular scenery; 4-wheel drive and raft trips; children's and teen's programs; 72-foot heated pool and hot tub; accommodating staff; nightly entertainment; clean air; fishing and waterskiing.

Profile of Summer Employees   Total number 30; average age 21. Employees are 50% female, 87% college students, 7% international, 7% local residents. Requires nonsmokers.

Employment Information   Openings are from May 1 to October 1. College credit possible. Jobs available: 10 *wranglers* with first aid certification and horse experience at $800 per month; 8 *cabins/kitchen staff* at $735 per month; 3 *children's counselors* with first aid certification at $800 per month; 2 *office/clerical persons* with clerical and computer experience at $770 per month; 1 *grounds/maintenance person* with electrical and woodworking experience at $735 per month; 1 *kitchen aide* with organizational skills and cooking experience at $735 per month.

Benefits   Preemployment training, on-the-job training, on-site room and board at no charge, laundry facilities, use of recreational/ranch facilities.

Contact   Applicant should send resume, write for application, or call for information by April 1 to Wilderness Trails Ranch, 776 County Road 300, Durango, Colorado 81301; 303-247-0722.

International students with work visas are welcome to apply for employment.

YMCA OF THE ROCKIES, CAMP CHIEF OURAY
Colorado

General Information   Christian-oriented residential camp for boys and girls ages 8–16. Operated by YMCA of the Rockies. Located 75 miles west of Denver. Features include beautiful mountain setting; backpacking; camping; horseback riding; hiking, nature activities; adventure and crafts.

Employment Information   Openings are from June to August 15. Jobs available: *assistant director; program director; nurses; cooks; maintenance travel person; counselor-in-training director; wranglers; senior counselors; junior counselors.*

Benefits   Preemployment training, on-site room and board at no charge, health insurance, returning staff members receive salary increase.

Contact   Applicant should send resume by March 1 to Director, YMCA of the Rockies, Camp Chief Ouray, Box 648, Granby, Colorado 80446.

Pleasant, fun-filled, Christian atmosphere. Two-week staff training provides orientation, team building, and guidance in child leadership. Come join an excellent, fun-filled camping program.

YMCA OF THE ROCKIES, ESTES PARK CENTER
Estes Park, Colorado 80511-2550

General Information   Large Christian-oriented family resort and conference center. Operated by YMCA of the Rockies. Located 70 miles west of Denver. Features include year-round operation; extensive staff activities such as dances, parties, movies, field trips, cookouts, and Bible studies; swimming; tennis; roller skating; miniature golf; horseback riding.

Profile of Summer Employees   Total number 320.

Employment Information   Openings are from May 15 to September 30. Jobs available: *front-desk clerk; switchboard operators; secretary/receptionists; chaplain; registered nurses; food-service personnel; room service (housekeeping) staff; maintenance workers; lodge/dormitory attendants; hosts/hostesses; soda fountain/snack bar staff; pool guards* with current certification; *day camp counselors; miniature golf and roller skating rink attendants; grocery store and gift shop salespersons.*

Benefits   On-site room and board at no charge, training programs for mountain guides, bonus and shared gratuity for those who complete their employment satisfactorily.

Contact   Applicant should write for application or call for information to Personnel Director, YMCA of the Rockies, Estes Park Center, Estes Park, Colorado 80511-2550; 303-586-3341.

Assistance in obtaining U.S. work visa (J-1) available for international applicants pursuing YMCA-related careers.

YMCA OF THE ROCKIES, SNOW MOUNTAIN RANCH
P.O. Box 169
Winter Park, Colorado 80482

General Information   YMCA conference center and family resort accommodating up to 1,700 guests a day. Established 1969. Operated by YMCA of the Rockies. Located 70 miles northwest of Denver on 4,500 acres. Features include year-round operation; location near Winter Park ski resort and Rocky Mountain National Park; Christian organization; extensive staff activities; staff from around the United States and many foreign countries.

Profile of Summer Employees   Total number 130; average age 21. Employees are 60% female, 10% minorities, 2% high school students, 45% college students, 15% retirees, 25% international, 3% local residents. Prefers nonsmokers.

Employment Information   Openings are from May 20 to August 28. Spring break, winter break, Christmas break, year-round positions also offered. Jobs available: 1 *chaplain* with seminary experience (preferred) at $120–$150 per week; 10 *lifeguards* with American Red Cross lifeguard certification at $85 per week; 2 *crafts shop instructors* at $75 per week; 1 *museum leader* at $75 per week; 1 *librarian* at $75 per week; 10 *day-camp counselors* at $75 per week; 32 *housekeeping personnel* at $75 per week; 28 *food-service personnel* at $75 per week; 10 *maintenance personnel* at $75 per week; 9 *retail sales personnel* at $75 per week; 12 *front-desk clerks* at $75 per week; 35 *resident-camp counselors* at $95 per week.

Benefits   On-the-job training, formal ongoing training, on-site room and board at no charge, laundry facilities, internships, free use of recreation facilities, discount in gift shop, 40 hour work week (normally) with two days off each week.

Contact   Applicant should write for application or call for information by June 1 to Julie Orr, Personnel Director, YMCA of the Rockies, Snow Mountain Ranch, P.O. Box 169, Winter Park, Colorado 80482; 303-887-2152, fax 303-449-6781.

Assistance in obtaining U.S. work visa (J-1) available for international applicants pursuing YMCA-related careers.

Connecticut

AWOSTING AND CHINQUEKA CAMPS
Litchfield, Connecticut

General Information Residential camps serving 140 boys and 125 girls in programs of two to eight weeks. Established 1900. Owned by Ebner Camps Inc. Affiliated with American Camping Association, Connecticut Camping Association. Located 10 miles south of Torrington on 200 acres. Features include location in foothills of Berkshires; Bantam Lake (3½ miles long); cabins with facilities for lodging; 7½ hours from New York City or Boston; excellent food program; family-owned and operated for over 40 years.

Profile of Summer Employees Total number 80; average age 22. Employees are 50% female, 10% minorities, 80% college students, 5% retirees, 30% international, 5% local residents. Prefers nonsmokers.

Employment Information Openings are from June 22 to August 22. College credit possible. Jobs available: 6 *swimming instructors* with WSI, LGT, or LGTI certificates (clinic available) at $1200–$1400 per season; 6 *small craft instructors* with certification in one or more of the following: canoeing, sailing, kayaking, and boating (clinic available) at $1200–$1400 per season; 3 *waterskiing instructors* with LGT and CPR certificates plus teaching experience at $1200–$1400 per season; 6 *sports instructors* with background in one or more of the following: softball, soccer, and tennis at $1000–$1300 per season; 2 *archery instructors* with certification (clinic available) at $1000–$1300 per season; 2 *riflery instructors* with NRA instructor certification (clinic available) and a minimum age of 21 at $1000–$1300 per season; 2 *go-carts/mini bikes personnel* with knowledge of equipment and racing at $1000–$1300 per season; 4 *black and white photography/video/filming instructors* with knowledge of equipment at $1000–$1300 per season; 3 *gymnastics instructors* with coaching experience at $1000–$1300 per season; 3 *dance/theater/music instructors* with some stage and music background at $1000–$1300 per season; 4 *computers and journalism staff* with journalism experience and the ability to operate Apple and IBM PC computers at $1000–$1300 per season; 2 *laundry workers* at $1250 per season; 2 *nurses or first aid persons* with RN, LPN, EMT, or standard first aid certificate and CPR certification at $1300–$1800 per season; 2 *maintenance personnel* with background in painting, carpentry, and ground maintenance at $1350 per season; 6 *kitchen aides* with food-service experience at $1250 per season; 3 *arts and crafts instructors* at $1200–$1400 per season; 2 *outdoor-camping staff* with hiking and camping experience (minimum age 21) at $1200–$1400 per season. International students encouraged to apply.

Benefits Preemployment training, on-the-job training, on-site room and board at no charge, laundry facilities, travel reimbursement, certification clinics, end-of-season bonus, tips.

Contact Applicant should write for application or call for information by May 15 to Oscar Ebner, Director, Awosting and Chinqueka Camps, Department SED, Breezy Hill, Harwinton, Connecticut 06791; 203-485-9566, fax 203-567-3641.

Our activity staff members are hired for their special ability to instruct one or more activity programs. We do not hire general counselors. In addition, the activity staff is also the cabin staff. We are seeking candidates with good prior experience or coaching and some previous camping background. Applicants with psychology, education, recreation, and sports majors in college make excellent candidates.

CAMP HEMLOCKS
P.O. Box 198
Hebron, Connecticut 06248

General Information Residential camp serving 100 persons with physical disabilities. Established 1950. Owned by Easter Seal Society of Connecticut. Affiliated with National Easter Seal Society, American Camping Association. Located 30 miles southeast of Hartford on 160 acres. Features include barrier-free design; indoor pool; modern facilities; location in central Connecticut.

Profile of Summer Employees Total number 60; average age 19. Employees are 67% female, 10% high school students, 55% college students, 25% international.

Employment Information Openings are from June 1 to August 17. Year-round positions also offered. Jobs available: *assistant program director* with three years of camp experience at $200 per week; *arts and crafts leader* at $150 per week; *nature/activity leader* at $150 per week; *outdoor-living skills instructor* at $150 per week; *physical recreation leader* at $150 per week; *assistant aquatic director* with WSI certificate at $160 per week; 6 *cabin leaders* with college junior or senior status at $130 per week; 48 *general counselors* with a minimum age of 18 at $110–$125 per week; 10 *counselors-in-training* with an age between 16–18 at $65 per week. International students encouraged to apply.

Benefits Preemployment training, on-the-job training, on-site room and board at no charge, laundry facilities.

Contact Applicant should write for application or call for information by May 15 to Mr. Sunny P. Ku, Summer Camp Director, Camp Hemlocks, Department SED, P.O. Box 198, Hebron, Connecticut 06248; 203-228-9496.

Camp Hemlocks is looking for staff members who want to learn about working with people with disabilities. We can provide internship supervision. The work is both challenging and rewarding, and we provide opportunities to learn, to explore, and to grow.

CAMP JEWELL YMCA
Prock Hill Road
Colebrook, Connecticut 06021

General Information Full-featured, coeducational, residential camp with teen adventure trips and year-round environmental education. Owned by YMCA of Metro Hartford. Affiliated with American Camping Association. Located 35 miles northwest of Hartford on 500 acres. Features include location in the foothills of the Berkshires; 50-acre private lake; cabins with fireplace and bathroom/shower; staff recruited from throughout the nation.

Profile of Summer Employees Total number 125; average age 21. Employees are 50% female, 10% minorities, 15% high school students, 65% college students, 1% retirees, 10% international, 25% local residents. Prefers nonsmokers.

Employment Information Openings are from June 19 to August 22. Year-round positions also offered. Jobs available: 2 *ropes-course directors* with previous experience at $1300–$1700 per season; 1 *waterfront director* with lifeguard/WSI certificate and experience at $1500–$2000 per season; 15 *teen trip leaders* with a minimum age of 21 at $1400–$1800 per season; 6 *village directors* with supervisory and camp experience at $1500–$2000 per season; 3 *crafts program specialists* at $1200–$1500 per season; 2 *sailing program specialists* at $1200–$1500 per season; 2 *tennis program specialists* at $1200–$1500 per season;

4 *aquatic program specialists* at $1200–$1500 per season; 1 *drama program specialist* at $1200–$1500 per season; 1 *naturalist.*

Benefits Preemployment training, on-site room and board at no charge, laundry facilities.

Contact Applicant should write for application by June 1 to Paul Kamin, Assistant Director, Camp Jewell YMCA, Department SED, Prock Hill Road, Colebrook, Connecticut 06021; 203-379-2782.

Program focuses on developing self-esteem through success-filled experiences with effective role models.

CAMP WASHINGTON
P.O. Box 161
Lakeside, Connecticut 06758

General Information Residential, coeducational camp serving a diverse population of 125 campers weekly. Established 1917. Located 50 miles west of Hartford on 300 acres. Features include new conference center; winterized, heated cabins; rural location.

Profile of Summer Employees Total number 60; average age 21. Employees are 50% female, 10% minorities, 20% high school students, 40% college students, 25% international, 25% local residents.

Employment Information Openings are from June 15 to August 25. Winter break, Christmas break positions also offered. Jobs available: 3 *waterfront staff* with WSI certificate and lifeguard training at $1000–$1500 per season; 16 *general counselors* with experience working with children at $800–$1300 per season; 10 *program coordinators* with ability to teach a specific activity at $1000–$1500 per season; *nurse* with RN license at $1500–$3000 per season. International students encouraged to apply.

Benefits Preemployment training, on-the-job training, formal ongoing training, on-site room and board, laundry facilities, travel reimbursement, health insurance.

Contact Applicant should send resume or write for application by April 1 to Richard Harris, Camp Director, Camp Washington, P.O. Box 161, Lakeside, Connecticut 06758; 203-567-9623.

CHANNEL 3 COUNTRY CAMP
73 Times Farm Road
Andover, Connecticut 06232

General Information Residential camp serving 480 boys and girls each session. Open enrollment, but preference given to Hartford area underprivileged children. Established 1910. Owned by Almada Lodge Times Farm Camp Corporation Board of Directors. Operated by WFSB–TV 3. Affiliated with American Camping Association. Located 20 miles east of Hartford on 300 acres. Features include stocked trout fishing stream; Olympic-size swimming pool; new playfield/ground; hardwood forest and trails setting; high rate of return of campers and staff.

Profile of Summer Employees Total number 40; average age 25. Employees are 50% female, 35% minorities, 75% college students, 15% international, 60% local residents. Prefers nonsmokers.

Employment Information Openings are from June 16 to August 17. Year-round positions also offered. Jobs available: 1 *alternate director* with B.S. degree and two years administrative/supervisory experience at $300–$350 per week; 2 *unit leaders* with A.A. or B.S. degree and one year supervisory experience at $150–$170 per week; 18 *counselors* with two years organizational camp experience (must be college junior or senior) at $100–$140 per week; 1 *swimming director* with American Red Cross BLS, CPR, and lifeguard training at $100–$160 per week; 1 *creative crafts instructor* with child-handicraft experience (must be college junior or senior) at $100–$130 per week; 1 *environmental education instructor* with interest and experience in nature (must be college junior or senior) at $100–$140 per week; 1 *outdoor-living skills instructor* with camping skills and experience (must be college junior or senior) at $100–$140 per week; 1 *archery instructor* with archery safety course certification (minimum age 18) at $100–$140 per week; 1 *health-care director* with American Red Cross standard first aid, BLS, and CPR certification (minimum age 21) at $155–$180 per week; 2 *swimming instructors* with American Red Cross ALS certification preferred (minimum age 19) at $100–$130 per week.

Benefits Preemployment training, on-the-job training, on-site room and board at no charge, laundry facilities, health insurance, 48 hour period off with entire staff every two weeks.

Contact Applicant should write for application or call for information by May 15 to Gary Turn, CCD, Director, Channel 3 Country Camp, 73 Times Farm Road, Andover, Connecticut 06232; 203-643-2494.

The challenge that awaits our staff comes from the freedom of individual programming and the task of meeting the special needs of the high percentage of underprivileged campers.

LAUREL RESIDENT CAMP
175 Clubhouse Road
Lebanon, Connecticut 06247

General Information Residential camp serving 200 Girl Scouts ages 6–17, with an informal, educational outdoor program. Established 1955. Owned by Connecticut Trails Girl Scout Council. Affiliated with American Camping Association, Camp Horsemanship Association, American Red Cross, National Wildlife Federation. Located 100 miles north of New York City on 300 acres. Features include large lake with extensive aquatic program; horseback riding in 2 lighted rings and trails; live-in cabins and tents; Girl Scout program and philosophy; international programming; implementation of innovative ideals.

Profile of Summer Employees Total number 60; average age 20. Employees are 95% female, 15% minorities, 5% high school students, 50% college students, 10% international, 20% local residents.

Employment Information Openings are from June 21 to August 16. Year-round positions also offered. College credit possible. Jobs available: 2 *program directors* with administrative/program experience at $2200–$3500 per season; 1 *assistant camp director* with administrative/program experience at $2200–$3500 per season; 1 *business manager* with business training and driver's license at $1200–$1500 per season; 2 *health directors* with nurse, LPN, or EMT license at $2000–$2500 per season; 2 *waterfront directors* with lifeguard, CPR, or FA certification (minimum age 21) at $1500–$1800 per season; 6 *waterfront assistants* with lifeguard, CPR, FA, or WSI certification at $900–$1200 per season; 8 *unit leaders* with experience supervising children at $1200–$1500 per season;

24 *unit assistants* with experience camping and working with children at $800–$1000 per season; 1 *food supervisor* with experience in menu planning and food preparation at $2000–$2500 per season; 2 *assistant cooks* with experience in food preparation at $1300–$1800 per season; 4 *kitchen assistants* with ability to assist cooks at $800–$1000 per season; 1 *horseback-riding director* with ability to develop and supervise equestrian programs at $1200–$1900 per season; 5 *horseback-riding staff* with experience in English and Western style riding at $800–$1800 per season; 1 *arts and crafts director* with experience in a specialty area at $1000–$1500 per season; 1 *ropes-course director* with experience in a specialty area at $1000–$1500 per season; 1 *naturalist* with experience in nature activities at $1000–$1500 per season; 1 *farm life director* with experience in farm animal care at $1000–$1500 per season; 1 *archery director* with experience in archery instruction at $1000–$1500 per season; 1 *trip leader* with experience in trip management at $1200–$1500 per season; 2 *maintenance assistants* with willingness to lift and to work outdoors at $800–$1000 per season; 2 *boating instructors* with experience teaching canoeing at $1000–$1200 per season. International students encouraged to apply.

Benefits Preemployment training, on-the-job training, on-site room and board at no charge, laundry facilities, travel reimbursement, health insurance, cultural exchange, recruitment bonus.

Contact Applicant should send resume, write for application, call for information, or apply in person by June 10 to Bridget Erin Healy, Outdoor Program/Property Director, Laurel Resident Camp, Department SED, 20 Washington Avenue, North Haven, Connecticut 06473; 203-239-2922.

Laurel Resident Camp sponsors a trip to Boston or New York City. We also offer competitive salaries and occasional transportation during staff time off. Our concerned campers and staff members are our greatest assets and are very valued.

SUNRISE RESORT
Route 151, P.O. Box 415
Moodus, Connecticut 06469

General Information Summer resort catering to families and outing groups. Established 1917. Owned by Bob Johnson. Affiliated with Hartford Convention Bureau, Middlesex Travel and Tourism Commission, Chamber of Commerce. Features include very social atmosphere; good work experience.

Profile of Summer Employees Total number 150; average age 20. Employees are 60% female, 5% minorities, 40% high school students, 40% college students, 5% retirees, 8% international, 75% local residents.

Employment Information Openings are from May 15 to October 15. College credit possible. Jobs available: 4 *lifeguards* with ALS or WSI certification at $2000–$3000 per season; 25 *waiters/waitresses* at $2000–$3500 per season; 15 *housekeeping staff* at $2000–$3000 per season; 4 *office personnel* with typing ability at $2000–$3500 per season. International students encouraged to apply.

Benefits On-the-job training, on-site room and board at $40 per week, laundry facilities, use of facilities.

Contact Applicant should send resume, write for application, call for information, or apply in person by April 1 to Jim Johnson, Director, Sunrise Resort, Department SED, P.O. Box 415, Moodus, Connecticut 06469; 203-873-8681.

UNITED CEREBRAL PALSY ASSOCIATION OF GREATER HARTFORD
80 Whitney Street
Hartford, Connecticut 06105

General Information Residential camping program serving the physically disabled, ages 8–adult. Offers an eight-week summer program. Operated by United Cerebral Palsy. Affiliated with Connecticut Parks and Recreation, National Parks and Recreation. Features include waterfront for boating and swimming on Long Island Sound; fully accessible location; horseback riding; field trips to tourist areas; trained staff for PCA work and excellent camper–staff ratio; individualized and group activities; heated cabins with full bathroom facilities.

Profile of Summer Employees Total number 23; average age 25. Employees are 20% minorities, 85% college students, 1% international, 55% local residents. Prefers nonsmokers.

Employment Information Openings are from January 15 to May 15. Year-round positions also offered. Jobs available: 1 *assistant director* with ability to interact with disabled individuals plus previous program and supervisory experience at $2000–$3000 per season; 1 *nurse (LPN or RN)* with experience caring for the disabled and Connecticut certification at $3000–$4000 per season; 2 *head counselors* with experience in personal care and working in a camp setting at $1400–$1600 per season; 5 *activity leaders* with experience in skill area and ability to work with others at $1300–$1450 per season; 14 *general counselors* with dedication and maturity, willingness to learn, a minimum age of 18, and previous experience working with disabled persons (preferred) at $1250–$1425 per season. International students encouraged to apply.

Benefits Preemployment training, on-the-job training, on-site room and board at no charge, laundry facilities, expenses paid on field trips.

Contact Applicant should send resume, write for application, call for information, or apply in person by May 15 to Janet Barry, Camp Coordinator, United Cerebral Palsy Association of Greater Hartford, 80 Whitney Street, Hartford, Connecticut 06105; 203-236-6201, fax 203-236-6205.

WESTPORT COUNTRY PLAYHOUSE
25 Powers Court
Westport, Connecticut 06880

General Information Professional summer theater producing six plays each year. Established 1931. Owned by Playhouse Limited Partnership. Operated by Connecticut Theatre Foundation. Affiliated with Actors' Equity Association, Council of Summer Theaters. Located 47 miles north of New York City on 3 acres. Features include historic site; red barn atmosphere.

Profile of Summer Employees Total number 50; average age 28. Employees are 50% female, 10% high school students, 40% college students, 50% local residents. Prefers nonsmokers.

Employment Information Openings are from June 8 to September 12. College credit possible. Jobs available: 8 *technical interns* at $60 per week; 2 *administrative/press interns* at $125 per week; 6 *box office staff* at $200 per week; 3 *carpentry staff* at $300–$400 per week. International students encouraged to apply.

Benefits On-the-job training.

Contact Applicant should send resume, write for application, call for information, or apply in person by May 1 to Julie Monahan, General Manager, Westport Country Playhouse, Department SED, P.O. Box 629, Westport, Connecticut 06881; 203-227-5137, fax 203-221-7482.

Internships qualify for points in Actors' Equity membership candidate program.

Delaware

CHESAPEAKE BAY GIRL SCOUT COUNCIL
501 South College Avenue
Newark, Delaware 19713

General Information Residential and day camps serving girls ages 6–16 during June, July, and August. Established 1912. Affiliated with American Camping Association, Girl Scouts of the United States of America, National Society of Fund Raising Executives. Located 40 miles south of Philadelphia on 265 acres. Features include location on Chesapeake Bay; environmentally pleasant surroundings; relaxed atmosphere; close proximity to Baltimore, Washington, D.C., and Philadelphia.

Profile of Summer Employees Total number 40; average age 20. Employees are 95% female, 10% minorities, 20% high school students, 60% college students, 20% international, 20% local residents. Prefers nonsmokers.

Employment Information Openings are from June 14 to August 12. Jobs available: 2 *swimming instructors* with WSI certificate at $1025–$1175 per season; 4 *lifeguards* with American Red Cross training at $1025–$1175 per season; 1 *sailing instructor* with American Red Cross training or equivalent at $1025–$1175 per season; *waterskiing instructor* with waterskiing certificate at $1025–$1175 per season. International students encouraged to apply.

Benefits Preemployment training, on-the-job training, on-site room and board, laundry facilities, reimbursement for program certificates.

Contact Applicant should send resume, write for application, call for information, or apply in person by June 1 to Suzanne Cash, Outdoor Program Manager, Chesapeake Bay Girl Scout Council, 501 South College Avenue, Newark, Delaware 19713; 302-456-7163, fax 302-456-7188.

District of Columbia

NATIONAL PARK SERVICE

Employment Information Jobs available: *clerical staff* with all DOL offices; *nonclerical staff* with Mine Safety, Health Administration, and Inspector General Offices; *nonclerical, professional, technical, or administrative staff* with Bureau of Labor Statistics, Employment Standards Administration, National Capital Service Center, Occupational Safety and Health Administration, and Office of the Solicitor agencies.

Contact   Applicant should write for application by March 1 to Summer Employment Coordinator, Department of Labor, Room N5470, National Park Service, 200 Constitution Avenue, NW, Washington, D.C. 20210.

Openings for students during summer and possibly part-time during school year. A limited number of positions available in Washington, D.C., and Arlington, Virginia. Interested applicants must apply directly to personnel offices of the individual agency to be considered. Jobs also available at regional offices in Boston, Massachusetts; New York, New York; Philadelphia, Pennsylvania; Atlanta, Georgia; Chicago, Illinois; Dallas, Texas; Kansas City, Missouri; Denver, Colorado; Seattle, Washington; San Francisco, California. Applications for outside Washington, D.C., and Arlington, Virginia must be submitted to the regional personnel office(s) for the area in which the candidate is interested. See state listings for addresses.

Florida

ACTIONQUEST PROGRAMS
P.O. Box 5507
Sarasota, Florida 34277

General Information   On-board program serving an average of 100 teenagers in each of three 2-week sessions in intensive sailing, dive training, and other water sports. Established 1970. Owned by James Stoll. Affiliated with American Sailing Association, American Waterskiing Association, United States Windsurfing Association. Features include foreign travel; 50-foot sailing yachts; high-quality training programs; stimulating work sessions; leadership/motivational programs; sailing/diving in Caribbean Waters.

Profile of Summer Employees   Total number 25; average age 28. Employees are 40% female, 50% college students, 10% international. Requires nonsmokers.

Employment Information   Openings are from June 15 to August 25. Jobs available: 12 *sailing teachers or British Yachtmasters* with USCG license or equivalent at $3000 per season; 12 *diving instructors* with PADI certification or equivalent at $2200 per season. International students encouraged to apply.

Benefits   On-site room and board at no charge, travel reimbursement, all expenses paid, plus the opportunity to travel in the British Virgin Islands.

Contact   Applicant should send resume, write for application, or call for information to James Stoll, Director, Actionquest Programs, Department SED, P.O. Box 5507, Sarasota, Florida 34277; 813-924-6789, fax 813-924-6075.

CAMP THUNDERBIRD
909 East Welch Road
Apopka, Florida 32712

General Information   Residential camp serving 96 campers with a 1:4 counselor–camper ratio. Offers summer fun mixed with social and independent living skills. Established 1985. Owned by Florida Foundation for Special Children. Affiliated with American Camping Association, Florida Association for Retarded Citizens. Located 20 miles northwest of

Orlando on 20 acres. Features include location on Wekiwa Springs State Park property; Florida pine and oak sandhill; swimming pool; new dorms with ceiling fans; out-stage and campfire area; sports court.

Profile of Summer Employees Total number 48; average age 25. Employees are 75% female, 10% minorities, 50% college students, 2% retirees, 50% international. Requires nonsmokers.

Employment Information Openings are from June 7 to August 16. College credit possible. Jobs available: 20 *cottage counselors* with experience working with mentally retarded persons at $1100–$1200 per season; 4 *swimming pool staff* with WSI/lifeguard certificate at $1100–$1300 per season; 3 *kitchen staff* with experience pertaining to food preparation at $1100–$1200 per season.

Benefits Preemployment training, on-the-job training, on-site room and board at no charge, laundry facilities, health insurance.

Contact Applicant should send resume, write for application, or call for information by April 15 to Suzanne Goltz Gagan, Camp Director, Camp Thunderbird, Department SED, 909 East Welch Road, Apopka, Florida 32712; 407-889-8088.

Good development opportunity for students in special education or related fields. In addition to summer positions, jobs are also available in November and from January to March. International students who wish to apply for employment should do so through a major counseling agency such as CCUSA/Camp America.

HOPP–INN GUEST HOUSE
5 Man-O-War Drive
Marathon, Florida 33050

General Information A bed-and-breakfast inn. Established 1981. Owned by Joan E. Hopp. Affiliated with Chamber of Commerce. Located 50 miles east of Key West. Features include oceanfront location in the heart of the Florida Keys; 5 rooms and 4 apartments.

Profile of Summer Employees Total number 2; average age 27. Employees are 50% female. Prefers nonsmokers.

Employment Information Openings are from June 6 to September 15. Winter break, Christmas break positions also offered. Jobs available: 1 *front-desk person* at $50 per week; 1 *manager* at $150–$165 per week; 1 *maid-service person* at $50 per week. International students encouraged to apply.

Benefits Preemployment training, on-the-job training, on-site room and board at no charge.

Contact Applicant should send resume, call for information, or apply in person by May 15 to Joan E. Hopp, President, Hopp–Inn Guest House, Department SED, 5 Man-O-War Drive, Marathon, Florida 33050; 305-743-4118, fax 305-743-9220.

Employment at Hopp–Inn Guest House is valuable on-the-job training for hotel/motel management and tourist relations majors.

NATIONAL PARK SERVICE

Contact   Applicant should write for application (must be 18 by May 13; U.S. citizenship required) to Regional Office of the National Park Service, Southeast Region, National Park Service, 75 Spring Street, SW, Atlanta, Georgia 30303.

Jobs located in Florida at the following facilities: Canaveral, Castillo de San Marcos/ Fort Matanzas, Everglades (including Biscayne, Big Cypress, and Fort Jefferson), Fort Caroline/Timucuan Preserve, Gulf Island. Also see District of Columbia listing.

OCEAN REEF CLUB
31 Ocean Reef Drive
Key Largo, Florida 33037

General Information   A private, full-service, year-round club and resort catering to the super-achievers of America. Established 1945. Located 50 miles south of Miami on 4,000 acres. Features include three 18-hole golf courses; 38 tennis courts; croquet; 6 restaurants; deep-sea fishing charters; full-size marina; only living coral reef in the northeast (offshore); excellent location and facilities.

Profile of Summer Employees   Total number 100; average age 25. Employees are 20% local residents. Prefers nonsmokers.

Employment Information   Openings are from May 15 to September 15. Spring break, Christmas break, year-round positions also offered. College credit possible. Jobs available: 20 *waiters/waitresses* with table-service experience at $200–$250 per week; 2 *lifeguards* with CPR and lifesaving training at $200–$250 per week; 4 *bellpersons* with outgoing, people-oriented personality at $200–$250 per week; 6 *housekeepers* at $175–$200 per week; 2 *cooks* with prior food preparation and cooking experience at $200–$250 per week.

Benefits   On-the-job training, formal ongoing training, on-site room and board at $56 per week, laundry facilities, a meal provided per shift, uniforms provided (excluding shoes), only 2 people per room.

Contact   Applicant should send resume, write for application, call for information, or apply in person by May 1 to John Chenhall, Vice President of Human Resources/Quality, Ocean Reef Club, Department SED, 31 Ocean Reef Drive, Key Largo, Florida 33037; 305-367-5820, fax 305-367-2333.

SEA WORLD OF FLORIDA
7007 Sea World Drive
Orlando, Florida 32821

General Information   Marine life theme park, open year-round, designed to entertain and educate guests. Established 1973. Owned by Anheuser-Busch Entertainment Corporation. Features include shows and exhibits; restaurants and gift shops.

Employment Information   Openings are from May to September. Spring break, Christmas break, year-round positions also offered. Jobs available: *counter persons; kitchen staff; buspersons; waiters/waitresses; warehouse personnel; prep cooks; dishwashers; gift shop personnel* with ability to operate cash register, assist guests, and stock shelves; *operations, crowd and traffic control personnel* with desire to maintain park cleanliness and assist at information center; *landscape personnel* with ability to work with a wide variety of plant material and design beds plus maintain drainage and irrigation (some experience preferred); *ticket sellers* with ability to sell and take tickets; *tour guides* with ability to narrate at animal exhibits throughout the park and conduct educational tours.

Benefits Employee lounge on premises for lunch and breaks, competitive salary, uniforms, complimentary tickets, employee discounts, end-of-season party.

Contact Applicant should write for application, call for information, or apply in person (information may be sent May through September) to Personnel Director, Sea World of Florida, Department SED, 7007 Sea World Drive, Orlando, Florida 32821; 407-351-3600.

Sea World of Florida offers staff members valuable and rewarding work experience in attractive surroundings. (Please note that employees can find housing in the several apartment complexes in the area.)

Georgia

CAMP LOW
1912 Rose Dhu Road
Savannah, Georgia 31419

General Information Residential girls' camp serving 96 campers per week. Established 1957. Operated by Girl Scout Council of Savannah. Affiliated with Girl Scouts of the United States of America, American Camping Association. Located 6 miles north of Savannah on 300 acres. Features include location on an island surrounded by salt marshes; lodge/dining hall, 4 units with platform tents or cabins, a unit house, swimming pool, dock for canoeing and crabbing; program based on girl's individual choices.

Profile of Summer Employees Total number 20; average age 22. Employees are 5% high school students, 90% college students, 5% international.

Employment Information Openings are from June 16 to August 10. College credit possible.

Benefits Preemployment training, on-the-job training, on-site room and board at no charge, laundry facilities, health insurance.

Contact Applicant should send resume, write for application, or call for information by May 31 to Julie Gonye, Outdoor Program Director, Camp Low, Department SED, P.O. Box 9389, Savannah, Georgia 31412; 912-236-1571.

Camp Low's program is based on individual choice. The girls select their program interests and, with staff guidance, plan their week's adventure.

GEORGIA STATE PARKS AND HISTORIC SITES
205 Butler Street, Suite 1352
Atlanta, Georgia 30334

General Information Conducts natural, cultural, and recreational programs for park visitors. Established 1928. Owned by State of Georgia. Features include Okefenokee

Swamp; Cloudland Canyon; Blue Ridge Mountain Land; 6 parks on major reservoirs; historic Indian mounds; Roosevelt's Little White House.

Profile of Summer Employees   Total number 30; average age 25. Employees are 60% female, 60% college students, 10% retirees, 30% local residents.

Employment Information   Openings are from March 1 to June 1. Year-round positions also offered. Jobs available: 20 *parks interpreters* with a background in natural science, recreation, or related fields at $175 per week; 10 *historic site interpreters* with a background in history at $175 per week. International students encouraged to apply.

Benefits   Preemployment training, on-the-job training, formal ongoing training, on-site room and board.

Contact   Applicant should write for application or call for information by April 1 to Chuck Gregory, Chief Naturalist, Georgia State Parks and Historic Sites, Department SED, 205 Butler Street, Suite 1352, Atlanta, Georgia 30334; 404-656-6539.

Salary is $4.40 an hour. Returning seasonal workers receive $4.65 an hour.

NATIONAL PARK SERVICE

Contact   Applicant should write for application (must be 18 by May 13; U.S. citizenship required) to Regional Office of the National Park Service, Southeast Region, National Park Service, 75 Spring Street, SW, Atlanta, Georgia 30303.

Jobs located in Georgia at the following facilities: Andersonville, Chattahoochee River, Chickamauga-Chattanooga National Military Park, Cumberland Island, Fort Frederica, Fort Pulaski, Jimmy Carter, Kennesaw Mountain, Martin Luther King, Jr., Ocmulgee. Also see District of Columbia listing.

Hawaii

CAMP MOKULEIA
68–729 Farrington Highway
Waialua, Hawaii 96791

General Information   Residential, coeducational camp serving 92 campers weekly. Established 1947. Owned by The Episcopal Church in Hawaii. Affiliated with American Camping Association. Located 37 miles northwest of Honolulu on 9 acres. Features include Hawaii beachfront location; excellent beach and reef for exploration; mountains nearby; new facilities; international mix of campers and staff; staff-camper ratio of 1:4.

Profile of Summer Employees   Total number 40; average age 24. Employees are 50% female, 35% minorities, 17% high school students, 35% college students, 5% retirees, 3% international, 50% local residents. Prefers nonsmokers.

Employment Information   Openings are from June 25 to August 16. Winter break positions also offered. Jobs available: 1 *assistant project director* with degree in recreation or physical education plus WSI, CPR, and AFA certification at $1200 per season; 1 *waterfront director* with study in related field plus WSI, CPR, and AFA certification at $1050 per season; 1 *ballfield director* with study in physical education or related field, plus CPR, AFA, and OLS certification at $1050 per season; 1 *arts director* with study in languages, drama, dance, art, crafts, or related fields at $1050 per season; 7 *senior counselors* with prior camping experience plus CPR and AFA certification at $950 per season; 7 *junior counselors* with counselor-in-training experience plus CPR and AFA certification at $750 per season; 5 *aides* with CPR and AFA certification. International students encouraged to apply.

Benefits On-the-job training, formal ongoing training, on-site room and board at no charge, laundry facilities, health insurance, accident insurance, worker's compensation insurance.

Contact Applicant should send resume, write for application, or call for information by April 15 to David T. Grout, Program Director–MSRA, Camp Mokuleia, Department SED, 68–729 Farrington Highway, Waialua, Hawaii 96791; 808-637-6241, fax 808-637-5505.

Camp Mokuleia provides our staff with opportunities for cultural exchange.

NATIONAL PARK SERVICE

Contact Applicant should write for application (must be 18 by May 13; U.S. citizenship required) to Regional Office of the National Park Service, Western Region, National Park Service, 450 Golden Gate Avenue, Box 36063, San Francisco, California 94102.

Jobs located in Hawaii at the following facilities: Haleakala, Hawaii Volcanoes, USS Arizona Memorial. Also see District of Columbia listing.

Idaho

NATIONAL PARK SERVICE

Contact Applicant should write for application (must be 18 by May 13; U.S. citizenship required) to Regional Office of the National Park Service, Pacific Northwest Region, National Park Service, 83 South King Street, Suite 212, Seattle, Washington 98104.

Jobs located in Idaho at the following facilities: Boise Interagency Fire Center, Craters of the Moon, Nez Perce. Also see District of Columbia listing.

REDFISH LAKE LODGE
Box 9
Stanley, Idaho 83278

General Information Family-oriented rustic lodge on a lake in the Sawtooth Mountains. Established 1929. Affiliated with National Restaurant Association, National Federation of Independent Businesses, Stanley and Sawtooth Chambers of Commerce. Located 160 miles northeast of Boise on 20 acres. Features include location on Redfish Lake; hiking and camping in the Sawtooth Mountains; Salmon River fishing and rafting; opportunity to participate in the Stanley Stomp; white sand beaches; waterskiing; windsurfing and volleyball.

Profile of Summer Employees Total number 50; average age 21. Employees are 50% female, 1% high school students, 98% college students, 1% retirees.

Employment Information   Openings are from May 1 to June 30. College credit possible. Jobs available: 6 *cooks* at $570 per month; 7 *waitresses* at $570 per month; 4 *buspersons* at $570 per month; 3 *dishwashers* at $570 per month; 8 *housekeepers* at $570 per month; 3 *service station persons* at $570 per month; 5 *marina personnel* at $570 per month; 1 *bartender* at $570 per month; 4 *store personnel* at $570 per month; 2 *front-desk persons* at $570 per month; 3 *maintenance persons* at $570 per month.

Benefits   On-the-job training, on-site room and board, laundry facilities, cash bonus for work through Labor Day, flexible scheduling, use of boats.

Contact   Applicant should write for application by May 15 to Jack See, Manager, Redfish Lake Lodge, Department SED, Box 9, Stanley, Idaho 83278; 208-774-3536.

Illinois

CAMP MEDILL MCCORMICK
Box 1616
Rockford, Illinois 61110

General Information   Girl Scout camp operated year-round for troop and group camping. Resident camping for girls ages 6–17 in one- and two-week sessions available in summer. Affiliated with American Camping Association. Features include hills and woods along river; deer in area; pool; canoes; teams course; tepees, platform tents, and lodges.

Employment Information   Openings are from June 10 to August 12. Year-round positions also offered. College credit possible. Jobs available: *general counselors* at $150–$200 per week; 1 *nurse* at $150–$200 per week; 4 *lifeguards* at $150–$200 per week; *assistant cook* at $150–$200 per week; *water safety instructor* at $150–$200 per week; *naturalist* at $150–$200 per week; *arts and crafts instructor* at $150–$200 per week.

Benefits   On-site room and board.

Contact   Applicant should send resume or write for application by May 1 to Susan Nichols, Camp Director, Camp Medill McCormick, Department SED, Box 1616, Rockford, Illinois 61110; 815-962-5591.

We provide a perfect environment for girls to develop independence and an increased respect for nature.

CAMP TAPAWINGO
Route 5
Metamora, Illinois 61548

General Information   Residential camp serving 120 Girl Scouts and non-Girl-Scouts per week. Established 1957. Owned by Kickapoo Council of Girl Scouts. Affiliated with American Camping Association. Located 20 miles east of Peoria on 640 acres. Features include pool; horseback riding; teams course; small lake.

Profile of Summer Employees   Total number 25; average age 20. Employees are 100% female, 1% minorities, 98% college students, 15% local residents.

Employment Information   Openings are from May 29 to August 11. Jobs available: 1 *assistant director* with a minimum age of 21 at $170–$200 per week; 1 *program director* with a minimum age of 21 at $155–$185 per week; 1 *business manager* with a minimum age of 21 at $155–$185 per week; 1 *health supervisor* with RN, LPN, or EMT license at $170–$200 per week; 1 *waterfront director* with WSI certificate (minimum age 21) at $155–$185 per week; 1 *lakefront director* with lifeguard certification and canoeing background at $155–$185 per week; 2 *waterfront assistants* with lifeguard certification at $133–$163 per week; 1 *teams course/campcraft instructor* with a minimum age of 21 at $155–$185 per week; 1 *riding instructor* with instruction experience (minimum age 21) at $155–$185 per week; 5 *unit leaders* with a minimum age of 21 at $138–$168 per week; 10 *unit assistants* with a minimum age 18 at $128–$158 per week.

Benefits   Preemployment training, on-the-job training, on-site room and board, health insurance.

Contact   Applicant should send resume, write for application, or call for information by April 30 to Val Isenhower, Director of Program and Properties, Camp Tapawingo, Department SED, 1103 West Lake, Peoria, Illinois 61614; 309-688-8671, fax 309-688-7358.

NATIONAL PARK SERVICE

Contact   Applicant should write for application (must be 18 by May 13; U.S. citizenship required) to Regional Office of the National Park Service, Midwest Region, National Park Service, 1709 Jackson Street, Omaha, Nebraska 68102.

Jobs located in Illinois at the following facility: Lincoln Home National Historic Site. Also see District of Columbia listing.

PEACOCK CAMP FOR CRIPPLED CHILDREN
38685 North Deep Lake Road
Lake Villa, Illinois 60046

General Information   Residential camp for 36 7–17 year-olds with physical disabilities. A new session is offered every two weeks. Established 1935. Owned by Peacock Camp. Affiliated with American Camping Association. Located 40 miles north of Chicago on 22 acres. Features include outdoor, heated pool with ramp; nature trail with wheelchair fitness course; lake; pontoon boat; arts and crafts cabin; recreation pavillion; lodge.

Profile of Summer Employees   Total number 23; average age 20. Employees are 5% high school students, 70% college students, 5% international, 5% local residents. Prefers nonsmokers.

Employment Information   Openings are from June 10 to August 15. College credit possible. Jobs available: 5 *counselors/aquatics instructors* with lifeguarding experience (preferred) at $1300 per season; 1 *counselor/aquatics team leader* with WSI certificate and lifeguard training at $1500 per season; 1 *counselor/arts and crafts team leader* at $1500 per season; 5 *counselors/arts and crafts instructors* at $1300 per season; 1 *counselor/recreation team leader* at $1500 per season; 5 *counselors/recreation personnel* at $1300 per season; 1 *head counselor* at $1800 per season; 1 *nurse* with RN license at $3500 per season; 2 *cooks* at $2000 per season; 1 *night attendant* at $2000 per season; 1 *maintenance person* at $1500 per season.

Benefits   Preemployment training, on-the-job training, on-site room and board at no charge, laundry facilities, tuition reimbursement.

Contact Applicant should send resume, write for application, or call for information to Dave and Peggy Bogenschutz, Camp Directors, Peacock Camp for Crippled Children, 38685 North Deep Lake Road, Lake Villa, Illinois 60046; 708-356-5201.

Peacock Camp offers a unique opportunity to work with children and teens with a wide variety of physical disabilities. Staff members are given freedom, with support, to plan and implement programs.

SHADY OAKS CEREBRAL PALSY CAMP
16300 Parker Road
Lockport, Illinois 60441

General Information Residential camp providing activities for 50–60 campers with cerebral palsy. Established 1947. Owned by Parents Association for Cerebral Palsy. Affiliated with United Way. Located 25 miles southwest of Chicago on 40 acres. Features include woodland setting; close proximity to Chicago; 1:1 camper-counselor ratio; field trips every week; sparkling heated pool; nature trail.

Profile of Summer Employees Total number 85; average age 19. Employees are 70% female, 2% minorities, 20% high school students, 80% college students, 60% local residents.

Employment Information Openings are from June 15 to August 15. College credit possible. Jobs available: 1 *lifeguard* with lifesaving certificate at $1000 per season; 1 *head cook* with food sanitation certificate and experience at $2000 per season; 1 *assistant cook* with food sanitation certificate and experience at $1500 per season; 1 *medication manager* with CPR and first aid certification plus RN license or certification to distribute medications at $2000 per season; 1 *medical technician* with CPR and first aid certification at $1800 per season; 70 *counselors* with willingness to help others at $850 per season. International students encouraged to apply.

Benefits On-the-job training, formal ongoing training, on-site room and board at no charge, laundry facilities, paid field trip fees, internships.

Contact Applicant should send resume, write for application, call for information, or apply in person by June 10 to Camp Director, Shady Oaks Cerebral Palsy Camp, Department SED, 16300 Parker Road, Lockport, Illinois 60441; 708-301-0816.

Shady Oaks is different because we offer a 1:1 camper-counselor ratio. We take numerous field trips to Chicagoland sites, and we always have fun.

Indiana

CAMP WAPI-KAMIGI
827 South Washington
Hagerstown, Indiana 47346

General Information Residential Girl Scout camp serving 72 girls weekly for six weeks. Open to all girls ages 7–17. Established 1952. Owned by Treaty Line Girl Scouts. Affiliated with American Camping Association. Located 45 miles east of Indianapolis on 200 acres.

Features include simple outdoor living; 13-acre lake; tents; nature program; unit centered program; secluded location but close to populated areas.

Profile of Summer Employees   Total number 20; average age 21. Employees are 100% female, 5% minorities, 20% high school students, 75% college students, 5% retirees, 5% international, 75% local residents. Prefers nonsmokers.

Employment Information   Openings are from June 15 to July 31. College credit possible. Jobs available: 1 *waterfront director* with WSI and ALS certificates at $750–$800 per season; 2 *waterfront assistants* with ALS certificate at $600–$650 per season; 1 *head cook* at $700–$800 per season; 1 *assistant cook* at $600–$700 per season; 1 *camp director* at $1600 per season; 4 *unit leaders* at $650–$800 per season; 6 *unit counselors* at $560–$625 per season; 1 *nurse* with RN license at $700–$800 per season; 1 *naturalist* at $700–$800 per season.

Benefits   Preemployment training, on-the-job training, on-site room and board at no charge, laundry facilities, health insurance.

Contact   Applicant should write for application, call for information, or apply in person to Pat Mayer, Program Director, Camp Wapi-Kamigi, Department SED, 713 Promenade, Richmond, Indiana 47374; 317-962-0225.

DUDLEY GALLAHUE VALLEY CAMPS
Morgantown, Indiana

General Information   Residential camp serving approximately 128–140 campers weekly and bi-weekly. Owned by Hoosier Capital Girl Scouts. Located 45 miles south of Indianapolis on 500 acres. Features include beautiful wooded area; man-made, 45-acre lake; location in the hills of scenic Brown County; horseback riding; aquatics program; opportunity to practice camping skills plus work in the arts and nature program; sleeping facilities are platform tents.

Profile of Summer Employees   Total number 30; average age 23. Employees are 98% female, 5% minorities, 5% high school students, 80% college students, 10% local residents. Prefers nonsmokers.

Employment Information   Openings are from June 8 to August 12. College credit possible. Jobs available: 1 *director* with Girl Scout, American Camping Association, or college camp director training course, successful experience in administrative and/or supervisory capacity, successful experience in planning and implementing outdoor living activity experiences in camps, ability to select, train, and supervise staff, administrative ability and flexibility, and college degree or equivalent; 1 *assistant director* with Girl Scout, American Camping Association, or college camp director training course, successful experience in administrative and/or supervisory capacity, successful experience in planning and implementing outdoor living activity experiences in camps, ability to select, train, and supervise staff, administrative ability and flexibility, and college degree or equivalent at $1000 per season; 1 *business manager* with business training (typing, bookkeeping, office practice) plus sound judgement in purchasing supplies and coordinating various business activities in camp at $1000 per season; 1 *health supervisor* with state license or registered as a physician, physician's assistant, RN, LPN, paramedic, camp health director, or EMT and advanced first aid and/or CPR certificate plus emotional stability to meet emergencies at $1000 per season; 1 *food supervisor* with minimum of two years of training in institutional management specializing in food service or a minimum of two years experience as a camp or food supervisor or equivalent experience plus ability to supervise and work with staff, campers, and trades people; 4 *cooks* with ability to prepare food and provide written records of health exams at $1000 per season; 9 *unit leaders* with experience as a girl leader, camper, or teacher, supervisory experience, ability to teach and guide campers, plus first aid and lifesaving training at $1000 per season; 12 *assistant unit leaders* with group leadership, counselor-in-training, or leader-in-training course plus experience as a camper or as youth leader at $1000 per season; *waterfront director* with current American National Red Cross WSI, ALS, and CPR training certification or YMCA Aquatic Leader Examiner or Boy Scouts of America National Aquatic Instructor certificate plus experience as a waterfront counselor and swimming and boating instructor at $1000 per season; *waterfront assistant* with current basic swimming instructor certificate issued by the American National Red Cross or equivalent from the YMCA or Boy Scouts of America at $1000 per season; *trip director* with leadership, outdoor, and program specialty training plus work experience as a teacher or counselor with children; *horseback director* with leadership, outdoor, and program specialty training plus work experience as a teacher or counselor at $1000 per season.

Benefits Preemployment training, on-the-job training, formal ongoing training, on-site room and board at no charge, laundry facilities.

Contact Applicant should send resume, write for application, call for information, or apply in person by June 1 to Bonnie Closey, Outdoor Program Specialist, c/o Hoosier Capital Girl Scout Council, Dudley Gallahue Valley Camps, Department SED, 615 North Alabama Street, Room 235, Indianapolis, Indiana 46204; 317-634-8393, fax 317-631-5440.

NATIONAL PARK SERVICE

Contact Applicant should write for application (must be 18 by May 13; U.S. citizenship required) to Regional Office of the National Park Service, Midwest Region, National Park Service, 1709 Jackson Street, Omaha, Nebraska 68102.

Jobs located in Indiana at the following facilities: George Rogers Clark, Indiana Dunes, Lincoln Boyhood National Memorial. Also see District of Columbia listing.

Iowa

CAMP HANTESA
RR 1
Boone, Iowa 50036

General Information Residential and day camp serving boys and girls ages 5–18. Established 1919. Operated by Camp Fire Boys and Girls. Affiliated with American Camping Association. Located 4 miles south of Boone on 144 acres. Features include swimming pool; river canoeing; nature exploration; campcraft, hand arts, and photography instruction.

Profile of Summer Employees Total number 40; average age 20. Employees are 70% female, 1% minorities, 99% college students, 80% local residents. Prefers nonsmokers.

Employment Information Openings are from June 10 to August 20. Spring break, winter break, Christmas break, year-round positions also offered. College credit possible. Jobs available: 20 *general counselors* with interest in children at $950 per season; 1 *swimming instructor* with WSI certificate at $950 per season; 1 *swimming guard* with lifeguard training at $950 per season; 6 *unit directors* with management skills at $950 per season; 1 *arts and crafts instructor* at $950 per season; 5 *cooks* at $950 per season; 3 *riding instructors* with riding skills (English or Western styles) at $950 per season. International students encouraged to apply.

Benefits Preemployment training, on-the-job training, on-site room and board at no charge, laundry facilities, health insurance.

Contact Applicant should send resume, write for application, call for information, or apply in person by March 31 to Suz Welch, Director, Camp Hantesa, Department SED, RR 1, Boone, Iowa 50036; 515-432-1417, fax 515-432-1294.

Pre-camp training allows all staff members to learn and participate in all areas. Inexperienced persons are welcome to apply.

NATIONAL PARK SERVICE

Contact Applicant should write for application (must be 18 by May 13; U.S. citizenship required) to Regional Office of the National Park Service, Midwest Region, National Park Service, 1709 Jackson Street, Omaha, Nebraska 68102.

Jobs located in Iowa at the following facilities: Effigy Mounds National Monument, Herbert Hoover National Historic Site. Also see District of Columbia listing.

Kansas

NATIONAL PARK SERVICE

Contact Applicant should write for application (must be 18 by May 13; U.S. citizenship required) to Regional Office of the National Park Service, Midwest Region, National Park Service, 1709 Jackson Street, Omaha, Nebraska 68102.

Jobs located in Kansas at the following facilities: Fort Larned National Historic Site, Fort Scott National Historic Site. Also see District of Columbia listing.

Kentucky

NATIONAL PARK SERVICE

Contact Applicant should write for application (must be 18 by May 13; U.S. citizenship required) to Regional Office of the National Park Service, Southeast Region, National Park Service, 75 Spring Street, SW, Atlanta, Georgia 30303.

Jobs located in Kentucky at the following facilities: Abraham Lincoln Birthplace, Big South Fork, Cumberland Gap, Mammoth Cave. Also see District of Columbia listing.

Louisiana

MARYDALE RESIDENT CAMP
HC 68, Box 429
St. Francisville, Louisiana 70775

General Information   Residential camp serving girls ages 8–18 with a general outdoor program. Established 1948. Owned by Audubon Girl Scout Council. Affiliated with Girl Scouts of the United States of America, American Camping Association, Camp Horsemanship Association. Located 35 miles north of Baton Rouge on 400 acres. Features include equestrian unit/barn, bunkhouse, and 2 arenas; location 2 hours from New Orleans in the heart of plantation country.

Profile of Summer Employees   Total number 40; average age 20. Employees are 99% female, 10% minorities, 5% high school students, 95% college students, 90% local residents. Prefers nonsmokers.

Employment Information   Openings are from June 1 to July 19. College credit possible. Jobs available: 5 *unit leaders* with a minimum age of 21 at $800–$850 per season; 14 *counselors* with a minimum age of 18 at $100 per week; 4 *waterfront personnel* with American Red Cross certificate at $100–$125 per week; 4 *riding personnel* with CHA certificate (minimum age 18) at $100–$125 per week; 2 *RN and EMT staff* with license (minimum age 21). International students encouraged to apply.

Benefits   Preemployment training, on-site room and board at no charge, laundry facilities, health insurance, time to explore own interest.

Contact   Applicant should send resume, write for application, call for information, or apply in person by May 1 to Gretchen Morgan, Camp Director, Marydale Resident Camp, Department SED, 8417 Kelwood Avenue, Baton Rouge, Louisiana 70806-4884; 504-927-8946.

NATIONAL PARK SERVICE

Contact   Applicant should write for application (must be 18 by May 13; U.S. citizenship required) to Regional Office of the National Park Service, Southwest Region, National Park Service, P.O. Box 728, Santa Fe, New Mexico 87501.

Jobs located in Louisiana at the following facility: Jean LaFitte National Historic Park. Also see District of Columbia.

Maine

ACADIA CORPORATION
85 Main Street, P.O. Box 24
Bar Harbor, Maine 04609

General Information National park concessioner operating a restaurant and 3 gift shops in Acadia National Park plus several gift shops in the town of Bar Harbor. Established 1932. Owned by David Woodside. Located 20 miles southeast of Ellsworth. Features include a national park setting; location near busy resort community; many outdoor and cultural activities; the unsurpassed natural beauty of Maine and Mt. Desert Island; people from all walks of life.

Profile of Summer Employees Total number 100; average age 21. Employees are 48% female, 3% minorities, 2% high school students, 88% college students, 10% retirees, 2% international, 20% local residents. Prefers nonsmokers.

Employment Information Openings are from May 1 to November 1. Jobs available: 36 *waiters/waitresses* with a pleasant personality and a calm demeanor; 5 *buspersons;* 15 *kitchen workers* with ability to perform food prep work, dishwashing, and cleaning duties; run cold food line and bakery; 3 *lead cooks* with strong creative cooking skills, including saute and sauces, plus two years supervisory experience or equivalent; 3 *bartenders* with ability to operate service bar and a cash register; 2 *cashiers* with ability to operate cash register, count money, and prepare bank accounts plus a valid driver's license; 6 *hosts* with a pleasant personality and calm demeanor to greet and seat customers and take reservations; 2 *guest relations personnel* with friendly personalities to orient arriving visitors, direct them to parking areas, and provide parking information; 32 *shop clerks* with ability to perform various duties, including operating a cash register, assisting with purchases, stocking and ordering merchandise, and orienting park visitors; 1 *maintenance person* with a willingness to perform a variety of tasks plus possession of a valid driver's license; 6 *building and grounds personnel* with ability to perform a variety of tasks (indoors and outdoors) and to interact well with park visitors; 3 *office clerks* with ability to perform work accurately, pay attention to detail, and type; must possess valid driver's license; 4 *warehouse clerks* with ability to maintain accurate records and pay attention to detail plus a good driving record and valid driver's license; 1 *dormitory cook* with ability to perform institutional cafeteria cooking for up to 60 people, plan menus, and prepare food plus possession of a valid driver's license. International students encouraged to apply.

Benefits On-the-job training, on-site room and board at $60 per week, laundry facilities, end-of-season bonus possible.

Contact Applicant should write for application or call for information by February to Rebecca Ghelli, Personnel, Acadia Corporation, P.O. Box 24, Bar Harbor, Maine 04609; 207-288-5592, fax 207-288-2420.

Wages range from $2.13 to $7 an hour depending on position and experience. Certain jobs also involve additional compensation in the form of tips and/or hourly bonuses.

ALFORD LAKE CAMP, INC.
RR 2, Box 6360
Union, Maine 04862

General Information   Residential facility offering a multi-activity program for 140 persons ages 7–15. Established 1907. Owned by McMullan Family. Affiliated with American Camping Association, Maine Youth Camping Association. Located 10 miles east of Camden on 416 acres. Features include clear, large lake; location 2½ hours from Acadia National Park; close proximity to rivers, mountains, forest, and fields.

Profile of Summer Employees   Total number 75; average age 21. Employees are 98% female. Requires nonsmokers.

Employment Information   Openings are from June 20 to August 15. Jobs available: 2 *swimming instructors* with WSI and American Red Cross lifeguard certification at $800–$1000 per season; 2 *sailing instructors* with WSI certificate or lifeguard training at $800–$1000 per season; 1 *nature counselor* with background in nature, ecology, etc. at $900–$1100 per season; 1 *tennis counselor* with teaching experience at $800–$1000 per season; 1 *gymnastics instructor* with teaching experience and certification at $800–$1000 per season; 1 *drama instructor* with teaching and production experience at $800–$1000 per season; 1 *sailboarding instructor* with sailboarding experience and ALS certificate (minimum) at $800–$1000 per season; 1 *campcraft instructor* with Maine trip-leading certification at $800–$1000 per season; 1 *canoeing instructor* with Red Cross canoeing (or equivalent) and ALS certificates (minimum) at $800–$1000 per season; 1 *riding instructor* with British Horse Society or Pony Club certification or equivalent at $800–$1000 per season; 1 *office person* with knowledge of computers and attention to detail at $800–$1000 per season. International students encouraged to apply.

Benefits   Preemployment training, on-the-job training, formal ongoing training, on-site room and board at no charge.

Contact   Applicant should send resume, write for application, or call for information and provide three references who know his/her work with children and who will supply evidence of his/her level of expertise in the activities the applicant hopes to teach by May 1 to Sue McMullan, Director, Alford Lake Camp, Inc., Department SED, 17 Pilot Point Road, Cape Elizabeth, Maine 04107; 207-799-3005, fax 207-799-7137.

Alford Lake Camp is one of the oldest girls' camps in the world, with long traditions, tremendous spirit, and a friendly, loyal staff. Employees have the opportunity to have fun and interact with a bright, creative, international community while experiencing valuable job training for future careers. Many of our counselors and campers return year after year. (Please note that compensation levels for all positions detailed in this listing depend upon the applicant's year in college or status as a college graduate.)

CAMP ANDROSCOGGIN
Wayne, Maine 04284

General Information   Private, residential camp serving 200 boys from the United States and abroad. Established 1907. Owned by Stanley Hirsch. Affiliated with American Camping Association, Maine Youth Camping Association. Located 50 miles northwest of Portland on 125 acres. Features include location on waterfront with 1,900 feet of shoreline; located in center of state with easy access to coast, mountains, and state parks.

Profile of Summer Employees   Total number 80; average age 21. Employees are 10% female, 80% college students, 10% international, 10% local residents. Prefers nonsmokers.

Employment Information   Openings are from June 16 to August 16. College credit possible. Jobs available: 10 *swimming instructors* with WSI certificate or lifeguard training at $850 per season; 3 *sailing instructors* at $850 per season; 3 *canoeing instructors* at $850 per season; 4 *waterskiing instructors* at $850 per season; 4 *baseball instructors* at $850 per season; 4 *basketball instructors* at $850 per season; 4 *soccer instructors* at $850 per season; 10 *tennis instructors* at $850 per season; 2 *lacrosse instructors* at $850 per season; 1 *drama instructor* at $850 per season; 1 *woodworking instructor* at $850 per season; 1 *photography instructor* at $850 per season; 1 *campcraft instructor* at $850 per season; 2 *nurses* at $2000–$2500 per season; 1 *archery instructor; riflery instructor; windsurfing instructor; radio staff; bicycling instructor; kayaking instructor.*

Benefits   Preemployment training, on-the-job training, on-site room and board at no charge, laundry facilities, travel reimbursement.

Contact   Applicant should send resume, write for application, or call for information by May to Peter Hirsch, Director, Camp Androscoggin, 733 West Street, Harrison, New York 10528; 914-835-5800.

Androscoggin offers one 8-week session with only 200 boys and 60 counselors, many of whom return year after year. Androscoggin also offers a full range of activities on and off campus. We hope to create an atmosphere in which campers and staff can make friends, experience new activities, improve their skills, and have the time of their lives in the process.

CAMP ARCADIA
Route 121
Casco, Maine 04015

General Information   Residential camp for girls serving 140–150 campers for seven weeks. Younger girls accepted for post-season. Established 1916. Owned by Anne H. Fritts and Louise L. Henderson. Affiliated with American Camping Association, Audubon Society, Camp Archery Association, Maine Youth Camping Association. Located 35 miles northeast of Portland on 365 acres. Features include over 1 mile of shorefront on Pleasant Lake with two natural sandy beaches; sunny fields and pine woods; 4 tennis courts; riding ring and stables; summer lodges; 45 minutes to mountains and ocean.

Profile of Summer Employees   Total number 58; average age 21. Employees are 86% female, 5% minorities, 70% college students, 5% international. Prefers nonsmokers.

Employment Information   Openings are from June 15 to August 12. College credit possible. Jobs available: 3 *swimming instructors* with WSI and lifeguard training certificates at $900 per season; 1 *archery instructor* at $1000 per season; 3 *canoeing instructors* with lifeguard training certificate and knowledge of lakes and rivers at $900 per season; 3 *tennis instructors* with ability to teach tennis at $900 per season; 1 *music instructor* with piano playing and camp song leadership ability at $900 per season; 3 *sailing instructors* with lifeguard training plus knowledge of sailing and racing at $900 per season; 2 *weaving instructors* with knowledge of floor, table, and hand looms at $1000 per season; 2 *riding instructors* with English balance seat riding and stable management ability at $950 per season; 2 *arts and crafts instructors* with silk screening, block printing, batik, drawing, and painting experience at $1000 per season; 1 *ceramics instructor* with electric kiln and potter's wheel experience at $950 per season; 2 *drama instructors* with experience in children's drama, directing, lighting, sets, etc. at $900 per season; 3 *trip instructors* with driver's license (minimum age 21) at $1000 per season; 1 *environmental (nature) instructor* with love and knowledge of nature and environment at $900 per season; 2 *office workers* with typing of 50 wpm and knowledge of computers at $900 per season; 1 *photography instructor* with black and white darkroom experience at $900 per season. International students encouraged to apply.

Benefits   On-the-job training, formal ongoing training, on-site room and board at no charge, laundry facilities, travel reimbursement, health insurance.

Contact   Applicant should send resume, write for application, call for information, or apply in person by May 1 to Anne H. Fritts, Director, Camp Arcadia, Department SED, Pleasantville Road, New Vernon, New Jersey 07976; 201-538-5409.

Camp Arcadia is seeking counselors who are interested in helping children discover who they are and where their talents lie. We have an unusually fine program of hiking and canoe trips. Qualified counselors are able to participate in this program if they desire.

CAMP LAUREL
Readfield, Maine 04355

General Information   Welcomes 300 boys and girls ages 7–16 who come from all over the United States as well as several foreign countries. The return rate for campers and staff is very high, owing partly to our efforts to make each summer slightly different, more challenging, a continuing growth experience and, most of all, fun. Established 1950. Owned by Ron and Ann Scott. Affiliated with American Camping Association, Maine Youth Camping Association. Located 17 miles west of Augusta on 150 acres. Features include location 1 hour from Maine seacoast; warm, friendly atmosphere.

Profile of Summer Employees   Total number 130; average age 23. Employees are 50% female. Prefers nonsmokers.

Employment Information   Openings are from June 10 to August 25. Jobs available: *swimming instructors* at $500 per month; *tennis instructors* with college team playing experience; *windsurfing/sailing instructors; waterskiing instructors; field sports instructors (volleyball, soccer, softball); dramatics instructor; horseback-riding instructor* with riding experience (English style); *arts and crafts instructor; ceramics instructor; gymnastics instructor; archery instructor; piano/music instructor; photography instructor; AM radio person; nature instructor; nurses.*

Benefits   Preemployment training, on-the-job training, formal ongoing training, on-site room and board, laundry facilities, travel reimbursement, health insurance, excellent facilities open to staff during time off (when available).

Contact   Applicant should send resume, write for application, or call for information to Ron Scott, Camp Director, Camp Laurel, Department SED, P.O. Box 4378, Boca Raton, Florida 33429; 407-391-1579, fax 407-391-4692.

Each year we choose the Laurel "Team" (students, graduates, and faculty) from prominent schools across the United States, Great Britain, and other parts of the world. We look for people with personality, character, maturity, professional training, experience, and most importantly, a sincere desire to work with children. Our counselor to camper ratio is approximately 1:3. If you love children and believe in their incredible potential, and if you feel good about yourself and the special talents you have to offer, if you thrive in outdoor surroundings and believe in an active, enthusiastic approach to life, then Camp Laurel is the perfect place to call your home for the summer.

CAMP MATOAKA FOR GIRLS
RFD 2
Oakland, Maine 04963

General Information Residential camp serving 200 girls in a variety of activities. Established 1951. Owned by Mike, Paula, and Sue Nathanson. Located 30 miles north of Augusta on 150 acres. Features include 1½ miles of shore frontage; largest recreation hall in New England; gym and dance complex; island on lake; 5 tennis courts.

Profile of Summer Employees Total number 120; average age 23. Employees are 80% female, 3% minorities, 10% high school students, 45% college students, 2% retirees, 30% international, 10% local residents. Prefers nonsmokers.

Employment Information Openings are from June 15 to August 17. College credit possible. Jobs available: 6 *swimming instructors* with WSI certificate at $1100–$1300 per season; 6 *arts and crafts instructors* with fine arts major at $1000–$1200 per season; 2 *sewing instructors* with home economic major at $1200 per season; 6 *tennis instructors* with college team level experience at $1000–$1400 per season; 3 *gymnastics instructors* with college team level experience at $1000–$1200 per season; 6 *ski instructors* with high skill level at $1100–$1500 per season; 3 *drama/music instructors* with theatre/drama major at $1100–$1300 per season; 4 *trip instructors* with outdoor experience at $1200–$1400 per season; 4 *land sports instructors* with physical education or health/recreation major at $1000–$1300 per season; 2 *ropes-course instructors* with Project Adventure or Outward Bound experience at $1500 per season; 3 *riding instructors* with high skill level at $1100–$1300 per season; 6 *small craft instructors* with Red Cross certificate at $1100–$1300 per season; 1 *pianist* with ability to sight read and accompany at $1100 per season; 2 *dance instructors* with dance/movement major at $1100–$1200 per season; 2 *photographers* with photography major at $1100–$1300 per season; 7 *video/radio personnel* with radio/communication major at $1150–$1400 per season. International students encouraged to apply.

Benefits Preemployment training, on-site room and board at no charge, laundry facilities, travel reimbursement.

Contact Applicant should send resume, write for application, or call for information by May 1 to Michael Nathanson, Director/Owner, Camp Matoaka for Girls, 8751 Horseshoe Lane, Boca Raton, Florida 33496; 407-488-6363, fax 407-488-6386.

Top-quality facilities and warm friendly work atmosphere makes Matoaka a great place to live and work.

CAMP NASHOBA NORTH
Raymond Hill Road
Raymond, Maine 04071

General Information International camp community of 150 boys and girls offering high-quality instruction in horsemanship, arts, sports, and aquatics. Established 1933. Owned by Janet Seaward Greene and Sarah Seaward Foley. Affiliated with American Camping Association, Maine Youth Camping Association, American Horse Show Association, National Archery Association, New England Horse Show Association, Maine Audubon Society, National Audubon Society. Located 30 miles northwest of Portland on 70 acres. Features include location on beautiful Crescent Lake in the Sebago Lakes and Mountain area; large modern cabins with running water; new 20-stall riding stable; numerous new craft centers; elective program offering lots of choice; supportive, friendly environment for first-time campers; nonsectarian.

Profile of Summer Employees   Total number 35; average age 20. Employees are 60% female, 10% minorities, 95% college students, 30% international. Requires nonsmokers.

Employment Information   Openings are from June 15 to August 17. College credit possible. Jobs available: 3 *swimming instructors* with LGT and WSI certificates at $1100–$1700 per season; 2 *sailing instructors* with LGT certificate at $1100–$1700 per season; 2 *windsurfing instructors* with LGT certificate at $1100–$1700 per season; 1 *boat driver/ waterskiing instructor* with LGT certificate at $1100–$1700 per season; 1 *canoeing instructor* with LGT certificate at $1100–$1700 per season; 4 *riding instructors* with Pony Club, eventing, or showing experience at $1100–$1700 per season; 2 *tennis instructors* with team and teaching experience at $1100–$1700 per season; 1 *ceramics/pottery instructor* at $1100–$1700 per season; 1 *photography instructor* at $1100–$1700 per season; 2 *dance instructors* at $1100–$1700 per season; 2 *theater instructors* at $1100–$1700 per season; 1 *archery instructor* at $1100–$1700 per season; 1 *music instructor* with ability to play guitar and piano at $1100–$1700 per season; 2 *trip instructors* at $1100–$1700 per season; 4 *kitchen helpers* at $1000–$1700 per season; 2 *chefs* at $3000–$4000 per season; 2 *nurses* with RN license at $2600 per season. International students encouraged to apply.

Benefits   Preemployment training, on-the-job training, formal ongoing training, on-site room and board at no charge, laundry facilities, travel reimbursement, health insurance, one day off each week, healthful cuisine, pre-camp training and certification opportunities available.

Contact   Applicant should send resume, write for application, or call for information to Janet Seaward Greene, Director, Camp Nashoba North, Nashoba Road, Littleton, Massachusetts 01460; 800-448-0136, fax 508-952-2442.

Staff members at Camp Nashoba North have the opportunity to meet people from all over the world.

CAMP PINECLIFFE
Harrison, Maine 04040

General Information   Traditional, residential camp offering high-quality instruction in skills at all levels. Established 1917. Owned by Helen Rosenthal and Susan Lifter. Affiliated with American Camping Association, Maine Youth Camping Association. Located 40 miles northwest of Portland on 150 acres. Features include location 1 hour from the ocean and less than an hour from the White Mountains; warm, capable staff and directors; location on a beautiful lake; salad bar twice a day; third generation ownership.

Profile of Summer Employees   Total number 75; average age 21. Employees are 80% female, 10% minorities, 95% college students, 25% international, 10% local residents. Prefers nonsmokers.

Employment Information   Openings are from June 15 to August 20. College credit possible. Jobs available: 5 *swimming instructors* with WSI certificate at $800–$1500 per season; 5 *waterskiing instructors* with lifesaving certificate at $800–$1500 per season; 3 *boating/sailing instructors* with Red Cross lifesaving certification at $800–$1500 per season; 1 *drama instructor* with experience at $1000 per season; 1 *dance instructor* at $800–$1200 per season; 1 *music instructor* with ability to play piano by ear at $1200–$1500 per season; 2 *arts and crafts instructors* at $800–$1200 per season; 1 *silversmithing instructor* at $1000–$1500 per season; 1 *ceramics instructor* at $800–$1100 per season; 4 *tennis* *instructors* with high school or college team experience at $1000 per season; 1 *riding instructor* with Pony Club experience at $800–$1000 per season; 3 *land sports instructors* at $800–$1000 per season; 1 *archery instructor* at $1000–$1200 per season; 1 *gymnastics instructor* at $1000–$1200 per season. International students encouraged to apply.

Benefits Preemployment training, on-the-job training, on-site room and board at no charge, laundry facilities, travel reimbursement.

Contact Applicant should send resume, write for application, or call for information by May 1 to Susan R. Lifter, Director, Camp Pinecliffe, Department SED, 277 South Cassingham, Bexley, Ohio 43209; 614-236-5698.

Central to our camp life is the individual child. What happens in the cabin is therefore of utmost importance. Our staff needs to be caring and warm, enjoy children, and be able to teach a particular activity.

CAMP RUNOIA
RR 1, Box 775, Point Road
Belgrade Lakes, Maine 04918

General Information Residential camp with traditional camp activities serving 75 campers. Established 1907. Owned by Philip J. and Elizabeth N. Cobb. Affiliated with American Camping Association, Maine Youth Camping Association. Located 83 miles north of Portland on 60 acres. Features include family atmosphere; location in central Maine lakes area; 1¼ hours from the Maine coast and mountains; excellent waterfront area; superior riding program; high-quality programs.

Profile of Summer Employees Total number 25; average age 25. Employees are 95% female, 10% high school students, 30% college students, 10% retirees, 15% international, 10% local residents.

Employment Information Openings are from June 15 to August 15. College credit possible. Jobs available: 5 *waterfront-trip instructors* with WSI certificate and lifeguard, basic sailing, canoeing, and campcraft skills at $1000–$1500 per season. International students encouraged to apply.

Benefits Preemployment training, on-the-job training, formal ongoing training, on-site room and board at no charge, laundry facilities.

Contact Applicant should write for application by February 10 to Mrs. Philip Cobb, Owner, Camp Runoia, Department SED, RR 1, Box 775, Point Road, Belgrade Lakes, Maine 04918; 207-495-2228, fax 207-495-2527.

CAMP SKYLEMAR
Route 114
Naples, Maine 04055

General Information Sports-oriented seven-week program for boys ages 8–16. Established 1949. Owned by Lee Horowitz and Herb Blumenfeld. Affiliated with American Camping Association, Maine Youth Camping Association, Private Independent Camps. Located 30 miles east of Portland on 200 acres. Features include excellent facilities and golf course; location on lake near White Mountains in an area with many tourist attractions; close family atmosphere with 120 campers and 40 counselors.

Profile of Summer Employees   Total number 40; average age 20. Employees are 90% college students, 5% international, 5% local residents. Prefers nonsmokers.

Employment Information   Openings are from June 24 to August 17. Winter break positions also offered. College credit possible. Jobs available: 4 *swimming instructors* with WSI certificate at $1200–$1500 per season; 15 *general sports counselors* with experience in sports at $1000–$1500 per season; 2 *arts and crafts instructors* with arts experience at $1000–$1200 per season; 2 *boating and skiing instructors* with small craft certificate at $1000–$1400 per season; 3 *lifeguards* with lifeguard certificate at $1000–$1400 per season; 1 *riflery instructor* with NRA instructor certification at $1000–$1400 per season; 2 *trip counselors* with trip experience at $1000–$1400 per season.

Benefits   Preemployment training, on-the-job training, formal ongoing training, on-site room and board at no charge, laundry facilities, travel reimbursement, use of all facilities, transportation to town every night, great food.

Contact   Applicant should send resume, write for application, or call for information by April 20 to Lee Horowitz, Director, Camp Skylemar, Department SED, 7900 Stevenson Road, Baltimore, Maryland 21208; 301-653-2480.

Our campers and staff members come from across the United States and abroad. Counselors have the opportunity to instruct in various areas rather than in just one specialty.

CAMP TAKAJO
Naples, Maine 04055

General Information   Residential boys' camp offering an eight-week session to 360 campers ages 7–16. Established 1947. Owned by Jeffrey A. Konigsberg. Affiliated with American Camping Association, Maine Youth Camping Association. Located 30 miles west of Portland on 75 acres. Features include picturesque lakefront location; exceptional facilities; location an hour from both the ocean and the mountains; campers and staff from all over the world; diverse program offering over thirty activity areas.

Profile of Summer Employees   Total number 150; average age 24. Employees are 5% female, 5% minorities, 1% high school students, 90% college students, 1% retirees, 25% international, 1% local residents. Prefers nonsmokers.

Employment Information   Openings are from June 18 to August 18. College credit possible. Jobs available: 10 *swimming instructors* with WSI certificate (training provided) at $800–$1200 per season; 6 *baseball instructors* with playing experience in high school or college baseball at $800–$1200 per season; 6 *basketball instructors* with playing experience in high school or college basketball at $800–$1200 per season; 20 *tennis instructors* with playing experience in high school or college tennis at $800–$1200 per season; 6 *soccer instructors* with playing experience in high school or college soccer at $800–$1200 per season; 2 *archery instructors* with no archery experience necessary (training provided) at $800–$1200 per season; 2 *riflery instructors* with no riflery experience necessary (training provided) at $800–$1200 per season; 1 *journalism instructor* with journalism experience at $800–$1200 per season; 1 *photography instructor* with photography experience at $800–$1200 per season; 2 *nature study instructors* with nature study experience at $800–$1200 per season; 12 *pioneering/trip instructors* with Boy Scout, Eagle Scout, Outward Bound, or other related types of experience at $800–$1200 per season; 8 *sailing instructors* with Red Cross certifications plus appropriate experience at $800–$1200 per season; 6 *arts and crafts instructors* with appropriate schooling and experience at $800–$1200 per season; 4 *waterskiing instructors* with appropriate experience with motorboats at $800–$1200 per season; 6 *general counselors* with ability to work well with children ages 7–10 at $800–$1200 per season. International students encouraged to apply.

Benefits Preemployment training, on-the-job training, on-site room and board at no charge, laundry facilities, travel reimbursement, health insurance.

Contact Applicant should send resume, write for application, or call for information by May 15 to Jeffrey A. Konigsberg, Owner/Director, Camp Takajo, 496 LaGuardia Place, Suite 381, New York, New York 10012; 212-979-0606, fax 212-982-4795.

Staff has use of all camp facilities. Staff members without cars are provided with transportation on days and evenings off. Each counselor leads or assists in one of the activity areas noted.

CAMP TAPAWINGO
Route 93
Sweden, Maine 04040

General Information Residential, private girls' camp offering an eight-week program. Established 1919. Owned by Jane Lichtman. Affiliated with American Camping Association, Appalachian Mountain Club, Maine Youth Camping Association, United States Lawn Tennis Association. Located 50 miles northwest of Portland on 200 acres. Features include 22 cabins and 2 historic lodges; highly individualized instruction (3 campers to 1 counselor); broad range of sports, water, arts, and backpacking activities; 8 tennis courts, riding rings (surrounded by extensive wood trails), regulation sports fields, and stables; beautiful setting on crystal-clear lake close to mountains.

Profile of Summer Employees Total number 55; average age 25. Employees are 90% female, 1% minorities, 2% high school students, 71% college students, 15% international, 2% local residents. Requires nonsmokers.

Employment Information Openings are from June 15 to August 19. College credit possible. Jobs available: 1 *art instructor* at $750 per season; 1 *stained glass instructor* at $750 per season; 1 *ceramics instructor* at $750 per season; 2 *gymnastics instructors* with teaching experience at $750 per season; 1 *piano accompanist* with sight-reading and transposing ability at $750 per season; 4 *tennis instructors* at $750 per season; 2 *sail/boardsail instructors* with lifeguard certificate and instructor rating at $750 per season; 2 *canoe instructors* with lifeguard certificate and instructor rating at $750 per season; 2 *waterskiing instructors* with lifeguard certificate and instructor rating at $750 per season; 4 *swimming instructors* with WSI and lifeguard certificate at $750 per season; 2 *nurses* with RN license at $750 per season; 1 *photography instructor* with knowledge of black and white photography and developing at $750 per season; 4 *trip leaders* with lifeguard, first aid, and CPR certificates at $750 per season; 4 *dramatics instructors* at $750 per season. International students encouraged to apply.

Benefits Preemployment training, on-the-job training, on-site room and board at no charge, laundry facilities, travel reimbursement, health insurance, use of facilities during free time.

Contact Applicant should send resume, write for application, or call for information to Becky Schumacher, Assistant Director, Camp Tapawingo, Department SED, P.O. Box 1353, Scarborough, Maine 04070-1353; 207-883-7052.

CAMP WAZIYATAH
RR 2, Box 465
Harrison, Maine 04040

General Information Traditional, residential camp serving 200 campers. Campers can choose their own activities. Established 1922. Owned by Tom and Nancy Armstrong. Affiliated with American Camping Association, Maine Youth Camping Association. Located 40 miles northwest of Portland on 150 acres. Features include 3½-mile crystal-clear lake; Old Farm House (arts media theater, dance room, studio, photo lab); gymnastics, martial arts, and theater programs; 10 tennis courts; riding stables, ring, and trails; trip programs, rifle range, 3 basketball courts, a volleyball court, 2 soccer fields, baseball and softball fields, and large dining room.

Profile of Summer Employees Total number 100; average age 23. Employees are 45% female, 2% minorities, 70% college students, 3% retirees, 45% international, 2% local residents. Prefers nonsmokers.

Employment Information Openings are from June 15 to August 23. Jobs available: 6 *swimming instructors* with WSI certificate at $900–$1200 per season; 2 *sailing instructors* with Red Cross sailing certificate at $900–$1200 per season; 2 *windsurfing instructors* with Red Cross sailing certificate at $900–$1200 per season; 4 *waterskiing instructors* with experience as a boat driver at $900–$1200 per season; 1 *canoe instructor* with certification at $900–$1200 per season; 2 *rifle instructors* with NRA certification at $900–$1200 per season; 1 *archery instructor* with certification at $900–$1200 per season; 2 *trip leaders* with CPR and first aid experience at $900–$1200 per season; 2 *baseball/softball instructors* with experience at $900–$1200 per season; 3 *arts and crafts instructors* with experience at $900–$1200 per season; 2 *theater personnel* with experience at $900–$1200 per season; 1 *song leader* with experience at $900–$1200 per season.

Benefits Preemployment training, on-the-job training, on-site room and board at no charge, laundry facilities, transportation on days off, staff lounge.

Contact Applicant should send resume, write for application, or call for information by April 15 to Tom and Nancy Armstrong, Directors, Camp Waziyatah, P.O. Box 86569, Madeira Beach, Florida 33738; 800-732-0223, fax 813-391-7119.

CAMP WEKEELA
RFD 1, Box 275, Route 219
Canton, Maine 04221

General Information Residential, traditional, coeducational camp serving 225 campers. The camp emphasizes sports, waterfront activities, and arts. Established 1922. Owned by Eric and Lauren Scoblionko. Affiliated with American Camping Association, United States Lawn Tennis Association, Maine Youth Camping Association. Located 10 miles southeast of Lewiston on 100 acres. Features include magnificent property/facilities; lakeside setting; campers from 38 states and 10 countries; location near ocean and mountains; close to Portland (1 hour) and Boston (3 hours).

Profile of Summer Employees Total number 110; average age 21. Employees are 50% female, 85% college students, 10% international, 5% local residents. Prefers nonsmokers.

Employment Information Openings are from June 15 to August 20. College credit possible. Jobs available: *ropes instructors; pioneering staff; tennis staff; gymnastics staff; folksingers; piano/music staff; land sports staff; creative arts staff; woodworking staff;*

ceramics staff; theatrical arts staff; radio staff; video/photo staff; waterfront staff; waterski-ing staff.

Benefits Preemployment training, on-site room and board at no charge, laundry facili-ties, travel reimbursement.

Contact Applicant should send resume, write for application, call for information, or apply in person by May 1 to Eric Scoblionko, Director, Camp Wekeela, Department SED, 130 South Merkle Road, Columbus, Ohio 43209; 614-235-3177, fax 614-235-3619.

The entire camp is cradled in a natural pine grove on the shores of beautiful Bear Pond with a 1,500-foot sandy beach. It has great facilities and a warm familylike atmos-phere.

HIDDEN VALLEY CAMP
Ireland Road
Freedom, Maine 04941

General Information Residential, international, noncompetitive camp offering a four-week session to 220 campers. Established 1947. Owned by Peter and Meg Kassen. Affiliat-ed with American Camping Association, Maine Youth Camping Association. Located 85 miles east of Portland on 200 acres. Features include farmlike environment; fields and forest; warm atmosphere; location near Atlantic Ocean; llama herd in residence.

Profile of Summer Employees Total number 90; average age 24. Employees are 60% female, 10% minorities, 5% high school students, 40% college students, 3% retirees, 20% international, 10% local residents. Requires nonsmokers.

Employment Information Openings are from June 15 to August 20. College credit possible. Jobs available: 3 *swimming instructors* with WSI/lifeguard certificate at $800–$1400 per season; 3 *ropes instructors* with experience teaching adventure courses at $800–$1400 per season; 3 *dance instructors* with experience teaching dance at $800–$1400 per season; 5 *horse instructors* with English riding experience at $800–$1400 per season; *soccer instructor* at $800–$1400 per season; *stained glass instructor* at $800–$1400 per season; *pottery instructor* at $800–$1400 per season; *animal-care person* with experience working with farm animals at $800–$1400 per season. International students encouraged to apply.

Benefits Preemployment training, on-the-job training, formal ongoing training, on-site room and board at no charge, laundry facilities, internships available, vegetarian diet.

Contact Applicant should send resume, write for application, or call for information by March 15 to Peter and Meg Kassen, Director/Owner, Hidden Valley Camp, Department SED, RR 1, Box 2360, Freedom, Maine 04941; 207-342-5177, fax 207-342-5685.

Directors work closely with staff members. Minimal hierarchy creates community feeling. Counselors must be hardworking and child-centered in addition to possessing skills in various camp areas.

IDLEASE GREAT RESORT
Route 9, P.O. Box 3086
Kennebunkport, Maine 04043

General Information Resort serving visitors to scenic Kennebunkport. Features include location several minutes from Dock Square, the hub of the beautiful seacoast village of

Kennebunkport; great restaurants, art galleries, antique shops, marinas, craft stores, deep-sea fishing/whale watching boat slips, and lovely historic homes (including the home of President George Bush); many fine sandy beaches located only minutes away.

Employment Information   College credit possible. Jobs available: 1 *assistant manager* with ability to perform desk work, scheduling, supervising hourly help, and general duties (should be able to work from May to September; applicant should be a college student, teacher, or foreign student–limited to French-speaking person) at $1200–$1400 per month; 8 *housekeeping associates* with ability to perform general work including chambermaid work (should be able to stay from March to December; applicants should be college or high school students or teachers) at $200–$240 per week.

Contact   Applicant should send resume or write for application to Ed Blake, General Manager, Idlease Great Resort, P.O. Box 3086, Kennebunkport, Maine 04043.

We offer good working conditions, opportunities to meet interesting people, interesting work, and a social atmosphere.

MAINE TEEN CAMP
RR 1, Box 39
Kezar Falls, Maine 04047

General Information   Residential camp for teenagers offering two sessions with 230 campers participating in each session. Established 1983. Owned by Bob Briskin and Kris Kamys. Affiliated with American Camping Association, Maine Youth Camping Association. Located 35 miles southwest of Portland on 50 acres. Features include 2 lakes; sailing and skiing; sports activities and tennis courts; international participation; fully elective program; advanced music technology and arts.

Profile of Summer Employees   Total number 70; average age 22. Employees are 55% female, 20% minorities, 50% college students, 2% retirees, 30% international, 2% local residents. Prefers nonsmokers.

Employment Information   Openings are from June 15 to August 23. College credit possible. Jobs available: *drum instructor* at $1000 per season; *keyboard instructor* at $1000 per season; *guitar instructor* at $1000 per season; *MIDI instructor* at $1000 per season; *tennis instructor* at $1000 per season; *swimming instructor* at $1000 per season; *jewelry-crafting instructor* at $1000 per season; *dance instructor* at $1000 per season; *theater instructor* at $1000 per season; *sailing/windsurfing instructor* at $1000 per season; *water-skiing instructor* at $1000 per season; *arts instructor* at $1000 per season; *land sports instructor* at $1000 per season; *ropes instructor* at $1000 per season. International students encouraged to apply.

Benefits   Preemployment training, on-the-job training, on-site room and board.

Contact   Applicant should send resume, write for application, or call for information by June 10 to Kris Kamys, Director, Maine Teen Camp, Department SED, RR 1, Box 39, Kezar Falls, Maine 04047; 207-625-8581, fax 207-627-7624.

We offer a fully equipped sound recording studio (MIDI equipment), computers, and instruction in keyboards, guitar, and drums.

NATIONAL PARK SERVICE

Contact   Applicant should write for application (must be 18 by May 13; U.S. citizenship required) to Regional Office of the National Park Service, North Atlantic Region, National Park Service, 15 State Street, Boston, Massachusetts 02109.

Jobs located in Maine at the following facility: Acadia. Also see District of Columbia listing.

WILD GOOSE...FOR BOYS
Great Moose Lake
Harmony, Maine 04942

General Information   Private, well-established, traditional boys' camp with an international clientele. Serves 68 boys ages 8–14. Established 1956. Owned by Lorna and William E. Trauth Jr. Located 50 miles west of Bangor on 1,000 acres. Features include all major land and water sports; a camper-counselor ratio of 3:1; trips to wilderness areas; first-class facilities and equipment; location on 8-mile long lake; a wide range of activities from which campers may choose, including archery, baseball, football, riflery, sailing, soccer, swimming, tennis, track and field, waterskiing, windsurfing, woodsmanship, wrestling, mountain climbing, canoeing, crafts, fishing, photography, and physical fitness.

Profile of Summer Employees   Total number 30; average age 25. Employees are 20% female, 50% college students. Prefers nonsmokers.

Employment Information   Openings are from June 15 to August 16. Jobs available: 5 *counselors* at $900 per season; *nurse; secretary/word processor.*

Benefits   Preemployment training, on-the-job training, on-site room and board at no charge, laundry facilities.

Contact   Applicant should write for application or call for information to William E. Trauth, Jr., Director, Wild Goose...for Boys, Department SED, 328 Summit Avenue, Leonia, New Jersey 07605; 201-944-6271.

WYONEGONIC CAMPS
RR 1, Box 186
Denmark, Maine 04022

General Information   Residential girls' camp. Established 1902. Owned by George and Carol Sudduth. Affiliated with American Camping Association, Maine Youth Camping Association. Located 40 miles west of Portland on 300 acres. Features include location on freshwater lake; 1 hour from mountains and ocean; rustic setting; pine woods.

Profile of Summer Employees   Total number 60; average age 21. Employees are 85% female, 5% high school students, 70% college students, 20% international, 5% local residents. Requires nonsmokers.

Employment Information   Openings are from June 8 to August 28. Christmas break positions also offered. College credit possible. Jobs available: *swimming instructor* with WSI and LGT certificates at $800–$1600 per season; *sailing instructor* with LGT certificate at $800–$1600 per season; *sailboarding instructor* with LGT certificate at $800–$1600 per season; *waterskiing instructor* with LGT certificate and driving experience at $800–$1600 per season; *tennis instructor* at $800–$1600 per season; *riding instructor* at $800–

$1600 per season; *pottery instructor* at $800–$1600 per season; *arts and crafts instructor* at $800–$1600 per season; *canoe trips instructor* with trip leader/SFA/LGT certificate (minimum age 21) at $800–$1600 per season; *hiking instructor* with trip leader/SFA/LGT certificate (minimum age 21) at $800–$1600 per season; *archery instructor* with Maine State certification at $800–$1600 per season; *riflery instructor* with NRA certification at $800–$1600 per season; *dramatics instructor* at $800–$1600 per season; *nurses* with RN license at $1800–$2000 per season; *kitchen workers.* International students encouraged to apply.

Benefits   Preemployment training, on-the-job training, formal ongoing training, on-site room and board at no charge, laundry facilities, travel reimbursement, certification training.

Contact   Applicant should send resume, write for application, or call for information by May 1 to Carol S. Sudduth, Director, Wyonegonic Camps, RR 1, Box 186, Denmark, Maine 04022; 207-452-2051, fax 207-452-2611.

Individuals who join us have the opportunity to work with children and staff members from forty different states and foreign countries.

Maryland

CAMPS AIRY AND LOUISE

General Information   Residential camps serving boys and girls. Established 1922. Owned by Aaron and Lilie Straus Foundation. Affiliated with American Camping Association. Located 60 miles north of Washington, D.C. on 950 acres. Features include great physical facilities; beautiful area close to the Appalachian Trail and the Blue Ridge Summit; wide selection of well-screened counselors.

Profile of Summer Employees   Total number 285; average age 25. Employees are 2% minorities, 95% college students, 3% retirees, 3% international, 10% local residents.

Employment Information   Openings are from June 20 to August 14. Jobs available: 30 *general counselors* at $700–$1200 per season; 15 *swimming instructors* with WSI or lifeguard certificate at $700–$1200 per season; 10 *outdoor-living instructors* at $700–$1200 per season; *music instructor; drama instructor; athletics instructors; karate instructor; riflery instructor; nature instructor; arts and crafts instructor; ceramics instructor.* International students encouraged to apply.

Benefits   Preemployment training, on-the-job training, on-site room and board at no charge, laundry facilities, travel reimbursement.

Contact   Applicant should write for application to Ed Cohen, Executive Director, Camps Airy and Louise, Department SED, 5750 Park Heights Avenue, Baltimore, Maryland 21215; 301-466-9010, fax 301-664-0551.

Come experience the family feeling at Camps Airy and Louise.

ELKS CAMP BARRETT
1001 Chesterfield Road
Annapolis, Maryland 21401

General Information Weekly residential camp serving 100–120 deserving boys and girls ages 9–15 during alternate weeks. Owned by Elks State Associations (Maryland, Delaware, and the District of Columbia). Affiliated with American Camping Association. Located 20 miles north of Washington, D.C. on 185 acres. Features include pleasant wooded atmosphere; proximity to two major metropolitan areas; opportunity for environmental experiences; modern base camp and outdoor camping programs; varied program for three age groups.

Profile of Summer Employees Total number 25; average age 19. Employees are 50% female, 8% minorities, 38% high school students, 42% college students, 30% international, 70% local residents.

Employment Information Openings are from June 15 to August 25. Jobs available: 10 *counselors (senior)* with some first aid and CPR training, arts and crafts experience, plus certification in archery, riflery, etc. at $1500–$1550 per season; 5 *counselors (junior)* with first aid training at $1000–$1100 per season; 2 *lifeguards (pool operators)* with pool operators' license, WSI certificate, plus first aid and CPR training at $1900 per season; 2 *lifeguards* with lifeguard, first aid, and CPR training at $1550 per season; 1 *cook* with previous experience at $250–$300 per week; 2 *kitchen helpers* with willingness to work at $1500 per season; 2 *program directors (base camp and wilderness programs)* at $2500 per season; 1 *nurse* with RN license. International students encouraged to apply.

Benefits Preemployment training, on-the-job training, on-site room and board at no charge, laundry facilities, weekly salary.

Contact Applicant should send resume, write for application, call for information, or apply in person by April 15 to Robert W. MacLellan, Chairman–Staff Hiring, Elks Camp Barrett, Department SED, 1001 Chesterfield Road, Annapolis, Maryland 21401; 301-224-2945.

MANIDOKAN OUTDOOR MINISTRY CENTER
1620 Harpers Ferry Road
Knoxville, Maryland 21758

General Information Residential camp with a variety of accommodations and programs for all ages. Established 1949. Owned by Baltimore Annual Conference of the United Methodist Church. Affiliated with American Camping Association, Christian Camping International, National Camp Leaders/United Methodist. Located 70 miles west of Washington, DC on 426 acres. Features include extensive ropes and initiatives course; canoe and rafting program; location adjacent to the Chesapeake and Ohio Canal, near Harpers Ferry and Antietam Battlefield.

Profile of Summer Employees Total number 14; average age 20. Employees are 50% female, 7% minorities, 7% high school students, 73% college students, 20% retirees, 35% local residents. Prefers nonsmokers.

Employment Information Openings are from June 7 to August 22. Jobs available: 4 *program resource personnel* with lifeguard training (preferred) at $150–$200 per week; 1 *lifeguard* with WSI certificate (preferred) at $150–$200 per week; 1 *canoe instructor* with Red Cross canoe instructor certificate at $175–$225 per week; 2 *cooks* at $200–$300 per week; 3 *kitchen aides* at $130–$150 per week; 1 *maintenance person* at $130–$150 per week; 1 *nurse* at $250–$350 per week; 1 *van driver* at $175–$225 per week.

Benefits   On-the-job training, on-site room and board at no charge, laundry facilities, health insurance.

Contact   Applicant should write for application or call for information by January 1 to Bruce A. VanDervort, Coordinator of Outdoor Ministries, Manidokan Outdoor Ministry Center, 5124 Greenwich Avenue, Baltimore, Maryland 21229; 301-233-7300, fax 301-233-7308.

NATIONAL PARK SERVICE

Contact   Applicant should write for application (must be 18 by May 13; U.S. citizenship required) to Regional Office of the National Park Service, Mid-Atlantic Region, National Park Service, 143 South Third Street, Philadelphia, Pennsylvania 19106.

Jobs located in Maryland at the following facilities: Antietam, Assateague Island, Catoctin Mountain Park, Chesapeake and Ohio Canal, George Washington Memorial Parkway/Clara Barton/Glen Echo Park, Fort McHenry, Fort Washington, Greenbelt Park, Hampton, Monocacy, Oxon Hill Farm, U.S. Park Police. Also see District of Columbia listing.

WEST RIVER UNITED METHODIST CENTER
Chalk Point Road, P.O. Box 429
Churchton, Maryland 20733

General Information   Residential camp on a mile-long waterfront near the Chesapeake Bay. Established 1951. Owned by Baltimore Annual Conference of the United Methodist Church. Affiliated with American Camping Association, Christian Camping International, National Camp Leaders/United Methodist. Located 15 miles south of Annapolis on 45 acres. Features include extensive sailing and boating program; swimming pool and athletics fields; comfortable lodges and retreat center; wetlands and shoreline nature study areas.

Profile of Summer Employees   Total number 16; average age 20. Employees are 60% female, 18% minorities, 12% high school students, 62% college students, 37% local residents. Prefers nonsmokers.

Employment Information   Openings are from June 7 to August 22. Jobs available: 3 *lifeguards* with Red Cross lifeguard training at $175–$200 per week; 1 *head lifeguard* with WSI certificate at $200–$250 per week; 1 *sailing instructor* with Red Cross sailing instructor certificate at $175–$225 per week; 2 *cooks* at $300–$400 per week; 4 *kitchen aides* at $130–$150 per week; 2 *maintenance personnel* at $130–$150 per week; 2 *program resource persons* with lifesaving training (preferred) at $175–$225 per week; 1 *nurse* at $250–$350 per week.

Benefits   On-the-job training, on-site room and board at no charge, laundry facilities, health insurance.

Contact   Applicant should write for application or call for information by January 1 to Bruce A. VanDervort, Coordinator of Outdoor Ministries, West River United Methodist Center, 5124 Greenwich Avenue, Baltimore, Maryland 21229; 301-233-7300, fax 301-233-7308.

YMCA CAMP LETTS
4003 Camp Letts Road, P.O. Box 208
Edgewater, Maryland 21037

General Information Residential camp serving 300 campers in sports and general activities during four 2-week sessions. Established 1906. Owned by YMCA of Metropolitan Washington. Affiliated with American Camping Association, Annapolis Chamber of Commerce, Young Men's Christian Association. Located 25 miles east of Washington, D.C. Features include location on 219-acre peninsula on Rhode River off of the Chesapeake Bay; sailing; waterskiing; horseback riding; 25-meter freshwater swimming pool; land-based activities.

Profile of Summer Employees Total number 100; average age 21. Employees are 50% female, 20% minorities, 10% high school students, 80% college students, 10% international, 5% local residents. Prefers nonsmokers.

Employment Information Openings are from May 1 to September 30. Spring break, winter break, Christmas break positions also offered. College credit possible. Jobs available: 5 *crew skippers* with a minimum age of 21 at $1380–$2185 per season; 30 *counselors* with first year of college completed or a minimum age of 19 at $1035–$1610 per season; 30 *assistant counselors* with high school graduate status or a minimum age of 18 at $750–$1180 per season; 1 *photographer/editor* with previous skill (resume required) at $1035–$1610 per season; 1 *administrative assistant* with college upperclassman or graduate status and managerial skills at $1610–$2185 per season; 1 *horsemanship director* with college upperclassman or graduate status, riding and teaching experience, and Pony Club background (preferred) at $1610–$2185 per season; 1 *land activities director* with college upperclassman or graduate status, background in physical fitness, plus CPR and first aid training at $1610–$2300 per season; 1 *small craft director* with college upperclassman or graduate status, WSI and AWSA certificates (preferred), plus lifeguarding and CPR certificates at $1610–$2415 per season; 1 *sailing director* with lifeguarding and CPR certificates plus USYRU certificate or USCG captain's license (preferred) at $1610–$2415 per season.

Benefits Preemployment training, on-the-job training, on-site room and board at no charge.

Contact Applicant should send resume, write for application, or call for information by April 30 to Jeffrey B. Butcher, Resident Camp Director, YMCA Camp Letts, Department SED, P.O. Box 208, Edgewater, Maryland 21037; 301-261-4286, fax 301-261-7336.

International students who wish to apply for employment should do so through an agency such as Camp America.

Massachusetts

BELVOIR TERRACE
Lenox, Massachusetts 01240

General Information Residential camp serving 180 girls with a focus on fine and performing arts. The program provides specific services for the academically talented and the gifted. Established 1954. Owned by Nancy S. Goldberg. Affiliated with American Camping Association. Features include programs in fine arts and crafts, dance, music, theater, and sports; close proximity to Tanglewood, Jacob's Pillow, and Williamstown Theatre.

Profile of Summer Employees Total number 80; average age 28. Requires nonsmokers.

Employment Information Openings are from June 16 to August 20. College credit possible.

Benefits Preemployment training, on-the-job training, on-site room and board, laundry facilities, travel reimbursement.

Contact Applicant should send resume to Nancy S. Goldberg, Director, Belvoir Terrace, Department SED, 145 Central Park West, New York, New York 10023.

We seek specialized staff and request that only skilled applicants apply.

BONNIE CASTLE RIDING CAMP
Stoneleigh–Burnham School
Greenfield, Massachusetts 01301

General Information Residential camp for girls ages 10–15. Established 1979. Owned by Stoneleigh-Burnham School. Affiliated with New England Association of Schools and Colleges, Independent Schools Association of Massachusetts, National Association of Independent Schools. Located 60 miles north of Hartford, Connecticut on 100 acres. Features include 60 horse stables; 2 indoor-riding rings; riding trails; event course; outdoor pool; 2 horse shows held on campus.

Profile of Summer Employees Total number 5; average age 22. Employees are 100% female, 10% high school students, 60% college students, 30% local residents. Prefers nonsmokers.

Employment Information Jobs available: 4 *riding instructors* with a minimum age of 18 at $900–$1200 per season; 1 *arts/photo instructor* with a minimum age of 18 at $700–$1200 per season; 1 *drama instructor* with a minimum age of 18 at $700–$1200 per season; 2 *swimming instructors* with WSI certificate at $600–$1200 per season. International students encouraged to apply.

Benefits On-site room and board at no charge, laundry facilities.

Contact Applicant should send resume or call for information by March 30 to Eileen Sullivan, Director, Bonnie Castle Riding Camp, Stoneleigh-Burnham School, Greenfield, Massachusetts 01301; 413-774-2711, fax 413-772-2602.

CAMP EMERSON
212 Longview Avenue
Hinsdale, Massachusetts 01235

General Information Residential camp serving 220 boys and girls ages 7–15. Established 1968. Owned by Marv and Addie Lein. Affiliated with American Camping Association, Massachusetts Camping Association, Western Massachusetts Camping Association. Located 150 miles northeast of New York City on 143 acres. Features include new heated pool; private lake; site near cultural centers of the Berkshires; facilities for all land and water sports; theater and art center.

Profile of Summer Employees   Total number 80; average age 23. Employees are 50% female, 80% college students. Prefers nonsmokers.

Employment Information   Openings are from June 21 to August 24. College credit possible. Jobs available: *creative arts instructors* with experience in fine arts/drawing and painting, ceramics, sculpting, batik, leather, jewelry, model rocketry, woodworking, photography, yearbook, newspaper/creative writing, video, and computers at $1000 per season; *performing arts instructors* with experience in dramatics/directing, stagecraft, costuming/sewing, skits and stunts, storytelling, music (all instruments), piano (play by ear and/or play for shows and transpose), dance (jazz/aerobic/ballet/modern), choreography, guitar (play, sing, teach), and puppetry at $1000 per season; *land sports instructors* with experience in archery, basketball, fencing, golf, gymnastics, hockey, judo, karate, soccer, softball, tennis, track, volleyball, and fitness at $1000 per season; *water sports instructors* with experience in swimming (WSI certificate), sailing (SCI certificate), canoeing, kayaking, water polo, windsurfing, water skiing, motorboat driving, and synchronized swimming at $1000 per season; *pioneering instructor* with experience in campcraft, fire building, outdoor cooking, overnight trips, forestry, nature, hiking, and fishing at $1000 per season; *nurses* with RN license; *secretary* at $1000 per season; *bookkeeper* at $1000 per season; *cooks/kitchen help* at $1000 per season; *driver* at $1000 per season.

Benefits   Preemployment training, on-the-job training, on-site room and board at no charge, laundry facilities, internships, healthful menu, salad bar.

Contact   Applicant should send resume, write for application, or call for information by June 1 to Marv and Addie Lein, Camp Directors, Camp Emerson, Department SED, 5 Brassie Road, Eastchester, New York 10707; 914-779-9406, fax 914-793-9334.

We provide a friendly atmosphere with emphasis on individual skill development in an elective program. Every camper is encouraged to become more self-confident and happy while nurturing all that is best within himself or herself. When it comes to our staff, we care and we show it! Whether it's an extended evening off, transportation to local shopping, special activities with staff from other nearby camps, or free video movies and snacks available nightly, we're working hard to provide our staff members with the little extras that will help make their summer camp experience the best it can be.

CAMP GOOD NEWS
Route 130
Forestdale, Massachusetts 02644

General Information   Residential, coeducational day camp serving 220 children ages 6–16. Established 1935. Owned by Society for Christian Activities. Affiliated with American Camping Association, Pioneers of Camping Club, Cape Cod Canal Region Chamber of Commerce. Located 13 miles east of Hyannis on 214 acres. Features include beautiful wooded area; a half mile of shorefront on fresh water pond; location 6 miles from ocean on beautiful Cape Cod; well-rounded program of recreation and work with a spiritual dimension; sailing, canoeing, and swimming activities.

Profile of Summer Employees   Total number 70; average age 25. Employees are 55% female, 3% minorities, 1% high school students, 58% college students, 1% retirees, 2% international, 5% local residents. Requires nonsmokers.

Employment Information   Openings are from June 27 to August 13. Jobs available: 35 *counselors* with college student status at $900–$1100 per season; 10 *kitchen staff* with a minimum age of 18 at $800–$1000 per season; 2 *arts and crafts instructors* with experience at $900–$1000 per season; *nurses* at $1000–$1100 per season; *store managers* at $800–$900 per season; *sports experts* with boating certification at $900–$1100 per season.

Benefits   Preemployment training, on-the-job training, on-site room and board at no charge, laundry facilities, tuition reimbursement.

Contact   Applicant should send resume, write for application, call for information, or apply in person by May 30 to Faith Willard, Director, Camp Good News, P.O. Box 95, Forestdale, Massachusetts 02644; 508-477-9731, fax 508-477-8016.

We have many campers from foreign countries—France, Japan, Mexico, and Canada—and this presents a good opportunity to utilize skills developed through language studies. In addition, one has the opportunity to impact lives of children and teenagers in a positive way.

CAMP PEMBROKE
Pembroke, Massachusetts 02359

General Information   Residential, Jewish cultural camp for girls serving 250. Established 1936. Operated by Cohen Foundation. Affiliated with American Camping Association, Massachusetts Camping Association, Private Independent Camps. Located 30 miles south of Boston on 68 acres. Features include Olympic-size pool; modern plant; proximity to Cape Cod and Boston.

Profile of Summer Employees   Total number 85; average age 19. Employees are 18% high school students, 80% college students, 2% international. Prefers nonsmokers.

Employment Information   Openings are from June 25 to August 24. College credit possible. Jobs available: 3 *arts and crafts instructors* at $1350–$1800 per season; 1 *arts and crafts head* at $2000–$2500 per season; 1 *music head* at $2000–$2500 per season; 2 *canoe instructors* at $1350–$2000 per season; 2 *sailing instructors* at $1350–$2000 per season; 3 *swimming instructors* at $1350–$2000 per season; 1 *swimming head* at $2000–$2500 per season; 1 *athletics head* at $2000–$2500 per season; 1 *waterskiing head* at $1500–$1900 per season; 1 *archery instructor* at $1500–$1900 per season.

Benefits   On-the-job training, formal ongoing training, on-site room and board at no charge, laundry facilities, gratuities.

Contact   Applicant should send resume or call for information by April 1 to Pearl Lourie, Director, Camp Pembroke, Department SED, 5 Birchmeadow Circle, Framingham, Massachusetts 01701; 508-788-0161, fax 508-881-1006.

Great summer opportunity working with children in a Jewish cultural setting. Work-study program is available.

CAMP WATITOH
Center Lake
Becket, Massachusetts 01223

General Information   Residential summer camp serving 200 children with a wide variety of land and water sports activities, including drama, nature, and trips to all Berkshire area attractions. Established 1937. Owned by Sandy, William, and Suzanne Hoch. Affiliated with American Camping Association, Massachusetts Camping Association, Western Massachusetts Camp Directors' Association. Located 150 miles north of New York City on

85 acres. Features include mountaintop location; attractive lake setting; noted summer cultural center.

Profile of Summer Employees   Total number 65; average age 20. Employees are 50% female, 85% college students, 10% international. Prefers nonsmokers.

Employment Information   Openings are from June 24 to August 21. Year-round positions also offered. College credit possible. Jobs available: 6 *swimming instructors* with WSI certificate at $1000–$1200 per season; 2 *sailing instructors* at $1000–$1200 per season; 2 *waterskiing instructors* at $1000–$1200 per season; 3 *arts and crafts instructors* with teaching experience (preferred) at $1500–$2500 per season; *sports instructor (general)* at $900–$1600 per season.

Benefits   Preemployment training, on-the-job training, on-site room and board at no charge, travel reimbursement, health insurance.

Contact   Applicant should send resume, write for application, or call for information by June 1 to William Hoch, Director, Camp Watitoh, 28 Sammis Lane, White Plains, New York 10605; 914-428-1894.

A warm, nurturing, familylike atmosphere, especially for younger, first-time campers.

CAPE COD SEA CAMPS
P.O. Box 1880
Brewster, Massachusetts 02631

General Information   Residential camp serving 320 campers for 3½ or 7 weeks and a day camp serving 220 weekly. Established 1922. Owned by Mrs. Berry D. Richardson. Affiliated with American Camping Association, Cape Cod Association of Children's Camps. Located 90 miles southeast of Boston on 125 acres. Features include 3 waterfronts (saltwater, lake, pool); location directly on Cape Cod Bay with a 1,000-foot beach; 9 tennis courts and 15 acres of playing fields; easy access to all of Cape Cod; exceptional variety of activities.

Profile of Summer Employees   Total number 120; average age 21. Employees are 50% female, 5% minorities, 80% college students, 4% international, 10% local residents. Prefers nonsmokers.

Employment Information   Openings are from June 12 to August 15. Jobs available: 3 *activity department heads* with teaching certification at $1500–$2100 per season; 10 *general counselors* with documented experience in camp activities at $900–$1500 per season; 5 *sailing staff* with instruction and racing experience at $900–$1500 per season.

Benefits   Preemployment training, on-the-job training, on-site room and board at no charge, laundry facilities.

Contact   Applicant should write for application or call for information and provide three written references with application by April 15 to Sherry Mernick, Associate Director, Cape Cod Sea Camps, Department SED, P.O. Box 1880, Brewster, Massachusetts 02631; 508-896-3451, fax 508-896-8272.

Cape Cod Sea Camps staff members have the opportunity to take part in an excellent growing and learning experience while performing interesting work.

COLLEGE LIGHT OPERA COMPANY
Highfield Theatre, P.O. Drawer F
Falmouth, Massachusetts 02541

General Information   Residential summer-stock music theater for training undergraduate and graduate students. Established 1969. Owned by College Light Opera Company Board of Trustees. Located 70 miles south of Boston on 6 acres. Features include excellent training in music theater and theater management; congenial environment; full pit orchestra; location on the beach on Cape Cod; largest resident theater company in the United States.

Profile of Summer Employees   Total number 85; average age 20. Employees are 50% female, 5% minorities, 2% high school students, 80% college students. Prefers nonsmokers.

Employment Information   Openings are from June 3 to August 25. College credit possible. Jobs available: 32 *vocalists* with previous experience; 18 *orchestra staff* with previous experience at $500 per season; 6 *stage crew* with previous experience at $500 per season; 5 *costume crew* with previous experience at $500 per season; 2 *box office treasurers* at $800 per season; 1 *assistant business manager* with business and word processing experience at $1000 per season; 1 *publicity director* with word processing and previous experience at $1000 per season; 1 *choreographer* with previous experience at $1200 per season; 2 *chorus masters* with previous experience at $900 per season; 2 *piano accompanists* with previous experience at $800 per season; 1 *costume designer* with previous experience at $2000 per season; 1 *set designer/technical director* with previous experience at $2000 per season; 1 *co-op work director* with previous experience at $1500 per season; 1 *cook* with previous experience at $1800 per season. International students encouraged to apply.

Benefits   Preemployment training, on-the-job training, on-site room and board at no charge, accident insurance.

Contact   Applicant should write for application or call for information by March 15 to Ursula P. Haslun, Producer, College Light Opera Company, 162 South Cedar Street, Oberlin, Ohio 44074; 216-774-8485.

CLOC welcomes both younger applicants seeking to gain experience in musical theater and the more mature performer, musician, and technician seeking to polish his or her craft by working with a professional staff and participating in nine different productions.

CRANE LAKE CAMP
State Line Road
West Stockbridge, Massachusetts 01266

General Information   Coeducational children's camp serving ages 6–15 with traditional sports and a full-cultural program. Established 1922. Owned by Ed and Barbara Ulanoff. Affiliated with American Camping Association. Located 12 miles south of Pittsfield on 120 acres. Features include private lake; swimming pool, 3 baseball fields, and 2 soccer fields; location 3 miles from Tanglewood Music Festival, 2½ hours from New York City and Boston, near the Berkshire Mountains; 10 tennis courts; modern cabins; gymnastics pavillion; 2 arts and crafts studios.

Profile of Summer Employees   Total number 125; average age 21. Employees are 48% female. Requires nonsmokers.

Employment Information   Openings are from June 20 to August 21. College credit possible. Jobs available: 10 *athletics counselors* with a physical education major or varsity athletics experience at $900–$1200 per season; 6 *waterfront instructors* with small crafts certificate and waterskiing, sailing, or canoeing experience at $900–$1200 per season; 4 *gymnastics instructors* with experience at $900–$1200 per season; 2 *arts and crafts instructors* at $900–$1200 per season; *nurse* with RN license at $1600 per season; *nature instructor* at $900–$1200 per season; *horseback-riding instructor* at $900–$1200 per season; *tennis instructor* with college playing experience at $1200 per season; *pioneering/hiking instructor* at $900–$1200 per season; *painting/sketching instructor* at $900–$1200 per season; *guitar instructor* at $900–$1200 per season; *piano instructor* with ability to play by ear at $900–$1200 per season; *dance staff.* International students encouraged to apply.

Benefits   Preemployment training, on-the-job training, formal ongoing training, on-site room and board at no charge, laundry facilities, travel reimbursement, health insurance.

Contact   Applicant should send resume or call for information by May 1 to Ed Ulanoff, Director, Crane Lake Camp, Department SED, 10 West 66th Street, New York, New York 10023; 212-362-1462.

ELLIOTT P. JOSLIN CAMP
P.O. Box 100
Charlton, Massachusetts 01507

General Information   Residential boys' camp serving an average of 75 diabetic campers per session for four sessions. Established 1948. Owned by Joslin Diabetes Center. Affiliated with American Camping Association, American Diabetes Association, International Diabetes and Camping Federation. Located 60 miles southwest of Boston on 300 acres. Features include outdoor pavillion; new outdoor tennis courts; 70-acre private pond; professional training by Joslin Diabetes Center staff; location in secluded area; staff to camper ratio of 1:2.

Profile of Summer Employees   Total number 54; average age 19. Employees are 20% female, 3% minorities, 25% high school students, 75% college students, 3% international, 85% local residents. Requires nonsmokers.

Employment Information   Openings are from June 12 to August 19. College credit possible. Jobs available: 3 *junior couselors* with a minimum age of 18 at $1000 per season; 3 *senior counselors* with a minimum age of 19 at $1300 per season; 4 *nurses (student/graduate/RN)* with certification or enrollment in a nursing program at $1700–$3500 per season; 1 *nutritionist* with certification or enrollment in nutrition program at $2200–$2600 per season; 1 *head cook* with previous experience at $2000–$2800 per season; 2 *assistant cooks* with previous experience at $1600–$1800 per season; 2 *kitchen aides* with a minimum age of 16 at $900–$1100 per season. International students encouraged to apply.

Benefits   Preemployment training, on-the-job training, formal ongoing training, on-site room and board at no charge, laundry facilities, health insurance.

Contact   Applicant should send resume or write for application by May 1 to Robert G. Gannon, Director, Elliott P. Joslin Camp, Department SED, Joslin Place, Boston, Massachusetts 02215; 617-732-2455.

4–H FARLEY OUTDOOR EDUCATION CENTER
Route 130, Forestdale Road
Mashpee, Massachusetts 02649

General Information Primary program offers overnight and day programs to boys and girls ages 7–14. There is limited mainstreaming of special needs children. Established 1934. Owned by Cape Cod 4-H Camp Corporation. Affiliated with University of Massachusetts Cooperative Extension, United States Department of Agriculture, Barnstable, Plymouth, Norfolk and Bristol County Cooperative Extension Service. Located 80 miles south of Boston on 32 acres. Features include freshwater lake (second largest on Cape Cod); adjacent woodland areas; location close to ocean; mini-farm with animals; auditorium/ outside amphitheater; nature classroom with native and domestic small animals.

Profile of Summer Employees Total number 25; average age 22. Employees are 75% female, 10% minorities, 20% high school students, 60% college students, 10% international, 10% local residents. Prefers nonsmokers.

Employment Information Openings are from June 23 to August 24. Jobs available: 1 *waterfront director* with WSI certificate (minimum age 21) at $200–$230 per week; 4 *lifeguards* with LGT certificate or equivalent at $140–$200 per week; 16 *counselors* with specialized program skills and camping experience at $75–$200 per week; 1 *child-care coordinator* with background in youth development at $250–$300 per week; 1 *health-care provider* with EMT, RN, or LPN license or special training in first aid at $250–$300 per week; 1 *secretary* with office skills at $200 per week. International students encouraged to apply.

Benefits Preemployment training, on-the-job training, formal ongoing training, on-site room and board at no charge, laundry facilities, health insurance, weekends off.

Contact Applicant should send resume, write for application, or call for information by April 15 to Michael Campbell, Executive Director, 4–H Farley Outdoor Education Center, Department SED, Box 97, Forestdale, Massachusetts 02644; 508-477-0181.

We provide training and ongoing support in the area of youth development. Early arrival and late departure are options for the staff. Training opportunities in program areas are offered. Lots of fun, opportunities for apprenticeships, and Native American cultural experiences make employment interesting and enjoyable.

MOUNT HOLYOKE COLLEGE SUMMER THEATRE
South Hadley, Massachusetts 01075

General Information Professional summer-stock company producing seven mainstage plays and three plays for children in one-week sessions. Established 1970. Affiliated with New England Theater Conference, East Central Theater Conference, Southeast Theater Conference. Closest major city is Springfield. Features include theater which operates under contract with Actor's Equity; directors and upper management drawn from New York City and finest regional theaters; excellent reputation and enthusiastic audience; commitment to family atmosphere in the company; beautiful facility at nation's oldest women's college; location close to Hartford, Boston, and New York City.

Profile of Summer Employees Total number 75; average age 22. Employees are 50% female, 5% minorities, 7% high school students, 30% college students, 2% international, 16% local residents.

Employment Information Openings are from May 31 to August 19. College credit possible. Jobs available: 12 *actors (non-Equity)* at $750 per season; 3 *carpenters* at $750 per season; 3 *prop artisans* at $750 per season; 2 *stitchers* at $750 per season; 1 *wardrobe mistress* at $850 per season; 1 *technical director* at $1200 per season; 1 *stage manager (non-Equity)* at $900 per season; 1 *prop master* at $1000 per season; 1 *box office manager* at $750 per season; 1 *house manager* at $750 per season; 1 *business manager* at $900 per season; 1 *publicity assistant* at $750 per season; 1 *sound designer* at $1000 per season; 1 *costume designer* at $1800 per season; 1 *master electrician* at $1000 per season. International students encouraged to apply.

Benefits On-site room and board at no charge, laundry facilities, health insurance, Equity membership candidate points.

Contact Applicant should send resume by March 1 to Michael Walker, Producing Director, Mount Holyoke College Summer Theatre, Department SED, South Hadley, Massachusetts 01075; 413-538-2632, fax 413-538-2512.

NATIONAL PARK SERVICE

Contact Applicant should write for application (must be 18 by May 13; U.S. citizenship required) to Regional Office of the National Park Service, North Atlantic Region, National Park Service, 15 State Street, Boston, Massachusetts 02109.

Jobs located in Massachusetts at the following facilities: Adams National Historic Site, Boston African American National Historic Site, Boston National Historic Park, Cape Cod, Longfellow, Lowell, Minute Man, Salem Maritime, Saugus Iron Works. Also see District of Columbia listing.

OFFENSE-DEFENSE TENNIS CAMP
Curry College
Milton, Massachusetts 02186

General Information Teaches tennis to boys and girls ages 10–18. Accommodates beginners to tournament players. Established 1972. Owned by Mike and Judy Meshken. Affiliated with New England Lawn Tennis Association, New England Camping Association, United States Tennis Association. Located 9 miles south of Boston on 150 acres. Features include college dorms; gymnasium; cafeteria and game room; wooded campus; New England setting; location near scenic and historical sites in and near Boston.

Profile of Summer Employees Total number 70; average age 23. Employees are 40% female, 85% college students, 10% local residents. Prefers nonsmokers.

Employment Information Openings are from June 20 to August 20. College credit possible. Jobs available: 16 *general counselors* with an age between 19–28 at $880–$1200 per season; 2 *bus drivers* with bus driver's license at $1200–$1800 per season; 24 *tennis instructors* with tennis instructor certification or varsity college player experience at $800–$1200 per season. International students encouraged to apply.

Benefits Preemployment training, on-the-job training, formal ongoing training, on-site room and board at no charge, laundry facilities, travel reimbursement, trips to Boston, full day off each week.

Contact Applicant should send resume or call for information by April 15 to Mike Meshken, Director, Offense-Defense Tennis Camp, Department SED, P.O. Box 295, Trumbull, Connecticut 06611; 203-374-7171.

*The camp is located on a college campus and has great facilities, food, and location.
A great staff that works with intelligent, healthy, and energetic children.*

WILLIAMSTOWN THEATER FESTIVAL
Williamstown, Massachusetts 01267

General Information   Summer theater using college facilities, including the theater, dormitories, and the snack bar. Features include location in a small college town in northwestern Massachusetts.

Employment Information   Openings are from June 1 to August 25. Jobs available: *staff members;* 65 *apprentices* with tuition charged by contract; *Equity and non-Equity actors;* 30 *interns.* International students encouraged to apply.

Benefits   Local eating facilities within walking distance (breakfast or lunch, $2–$5; dinner, $5–$10).

Contact   by March 15 to Intern Coordinator, Williamstown Theater Festival, P.O. Box 517, Williamstown, Massachusetts 01267; 413-458-3200.

*"If you are at all serious about professional theater, all roads lead to Williamstown.
Somewhere in your past, present, or future, there is the Williamstown Theater Festival."
— Christopher Reeve*

YMCA CAMP LYNDON
117 Stowe Road
Sandwich, Massachusetts 02563

General Information   Day camp serving 400 youth. Established 1912. Owned by Cape Cod YMCA. Affiliated with Young Men's Christian Association. Located 60 miles south of Boston on 100 acres. Features include location on Cape Cod; proximity to beaches; cool summer weather.

Profile of Summer Employees   Total number 100; average age 20. Employees are 60% female, 2% minorities, 35% high school students, 55% college students, 10% international, 65% local residents. Prefers nonsmokers.

Employment Information   Openings are from June 24 to September 1. Spring break, winter break, Christmas break positions also offered. College credit possible. Jobs available: 60 *counselors* with youth experience at $120–$150 per week; 2 *archery specialists* with experience and certificate at $150–$190 per week; 10 *boating instructors* with experience and small craft or equivalent certificate at $140–$165 per week; 3 *nature specialists* with experience and degree in related subject at $150–$190 per week; 2 *waterfront directors* with WSI and LGI certificates at $150–$190 per week; 3 *arts and crafts specialists* with experience and teaching certificate at $150–$190 per week; 12 *swimming instructors* with LGT certificate (minimum) at $120–$150 per week; 3 *horseback-riding instructors* with Massachusetts riding license at $150–$190 per week; 2 *ropes/initiative specialists* with experience and completion of course at $150–$190 per week. International students encouraged to apply.

Benefits   On-the-job training, formal ongoing training, on-site room and board at no charge, laundry facilities, travel reimbursement, 36-hour work week.

Contact Applicant should send resume, write for application, or call for information by May 15 to G. Ray Millsap, Camp Executive, YMCA Camp Lyndon, Department SED, 117 Stowe Road, Sandwich, Massachusetts 02563; 508-428-9251.

Camp Lyndon is searching for young adults who wish to work with youth in order to broaden their experience and skills. A great opportunity for those in child education, social services, or child-care development programs. Located near transportation to major attractions in the New England area and Canada.

Michigan

AMERICAN YOUTH FOUNDATION–CAMP MINIWANCA
1 Miniwanca Road
Shelby, Michigan 49455

General Information Camp with a goal of helping participants achieve their best, live in a balanced way, and learn to serve others. Established 1924. Owned by American Youth Foundation. Affiliated with American Camping Association, Association for Experimental Education. Located 70 miles northwest of Grand Rapids on 360 acres. Features include a mile of Lake Michigan beach; sand dunes; wooded hills; liberal arts approach to camping; leadership education and skill development.

Profile of Summer Employees Total number 200; average age 23. Employees are 60% female, 3% minorities, 10% high school students, 55% college students, 5% retirees, 1% international, 10% local residents. Prefers nonsmokers.

Employment Information Openings are from June 7 to August 26. College credit possible. Jobs available: 90 *leaders* with college student or teacher status at $115–$220 per week; 26 *central summer staff* with teacher status at $200–$300 per week; 20 *kitchen personnel* with high school student or retired person status at $90–$105 per week; 10 *camp cleaning personnel* with high school student or retired person status at $90–$105 per week; 16 *building/grounds personnel* with high school student or retired person status at $90–$105 per week. International students encouraged to apply.

Benefits Preemployment training, on-the-job training, formal ongoing training, on-site room and board at no charge, laundry facilities, travel reimbursement.

Contact Applicant should write for application or call for information by April 1 to Mark Pawlowski, Director, American Youth Foundation–Camp Miniwanca, Department SED, Box 216, Three Rivers, Michigan 49093; 616-273-8845, fax 616-279-7740.

Advantages of working at Camp Miniwanca include the diverse backgrounds and experiences of coworkers as well as campers. In a typical summer, almost all fifty states are represented as well as several foreign countries. Our purpose is to provide an opportunity for personal growth.

BAY CLIFF HEALTH CAMP
Big Bay, Michigan 49808

General Information Residential therapy camp serving 200 handicapped children ages 3–11 per two-week session. Established 1934. Located 300 miles north of Milwaukee on

170 acres. Features include beautiful natural area; location on Lake Superior; physical, occupational, speech, hearing, and music therapy.

Profile of Summer Employees   Total number 125; average age 25. Employees are 70% female, 5% minorities, 5% high school students, 50% college students, 5% retirees, 15% local residents. Prefers nonsmokers.

Employment Information   Openings are from June 14 to August 9. College credit possible. Jobs available: 5 *unit leaders* with teaching experience and special education degree (preferred); 50 *counselors* with a year of college completed (preferably in the study of special education, therapy, nursing, or human services) and a minimum age of 18 at $1000 per season; 8 *roving counselors* with a year of college completed (preferably in the study of special education, therapy, nursing, or human services) and a minimum age of 18; 3 *hearing therapists* with certification; 1 *music therapists* with certification; 4 *occupational therapists* with certification; 4 *physical therapists* with certification; 8 *speech therapists* with certification; 12 *student therapists* with ability to work under a supervising therapist; 3 *nurses* with RN or LPN license; 1 *nurse's aide* with student nurse status; 1 *dentist* with license and professional training; 1 *dental assistant* with license and professional training; 1 *dental hygienist* with license and professional training; 2 *arts and crafts instructors* with ability to plan and implement classes for all camp units; 1 *nature instructor* with ability to plan and implement classes for all camp units; 1 *recreation instructor* with ability to plan and implement classes for all camp units; 4 *waterfront staff* with ability to both guard and instruct campers; 1 *advanced lifesaving/waterfront safety instructor;* 1 *head cook* with ability to supervise kitchen operation; 1 *assistant cook;* 1 *baker;* 12 *kitchen and dining room aides;* 3 *laundry/housekeeping personnel;* 2 *linen-room personnel;* 4 *maintenance personnel* with a minimum age of 18; 1 *secretary.*

Benefits   On-site room and board at no charge, laundry facilities, travel reimbursement.

Contact   Applicant should send resume, write for application, call for information, or apply in person by May 1 to Tim Bennett, Assistant Director, Bay Cliff Health Camp, 104 Coles Drive–G, Marquette, Michigan 49855; 906-228-5770.

Bay Cliff Health Camp provides a learning experience for people interested in learning about the special needs of handicapped children.

CAMP SANCTA MARIA
5361 M–32 West, P.O. Box 338
Gaylord, Michigan 49735

General Information   Residential camp serving a normal population in a generalist and character-building fashion. Established 1933. Owned by Camp Sancta Maria Corporation. Operated by Rev. Gerard S. Brennan. Affiliated with American Camping Association. Located 7 miles west of Gaylord. Features include rolling hills; lakes area; golf mecca; location in the heart of the northern lower penninsula; great food; horseback riding.

Profile of Summer Employees   Total number 40; average age 23. Employees are 10% minorities, 35% high school students, 65% college students, 10% international, 90% local residents. Prefers nonsmokers.

Employment Information   Openings are from June 22 to August 14. College credit possible. Jobs available: 20 *general counselors* with willingness to assume cabin responsibilities and coach most sports at $925–$1000 per season. International students encouraged to apply.

Benefits On-the-job training, formal ongoing training, on-site room and board at no charge, laundry facilities, use of the kitchen after hours, one day plus certain evenings off per week, van use and a half of a tank of gas on day off.

Contact Applicant should send resume, write for application, or call for information by May 31 to Mr. Michael Hickey, Camp Director, Camp Sancta Maria, Department SED, 3002 Connecticut, Royal Oak, Michigan 48073; 313-589-2306.

At Camp Sancta Maria counselors experience great camaraderie as demonstrated by a strong alumni association.

CAMP SHERWOOD
1789 Horton Lake Road
Lapeer, Michigan 48446

General Information Residential camp serving girls ages 7–16. Special trips include canoeing and biking. Established 1929. Owned by Northern Oakland County Girl Scout Council. Affiliated with American Camping Association. Located 25 miles east of Flint on 297 acres. Features include location on Davis Lake; modern dining hall; primitive living units (platform canvas tents and cabins) and outdoor cooking; trips away from central camp.

Profile of Summer Employees Total number 25; average age 21. Employees are 95% female, 80% college students, 25% local residents.

Employment Information Openings are from June 24 to August 15. College credit possible. Jobs available: 6 *unit leaders* with a minimum age of 21 at $770 per season; 10 *unit counselors* with high school graduate status at $700 per season; 2 *lifeguards* with LGI, WSI, CPR, and FA certification at $700 per season; 1 *health supervisor* with LPN, RN, or EMT license plus CPR and FA certification at $1500 per season; 2 *program specialists* with arts and crafts and nature experience at $725 per season.

Benefits Preemployment training, on-the-job training, on-site room and board at no charge, health insurance, bonus for completing summer, first aid and CPR certification, basic water-safety training.

Contact Applicant should send resume, write for application, call for information, or apply in person by June 1 to Susan Barnes, Outdoor Education Director, Camp Sherwood, Department SED, P.O. Box 430659, Pontiac, Michigan 48343; 313-666-3880, fax 313-666-4971.

Working at Camp Sherwood gives you an opportunity to make a difference in the life of a girl.

CAMP WALDEN
5607 South River Road
Cheboygan, Michigan 49721

General Information Residential, coeducational camp serving children ages 7–16. A full recreational program is offered. Established 1959. Owned by Larry Stevens and Tom Lurie. Affiliated with American Camping Association, Private Independent Camps, Camp Horsemanship Association. Located 8 miles west of Cheboygan on 160 acres. Features include Mackinaw Island and Bridge; location on Michigan's upper pennisula; Great Lakes shorelines; beautiful wooded camp environment.

Profile of Summer Employees Total number 100; average age 23. Employees are 50% female. Requires nonsmokers.

Employment Information Openings are from June 15 to August 20. College credit possible. Jobs available: *riding instructor* with CHA certification or equivalent at $1000–$2000 per season; *windsurfing instructor* with certification at $1000–$2000 per season; *sailing instructor* with certification at $1000–$2000 per season; *kayaking instructor* with certification at $1000–$2000 per season; *waterskiing instructor* with certification at $1000–$2000 per season; *tennis instructor* with coaching experience at $1000–$2000 per season; *archery instructor* with certification at $1000–$2000 per season; *gymnastics instructor* with gymnastics and coaching experience at $1000–$2000 per season; *theater instructor* with training, acting, and directing experience at $1000–$2000 per season; *dance instructor* with dance training and teaching experience at $1000–$2000 per season; *fencing instructor* with fencing training and teaching experience at $1000–$2000 per season; *arts and crafts instructor* with arts and crafts training plus teaching experience at $1000–$2000 per season; *natural science instructor* with natural sciences training and teaching experience at $1000–$2000 per season; *mountain-biking instructor* with experience and maintenance skills at $1000–$2000 per season; *backpack/canoe/trip instructor* with trip leader experience at $1000–$2000 per season; *swimming instructor* with lifeguard and/or WSI certificate at $1000–$2000 per season.

Benefits On-the-job training, formal ongoing training, on-site room and board at no charge, travel reimbursement.

Contact Applicant should send resume, write for application, or call for information by May 15 to Larry Stevens, Director, Camp Walden, Department SED, 31070 Applewood Lane, Farmington Hills, Michigan 48331; 313-661-1890.

CEDAR LODGE
47138 52nd Street
Lawrence, Michigan 49064

General Information Residential, coeducational camp serving 44 campers in a relaxed, loosely structured program. Established 1964. Affiliated with American Camping Association, Association for Horsemanship Safety and Education. Located 105 miles west of Chicago on 160 acres. Features include excellent riding program; low pressure, family-type atmosphere; small operation; private lake; location in the heart of fruit country; rustic setting.

Profile of Summer Employees Total number 11; average age 20. Prefers nonsmokers.

Employment Information Openings are from June 15 to August 15. College credit possible. Jobs available: *swimming instructor; riding instructor;* 1 *arts and crafts instructor;* 1 *music/dance/drama instructor;* 1 *biking/trip instructor; sports instructor;* 1 *kitchen assistant.* International students encouraged to apply.

Benefits Preemployment training, on-the-job training, formal ongoing training, on-site room and board, pre-camp certification for riding and swimming instructors.

Contact Applicant should send resume, write for application, call for information, or apply in person by June 15 to Amy Edwards, Program Director, Cedar Lodge, P.O. Box 218, Lawrence, Michigan 49064; 616-674-8071.

Maintenance work is available prior to camp.

CIRCLE PINES
8650 Mullen Road
Delton, Michigan 49046

General Information A small, coeducational, residential, multicultural camp for children ages 8–17 promoting peace, cooperation, and social justice. Established 1938. Owned by Circle Pines Center. Affiliated with American Camping Association, Michigan Federation of Food Co-ops, Co-op America. Located 25 miles northeast of Kalamazoo on 284 acres. Features include spring-fed lake with sandy beach; rolling hills, meadows, and forests; location an hour from Lake Michigan; miles of hiking trails; proximity to 10,000 acres of state land.

Profile of Summer Employees Total number 30; average age 24. Employees are 55% female, 10% minorities, 40% college students, 5% retirees, 5% international, 5% local residents. Prefers nonsmokers.

Employment Information Openings are from June 20 to August 30. Spring break, year-round positions also offered. College credit possible. Jobs available: 1 *waterfront director* with WSI, CPR, and lifeguard training/certification (minimum age 21) at $700–$1000 per season; 1 *waterfront assistant* with CPR certificate plus lifeguard and first aid training at $600–$800 per season; 1 *health officer* with RN, LPN, or EMT license (RN preferred) at $100–$125 per week; 14 *counselors* with experience with children at $500–$700 per season; 4 *cooks* with experience working with whole foods at $500–$1000 per season; 2 *maintenance staff* with ability to work with children at $300–$400 per month; 1 *gardener* with organic-gardening experience at $200–$400 per month; 1 *office manager* with office experience at $600–$800 per season; 1 *drama specialist* with children's theater experience at $600–$800 per season; 1 *arts and crafts director* with experience as an instructor (preferred) at $600–$800 per season; 1 *activity coordinator* with good organizational ability at $600–$700 per season; 1 *work-project coordinator* with knowledge of tools and materials at $600–$800 per season; 1 *housekeeper* with ability to work with children at $600–$700 per season. International students encouraged to apply.

Benefits Preemployment training, on-the-job training, on-site room and board at no charge, laundry facilities, whole food, vegetarian meals, on-site medical care.

Contact Applicant should send resume, write for application, or call for information by March 15 to Tom VanHammen, Camp Director, Circle Pines, Department SED, 8650 Mullen Road, Delton, Michigan 49046; 616-623-5555.

Circle Pines' summer camp program includes morning work projects, afternoon activities such as art, crafts, theater, swimming, soccer, sign language, and photography, and other activities, including folk dancing, nature, rock-climbing, canoeing, and storytelling.

CRYSTALAIRE CAMP
1327 South Shore Road East
Frankfort, Michigan 49635

General Information A small, coeducational, loosely structured residential camp with an emphasis on individual growth. Established 1921. Owned by David B. Reid. Affiliated with American Camping Association. Located 35 miles west of Traverse City on 145 acres. Features include location on Crystal Lake; proximity to Sleeping Bear National Lakeshore; rustic nature; excellent waterfront, sailing, and windsurfing programs; large, varied program; wilderness trips (backpack, canoe, bike).

Profile of Summer Employees Total number 30; average age 22. Employees are 50% female, 5% minorities, 20% high school students, 65% college students, 5% retirees, 10% international, 5% local residents. Prefers nonsmokers.

Employment Information Openings are from June 18 to August 18. College credit possible. Jobs available: 14 *counselors* with lifesaving training also art, sailing trip, and sports skills desired at $850–$1500 per season; 1 *riding instructor* with experience and ability to manage riding program at $950–$1600 per season; 3 *sailing/windsurfing instructors* with lifesaving training and appropriate experience at $950–$1600 per season; 1 *art specialist* with ability to organize art program (teacher preferred) at $1000 per season; 1 *nurse* with RN, LPN, or EMT license at $1000–$2000 per season; 1 *trip coordinator* with ability to organize trips and train staff at $950–$2000 per season; 2 *cooks* with quantity cooking experience at $1200–$2500 per season; 1 *waterfront director* with WSI certificate and experience with large waterfront at $1200–$2000 per season; 1 *stable helper* at $60–$150 per week; 5 *junior counselors (high school students)* at $500–$700 per season. International students encouraged to apply.

Benefits Preemployment training, formal ongoing training, on-site room and board at no charge, CPR/first aid training offered, vegetarian menu available.

Contact Applicant should write for application or call for information by June 20 to David B. Reid, Director, Crystalaire Camp, 1327 South Shore Road East, Frankfort, Michigan 49635; 616-352-7589.

We need open, flexible, child-oriented staff members. If you have sports, art, trip, swimming, sailing/windsurfing, riding, or other camp skills and interests, you'll be able to teach your speciality, try other activity areas, and work with 30 other great people.

DOUBLE JJ RESORT RANCH
P.O. Box 94
Rothbury, Michigan 49452

General Information Resort ranch exclusively for adults. Established 1937. Owned by Joan and Bob Lipsitz. Affiliated with Circle Michigan, West Michigan Tourist Association, White Lake Muskegon Chamber of Commerce. Located 20 miles north of Muskegon on 1,000 acres. Features include horseback riding; nightly entertainment; beautiful wooded acres; location near to sand dunes of Lake Michigan; wonderful guests and staff; full-service resort.

Profile of Summer Employees Total number 50; average age 25. Employees are 50% female, 36% college students, 2% retirees, 6% international, 6% local residents.

Employment Information Openings are from May 1 to November 1. College credit possible. Jobs available: 6 *entertainers (guitarists, singers, etc.)* with musical talent and outgoing personality at $130 per week; 6 *waiters/waitresses* with prior experience preferred (training available) at $130 per week; 3 *prep cooks/bakers* with prior experience at $130–$160 per week; 4 *lawn maintenance persons* at $130 per week; 1 *disc jockey* with prior experience at $130–$150 per week; 6 *housekeepers* at $130 per week; 6 *wranglers* with previous experience with horses at $130–$160 per week; 3 *snack bar/gift shop clerks* at $130 per week; 2 *dishwashers* at $130 per week; 1 *dining room manager* with previous waitressing experience at $150 per week. International students encouraged to apply.

Benefits On-the-job training, on-site room and board at no charge, laundry facilities, use of all facilities.

Contact Applicant should send resume, write for application, or call for information by April 1 to Joan Lipsitz, Owner, Double JJ Resort Ranch, Department SED, P.O. Box 94, Rothbury, Michigan 49452; 616-894-4444.

Our jobs offer employees a fun-filled summer in which they can meet thousands of other people their own age. We encourage everyone to work hard, but it's also a great place to play. We hire staff that like being around people and are willing to take initiative and be involved in all activities.

EL RANCHO STEVENS
2332 East Dixon Lake Road
Gaylord, Michigan 49735

General Information Family resort specializing in horses, waterskiing, and children's programs. Serves 800 people weekly. Established 1947. Owned by Steven S. Stevens. Affiliated with West Michigan Tourist Association, Gaylord Chamber of Commerce, Michigan Lodging Association. Located 3 miles southeast of Gaylord on 1,000 acres. Features include horseback riding; waterskiing; lake; interaction with the guests.

Profile of Summer Employees Total number 25; average age 25. Employees are 80% female, 10% minorities, 10% high school students, 75% college students, 10% retirees, 25% local residents. Prefers nonsmokers.

Employment Information Openings are from May 29 to September 5. College credit possible. Jobs available: 5 *waitresses/waiters* at $130–$150 per week; 2 *cooks* with cooking experience at $150–$200 per week; 2 *kitchen helpers* at $130–$150 per week; 3 *housekeepers* at $130–$150 per week; 1 *waterskiing instructor/boat driver* with knowledge of water safety rules (minimum age 18) at $130–$150 per week; 2 *riding instructors/trail guides* with experience with horses (minimum age 18) at $130–$150 per week; 3 *children's counselors* with aptitude for working with children at $130–$150 per week; 1 *recreational director* with ability to work with people of all ages and knowledge of various sports and games at $130–$150 per week; 2 *bartenders* with a minimum age of 18 at $130–$150 per week; 2 *office personnel* with good phone, typing, and bookkeeping skills at $130–$150 per week.

Benefits On-the-job training, on-site room and board at no charge.

Contact Applicant should send resume or write for application by May 15 to Personnel Department, El Rancho Stevens, P.O. Box 495, Gaylord, Michigan 49735; 517-732-5090.

Staff members have the opportunity to participate in ranch activities such as riding.

LAKE OF THE WOODS AND GREENWOODS CAMPS
Decatur, Michigan 49045

General Information Private, residential camp for children ages 7–15 in a recreational environment. Established 1935. Owned by Marc Seeger. Affiliated with American Camping Association, Midwest Association of Private Camps. Located 20 miles southwest of Kalamazoo on 57 acres. Features include modern facilities; long-standing reputation; beautiful location on 6¼-mile lake frontage; high staff to camper ratio.

Profile of Summer Employees   Total number 65; average age 21. Employees are 50% female, 90% college students. Prefers nonsmokers.

Employment Information   Openings are from June 14 to August 17. Year-round positions also offered. College credit possible. Jobs available: 8 *swimming instructors* with lifeguard training and/or WSI certificate at $1000 per season; 2 *sail instructors* at $1000 per season; 3 *riding instructors* at $1050 per season; 1 *computer instructor* at $1050 per season; 7 *waterskiing instructors* at $1000 per season; 2 *tennis instructors* at $1000 per season; 1 *golf instructor* at $1000 per season; 1 *gymnastics instructor* at $1000 per season; 2 *arts and crafts instructors* at $1000 per season; 1 *dramatics instructor* at $1000 per season; 1 *dance/aerobics instructor* at $1000 per season; 2 *sports coaches* at $1000 per season; 2 *nurses* with RN license (preferred) at $2400 per season; 2 *office persons* with experience at $1000 per season; *kitchen personnel (cooks and assistants)* at $135–$350 per week; *riflery instructor* with a minimum age of 19 at $1000 per season; *archery instructor* with a minimum age of 19 at $1000 per season; *rowing/canoe instructor* with a minimum age of 19 at $1000 per season; *model rocketry instructor* with a minimum age of 19 at $1000 per season. International students encouraged to apply.

Benefits   Preemployment training, on-site room and board at no charge.

Contact   Applicant should write for application or call for information by July 15 (interviews will be conducted at selected Midwest universities in the spring) to Marc Seeger, Owner/Director, Lake of the Woods and Greenwoods Camps, Department SED, 1765 Maple Street, Northfield, Illinois 60093; 708-446-2444, fax 708-446-7342.

MCGAW YMCA CAMP ECHO
2000 West 32nd Street
Fremont, Michigan 49412

General Information   Residential, coeducational camp serving 230 youngsters in two-week sessions; emphasis is on building self-esteem. Established 1899. Owned by McGaw YMCA. Located 40 miles north of Muskegon on 400 acres. Features include peninsula with 400 acres; fireplace and porch in every cabin; forested and field areas; nature trail; separate beaches for sailing, canoeing, and waterskiing; pine and beech forests.

Profile of Summer Employees   Total number 75; average age 22. Employees are 50% female, 40% minorities, 25% high school students, 75% college students, 1% international, 75% local residents.

Employment Information   Openings are from June 10 to August 25. College credit possible. Jobs available: 15 *senior counselors* with standard first aid and CPR certificates at $95–$150 per week; 1 *aquatic director* with lifeguard, first aid, and CPR certificates at $125–$150 per week; 1 *arts and crafts director* with standard first aid and CPR certificates at $100–$125 per week; 1 *trip director* with lifeguard, first aid, and CPR class C licenses at $125–$150 per week; 4 *adventure trip leaders* with lifeguard, first aid, and CPR class C licenses at $125–$150 per week; 2 *pioneer village leaders* with lifeguard, first aid, and CPR certificates at $120–$140 per week; 2 *outpost leaders* with lifeguard, first aid, and CPR certificates at $120–$140 per week; 1 *wrangler* with standard first aid and CPR certificates plus CHA training at $140–$160 per week; 1 *assistant wrangler* with standard first aid and CPR certificates at $120–$140 per week; 5 *health officers* with RN or LPN license and CPR and standard first aid certificates at $250 per week; 1 *van drivers* with standard first aid and CPR class C licenses at $100–$125 per week; 3 *cooks* with CPR certificate and experience with large groups at $100–$300 per week; 3 *sail/canoe/*

waterski directors with standard first aid, CPR, and lifeguard certificates at $95–$150 per week. International students encouraged to apply.

Benefits Preemployment training, on-the-job training, on-site room and board at no charge, use of facility, party night, YMCA membership.

Contact Applicant should send resume, write for application, call for information, or apply in person by June 1 to Sally Courtney, Director, McGaw YMCA Camp Echo, Department SED, 1000 Grove Street, Evanston, Illinois 60201; 708-475-7400, fax 708-475-7959.

We offer family camps and environmental education. A youth-at-risk program is offered for boys and girls in grades 7 and 9. This program includes a high-ropes course. We are a caring staff that seeks to build self-esteem in our campers through safe and fun activities.

MICHILLINDA BEACH LODGE
5207 Scenic Drive
Whitehall, Michigan 49461

General Information Modified American-plan resort with 50 guest units overlooking Lake Michigan. Established 1928. Owned by Donald E. Eilers. Affiliated with West Michigan Tourist Association, Michigan Lodging Association, American Hotel Association. Located 25 miles north of Muskegon on 22 acres. Features include close proximity to Lake Michigan Beach; tennis courts; swimming and wading pools; miniature golf; family-oriented atmosphere.

Profile of Summer Employees Total number 35; average age 18. Employees are 80% female, 60% high school students, 40% college students, 90% local residents. Prefers nonsmokers.

Employment Information Openings are from June 15 to September. Spring break positions also offered. College credit possible.

Benefits Preemployment training, on-the-job training, on-site room and board at $30 per month, laundry facilities, bonus in place of tips.

Contact Applicant should send resume, write for application, call for information, or apply in person by April 1 to Don Eilers, General Manager, Michillinda Beach Lodge, Department SED, 5207 Scenic Drive, Whitehall, Michigan 49461; 616-893-1895.

NATIONAL PARK SERVICE

Contact Applicant should write for application (must be 18 by May 13; U.S. citizenship required) to Regional Office of the National Park Service, Midwest Region, National Park Service, 1709 Jackson Street, Omaha, Nebraska 68102.

Jobs located in Michigan at the following facilities: Isle Royale, Pictured Rocks National Lakeshore, Sleeping Bear Dunes. Also see District of Columbia listing.

PANCAKE CHEF RESTAURANT
327 Central, P.O. Box 476
Mackinaw City, Michigan 49701

General Information   Full-service restaurant. Established 1964. Owned by R. J. Fisher. Affiliated with National Restaurant Association, Mackinaw Chamber of Commerce, Michigan Retailers' Association. Located 40 miles north of Petoskey. Features include good working conditions; beautiful surrounding area; fishing, sailing, tennis, golf, and major historical attractions nearby; seating capacity of 175.

Profile of Summer Employees   Total number 65; average age 25. Employees are 50% female, 10% minorities, 20% high school students, 25% college students, 5% retirees, 40% local residents.

Employment Information   Openings are from May 15 to October 15. College credit possible. Jobs available: 4 *cashiers/hostesses* at $720–$800 per month; 8 *short order cooks* at $800–$1000 per month; 8 *buspersons* at $600–$800 per month; 6 *dishwashers* at $800–$900 per month; 16 *wait staff* at $1200–$1700 per month.

Benefits   Preemployment training, on-the-job training, formal ongoing training, externships, end-of-season bonus possible.

Contact   Applicant should send resume or call for information by June 30 (foreign students should apply 8–12 months prior to desired work season) to Jane Magers, Manager, Pancake Chef Restaurant, Department SED, P.O. Box 476, Mackinaw City, Michigan 49701; 616-436-5578.

SUNNY BROOK FARM RESORT
South Haven, Michigan

General Information   Family resort offering a variety of facilities. Located 120 miles northeast of Chicago, Illinois. Features include 2 heated pools; tennis courts; shuffleboard; volleyball.

Employment Information   Openings are from June to September. Jobs available: *waitresses/waiters* at $2000–$3000 per season; *cooks* at $2000–$3000 per season; *desk clerks* with business or hotel major (preferred) at $2000–$3000 per season; *lifeguard* with lifesaving certificate (required) and CPR certificate (preferred) at $2000–$3000 per season; *kitchen helpers* at $2000–$3000 per season; *children's counselors* with lifesaving certificate (required) and CPR certificate (preferred) at $2000–$3000 per season; *maintenance helpers* at $2000–$3000 per season; *yardman* at $2000–$3000 per season; *night watchman* at $2000–$3000 per season; *refreshment stand workers* at $2000–$3000 per season; *assistant maintenance foreman* at $2000–$3000 per season.

Benefits   On-site room and board.

Contact   Applicant should write for application and send business size self-addressed stamped envelope by May 1 to Mary C. Ott, Sunny Brook Farm Resort, 68300 County Road 388, South Haven, Michigan 49090.

THE TIMBERS GIRL SCOUT CAMP
8195 Timbers Trail Drive
Traverse City, Michigan 49684

General Information   Trip camp offering four 2-week sessions for 100 girls ages 12–18. Established 1962. Owned by Fair Winds Girl Scout Council. Affiliated with Girl Scouts of the United States of America, American Camping Association. Located 6 miles west of Traverse City on 262 acres. Features include trips to three states and Canada; large waterfront with windsurfing, sailing, canoeing, swimming, and more; backpacking, biking, and sailing trips; location near Grand Traverse Bay resort area; beautiful tourist area.

Profile of Summer Employees   Total number 40; average age 40. Employees are 100% female, 5% minorities, 5% international, 2% local residents. Prefers nonsmokers.

Employment Information   Openings are from June 10 to August 15. College credit possible. Jobs available: 11 *counselors (level one)* with the ability to pass a 20 minute swimming test at $855–$1200 per season; 11 *counselors (level two)* with the ability to pass a 20 minute swimming test at $1035–$1400 per season; 1 *business manager* with driver's license and bookkeeping and typing experience at $1170–$1600 per season; 1 *arts and crafts instructor* with expertise in woodworking, stained glass, silk-screening, and nature crafts at $1125–$1600 per season; 1 *waterfront director* with WSI and ALS or LGT certificates at $1170–$1600 per season; 1 *small craft director* with ALS or LGT and small craft instructor certificates or equivalent at $1170–$1600 per season; 1 *trip outfitter* at $1575–$1900 per season; 1 *assistant camp director* at $1350–$2000 per season; 1 *head cook* at $1575–$1900 per season; 1 *assistant cook* at $1170–$1700 per season; 2 *kitchen aides* at $765–$1000 per season; *packout supervisor* at $1125–$1600 per season; *assistant ranger* at $1035–$1300 per season; *camp nurse* with RN or EMT license at $205 per week; *initiatives director* at $1125–$1400 per season.

Benefits   On-site room and board at no charge, laundry facilities, health insurance.

Contact   Applicant should write for application or call for information to Joann Downing, Director of Outdoor Education, The Timbers Girl Scout Camp, Department SED, 2029-C South Elms Road, Swartz Creek, Michigan 48473; 313-230-0244.

Minnesota

BLUE BELL ICE CREAM INC.
3218 Snelling Avenue
Minneapolis, Minnesota 55406

General Information   Blue Bell Ice Cream has been in business since 1976. Known as the "Ice-Cream Man" in the Twin Cities. The company also operates the concession stands at the city zoo in St. Paul. Owned by Blue Bell Ice Cream Inc. Affiliated with International Association of Ice Cream Vendors, Como Zoological Society. Features include fun summer jobs; location on the bus lines; location in Minneapolis, a city of great diversity and interest.

Profile of Summer Employees   Total number 100; average age 23. Employees are 40% female, 30% minorities, 20% high school students, 70% college students, 5% retirees, 80% local residents.

Employment Information   Openings are from March 15 to July 1. Spring break positions also offered. Jobs available: 15 *ice cream truck drivers* with good driving record, hard working attitude, and a liking for children at $250–$500 per week; 7 *Como Zoo concession stand workers* with hard working attitude, a liking for children, and food service experience (helpful but not necessary) at $200–$275 per week; 2 *Como Zoo Grill Cooks* with grill work experience at $200–$275 per week; 3 *hot dog cart vendors* with cash handling experience, hard working attitude, plus enjoys people and working outside at $220–$275 per week. International students encouraged to apply.

Benefits   On-the-job training.

Contact   Applicant should send resume or write for application by July 1 to Glenn Baron, Blue Bell Ice Cream Inc., Department SED, 3218 Snelling Avenue South, Minneapolis, Minnesota 55406; 612-729-5205, fax 612-729-6454.

Blue Bell Ice Cream has a high percentage of employees who return summer after summer to drive ice cream trucks and work at the Como Zoo in St. Paul. We help job applicants find convenient, affordable housing.

CAMP BUCKSKIN
Box 389
Ely, Minnesota 55731

General Information   Residential camp offering two 32-day sessions for emotionally/behaviorally challenged youth. Established 1959. Owned by Mr. and Mrs. R. S. Bauer. Affiliated with American Camping Association. Located 80 miles northeast of Duluth on 165 acres. Features include location on lake and river in the Superior National Forest; academic and traditional camp activities; separate canoe trip program in Boundary Water Canoe Area Wilderness.

Profile of Summer Employees   Total number 80; average age 22. Employees are 50% female, 5% minorities, 12% high school students, 70% college students, 5% international, 15% local residents. Requires nonsmokers.

Employment Information   Openings are from June 4 to August 19. College credit possible. Jobs available: 8 *counselors/swimming instructors* with WSI certificate, lifeguard training, and standard first aid training at $1050–$1350 per season; 10 *counselors/canoeing instructors* with lifeguard training and standard first aid training at $1050–$1350 per season; 6 *counselors/nature and environment instructors* with experience at $1050–$1350 per season; 6 *counselors/arts and crafts instructors* with experience at $1050–$1350 per season; 3 *counselors/archery instructors* with experience at $1050–$1350 per season; 3 *counselors/riflery instructors* with experience (NRA safety training preferred) at $1050–$1350 per season; 8 *reading teachers* with teacher's license at $1350–$1550 per season; 2 *office assistants* with typing skills and phone experience at $1050–$1350 per season; 5 *kitchen assistants* at $800–$1000 per season; 8 *trip counselors* with lifeguard, CPR, and standard first aid training at $1050–$1350 per season; 2 *registered nurses* with RN license at $1450–$1650 per season. International students encouraged to apply.

Benefits   Preemployment training, on-the-job training, on-site room and board at no charge, internship/college credits, end-of-season bonus possible.

Contact   Applicant should write for application, call for information, or apply in person by May 30 to Thomas Bauer, Assistant Director, Camp Buckskin, Department SED, 3811 West Broadway, Minneapolis, Minnesota 55422; 612-536-9749.

Buckskin is looking for staff members who are genuinely interested in our campers. Interest, patience, and understanding are extremely important characteristics to possess for this job.

CAMP COURAGE
Route 1, Box 258
Maple Lake, Minnesota 55358

General Information Programs offered for physically disabled children and adults. Adventure camping for the deaf and speech therapy for speech/language impaired children. Established 1955. Owned by Courage Center. Affiliated with American Camping Association. Located 50 miles west of Minneapolis on 300 acres. Features include 2 lakes; pool; gymnasium; forest areas; accessible site; horse program.

Profile of Summer Employees Total number 100; average age 22. Employees are 50% female, 5% minorities, 10% high school students, 80% college students, 1% retirees, 1% international, 60% local residents.

Employment Information Openings are from June 5 to August 29. Year-round positions also offered. College credit possible. Jobs available: 6 *waterfront personnel* with WSI/ lifeguard certification at $110–$140 per week; 36 *counselors* at $110–$140 per week; 3 *nurses* with RN, LPN, or GN license at $300 per week; 20 *program specialists* with appropriate certification for area at $115–$140 per week; 10 *speech clinicians* with M.S. in speech pathology/communications disorders at $220 per week. International students encouraged to apply.

Benefits Preemployment training, on-the-job training, formal ongoing training, on-site room and board at no charge, laundry facilities, health insurance, tuition reimbursement, scholarships.

Contact Applicant should write for application or call for information by May to Roger Upcraft, Program Manager, Camp Courage, Department SED, Route 1, Box 258, Maple Lake, Minnesota 55358; 612-963-3121.

Camp Courage is the largest program of its kind in the country. Students interested in medical fields, special education, or recreation can gain valuable experience with special needs groups in a fun, outdoor setting.

CAMP FRIENDSHIP
Route 3, Box 162
Annandale, Minnesota 55302

General Information Residential camp serving children and adults with developmental disabilities. Established 1964. Affiliated with American Camping Association. Located 60 miles north of Minneapolis on 100 acres. Features include location on a large lake; 80-wooded acres; resort-style camping.

Profile of Summer Employees Total number 100; average age 20. Employees are 75% female, 5% minorities, 15% high school students, 85% college students, 10% international, 20% local residents. Prefers nonsmokers.

Employment Information Openings are from June 1 to August 30. Winter break, Christmas break positions also offered. College credit possible. Jobs available: 6 *unit leaders* with leadership skills and previous camp experience at $160 per week; 50 *counselors* with ability to provide campers with a recreational experience at $140 per week; 1 *waterfront director* with WSI and lifeguard certificates at $150 per week; 2 *waterfront lifeguards* with WSI and lifeguard certificates at $140 per week; 1 *boating director* with experience with outboard motors, canoes, rowboats, and pontoon boats at $140 per week; 12 *program specialists* with arts and crafts, music, recreation, and nature expertise at $140 per week; 1 *canteen manager* with record keeping skills at $140 per week; 2 *seasonal support personnel* with computer, typing, and filing experience; 1 *nurse* with current RN license (must be graduate of an accredited nursing school); 3 *assistant nurses* with RN, LPN, or GN license; or B.S.N. degree; 1 *cook* with food-service experience; 3 *weekend counselors* with physical strength, mental alertness, and at least one year of college completed; 12 *junior counselors* with physical and emotional strength, mental alertness, creativity, flexibility, and high school student status (successful volunteer experience may be substituted for the age requirement) at $75 per week; 2 *arts and crafts specialists* with current major in therapeutic recreation, occupational therapy, or art education/therapy or experience planning and implementing arts and crafts activities/projects at $140 per week; 2 *music specialists* with current major in music, music therapy, or special education plus experience planning and implementing activities at $140 per week; 2 *nature specialists* with leadership skills, experience working with people with mental retardation, and academic major in an environmental, outdoor, or education field at $140 per week; 2 *recreation specialists* with current major in recreation, physical education, or adaptive physical recreation plus leadership skills involving small and large group activities for people with mental retardation at $140 per week; 1 *public-relations assistant* with current major in journalism, photography, or related field plus experience with a 35mm camera at $140 per week; *dining hall workers* with experience in kitchen and/or dining hall clean-up. International students encouraged to apply.

Benefits   Preemployment training, on-the-job training, formal ongoing training, on-site room and board at no charge, laundry facilities.

Contact   Applicant should write for application or call for information by May 1 to Program Director, Camp Friendship, Route 3, Box 162, Annandale, Minnesota 55302; 612-274-8376.

Camp Friendship provides a full range of recreational services, including summer and winter residential camps, Ventures Travel Service, respite care, and family camping to individuals with mental retardation or other developmental disabilities and their families.

CAMP MISHAWAKA FOR BOYS/GIRLS
P.O. Box 368
Grand Rapids, Minnesota 55744

General Information   Established 1910. Owned by Camp Mishawaka. Affiliated with American Camping Association, Midwest Association of Private Camps, Grand Rapids Chamber of Commerce. Located 5 miles south of Grand Rapids on 250 acres. Features include beautiful facility; diverse program; international clientele; experienced staff; eighty-two year tradition; secluded setting but near town.

Profile of Summer Employees   Total number 40; average age 29. Employees are 37% female, 4% minorities, 20% college students, 6% retirees, 3% international, 7% local residents.

Employment Information   Openings are from June 10 to August 12. College credit possible. Jobs available: 12 *cabin counselors (boys and girls)* with WSI certificate and general skills in tennis, swimming, canoeing, sailing, arts and crafts, boating, and music at $600–$850 per season; 2 *food-service personnel* at $160–$180 per week; 1 *riding director* with HSA certificate at $850–$1000 per season. International students encouraged to apply.

Benefits Preemployment training, on-site room and board at no charge, travel reimbursement, use of facilities during time off, cordial atmosphere, interesting trips.

Contact Applicant should send resume, write for application, or call for information by May 15 to Jon Erickson, Director, Camp Mishawaka for Boys/Girls, Department SED, P.O. Box 368, Grand Rapids, Minnesota 55744; 218-326-5011.

Brother-sister camp with separate facilities and programs, but many activities are shared. An opportunity for per diem work before and after season is also available.

CAMP THUNDERBIRD FOR BOYS/CAMP THUNDERBIRD FOR GIRLS
Route 2, Box 225
Bemidji, Minnesota 56601

General Information Separate residential facilities serving 150 girls and 200 boys from forty U.S. cities and five foreign countries. Established 1946. Owned by Camp Thunderbird, Inc. Affiliated with American Camping Association, Green Peace/Defender of Wildlife, Nature Conservancy. Located 12 miles south of Bemidji on 700 acres. Features include cheerful, supportive workplace; 7½ miles of shoreline; pristine pine and hardwood forest; noncompetitive philosophy; unique, colorful, child-oriented counselors.

Profile of Summer Employees Total number 200; average age 24. Employees are 45% female, 5% minorities, 12% high school students, 60% college students, 2% retirees, 10% international, 3% local residents. Prefers nonsmokers.

Employment Information Openings are from June 10 to August 15. College credit possible. Jobs available: *cabin counselor* with freshman year of college completed (minimum age 19); *riflery specialist* with riflery instructor certification (minimum age 21); *arts and crafts specialist* with experience as an art teacher, industrial arts teacher, or student preferred (minimum age 21 and completion of junior year of college required); *horseback specialist* with experience in Western and English Hunt Seat specialties (minimum age 21 and completion of junior year of college required); *waterfront director* with WSI certificate (minimum age of 25 and college graduate required); *swimming director* with WSI certificate (minimum age 22); *sailing specialist* with WSI certificate and Red Cross small crafts sailing instructor certification preferred (minimum age 21); *unit directors* with experience encompassing staff supervision and direct leadership of children in outdoor recreation/camp activities (minimum age 22 and college graduate required); *program director* with experience encompassing staff supervision and direct leadership of children in outdoor recreation/camp activities (minimum age 21 and college graduate required); *trip director* with experience pertaining to diverse kinds of wilderness tripping and equipment use (minimum age 21 and college graduate required); *wilderness and trip leaders* with current certifications in CPR, WSI, and advanced first aid (minimum age 21 and must be comfortable and confident living in wilderness); *nurse* with RN or LPN license; *kitchen personnel* with ability to assist with kitchen operations, food preparation, dishwashing, and cleanup (minimum age 19 and completion of freshman year of college required); *laundry personnel* with ability to operate camp laundry (minimum age 19 and completion of freshman year of college required); *maintenance staff* with ability to work with caretaker to prepare camp and maintain it throughout the summer; *office personnel* with bookkeeping and computer knowledge and ability to handle camper/staff cash accounts (minimum age 20, completion of sophomore year of college, and average or above typing skills required).

Benefits Preemployment training, on-the-job training, on-site room and board at no charge, laundry facilities, travel reimbursement, medical services.

Contact Applicant should send resume or write for application by March 30 to Carol A. Sigoloff, Director of Girls' Camp, Michael O'Grady, Associate Director of Boys' Camp, Camp Thunderbird for Boys/Camp Thunderbird for Girls, Department SED, 10976 Chambray Court, St. Louis, Missouri 63141; 314-567-3167.

Thunderbird is a place where children experience challenge without feeling pressured and where they are accepted unconditionally as people of worth. Because Thunderbird is foremost a children's environment, we strive to provide a comfortable arena in which children can freely experience the joy of self-discovery and accomplishment. Learning is fun at Thunderbird. Activities are used to build a child's self-esteem, helping him develop skills for later life. Each camper is given the personal guidance and support that is needed to broaden his interest, learn to live with others, and to grow in the art of self-expression.

EDEN WOOD CAMPING AND RETREAT CENTER
6350 Indian Chief Road
Eden Prairie, Minnesota 55346

General Information Residential, coeducational camp serving 40 participants with developmental disabilities and an additional 6–18 off-site weekly. Established 1958. Owned by ARC of Hennepin County. Affiliated with American Camping Association. Located 20 miles southwest of Minneapolis on 11 acres. Features include off-site trip program; location in heavily wooded area surrounded by wetlands.

Profile of Summer Employees Total number 50; average age 21. Prefers nonsmokers.

Employment Information Openings are from June 1 to September 1. Christmas break, year-round positions also offered. College credit possible. Jobs available: 1 *waterfront director* with lifeguard certification at $100–$150 per week; 8 *team leaders* with ability to supervise 8 participants and 2–8 staff members at $125–$130 per week; 20 *counselors* with ability to supervise 8 participants at $100–$105 per week; 6 *program staff* with experience in arts and crafts, camping, nature, music, wellness, barnyard, etc. at $100–$125 per week; 4 *trip leaders* with five years driving experience and a clean record at $130–$150 per week; 1 *trip coordinator* with ability to supervise staff plus handle trip planning and budget responsibilities at $140–$200 per week; 1 *secretary* with good communication skills and ability to handle light secretarial duties at $100–$150 per week; 3 *laundry/dishwashing/housekeeping staff* with a minimum age of 16 at $100–$150 per week; 2 *assistant cooks* with prep cook experience at $125–$150 per week; 2 *integration specialist* with ability to integrate disabled children into camps that do not traditionally serve youngsters with disabilities at $125–$150 per week; 6 *weekend counselors* at $125–$150 per week; 1 *summer maintenance person* with ability to perform light maintenance duties at $125–$180 per week. International students encouraged to apply.

Benefits Preemployment training, on-the-job training, formal ongoing training, on-site room and board at no charge, laundry facilities, one-week orientation covering disabilities and leadership, weekly in-service training.

Contact Applicant should send resume, write for application, or call for information by June 1 (those outside of Minnesota may call toll free at 1-800-747-7832) to Michael Levandowski, Director, Eden Wood Camping and Retreat Center, Department SED, 6350 Indian Chief Road, Eden Prairie, Minnesota 55346; 612-934-2771, fax 612-934-3707.

Eden Wood Camping and Retreat Center provides staff members with the opportunity to gain experience working with disabled individuals of all ages and ability levels.

GRAND VIEW LODGE GOLF AND TENNIS CLUB
South 134 Nokomis Avenue
Nisswa, Minnesota 56468

General Information Grand View Lodge is a resort that caters to families and business conventions. Established 1919. Owned by ETOC Corp. Affiliated with Minnesota Resort Association. Located 140 miles north of Minneapolis on 900 acres. Features include historic main lodge and 60 cabins; full-service conference center; 1,500 feet of beach; 2 golf courses and 11 tennis courts; full-service dining; family atmosphere.

Profile of Summer Employees Total number 200; average age 21. Employees are 10% minorities, 20% high school students, 70% college students, 10% retirees, 20% international, 20% local residents.

Employment Information Openings are from April 20 to October 30. Jobs available: 25 *dining room personnel* with no experience required at $155–$175 per week; 5 *bartenders* with experience at $155–$175 per week; 5 *beach staff* with good swimming skills at $155–$175 per week; 15 *housekeepers* with desire to clean at $165–$185 per week; 3 *desk clerks* with good basic math skills at $165–$185 per week; 3 *children's program instructors* with love of children at $155–$175 per week. International students encouraged to apply.

Benefits On-the-job training, formal ongoing training, on-site room and board at $140 per month, laundry facilities, bonus (if work contract is completed), employees permitted to use resort facilities at little or no charge (golf, tennis, boating, jacuzzi, indoor pool, and so on).

Contact Applicant should write for application, call for information, or apply in person by July 1 to Paul Welch, Operations Manager, Grand View Lodge Golf and Tennis Club, Department SED, South 134 Nokomis Avenue, Nisswa, Minnesota 56468; 218-963-2234, fax 218-963-2269.

MENOGYN–YMCA WILDERNESS ADVENTURES
HC 64, Box 492
Grand Marais, Minnesota 55604

General Information Wilderness base camp specializing in canoe and backpacking trips in wilderness areas. Established 1922. Owned by YMCA of Metropolitan Minneapolis. Affiliated with American Camping Association. Located 32 miles north of Grand Marais on 80 acres. Features include location 2 miles from Canada bordering the Boundary Waters Canoe Area Wilderness.

Profile of Summer Employees Total number 32; average age 22. Employees are 50% female, 5% minorities, 90% college students, 5% international, 75% local residents. Requires nonsmokers.

Employment Information   Openings are from June 4 to August 26. Spring break, winter break, Christmas break positions also offered. Jobs available: 24 *trail counselors* with CPR, first aid, and lifeguard training at $78–$108 per week; 1 *cook* with references verifying past cooking experience at $1000–$1330 per season; 1 *program director* with CPR, first aid, and lifeguard training at $78–$108 per week; 3 *in-camp staff* with CPR, first aid, and lifeguard training at $78–$108 per week; 1 *nurse* with current license at $1200 per season; 1 *maintenance person* with CPR, first aid, lifeguard training at $1200 per season. International students encouraged to apply.

Benefits   On-the-job training, formal ongoing training, on-site room and board at no charge.

Contact   Applicant should write for application or call for information by March 15 to David L. Palmer, Executive Director, Menogyn–YMCA Wilderness Adventures, Department SED, 4 West Rustic Lodge Avenue, Minneapolis, Minnesota 55409; 612-823-5282, fax 612-827-3887.

Menogyn also offers winter programs of cross-country skiing, snowshoeing, dogsledding, and winter camping.

NATIONAL PARK SERVICE

Contact   Applicant should write for application (must be 18 by May 13; U.S. citizenship required) to Regional Office of the National Park Service, Midwest Region, National Park Service, 1709 Jackson Street, Omaha, Nebraska 68102.

Jobs located in Minnesota at the following facilities: Grand Portage National Monument, Mississippi National River and Recreation Area, Pipestone National Monument, Voyageurs National Park. Also see District of Columbia listing.

NELSON'S RESORT
7632 Nelson Road
Crane Lake, Minnesota 55725

General Information   Family resort with conventions in the fall. Established 1931. Located 75 miles north of Hibbina on 84 acres. Features include 28 cabins; dining room/cocktail lounge; gift shop; marina; fishing guides; American plan and modified American plan.

Profile of Summer Employees   Total number 32; average age 20. Employees are 56% female, 25% college students, 2% retirees, 1% international, 6% local residents.

Employment Information   Openings are from May 1 to October 15. Jobs available: 6 *waiters/waitresses* at $800–$900 per month; 5 *cabin maids* at $800–$900 per month; 3 *pack boys* at $800–$900 per month; 1 *bellman* at $800–$900 per month; 3 *kitchen helpers* at $800–$900 per month; 1 *office/front-desk person* at $800–$900 per month; 1 *store clerk* at $800–$900 per month; 1 *bartender* at $800–$1000 per month. International students encouraged to apply.

Benefits   On-the-job training, on-site room and board at $240 per month, laundry facilities, use of facilities, bonus.

Contact   Applicant should send resume, write for application, or call for information and send dates of availability by April 30 to G. N. Pohlman, Owner, Nelson's Resort, Department SED, 7632 Nelson Road, Crane Lake, Minnesota 55725; 218-993-2295.

VALLEYFAIR FAMILY AMUSEMENT PARK
1 Valleyfair Drive
Shakopee, Minnesota 55379

General Information Family amusement park offering a variety of entertainment attractions. Established 1976. Owned by Cedar Fair Limited Partnership. Located 30 miles south of Minneapolis/St. Paul on 75 acres. Features include location along the Minnesota River; fun atmosphere; more than two dozen thrilling rides and an equal number of special attractions.

Profile of Summer Employees Total number 1,000. Employees are 50% female.

Employment Information Openings are from May 1 to September 30. College credit possible. Jobs available: 200 *ride hosts/hostesses* at $2500–$3500 per season; 270 *food hosts/hostesses* at $2500–$3500 per season; 90 *merchandise attendants* at $2500–$3500 per season; 140 *game attendants* at $2500–$3500 per season; 1 *accounting clerk* at $2500–$3500 per season; 1 *employee relations person* at $2500–$3500 per season; 1 *marketing assistant* at $2500–$3500 per season; 25 *park-service attendants* at $2500–$3500 per season; 28 *security officers* at $2500–$3500 per season; 40 *admissions cashiers* at $2500–$3500 per season; 40 *ticket takers* at $2500–$3500 per season; *landscaper* with landscape background at $2500–$3500 per season; *mechanic's assistant* with mechanical background at $2500–$3500 per season; 4 *seasonal group-sales representatives* at $2500–$3500 per season; 4 *personnel clerks* at $2500–$3500 per season. International students encouraged to apply.

Benefits Preemployment training, free admission to the park with Valleyfair identification, free admission passes for relatives and friends, free uniforms and laundry, internships possible for certain positions.

Contact Applicant should write for application, call for information, or apply in person by June 15 to Carol Wacker, Personnel Manager, Valleyfair Family Amusement Park, Department SED, 1 Valleyfair Drive, Shakopee, Minnesota 55379; 612-445-7600, fax 612-445-9333.

Valley Fair Amusement Park offers staff members the opportunity to gain valuable employment experience while working in an exciting outdoor atmosphere with people who know how to mix work with pleasure. Weekly social activities are planned, a scholarship program is offered, and community-wide discounts are available. (Please note that a housing coordinator is available to help locate affordable housing and match roommates. Rent reimbursements are available).

WIDJIWAGAN–YMCA WILDERNESS ADVENTURES
3788 North Arm Road
Ely, Minnesota 55731

General Information Offers summer wilderness trips for teens as well as school-year wilderness environmental education. Established 1929. Owned by YMCA of Greater St. Paul. Affiliated with American Camping Association, Young Men's Christian Association. Located 250 miles north of St. Paul on 400 acres. Features include wilderness setting; proximity to Boundary Waters Canoe Area; location among pristine lakes and forests; small capacity.

Profile of Summer Employees Total number 70; average age 23. Employees are 40% female, 5% minorities, 60% college students, 2% international, 2% local residents. Requires nonsmokers.

Employment Information   Openings are from June 5 to August 31. Year-round positions also offered. Jobs available: 50 *trail counselors* with CPR, first aid, and lifeguard certificates at $100–$150 per week; 1 *nurse* with RN license at $180–$280 per week. International students encouraged to apply.

Benefits   Preemployment training, on-the-job training, formal ongoing training, on-site room and board at no charge, laundry facilities.

Contact   Applicant should write for application or call for information by February 15 to Rolf Thompson, Executive Director, Widjiwagan–YMCA Wilderness Adventures, Department SED, 1761 University Avenue, St. Paul, Minnesota 55104; 612-645-6605, fax 612-646-5521.

Trail counselors lead and instruct groups of 3–6 teens on wilderness canoeing, backpacking, or sea-kayaking trips from ten to forty days in length.

YMCA CAMP IHDUHPI
Box 37
Loretto, Minnesota 55357

General Information   Residential camp serving 150 boys and girls. Established 1930. Owned by YMCA of Metropolitan Minneapolis. Located 25 miles west of Minneapolis on 200 acres. Features include beautiful Minnesota location; high adventure center; kayaking, sailing, and windsurfing; horseback riding; rich tradition; professional opportunities available.

Profile of Summer Employees   Total number 50; average age 21. Employees are 50% female, 15% minorities, 30% high school students, 70% college students, 5% international, 50% local residents. Requires nonsmokers.

Employment Information   Openings are from June 7 to August 24. Year-round positions also offered. College credit possible. Jobs available: 1 *program director* at $1500–$1800 per season; 2 *unit directors* at $1400–$1700 per season; 1 *waterfront director* with WSI certificate at $1400–$1700 per season; 1 *riding director* at $1350–$1600 per season; 1 *business manager* at $1150–$1400 per season; 20 *counselors* at $1150–$1400 per season; 1 *nurse* with RN license at $1600–$1800 per season; 3 *cooks* at $1400–$1700 per season; 1 *ropes-course director* at $1200–$1450 per season; 1 *nature director* at $1200–$1450 per season; 1 *arts and crafts director* at $1200–$1450 per season; 1 *trip director* at $1200–$1500 per season.

Benefits   Preemployment training, on-the-job training, formal ongoing training, on-site room and board at no charge, laundry facilities.

Contact   Applicant should write for application or call for information by April 1 to Mark Hennessy, Executive Director, YMCA Camp Ihduhpi, Department SED, Box 37, Loretto, Minnesota 55357; 612-479-1146, fax 612-479-1966.

Mississippi

NATIONAL PARK SERVICE

Contact Applicant should write for application (must be 18 by May 13; U.S. citizenship required) to Regional Office of the National Park Service, Southeast Region, National Park Service, 75 Spring Street, SW, Atlanta, Georgia 30303.

Jobs located in Mississippi at the following facilities: Gulf Island, Natchez Trace, Vicksburg National Military Park. Also see District of Columbia listing.

Missouri

NATIONAL PARK SERVICE

Contact Applicant should write for application (must be 18 by May 13; U.S. citizenship required) to Regional Office of the National Park Service, Midwest Region, National Park Service, 1709 Jackson Street, Omaha, Nebraska 68102.

Jobs located in Missouri at the following facilities: George Washington Carver National Monument, Harry S. Truman National Historic Site, Jefferson National Expansion Memorial, Ozark National Scenic Riverway, Wilson's Creek National Battlefield. Also see District of Columbia listing.

Montana

BIG SKY OF MONTANA SKI AND SUMMER RESORT
P.O. Box 1
Big Sky, Montana 59716

General Information Montana's largest winter and summer resort attracting both families and conventions. Established 1974. Owned by John E. Kircher. Affiliated with Montana Innkeepers' Association, Montana Taverns Association, Ski the Rockies. Located 45 miles south of Bozeman on 10,000 acres. Features include location just 18 miles north of Yellowstone National Park; Rocky Mountain resort surrounded by millions of acres of national forest and wilderness; Alpine and Nordic skiing, snowmobiling, and snowboarding in winter; fly-fishing on blue ribbon trout streams, golf, tennis, hiking, horseback riding, and white-water rafting in summer; 15 restaurants and night spots; accommodations for over 3,000 guests.

Profile of Summer Employees Total number 200; average age 21. Employees are 50% female, 5% minorities, 5% high school students, 80% college students, 5% local residents.

Employment Information Openings are from June 2 to October 15. Spring break, winter break, Christmas break positions also offered. Jobs available: 50 *housekeepers* at $170 per week; 75 *food and beverage positions* with experience preferred at $160 per week; 10 *accountants* with experience preferred at $200 per week; 2 *night auditors* with experience preferred at $200 per week; 7 *front-desk personnel* with experience preferred at $180 per week; 5 *bellmen* at $180 per week; 15 *retail sales personnel* at $180 per week; 30 *golf course maintenance persons* at $190 per week; 3 *conference services personnel* at $190 per week; 3 *reservations staff* with experience preferred at $200 per week; 3 *hotel maintenance personnel* at $200 per week. International students encouraged to apply.

Benefits   On-the-job training, on-site room and board at $88 per month, laundry facilities, employee discounts on meals.

Contact   Applicant should write for application or call for information by May 20 to Jeane S. Alm, Hotel Manager, or Brian D. Wheeler, Food and Beverage Director, Big Sky of Montana Ski and Summer Resort, Department SED, P.O. Box 1, Big Sky, Montana 59716; 406-995-4211, fax 406-995-4860.

GLACIER PARK, INC.
Glacier National Park
Montana

General Information   National park concessioner. Established 1912. Features include 1,000 miles of hiking trails; glacier, forest, and wildlife; 60 concessions employing students from every state; location in Big Sky Country.

Profile of Summer Employees   Total number 936; average age 20. Employees are 50% female. Prefers nonsmokers.

Employment Information   Openings are from June to September. Jobs available: *waiters/ waitresses; buspersons; bartenders; front-office clerks; cashiers; night auditors; bell porters; room attendants; housepersons; porters; line cooks; kitchen workers; gift shop and camp store clerks; reservation clerks; general office personnel; accounting clerks; under-gardeners; laundry workers; warehouse clerks; truck drivers; bus drivers/tour guides* with ability to qualify for, or already have, a Class A chauffeur's license (minimum age 21); *dormitory supervisors.* International students encouraged to apply.

Benefits   Preemployment training, on-the-job training, formal ongoing training, on-site room and board at $49 per week, laundry facilities, travel reimbursement, opportunity for internships, employee cafeterias, including extensive salad bar, paid transportation (bus pass) for culinary arts majors, group tour gratuity share or bonus program for all positions at contract completion.

Contact   Applicant should send resume, write for application, or call for information to Mr. Ian B. Tippet, Executive Director, Personnel, Glacier Park, Inc., Greyhound Lower Mail Station, 1210, Phoenix, Arizona 85077; 602-248-2612.

Guest entertainment programming is an important part of each summer and Glacier is renowned for its presentations. Music and voice majors, as well as hotel and restaurant, culinary art, and accounting majors are given additional consideration when applying. (An Equal Opportunity Employer. Affirmative action; minorities are encouraged to apply.)

GRANITE PARK AND SPERRY CHALETS
Glacier National Park
West Glacier, Montana 59936

General Information   Offers meals and lodging for backcountry visitors in Glacier National Park. Established 1914. Owned by National Park Service. Operated by Belton

Chalets, Inc. Located 50 miles northeast of Kalispell. Features include registered National Historic Landmark buildings; pristine wilderness location (reached by trail only).

Profile of Summer Employees   Total number 22; average age 21. Employees are 90% college students. Prefers nonsmokers.

Employment Information   Openings are from June 18 to September 8. Jobs available: 2 *cooks;* 2 *bakers;* 2 *dishwashers;* 4 *waiters/waitresses;* 2 *laundry persons;* 4 *housekeeping persons.*

Benefits   Preemployment training, on-site room and board at no charge, laundry facilities, health insurance.

Contact   Applicant should write for application by June 1 to L. R. Luding, Chalet Coordinator, Granite Park and Sperry Chalets, Department SED, P.O. Box 188, West Glacier, Montana 59936; 406-387-5654.

HAMILTON STORES, INC.
P.O. Box 250
West Yellowstone, Montana 59758

General Information   Fifteen general stores located throughout Yellowstone National Park with general offices and a distribution center in West Yellowstone, Montana. Established 1915. Affiliated with National Park Conference of Concessioners. Closest major city is Bozeman. Features include backpacking, rafting, and fishing; excellent quality, family-style meals.

Profile of Summer Employees   Total number 900. Employees are 51% female, 22% college students, 55% retirees.

Employment Information   Openings are from March 15 to October 15. College credit possible. Jobs available: *sales clerks; grocery clerks; food-service clerks;* 20 *employee dining room cooks* with previous experience in large volume food preparation; *dining room assistants; dishwashers; custodians;* 12 *dormitory managers;* 20 *auditors* with background in bookkeeping and/or money handling; 2 *maintenance workers* with general maintenance experience in plumbing, electrical work, etc.; *distribution center workers;* 5 *clerical personnel; security guards.*

Benefits   On-the-job training, on-site room and board at $58 per week, laundry facilities, health insurance, employee discount, college classes (limited subjects), active employee recreation co-op, two consecutive days off to explore Yellowstone National Park, guaranteed 7–8 hour day, trailer sites available for RVs.

Contact   Applicant should write for application or call for information by August 15 to Personnel Department, Hamilton Stores, Inc., Department SED, 1705 West College, Bozeman, Montana 59715; 406-587-2208, fax 406-587-3105.

Hamilton Stores, Inc., has over a 50 percent return rate, so applicants are urged to apply by January for placement. Returning employees are given choice of jobs and location wherever possible. All jobs start at $4.25 and up. Students attending summer school who can work August to October are encouraged to apply.

KLICK'S K BAR L RANCH
Augusta, Montana 59410

General Information   Established 1927. Owned by Dick Klick.

Profile of Summer Employees   Total number 10. Prefers nonsmokers.

Employment Information Openings are from June 1 to September 1. Jobs available: *domestic staff.*
Benefits On-the-job training, on-site room and board, laundry facilities.
Contact Applicant should send resume by March 1 to Nancy Klick, Klick's K Bar L Ranch, Box 287, Augusta, Montana 59410; 406-562-3589.

LAZY K BAR RANCH
P.O. Box 550
Big Timber, Montana 59011

General Information Operating cattle and horse ranch, 111 years old, accommodating selected guests for sixty-nine summers. Established 1922. Owned by Van Cleve Family. Affiliated with Dude Ranchers' Association. Located 100 miles west of Billings on 22,000 acres. Features include well-run operation; very rural setting, isolated mountain environment; an authentic ranch; nice group of employees; swimming pool; horses.
Profile of Summer Employees Total number 19; average age 18. Employees are 40% female, 45% high school students, 40% college students, 5% retirees, 5% international, 5% local residents.
Employment Information Openings are from June 12 to September 1. Jobs available: 1 *head cook* at $600 per month; 1 *second cook* at $350–$450 per month; 3 *waiters/ waitresses* at $325–$350 per month; 2 *housekeeping persons* at $350–$375 per month; 1 *laundress* at $350 per month; 1 *split-shift worker* at $375 per month; 1 *storekeeper* at $325 per month; 1 *choreman (male)* with experience with milk cows at $325 per month; 3 *wranglers (male)* with experience at $350–$450 per month; 1 *children's wrangler* with experience with horses and children at $400 per month; 1 *head wrangler (male)* with maturity and experience with horses; 1 *dishwasher* at $325 per month; 1 *waiter/caretaker* with desire for solitude at $444 per month. International students encouraged to apply.
Benefits On-the-job training, on-site room and board at no charge, laundry facilities, occasional riding, end-of-season bonus.
Contact Applicant should write for application and include a stamped, self-addressed envelope by March to Lazy K Bar Ranch, Department SED, P.O. Box 550, Big Timber, Montana 59011; 406-537-4404.
   Lazy K Bar Ranch is the oldest dude ranch in Montana. Employees have the opportunity to meet interesting guests and collect good tips.

NATIONAL PARK SERVICE

Contact Applicant should write for application (must be 18 by May 13; U.S. citizenship required) to Regional Office of the National Park Service, Rocky Mountain Region, National Park Service, P.O. Box 25287, Denver, Colorado 80225-0287.
   Jobs located in Montana at the following facilities: Big Hole National Battlefield, Bighorn Canyon, Custer Battlefield, Glacier National Park, Grant Kohrs Ranch. Also see District of Columbia listing.

ST. MARY LODGE & RESORT
Glacier National Park
St. Mary, Montana 59417

General Information   One of Montana's most notable, full-service high country resorts. Established 1932. Owned by Roscoe Black. Located 89 miles west of Kalispell on 100 acres. Features include location at the east entrance to Glacier National Park; 600 miles of hiking trails; internationally famous dining room; famous fishing; white-water rafting and horseback riding; close proximity to Canada.

Profile of Summer Employees   Total number 180; average age 21. Employees are 60% female, 5% high school students, 85% college students, 10% retirees, 20% local residents. Prefers nonsmokers.

Employment Information   Openings are from May 1 to October 1. Year-round positions also offered. College credit possible. Jobs available: 26 *waiters/waitresses* with experience at $760 per month; 12 *pantry/fry cooks* with some experience at $824–$840 per month; 5 *gas station attendants* at $792 per month; 15 *housekeepers* at $824 per month; 10 *gift shop clerks* with some experience at $792 per month; 3 *sporting-goods clerks* at $792 per month; 6 *bartenders/cocktail servers* with some experience at $760 per month; 4 *pizza parlor staff* at $792–$824 per month; 9 *supermarket staff* at $792 per month; 4 *front-desk clerks* at $792 per month; 10 *maintenance personnel* at $792 per month; 14 *dishwashing/kitchen personnel* at $792 per month; 11 *deli cooks* at $792 per month; 4 *accounting/secretarial staff* with some experience at $792 per month; 5 *clerical staff* at $792 per month; *hostesses/bussers* at $760 per month. International students encouraged to apply.

Benefits   On-the-job training, on-site room and board at $245 per month, laundry facilities, guaranteed year-end bonuses, retail discount, internships.

Contact   Applicant should send resume, write for application, or call for information by April 10 to Director of Human Resources, St. Mary Lodge & Resort, Department SED, P.O. Box 1808, Sun Valley, Idaho 83353; 208-726-6279, fax 208-726-6282.

The resort is the most centrally located guest facility in Glacier National Park. Opportunity to become a member of an innovative team that is well-known in the region for the highest quality products and services.

63 RANCH
P.O. Box 979
Livingston, Montana 59047

General Information   Working cattle and dude ranch with capacity for 30 guests from June to September. Established 1929. Owned by Sandra C. Cahill. Affiliated with Dude Ranchers' Association, The Montana Outfitters and Guides Association, Livingston Chamber of Commerce, Gallatin Outfitters' Association, Montana Chamber of Commerce, Trout Unlimited, Federation of Fly Fishermen, Montana Farm Bureau, National Rifle Association, National Wildlife Federation. Features include location in Big Sky country bordering national forest and wilderness; clean air and water; proximity to Yellowstone National Park; blue ribbon trout streams; location far from town.

Profile of Summer Employees   Total number 15; average age 25. Employees are 53% female. Requires nonsmokers.

Employment Information   Openings are from June 1 to September 20. Jobs available: 1 *head cook* with extensive experience and the ability to run a kitchen and cook for 50 people at $1000 per month; 1 *second cook* with extensive experience at $800 per month; 1 *dishwasher* at $600 per month; 2 *waiters/waitresses* at $600 per month; 1 *kitchen helper* at $600 per month; 1 *head housekeeper* with extensive housecleaning and supervisory experience at $800 per month; 2 *cabin cleaners* at $600 per month; 1 *chore boy/girl* with physical strength (lifting involved) at $600 per month.

Benefits On-the-job training, on-site room and board, laundry facilities, end-of-season bonus possible, workman's compensation, use of all ranch facilities during time off, food same as guests, transportation to and from town and airport.

Contact Applicant should write for application by August 30 (College students need not apply unless they can stay until September 15.) to Sandra C. Cahill, President, 63 Ranch, Department SED, P.O. Box 979, Livingston, Montana 59047; 406-222-0570.

We hire a lot of young people without experience who receive on-the-job training. This valuable experience can be utilized in the future and can help to establish good work habits. Additionally, our staff members can enjoy the wide open spaces of the West.

STAGE COACH INN
209 Madison Avenue
West Yellowstone, Montana 59758

General Information Full-service, luxury hotel with Western atmosphere. Established 1948. Owned by Hamilton Stores, Inc. Affiliated with Montana Innkeepers' Association, West Yellowstone Chamber of Commerce. Located 89 miles south of Bozeman. Features include location at west entrance to Yellowstone; blue ribbon trout fishing; unparalleled scenic beauty; abundant wildlife; easy access to wilderness.

Profile of Summer Employees Total number 50; average age 21. Employees are 50% female, 10% high school students, 30% college students, 5% retirees, 5% local residents.

Employment Information Openings are from June 1 to September 20. Winter break, Christmas break, year-round positions also offered. College credit possible. Jobs available: 3 *first and second cooks;* 4 *waiters/waitresses;* 4 *dining room attendants;* 2 *bartenders;* 2 *pizza servers;* 4 *room attendants.* International students encouraged to apply.

Benefits On-the-job training, on-site room and board at $100 per month, laundry facilities.

Contact Applicant should write for application, call for information, or apply in person by June 30 to Tita Norris, Administrative Assistant, Stage Coach Inn, Department SED, P.O. Box 160, West Yellowstone, Montana 59758; 406-646-7381, fax 406-646-9575.

The Stage Coach Inn has Old West charm and hospitality. A wide variety of clientele from all over the world stay at our hotel while visiting the Yellowstone area. Our staff members can explore and enjoy Yellowstone Park and Montana on their days off. Employee wages range from $4.25 to $6.00 per hour, depending on experience.

SWEET GRASS RANCH
Melville Route, Box 161
Big Timber, Montana 59011

General Information Working cattle ranch that accepts 20 guests to live ranch life. Established 1926. Owned by Bill and Shelly Carroccia. Affiliated with National Register of Historic Places, Dude Ranchers' Association, National Cattlemen's Association. Located 120 miles northwest of Billings on 12,000 acres. Features include unlimited riding on good horses; chance to live without social organization (no TV); pack trips into the mountains; fishing in clear lakes and streams; ranch-raised meat, milk, cream, and vegetables; beautiful, unspoiled scenery.

Profile of Summer Employees   Total number 8; average age 21. Employees are 50% female, 100% college students, 25% local residents. Prefers nonsmokers.

Employment Information   Openings are from June 1 to September 10. Jobs available: 2 *cooks* with cooking experience or training as a baker and ability to work well with others at $500–$600 per month; 2 *cabin girls* with organizational and interpersonal skills and an attention to cleanliness at $450 per month; 4 *wranglers* with horse experience at $500 per month.

Benefits   On-the-job training, on-site room and board at no charge, laundry facilities, tips.

Contact   Applicant should send resume, write for application, or call for information by February 15 to Mrs. William Carroccia, Owner, Sweet Grass Ranch, Department SED, Melville Route, Box 161, Big Timber, Montana 59011; 406-537-4497.

Sweet Grass Ranch provides individuals with the opportunity to ride one day a week, meet interesting guests from the United States and Europe, have a challenging and rewarding employment experience, and learn about life on a cattle ranch. It is located 40 miles from town and provides a clean living environment. Our staff members and a large percentage of our guests return each year.

YELLOWSTONE PARK SERVICE STATIONS
Yellowstone National Park
Montana

General Information   YPSS operates automotive service facilities in Yellowstone National Park. Established 1947. Affiliated with Montana Chamber of Commerce, Gardiner Chamber of Commerce, National Park Conference of Concessioners. Located 90 miles south of Bozeman. Features include opportunity to work outdoors in one of the world's premier parks; world's greatest concentration of geysers; spectacular waterfalls, mountains, and canyons; Yellowstone Lake, the largest Alpine lake in the United States; proximity to Teton National Park and several national forests.

Profile of Summer Employees   Total number 95; average age 23. Employees are 29% female, 2% minorities, 63% college students, 4% retirees, 1% international, 10% local residents. Prefers nonsmokers.

Employment Information   Openings are from May 1 to October 15. College credit possible. Jobs available: 50 *service station attendants* with good people and communication skills at $178 per week; 18 *automobile mechanics* with ASE certification or current enrollment in ASE program at $240 per week; 3 *accounting clerks* with ability to operate 10-key adding machine by touch, computer skills, and communication skills at $182 per week; 1 *warehouse helper* with good driving record and communication skills at $182 per week.

Benefits   Preemployment training, on-the-job training, on-site room and board at $58 per week, laundry facilities, health insurance, recreation program, accident insurance, advancement potential.

Contact Applicant should write for application or call for information by May 1 to Yellowstone Park Service Stations, P.O. Box 11, Department WDW, Gardiner, Montana 59030-0011; 406-848-7333.

We operate eleven retail establishments located throughout the 2.2- million acres of Yellowstone National Park. We present our employees with opportunities for advancement; all of our managers are promoted from within. In addition, staff members have the opportunity to meet and work with people from across the United States and other parts of the world.

Nebraska

NATIONAL PARK SERVICE

Contact Applicant should write for application (must be 18 by May 13; U.S. citizenship required) to Regional Office of the National Park Service, Midwest Region, National Park Service, 1709 Jackson Street, Omaha, Nebraska 68102.

Jobs located in Nebraska at the following facilities: Agate Fossil Beds, Homestead National Monument of America, Scotts Bluff. Also see District of Columbia listing.

Nevada

NATIONAL PARK SERVICE

Contact Applicant should write for application (must be 18 by May 13; U.S. citizenship required) to Regional Office of the National Park Service, Western Region, National Park Service, 450 Golden Gate Avenue, Box 36063, San Francisco, California 94102.

Jobs located in Nevada at the following facilities: Great Basin, Lake Mead. Also see District of Columbia listing.

New Hampshire

THE BALSAMS GRAND RESORT HOTEL
Route 26
Dixville Notch, New Hampshire 03576

General Information A four-star, four-diamond facility catering to vacationers (July, August, and winter) as well as convention groups (spring and fall). Established 1873. Owned by Balsams Corporation. Affiliated with American Hospitality Association, American Culinary Federation, Chaines Des Rotisseurs. Located 300 miles north of Boston, Massachusetts on 15,000 acres. Features include location in the White Mountains of New Hampshire 13 miles south of Canada; panoramic golf courses; Lake Gloriette; hiking trails; tennis courts; swimming pool.

Profile of Summer Employees Total number 450; average age 21. Employees are 50% female, 11% minorities, 4% high school students, 22% college students, 6% retirees, 6% international, 53% local residents.

Employment Information Openings are from May 22 to October 20. Winter break positions also offered. Jobs available: 3 *recreation staff (lifeguards)* at $720 per month; 30 *dining room wait staff* at $200–$400 per week; 10 *housekeeping staff* at $200–$300 per week; 5 *beverage servers* at $200–$300 per week; 5 *bellpersons;* 5 *kitchen staff;* 5 *laundry staff; bartenders.* International students encouraged to apply.

Benefits Preemployment training, on-the-job training, formal ongoing training, on-site room and board at $30 per week, laundry facilities, free use of lake, golf course, tennis courts, and hiking trails.

Contact Applicant should send resume, write for application, or call for information and give information with regards to his/her earliest possible starting dates plus departure dates by April 1 to Suzanne Noyes, Director of Personnel, The Balsams Grand Resort Hotel, Department SED, Route 26, Dixville Notch, New Hampshire 03576; 603-255-3400 Ext. 2666, fax 603-255-4670.

We operate two seasons of the year, from mid-May through the middle of October, and then again from mid-December through the end of March.

CAMP ALBANY
RFD 1
Conway, New Hampshire 03818

General Information Residential Girl Scout camp serving 100 girls ages 6–12 in one- and two-week sessions. Especially suited for those who are away from home for the first time. Established 1984. Owned by Swift Water Girl Scout Council. Affiliated with American Camping Association. Located 150 miles north of Boston on 100 acres. Features include location in White Mountains of New Hampshire; small, family atmosphere; sandy beach on beautiful Iona Lake; cabin sleeping; girls get to make decisions about program; waterfront with panoramic view of Mt. Chocorua.

Profile of Summer Employees Total number 35; average age 20. Employees are 100% female, 5% minorities, 70% college students, 10% international, 20% local residents. Prefers nonsmokers.

Employment Information Openings are from June 15 to August 22. Jobs available: 1 *program director* with administrative and supervision experience at $2300–$3700 per season; 1 *health director* with RN license at $1600–$2800 per season; 1 *waterfront director* with WSI and LGT certificates plus supervision experience at $1600–$2800 per season; 4 *waterfront assistants* with WSI and LGT certificates at $1200–$1600 per season; 5 *unit leaders* with supervisory experience at $1600–$2100 per season; 15 *unit assistants* with experience with children at $1200–$1600 per season; 1 *food supervisor* with menu planning and quantity cooking experience at $2300–$3700 per season; 2 *cooks* with quantity cooking experience at $1600–$2600 per season; 1 *arts director* with arts program experience at $1600–$2600 per season.

Benefits Preemployment training, on-the-job training, on-site room and board at no charge, laundry facilities, health insurance.

Contact Applicant should send resume, write for application, or call for information by June 15 to Nancy Frankel, Director of Outdoor Education, Camp Albany, Department SED, 88 Harvey Road, #4, Manchester, New Hampshire 03103; 603-627-4158.

CAMP CODY FOR BOYS
Ossipee Lake Road
Freedom, New Hampshire 03836

General Information   Multispecialty programs of play and skill development in all land and water sports, shop, arts and sciences, and adventure trips. Established 1926. Owned by Camp Cody, Inc. Affiliated with American Camping Association, New Hampshire Camp Directors' Association. Located 40 miles west of Portland, Maine on 140 acres. Features include superb site near ocean and Boston, at the edge of White Mountain National Forest; warm sand-bottom lake; national clientele; family ownership; super facilities and equipment.

Profile of Summer Employees   Total number 75; average age 24. Employees are 10% female, 15% minorities, 10% high school students, 75% college students, 5% retirees, 20% international, 10% local residents. Prefers nonsmokers.

Employment Information   Openings are from June to August. College credit possible. Jobs available: *swimming instructors and assistants* with experience in all waterfront skills (swimming, waterskiing, sailing, scuba, windsurfing, lifesaving, canoeing, kayaking, etc.); *canoe and kayak trip leaders; coaches and assistants* with experience in all land team sports (baseball, basketball, soccer, volleyball, street hockey) and individual sports (tennis, archery, riflery, track, bicycling); *outdoor-skills and trip leaders* with experience in natural sciences/nature/ecology, camp craft, scouting, overnight backpacking, and bicycle trips; *art and science instructors* with experience in woodshop, model rocketry, computers, videos, photography/darkroom, ham radios, and fishing; *general counselors and assistants; nurse* with RN license; *chef's assistants; office staff; housekeeping staff; nannies; maintenance and groundskeepers; food-service workers.* International students encouraged to apply.

Benefits   Preemployment training, on-the-job training, formal ongoing training, on-site room and board at no charge, laundry facilities, travel reimbursement, health insurance, use of facilities, wonderful local vacation areas, no state taxes or deductions.

Contact   Applicant should send resume, write for application, call for information, or apply in person by July 1 to Alan J. Stolz, CCD, Director, Camp Cody for Boys, Department SED, 5 Lockwood Circle, Westport, Connecticut 06880; 203-226-4389, fax 203-454-5519.

We offer a busy, exciting, and funfilled summer that includes intercamp and sports events, adventure trips from Boston to Canada, elaborate facilities, and great camaraderie. We are located at a superb site in the heart of New England's vacation areas. We have a national reputation for providing leadership. We offer many activities and support positions to both experienced counselors and those new to summer camp work.

CAMP KENWOOD–EVERGREEN
Potter Place, P.O. Box 501
Andover, New Hampshire 03216

General Information   Residential camp serving boys and girls who want a great summer. Established 1930. Owned by Judy and Arthur Sharenow. Affiliated with American Camping Association, Private Independent Camps, New Hampshire Camp Directors' Association. Located 100 miles northwest of Boston, Massachusetts on 160 acres. Features include setting in mountain valley; beautiful pond; rolling hills; 11 tennis courts and major indoor gymnasium.

Profile of Summer Employees   Total number 100; average age 23. Employees are 50% female, 2% minorities, 20% high school students, 70% college students, 10% international, 10% local residents. Prefers nonsmokers.

Employment Information   Openings are from June 20 to August 20. Jobs available: 2 *waterfront directors* with college graduate status plus WSI and lifeguard certificates at $2500 per season; 1 *tennis director* with club teaching experience at $3000 per season; 1 *arts and crafts instructor* with college graduate status at $2000 per season; 1 *drama director* with college graduate status and directing experience at $2000 per season; 4 *swimming instructors* with WSI and lifeguard certificates at $1200–$1500 per season; 1 *gymnastics instructor* with college graduate status and teaching experience at $1200–$1500 per season; *general athletics counselors* at $1100–$1800 per season. International students encouraged to apply.

Benefits   Preemployment training, on-the-job training, on-site room and board, laundry facilities, travel reimbursement.

Contact   Applicant should send resume, write for application, or call for information to Arthur Sharenow, Director, Camp Kenwood–Evergreen, 10 Partridge Road, Lexington, Massachusetts 02173; 617-862-7537.

CAMP MERRIMAC
Route 2
Contoocook, New Hampshire 03229

General Information   Residential camp serving over 200 highly motivated boys and girls. Established 1919. Owned by Robert M. Martin. Affiliated with American Camping Association, New England Camping Association. Located 10 miles northwest of Concord on 400 acres. Features include magnificent lake; pollen-free air; location 72 miles from Boston; modern cabins; pine forest location.

Profile of Summer Employees   Total number 100; average age 21. Employees are 40% female, 40% college students, 60% international. Requires nonsmokers.

Employment Information   Openings are from June 28 to August 25. College credit possible. Jobs available: 1 *archery instructor* with previous experience at $800–$1200 per season; 1 *riflery instructor* with previous experience at $800–$1200 per season; 3 *swimming instructors* with WSI certificate at $800–$1200 per season; 1 *canoe instructor* at $800–$1200 per season; 2 *waterskiing instructors* at $800–$1200 per season; 1 *sailing instructor* at $800–$1200 per season; 1 *athletics director* at $800–$1200 per season; 1 *head of waterfront* with WSI certificate at $800–$1200 per season; 2 *soccer instructors* at $800–$1200 per season; 2 *softball instructors* at $800–$1200 per season; 2 *basketball instructors* at $800–$1200 per season; 4 *group leaders* at $1200–$1500 per season; 1 *fine arts instructor* at $800–$1200 per season; 1 *crafts instructor* at $800–$1200 per season; 3 *science instructors* at $1200–$1400 per season; 6 *bus drivers* at $800–$1200 per season; *tennis instructors* at $800–$1200 per season. International students encouraged to apply.

Benefits   Preemployment training, on-site room and board at no charge, laundry facilities, workman's compensation.

Contact   Applicant should send resume, write for application, or call for information by March to Robert M. Martin, President, Camp Merrimac, Department SED, 46 Standish Drive, Scarsdale, New York 10583; 914-725-1215, fax 914-723-7105.

Camp Merrimac has provided outstanding leadership and support for its counselors. Transportation is provided for trips out of camp. We are located near Boston and the Lakes Region in New Hampshire, allowing for many cultural experiences for the staff.

CAMP TEL NOAR
Hampstead, New Hampshire 03841

General Information   Jewish, coeducational, cultural, residential camp serving 265 children. Established 1952. Operated by Cohen Foundation. Affiliated with American Camping Association, New Hampshire Camping Association, Private Independent Camps. Located 50 miles north of Boston, Massachusetts on 60 acres. Features include unique housing; spring-fed lake.

Profile of Summer Employees   Total number 95; average age 19. Employees are 16% high school students, 82% college students, 2% international. Prefers nonsmokers.

Employment Information   Openings are from June 25 to August 24. College credit possible. Jobs available: 3 *arts and crafts instructors* at $1350–$1800 per season; 1 *arts and crafts head* at $2000–$2500 per season; 1 *music head* at $2000–$2500 per season; 2 *canoe instructors* at $1350–$2000 per season; 2 *sailing instructors* at $1350–$2000 per season; 3 *swimming instructors* at $1350–$2000 per season; 1 *swimming head* at $2000–$2500 per season; 1 *athletics head* at $2000–$2500 per season; 1 *waterskiing head* at $1500–$1900 per season; 1 *archery instructor* at $1500–$1900 per season.

Benefits   On-the-job training, formal ongoing training, on-site room and board at no charge, laundry facilities, gratuities.

Contact   Applicant should send resume or call for information by April 1 to Marty Wiadro, Director, Camp Tel Noar, Department SED, 131 Victoria Road, Sudbury, Massachusetts 01776; 508-443-3655, fax 508-881-1006.

Great summer opportunity to work with children. Work-study program available.

CAMP TEVYA
Brookline, New Hampshire 03033

General Information   Jewish, coeducational, cultural camp serving 325 campers. Established 1940. Operated by Cohen Foundation. Affiliated with American Camping Association, New Hampshire Camping Association. Located 65 miles north of Boston, Massachusetts on 650 acres. Features include outstanding waterfront.

Profile of Summer Employees   Employees are 16% high school students, 82% college students, 2% international. Prefers nonsmokers.

Employment Information   Openings are from June 25 to August 24. College credit possible. Jobs available: 3 *arts and crafts instructors* at $1350–$1800 per season; 1 *arts and crafts head* at $2000–$2500 per season; 1 *music head* at $2000–$2500 per season; 2 *canoe instructors* at $1350–$2000 per season; 2 *sailing instructors* at $1350–$2000 per season; 3 *swimming instructors* at $1350–$2000 per season; 1 *swimming head* at $2000–$2500 per season; 1 *athletics head* at $2000–$2500 per season; 1 *waterskiing head* at $1500–$1900 per season; 1 *archery instructor* at $1500–$1900 per season.

Benefits   On-the-job training, formal ongoing training, on-site room and board at no charge, laundry facilities, gratuities.

Contact   Applicant should send resume or call for information by April 1 to Shelley Shapiro, Director, Camp Tevya, Department SED, 4 Willey Road, Durham, New Hampshire 03824; 603-868-5544, fax 508-881-1006.

Great summer opportunity to work with children. Work-study program available.

CAMP WALT WHITMAN
Pike, New Hampshire 03780

General Information Coeducational, residential camp serving 260 campers and offering a strong general program. Established 1948. Owned by Jancy and Bill Dorfman. Affiliated with American Camping Association, Private Independent Camps. Located 120 miles north of Boston on 300 acres. Features include location in White Mountains on crystal-clear lake; 11 clay tennis courts; beautiful playing fields; excellent indoor facilities and modern cabins; beautiful natural environment.

Profile of Summer Employees Total number 120; average age 21. Employees are 50% female, 5% high school students, 60% college students, 2% retirees, 10% international. Requires nonsmokers.

Employment Information Openings are from June 15 to August 22. College credit possible. Jobs available: 20 *general counselors* with experience working with children at $800–$1200 per season; 6 *sports coaches* with experience coaching on elementary, junior/senior high school, or college levels at $1200–$1800 per season; 6 *tennis instructors* with experience teaching tennis at $1000–$1800 per season; 6 *swimming instructors* with WSI certificate at $1000–$1800 per season; 3 *hiking and camping specialists* with wilderness and trip leading experience at $1000–$1800 per season; 6 *kitchen and maintenance personnel* with experience at $1200–$2500 per season; 2 *dance/gymnastics instructors* with experience at $1200–$1500 per season; 3 *art/woodshop instructors* with experience at $1200–$1500 per season; 3 *sailing, canoeing, and windsurfing instructors* with experience at $1000–$1800 per season.

Benefits Preemployment training, on-the-job training, formal ongoing training, on-site room and board, travel reimbursement, health insurance, staff recreation program, staff lounge and kitchen.

Contact Applicant should send resume, write for application, or call for information to Jancy Dorfman, Director, Camp Walt Whitman, Department SED, P.O. Box 558, Armonk, New York 10504; 800-657-8282.

Family-run since 1948 with committed, involved directors. Opportunity to travel throughout New England and Canada. Great team and camp spirit with 90 percent of campers and 50 percent of staff members returning annually.

INTERLOCKEN CENTER FOR EXPERIENTIAL LEARNING
RR 2, Box 165
Hillsboro, New Hampshire 03244

General Information Residential, international summer camp serving 130 campers from a variety of countries in a cross-cultural atmosphere. Also offers travel programs throughout the world for junior high and high school age students. Established 1961. Owned by Richard Herman. Affiliated with Association for Experimental Education. Located 75 miles northwest of Boston on 500 acres. Features include wilderness area; full ropes course; lakefront and boating; strong performing arts program; all sports activities.

Profile of Summer Employees Total number 45; average age 26. Employees are 50% female, 20% minorities, 40% college students, 20% international. Requires nonsmokers.

Employment Information   Openings are from June 20 to August 25. International students encouraged to apply.

Benefits   Preemployment training, on-the-job training, on-site room and board at no charge, laundry facilities.

Contact   Applicant should send resume or write for application by March 1 to Staffing Coordinator, Interlocken Center for Experiential Learning, Department SED, RR 2, Box 105, Hillsboro, New Hampshire 03244; 603-478-3166, fax 603-478-5260.

Interlocken staff members design their own programs in a creative, supportive environment.

NATIONAL PARK SERVICE

Contact   Applicant should write for application (must be 18 by May 13; U.S. citizenship required) to Regional Office of the National Park Service, North Atlantic Region, National Park Service, 15 State Street, Boston, Massachusetts 02109.

Jobs located in New Hampshire at Saint Gaudens National Historic Site. Also see District of Columbia listing.

ROCKYWOLD–DEEPHAVEN CAMPS INC. (RDC)
Pinehurst Road, P.O. Box B
Holderness, New Hampshire 03245

General Information   A family vacation camp since 1897. RDC provides its guests with a unique family living experience offering rustic simplicity, high-quality services, and a beautiful natural setting. Owned by Rockywold-Deephaven Camps Inc. Affiliated with New England Innkeepers' Association, American Camping Association, Squam Lake Association. Located 45 miles north of Concord on 115 acres. Features include location at the southern edge of the White Mountains on Squam Lake; 8 tennis courts, basketball court, and sports field; unlimited miles of hiking trails; 1½ miles of shore front with a large fleet of canoes, kayaks, rowboats, and sailboats.

Profile of Summer Employees   Total number 80; average age 23. Employees are 50% female, 5% minorities, 5% high school students, 70% college students, 5% retirees, 5% international, 10% local residents. Prefers nonsmokers.

Employment Information   Openings are from May 20 to October 15. Jobs available: 22 *housekeeping personnel* with a positive and flexible attitude and high work standards at $176–$280 per week; 20 *food-service personnel* with a positive and flexible attitude and high work standards at $176–$360 per week; 10 *grounds/maintenance personnel* with experience in soft surface tennis court maintenance and carpentry at $176–$280 per week; 5 *recreation staff* with experience in tennis, water sports, and working with various age groups at $200–$250 per week; 6 *office staff* with experience with the public plus word processing and money handling skills at $184–$280 per week.

Benefits   Preemployment training, on-the-job training, on-site room and board at no charge, laundry facilities, end-of-season bonus possible, limited use of recreational facilities and equipment.

Contact   Applicant should send resume, write for application, or call for information by March 15 to John Jurczynski, General Manager, Rockywold–Deephaven Camps Inc. (RDC), Department SED, P.O. Box B, Holderness, New Hampshire 03245; 603-968-3313.

Rockywold-Deephaven Camps are highly regarded by guests, staff, and the resort community. The camps are proud of their traditions and high-quality services, but most important to the success of RDC is the accommodating nature of its staff members towards guests and each other.

WA-KLO
Thorndike Lake, Jaffrey Center
Jaffrey, New Hampshire 03452

General Information   Private girls' camp accomodating 125 girls. Established 1938. Owned by Ethel T. Kloberg and Marie J. Jensen. Affiliated with American Camping Association, New Hampshire Camp Directors' Association. Located 70 miles west of Boston, Massachusetts on 150 acres. Features include location on beautiful Thorndike Lake, at the base of Mount Monadnock; excellent facilities for all land and water sports; international community; performing arts activities.

Profile of Summer Employees   Total number 35; average age 20. Employees are 90% female, 100% college students, 50% international. Prefers nonsmokers.

Employment Information   Openings are from June 15 to August 15. College credit possible. Jobs available: *swimming instructor* with lifeguard and WSI certificates at $1200–$1500 per season; *sailing instructor* at $1200–$1500 per season; *waterskiing instructor* at $1200–$1500 per season; *nurse* at $1200–$1500 per season; *tennis instructor* at $1200–$1500 per season; *riding instructor* at $1200–$1500 per season; *windsurfing instructor* at $1200–$1500 per season; *dance instructor* at $1200–$1500 per season; *drama instructor* at $1200–$1500 per season; *kayaking instructor* at $1200–$1500 per season; *gymnastics instructor* at $1200–$1500 per season; *pet care instructor* at $1200–$1500 per season; *tutor* at $1200–$1500 per season; *arts and crafts instructor* at $1200–$1500 per season; *piano instructor* at $1200–$1500 per season; *bugle instructor* at $1200–$1500 per season. International students encouraged to apply.

Benefits   Preemployment training, on-the-job training, on-site room and board, health insurance, tuition reimbursement, 24-hour leave each week, free evenings.

Contact   Applicant should send resume, write for application, or call for information by June 1 to Ethel T. Kloberg, Owner/Director, Wa-Klo, Department SED, 3638 Lorrie Drive, Oceanside, New York 11572; 516-678-3174.

New Jersey

AMERICAN CAMPING ASSOCIATION/NEW JERSEY SECTION
RD 2, O'Brien Road
Hackettstown, New Jersey 07840

General Information   Referral services for camps and educational sponsor for camping personnel. Operated by American Camping Association. Located 3 miles west of Hackettstown.

Employment Information   Openings are from June 7 to September 1.

Contact   Applicant should write for application or call for information by June 1 to American Camping Association/New Jersey Section, Department SED, RD 2, O'Brien Road, Hackettstown, New Jersey 07840; 908-852-3896, fax 908-852-9263.

We are part of a national organization whose purpose is to assure the highest professional practices for the administration and extension of organized camping.

APPEL FARM ARTS AND MUSIC CENTER
Elmer-Shirley Road
Elmer, New Jersey 08318

General Information   Residential camp offering instruction in the fine and performing arts. Established 1960. Owned by Appel Farm Arts and Music Center. Operated by National Guild of Community Schools of the Arts. Affiliated with American Camping Association. Located 30 miles south of Philadelphia, Pennsylvania on 176 acres. Features include international, intercultural community; rural area; playing fields; air-conditioned practice/rehearsal spaces; professional staff with a 1:2 ratio; supportive, nurturing community; 2-acre organic garden.

Profile of Summer Employees   Total number 90; average age 29. Employees are 60% female, 20% minorities, 15% college students, 20% international, 10% local residents. Requires nonsmokers.

Employment Information   Openings are from June 23 to August 19. Jobs available: 3 *dance instructors* with knowledge of modern, jazz, and ballet dancing at $1100–$1400 per season; 10 *music instructors* with experience in electronic music, rock, woodwinds, piano, strings, percussion, voice, and brass at $1100–$1500 per season; 3 *photography instructors* with teaching experience at $1100–$1300 per season; 2 *video instructors* with teaching experience at $1100–$1300 per season; 1 *radio instructor* with teaching experience at $1100–$1300 per season; 5 *theater instructors* with directing experience at $1100–$1400 per season; 3 *technical theater personnel* with experience in stage craft, set design, costumes, and lighting at $1100–$1500 per season; 10 *art instructors* with experience in painting, drawing, printmaking, sculpture, weaving, film animation, and ceramics at $1100–$1500 per season; 4 *swimming instructors* with lifeguard training or WSI certificate at $1100–$1500 per season; 3 *sports staff* with experience in tennis and other noncompetitive sports at $1100–$1400 per season; 1 *community-outreach instructor* with organizational ability and office work experience at $1100–$1300 per season.

Benefits   On-site room and board at no charge, laundry facilities, week-long staff orientation, working in a community of artists, rehearsal space/studio space.

Contact Applicant should send resume, write for application, or call for information to Rena Levitt, Camp Director, Appel Farm Arts and Music Center, P.O. Box 888, Elmer, New Jersey 08318; 609-358-2472.

CAMP MERRY HEART/EASTER SEALS
RD 2, O'Brien Road
Hackettstown, New Jersey 07840

General Information Residential camp for disabled people ages 5–60 and day camp for nondisabled children ages 5–12. Established 1949. Operated by Easter Seal Society of New Jersey. Affiliated with American Camping Association. Located 3 miles west of Hackettstown on 121 acres. Features include pool; lake for boating and fishing; cabins; accessibility for disabled people; low camper-staff ratio.

Profile of Summer Employees Total number 61; average age 21. Employees are 50% female, 25% minorities, 10% high school students, 75% college students, 25% international, 10% local residents. Prefers nonsmokers.

Employment Information Openings are from June 15 to August 15. Christmas break positions also offered. College credit possible. Jobs available: 1 *swimming instructor* with WSI/lifeguard certification at $1050–$1200 per season; 1 *nature specialist* with ecology background at $1050–$1200 per season; 1 *recreation specialist* with theraputic background at $1050–$1200 per season; 1 *boating specialist* with small craft certificate at $1050–$1200 per season; 20 *counselors (female)* with college student status and special education background at $1000–$1200 per season; 20 *counselors (male)* with college student status at $1000–$1200 per season; 2 *cooks* with knowledge of cooking for groups at $2000–$3000 per season; 1 *program specialist* with program organizational skills at $2000–$3000 per season; 2 *nurses* with RN license plus first aid and CPR certification at $2000–$3000 per season. International students encouraged to apply.

Benefits Preemployment training, formal ongoing training, on-site room and board at no charge, laundry facilities.

Contact Applicant should write for application, call for information, or apply in person by May 15 to Mary Ellen Ross, Director of Camping, Camp Merry Heart/Easter Seals, Department SED, RD 2, O'Brien Road, Hackettstown, New Jersey 07840; 908-852-3896, fax 908-852-9263.

Our staff obtains the best practical experience for career development.

CAMP NEJEDA
Saddleback Road
Stillwater, New Jersey 07875-0156

General Information Residential summer camp serving 72 campers with diabetes in one- or two-week sessions. Established 1958. Owned by Camp Nejeda Foundation, Inc. Affiliated with American Camping Association. Located 50 miles west of New York City on 72 acres. Features include caring environment; lake for boating and fishing; 20x60-foot pool; medical staff on site; location in scenic area of New Jersey.

Profile of Summer Employees Total number 50; average age 19. Employees are 60% female, 10% high school students, 30% college students.

Employment Information Openings are from June 22 to August 16. Jobs available: 2 *swimming instructors* with WSI certificate; 18 *senior counselors* with a minimum age of 18 at $1000 per season; 9 *junior counselors* with a minimum age of 17 at $700 per season; 4 *kitchen staff* with a minimum age of 17 at $800 per season; 1 *dietitian* with RD license or eligibility at $3000 per season; 1 *program director* with camping and program experience at $2600 per season. International students encouraged to apply.

Benefits On-the-job training, formal ongoing training, on-site room and board at no charge, laundry facilities.

Contact Applicant should send resume, write for application, or call for information by March 31 (no actual deadline, date is recommended) to Camp Director, Camp Nejeda, P.O. Box 156, Stillwater, New Jersey 07875-0156; 201-383-2611, fax 201-383-9891.

Great experience in helping children with diabetes learn to cope.

CAMP VACAMAS
256 Macopin Road
West Milford, New Jersey 07480

General Information Serves the needs of children from low- and moderate-income families. Established 1924. Operated by Camp Vacamas Association. Affiliated with American Camping Association. Features include beautiful natural surrounding; 1 hour from New York.

Profile of Summer Employees Total number 160; average age 21. Employees are 60% female, 30% minorities, 5% high school students, 95% college students, 30% international, 15% local residents. Prefers nonsmokers.

Employment Information Openings are from June 15 to August 24. Year-round positions also offered. College credit possible. Jobs available: *head counselor* with M.S.W. degree and camp experience (minimum age 21) at $2000–$3000 per season; *camper counselor* with B.S.W. or B.A. degree in psychology or sociology at $1800–$2000 per season; *teen coordinator* with education degree (minimum age 21) at $1800–$2000 per season; *waterfront director* with WSI certificate plus experience with staff supervision (minimum age 21) at $1800–$2000 per season; *teen trip leaders* with college senior status and expedition experience at $1300–$1500 per season; *teen theater arts director* with B.A. degree and theater experience at $1200–$1500 per season; *teen leadership-in-training person* with B.A. degree and three years camp experience at $1200–$1500 per season; *creative arts director* with experience in diverse art forms at $900–$1400 per season; *woodshop/construction instructor* with extensive experience with hand tools and children (minimum age 21) at $900–$1000 per season; *nature/campcraft instructor* with outdoors experience at $800–$1000 per season; *library counselor* with B.A. degree in education or psychology at $800–$1000 per season; *ropes-course instructor* with college junior status and experience in rock-climbing at $1000–$1500 per season; *farm/garden director* with livestock and gardening experience; *head nurse* with RN license and an interest in working with children at $2000 per season; *nurse* with RN or LPN license at $1500–$2000 per season. International students encouraged to apply.

Benefits Preemployment training, on-the-job training, formal ongoing training, on-site room and board at no charge, laundry facilities, travel reimbursement, health insurance.

Contact Applicant should send resume or write for application by May 31 to Michael H. Friedman, Executive Director, Camp Vacamas, 256 Macopin Road, West Milford, New Jersey 07480; 201-838-1394, fax 201-838-7534.

Camp Vacamas is based on a decentralized, noncompetitive philosophy geared toward the individuality of each child. We are committed to serving a diverse population on every level: by gender, religiously, ethnically, culturally, racially, and socioeconomically. Our mission is to provide a meaningful summer and year-round experience to the families with whom we work. Additionally, we have developed unique dropout prevention programs and offer food service at the camp that follows simple dietary laws/kosher style meals.

FELLOWSHIP DEACONRY, INC. (DAY CAMP SUNSHINE AND FELLOWSHIP CONFERENCE CENTER)
3575 Valley Road
Liberty Corner, New Jersey 07938

General Information A well-balanced program seeking to meet the spiritual and physical needs of young and old participants by providing the study of God's word, rest, and recreation. Owned by Fellowship Deaconry, Inc. Affiliated with Christian Camping International. Located 40 miles southwest of New York City on 120 acres. Features include location surrounded by beautiful, historic Watchung Mountains; Christ-centered atmosphere; daily Bible study and dynamic speakers; Christian concerts; swimming, miniature golf, and other sports.

Profile of Summer Employees Requires nonsmokers.

Employment Information Openings are from June 20 to September 1. Christmas break, year-round positions also offered. Jobs available: 10 *counselors* at $95–$180 per week; 10 *counselors-in-training* at $65–$90 per week; 2 *kitchen crew (day camp)* at $65–$120 per week; 2 *housekeeping staff* at $45–$180 per week; 5 *waitresses* at $45–$180 per week; 1 *pantry person* at $60–$180 per week; 5 *lifeguards* with Red Cross advanced lifesaving certificate at $120–$180 per week.

Benefits Preemployment training, on-the-job training, on-site room and board, laundry facilities.

Contact Applicant should send resume, write for application, or call for information by May 15 to Rita Krohn, Directing Deaconess, Fellowship Deaconry, Inc. (Day Camp Sunshine and Fellowship Conference Center), Department SED, P.O. Box 204, Liberty Corner, New Jersey 07938; 908-647-1777.

We offer the opportunity for good Christian fellowship, friendship, and growth.

THE GREAT GORGE RESORT/ACTION PARK
Box 848
McAfee, New Jersey 07428

General Information Resort and theme park for the general public with a winter ski area. Established 1966. Affiliated with United Ski Areas of America. Located 50 miles west of New York City on 600 acres. Features include over 70 rides and attractions; health spa; restaurants and hotel complex; ethnic festivals; location in the Appalachian Mountains; golf and tennis.

Profile of Summer Employees Total number 2,000; average age 19. Employees are 20% minorities, 50% high school students, 25% college students, 5% retirees, 20% international, 80% local residents.

Employment Information Openings are from May 30 to September 15. Spring break, winter break, Christmas break, year-round positions also offered. College credit possible. Jobs available: 50 *ride attendants* at $175–$200 per week; 50 *food and beverage servers* at $175–$200 per week; 30 *maintenance workers* at $240–$300 per week; 10 *mechanics* with experience at $240–$300 per week; 50 *lifeguards* with lifesaving certificate at $240–$300 per week; *retail clerks* at $175–$250 per week; *housekeepers* at $175–$250 per week; *security guards* at $175–$250 per week; *EMTs* at $175–$250 per week; *cooks* at $175–$250 per week; *landscapers* at $175–$250 per week. International students encouraged to apply.

Benefits Preemployment training, on-the-job training, formal ongoing training, on-site room and board at $50 per week, free use of facilities, food discounts, bonuses, special employee events, softball games, transportation to laundry, shopping, etc.

Contact Applicant should write for application by May 1 to Personnel Office, VVRA, The Great Gorge Resort/Action Park, Department SED, Box 848, McAfee, New Jersey 07428; 201-827-2000.

NATIONAL PARK SERVICE

Contact Applicant should write for application (must be 18 by May 13; U.S. citizenship required) to Regional Office of the National Park Service, North Atlantic Region, National Park Service, 15 State Street, Boston, Massachusetts 02109.

Jobs located in New Jersey at the following facilities: Gateway/Sandy Hook, Morristown. Also see District of Columbia listing.

NEW JERSEY 4–H CAMPS
50 Nielson Road, RD 6, Box 250
Sussex, New Jersey 07461

General Information Two residential camp facilities with a total weekly capacity of 300 campers ages 9–13. Established 1951. Owned by Rutgers University. Operated by Rutgers Cooperative Extension System. Located 70 miles northwest of New York City on 700 acres. Features include horseback riding; farm animals (working farm); 6-acre lake; proximity to Stokes State Forest, High Point State Park, and the Delaware River.

Profile of Summer Employees Total number 30; average age 19. Employees are 60% female, 10% minorities, 35% high school students, 35% college students, 10% international, 10% local residents. Prefers nonsmokers.

Employment Information Openings are from June 20 to August 20. College credit possible. Jobs available: 2 *waterfront supervisors* with lifeguard certification (minimum age 18) at $210–$240 per week; 4 *lifeguards* with lifeguard certification at $180–$210 per week; 2 *boating/canoeing instructors* with lifeguard certification and boating experience (minimum age 18) at $180–$210 per week; 2 *chefs* with kitchen, cooking, ordering, and supervisory experience at $210–$240 per week; 2 *cooks* with kitchen and cooking experience at $180–$210 per week; 2 *assistant cooks* with kitchen experience at $160–$180 per week; 2 *health directors* with at least Red Cross advanced first aid and CPR certification (minimum age 18) at $250–$325 per week; 2 *horseback-riding instructors* with horseback-riding experience (minimum age 18) at $180–$210 per week; 2 *animal-science instructors* with experience working with farm animals (minimum age 18) at $180–$210 per week;

2 *nature instructors* with a minimum age of 18 at $180–$210 per week; 1 *hiking/camping instructor* with Red Cross standard first aid and CPR certification (minimum age 18) at $180–$210 per week; 1 *fishing instructor* with a minimum age of 18 at $180–$210 per week; 2 *crafts shop managers* with experience maintaining inventories (minimum age 18) at $180–$210 per week; 1 *horse-care person* with experience taking care of horses at $160–$180 per week. International students encouraged to apply.

Benefits Preemployment training, on-the-job training, formal ongoing training, on-site room and board at no charge, laundry facilities, first aid training, 1½ days off each week, end-of-season bonus possible.

Contact Applicant should send resume, write for application, or call for information by June 15 to Kevin Mitchell, Director, 4–H Outdoor Education Centers, New Jersey 4–H Camps, Department SED, 50 Nielson Road, Sussex, New Jersey 07461; 201-875-4715, fax 201-875-1289.

The New Jersey 4-H Camps consist of two facilities. The Lindley G. Look 4-H Camp is located in Stokes State Forest and is situated on 100 wooded acres. The Beemerville 4-H Camp is situated on 600 acres on the former site of the Rutgers University dairy farm. Staff quarters are in a separate building from the camper's quarters. Volunteer counselors supervise the camper's quarters.

SOMERSET COUNTY PARK COMMISSION ENVIRONMENTAL EDUCATION CENTER
190 Lord Stirling Road
Basking Ridge, New Jersey 07920

General Information Environmental educational programs for children, adults, and families. Established 1970. Owned by Somerset County Park Commission. Located 35 miles west of New York City on 430 acres. Features include location within the Great Swamp Basin; 8½ miles of trails and boardwalk; 18,000 square-foot education building.

Profile of Summer Employees Total number 5; average age 20. Employees are 50% female, 100% college students, 80% local residents. Prefers nonsmokers.

Employment Information Openings are from June 16 to August 31. Year-round positions also offered. Jobs available: 5 *seasonal naturalists* with college upperclassman or college graduate status at $240 per week.

Benefits On-the-job training.

Contact Applicant should send resume to Ross A. Zito, Supervisor, Somerset County Park Commission Environmental Education Center, Department SED, 190 Lord Stirling Road, Basking Ridge, New Jersey 07920; 908-766-2489.

Personal interview required and local college students encouraged to apply. Extensive opportunities for teaching environmental programs to children. Several permanent staff members started here as interns.

CITY OF WILDWOOD
4400 New Jersey Avenue
Wildwood, New Jersey 08260

General Information Municipal government serving the needs of the people of Wildwood. Established 1912. Operated by John Nestor. Affiliated with British Universities North America Club, Council on International Educational Exchange. Located 40 miles north of Atlantic City. Features include location on Atlantic Ocean; world's largest, safest beach; 2½ miles of world famous boardwalk with more amusement rides than Disneyworld; inland waterways, great for water sports.

Profile of Summer Employees Total number 200. Employees are 20% female, 50% minorities, 30% high school students, 65% college students, 5% retirees, 5% international, 70% local residents.

Employment Information Openings are from May 1 to September 1. Jobs available: 80 *lifeguards* with ability to pass lifeguard test; 30 *laborers;* 6 *truck drivers* with valid driver's license; 10 *EMTs* with certification; 6 *equipment operators* with valid driver's license; 10 *recreation attendants;* 8 *meter maids* with a minimum age of 18; 50 *police officers* with a major in criminal justice; 10 *parking lot attendants;* 5 *inspectors* with some public relations experience. International students encouraged to apply.

Benefits On-the-job training.

Contact Applicant should send resume, write for application, or apply in person by July 30 to John Nestor, Personnel Officer, City of Wildwood, Department SED, 4400 New Jersey Avenue, Wildwood, New Jersey 08260; 609-522-2444 Ext. 248, fax 609-522-9239.

Wages range from $4.50 to $7.50 an hour depending on position. (Please note that lifeguards are paid $48 per day.)

New Mexico

BRUSH RANCH CAMPS FOR GIRLS AND BOYS
Tererro, New Mexico 87573

General Information Residential camp serving 80 girls, ages 8–16, and 50 boys, ages 8–14, by providing camp programs in a noncompetitive atmosphere. Established 1957. Owned by Scott and Kay Rice. Affiliated with American Camping Association, Western Association of Independent Camps, Camp Horsemanship Association. Located 35 miles east of Santa Fe on 290 acres. Features include beautiful environment; well-maintained camp and grounds; log cabins and buildings in the mountains.

Profile of Summer Employees Total number 49; average age 23. Employees are 25% female, 1% high school students, 90% college students, 1% local residents. Prefers nonsmokers.

Employment Information Openings are from June 16 to August 15. College credit possible. Jobs available: 2 *dance instructors* at $850–$1000 per season; 2 *drama instructors* at $900–$2500 per season; 1 *music instructor* at $850–$950 per season; 3 *art instructors* at $850–$950 per season; 3 *swimming instructors* with WSI certificate at $850–$950 per season; 2 *fencing instructors* at $850–$950 per season; 2 *tennis instructors* at $850–$950 per season; 2 *riding instructors (English style)* at $850–$1000 per season; 2 *riding instruc-*

tors *(Western style)* at \$850–\$1000 per season; 1 *shooting instructor* at \$850–\$950 per season; 3 *ropes challenge-course instructors* with experience and certification at \$850–\$1500 per season; 2 *nature instructors* at \$850–\$950 per season; 1 *archery instructor* at \$850–\$950 per season; 1 *fishing instructor* with fly-fishing experience at \$850–\$950 per season. International students encouraged to apply.

Benefits Preemployment training, on-the-job training, on-site room and board at no charge, travel reimbursement, cost-sharing or full tuition of training courses after first summer.

Contact Applicant should send resume, write for application, or call for information by May 10 to Scott Rice, Owner/Director, Brush Ranch Camps for Girls and Boys, Department SED, P.O. Box 5759, Santa Fe, New Mexico 87502-5759; 505-757-8821.

At Brush Ranch Camps, one of our primary goals is to see that each camper and staff member feels secure and loved within our community. Our camp is small enough for us to know the campers and staff well, yet large enough for children and staff members from different backgrounds to feel right at home. We welcome children and staff members of all races, creeds, and national origins who wish to explore the wonders of nature in our beautiful mountain setting.

CAMP MARY WHITE
Mayhill, New Mexico 88339

General Information Residential camp for Girl Scouts and non-Girl-Scouts from the third grade. Established 1927. Owned by Girl Scouts. Operated by Zia Girl Scout Council. Affiliated with American Camping Association. Closest major city is Alamogordo. Features include primitive outdoor living; nature at its best; camp ranger living on site; location 8,000 feet in the Sacramento Mountains.

Profile of Summer Employees Total number 25; average age 23. Employees are 95% female, 40% minorities, 2% high school students, 98% college students. Prefers nonsmokers.

Employment Information Openings are from June 2 to August 3. College credit possible. International students encouraged to apply.

Benefits Preemployment training, on-the-job training, formal ongoing training, on-site room and board at no charge, laundry facilities, health insurance.

Contact Applicant should send resume, write for application, call for information, or apply in person to Linda Bentley, Camping Services Coordinator, Camp Mary White, Department SED, Drawer K, Artesia, New Mexico 88211; 505-746-9846.

GLORIETA BAPTIST CONFERENCE CENTER
Glorieta, New Mexico 87535

General Information Provides support facilities and services for approximately 28,000 guests attending summer conferences. Established 1952. Owned by The Sunday School Board of the Southern Baptist Convention. Located 18 miles east of Santa Fe on 2,271 acres. Features include accommodation of 3,000 guests; 37,530 square feet of conference space; tennis courts, hiking, and recreation fields; location in the Sangre de Cristo Mountains at 7,500-foot elevation.

Profile of Summer Employees   Total number 238; average age 21. Employees are 60% female, 15% minorities, 35% high school students, 60% college students, 5% retirees, 2% international, 18% local residents.

Employment Information   Openings are from May 24 to August 22. Year-round positions also offered. College credit possible. Jobs available: 1 *recreation director;* 8 *recreation workers;* 5 *sound and lighting technicians;* 12 *day-camp workers;* 25 *preschool workers;* 14 *chuckwagon workers;* 48 *food-service workers;* 47 *housekeepers;* 26 *conference support workers;* 7 *preschool faculty;* 10 *business-section workers;* 1 *tape duplicator;* 11 *media/ library workers;* 7 *guest relations workers;* 2 *security workers;* 9 *maintenance/grounds workers;* 1 *vending route worker;* 1 *money-room clerk;* 1 *bike-shop technician;* 2 *post office clerks;* 1 *religious emphasis coordinator;* 1 *music coordinator;* 1 *special activities coordinator;* 2 *residence-hall coordinators;* 4 *registered nurses.* International students encouraged to apply.

Benefits   On-the-job training, on-site room and board, travel reimbursement, a wide range of activities available during off duty hours including worship, discipleship opportunities, recreation, camp-outs, and many special events, pay rate of $4.47 per hour and up.

Contact   Applicant should write for application, call for information, or apply in person by March 1 to Glenn Compton, Personnel Services Administrator, Glorieta Baptist Conference Center, Department SED, P.O. Box 8, Glorieta, New Mexico 87535; 505-757-6161, fax 505-757-6149.

Employment at Glorieta is a wonderful opportunity to grow spiritually and to make new friends. The rewards are numerous, and year after year employees return to work here. All applicants must be at least 17 years old by May 24. Some positions must be filled with Southern Baptists.

NATIONAL PARK SERVICE

Contact   Applicant should write for application (must be 18 by May 13; U.S. citizenship required) to Regional Office of the National Park Service, Southwest Region, National Park Service, P.O. Box 728, Santa Fe, New Mexico 87501.

Jobs located in New Mexico at the following facility: Chaco Culture National Historic Park. Also see District of Columbia listing.

PHILMONT SCOUT RANCH
Cimarron, New Mexico 87714

General Information   Camp and family conference center offering mountain backpacking with a wide variety of outdoor and historical experiences. Established 1938. Owned by Boy Scouts of America. Affiliated with American Camping Association. Located 200 miles northeast of Albuquerque on 137,493 acres. Features include mountain/high-country location, elevation from 6,500 feet to 12,441 feet; wilderness atmosphere; rugged, challenging, positive team-building experiences; fellowship with people from throughout the U.S. and other countries; conference facilities for the whole family in a friendly, relaxed atmosphere.

Profile of Summer Employees Total number 728; average age 21. Employees are 25% female, 7% high school students, 82% college students, 1% international, 3% local residents. Prefers nonsmokers.

Employment Information Openings are from May 25 to August 25. Winter break positions also offered. College credit possible. Jobs available: *bookkeeping clerk, clerk/typists; business and food services staff: production manager, cook, assistant cook, backcountry cook, food services manager, food services assistant manager, and food services staff; commissary staff: manager, backcountry manager, and clerk; truck driver* with experience driving a two-ton truck over dirt roads (minimum age 21); *trading post managers for headquarters, training center, and backcountry; warehouse manager; snack bar clerks; quartermaster staff: equipment and tent repair manager, tent repair helper, warehouse clerk; custodial staff: custodian, housekeeper/laundress, and lawn maintenance personnel; seasonal registrar for the camp; security supervisor and staff; conservation staff: director of conservation, associate director of conservation, conservation crew foreman, trail crew foreman, assistant trail crew foreman, trail construction supervisor, conservation staff; logistic services manager, assistant manager, and staff; transportation manager; headquarters activities manager and staff; headquarters services manager, assistant manager, and staff; postmaster; news and information staff: manager, assistant manager, photo lab manager, and photographer; medical/health lodge staff: administrator, medics, medical secretary, nurse, and health lodge drivers; headquarters maintenance staff; chief ranger, associate chief ranger, Rayado Trek coordinator, Mountain Trek coordinator, training rangers, and approximately 200 rangers; backcountry manager; camp directors; program counselors* with knowledge of and experience in one or more of the following: adobe construction, archeology, black powder weapons, blacksmithing, burro packing and racing, challenge events, environmental ecology and nature studies, fishing and fly-tying, gold mining and panning, Indian ethnology, logging skills, mountain living and homesteading, no-trace camping, riflery, rock-climbing, shotgun instruction, trapping, Western lore; *museum receptionist and sales clerks; ranch staff: horsemen and wranglers; training center administrative staff; support services manager and staff; tent city manager and assistant manager; family programs manager and assistant manager, nursery leader, leaders and assistant leaders for activities for various age groups from toddlers to adults; arts and crafts manager and staff; Rocky Mountain Scout Camp director, scout master, and staff.* International students encouraged to apply.

Benefits Preemployment training, on-the-job training, formal ongoing training, on-site room and board at no charge, laundry facilities, health insurance.

Contact Applicant should write for application or call for information by May 30 (most hiring takes place by April 1) to Seasonal Personnel, Philmont Scout Ranch, Department SED, Cimarron, New Mexico 87714; 505-376-2281.

A high volume of people are spread out on a large area of land to preserve a wilderness atmosphere. Backpackers stay for twelve days; we will host about 18,000 in 1991. Conference center participants stay for ten 1-week sessions, and about 4,300 will attend in the summer of 1991.

New York

ADIRONDACK WOODCRAFT CAMPS
Rondaxe Road, P.O. Box 219
Old Forge, New York 13420

General Information   Residential, coeducational camp and environmental education center offering teaching, learning, and outdoor activities. Established 1923. Owned by The Leach Family. Located 60 miles north of Utica on 400 acres. Features include 2 private lakes and 1½ miles of riverfront; location in the Adirondacks; one of the oldest camps in the United States; location surrounded by hundreds of miles of prime hiking and canoeing routes.

Profile of Summer Employees   Total number 30; average age 22. Employees are 30% female, 10% high school students, 55% college students, 20% international, 15% local residents. Prefers nonsmokers.

Employment Information   Openings are from May 3 to August 30. Jobs available: 16 *counselors* with experience working with children at $850–$1200 per season; 2 *kitchen assistants* at $110–$130 per week; 1 *office assistant* with typing, computer, and good communications skills at $120–$150 per week; 2 *wilderness trip leaders* with trip leading experience at $1000–$1400 per season; 2 *waterfront staff* with lifeguarding/BLS certificate at $900–$1400 per season. International students encouraged to apply.

Benefits   Preemployment training, on-the-job training, on-site room and board, laundry facilities, tuition reimbursement.

Contact   Applicant should send resume, write for application, or call for information by May 1 to Chris Clemans, Program Director, Adirondack Woodcraft Camps, Department SED, P.O. Box 219, Old Forge, New York 13420; 315-369-6031.

Adirondack Woodcraft Camp functions as an environmental education center during the months of May and June.

AMERICAN CAMPING ASSOCIATION
12 West 31st Street
New York, New York 10001

General Information   Employment clearinghouse for camps that offers a free referral service for college students and faculty, teachers, and school administrators who desire a summer job outdoors.

Profile of Summer Employees   Employees are 50% female, 10% minorities, 90% college students, 2% retirees. Prefers nonsmokers.

Employment Information   Openings are from June 15 to August 25. College credit possible. Jobs available: *drama staff; music staff; team sports staff; individual sports staff; kitchen staff; registered nurse; medical doctor; EMT; general counselors; land and water sports staff; visual and performing arts staff; secretarial staff; maintenance staff.*

Benefits   Preemployment training, on-the-job training, formal ongoing training, on-site room and board, laundry facilities, travel reimbursement, end-of-season bonus possible.

Contact   Applicant should send resume, write for application, call for information, or apply in person by June to Adele A. Selik, Director of Placement Services, American Camping Association, Department SED, 12 West 31st Street, New York, New York 10001; 800-777-2267, fax 212-594-1684.

We are a clearinghouse for over 300 camps in the Northeast. One employment application is put on file for all camp directors to see and use. College students are urged to apply regardless of their major field of study. Prior certifications are not necessary.

ANTONIO'S RESORT
Dale Lane
Elka Park, New York 12427

General Information Family resort providing a variety of activities for guests. Established 1973. Owned by Nat Manzella. Located 40 miles south of Albany on 7 acres. Features include indoor/outdoor pools, jacuzzi, and steam showers; indoor/outdoor sports (tennis); restaurant/lounge; location convenient to nearby downhill and cross-country skiing areas, hiking, horseback riding, festivals, and various other attractions.

Profile of Summer Employees Total number 35; average age 22. Prefers nonsmokers.

Employment Information Openings are from May to October. Spring break, winter break, Christmas break, year-round positions also offered. College credit possible. Jobs available: 2 *social directors* with knowledge of sports and social games at $140 per week; 2 *child counselors* with knowledge of sports and social games at $140 per week; 2 *pool attendants* with junior Red Cross certificate at $205 per week; 3 *maintenance/grounds persons* at $205 per week; 2 *office personnel* at $205 per week; 4 *chambermaids* at $140 per week; 1 *laundry person/floater* at $205 per week; 1 *cocktail waitress* at $140 per week; 6 *waiters/waitresses* at $140 per week; 2 *subwaitresses* at $140 per week; 5 *kitchen helpers* at $205 per week; 2 *dish and pot washers* at $205 per week; 1 *floater* at $205 per week; 1 *host/office person* at $205 per week. International students encouraged to apply.

Benefits On-the-job training, on-site room and board at $67 per week, end-of-season bonus.

Contact Applicant should send resume, write for application, or call for information to Cathy Manzella, Receptionist, Personnel, Antonio's Resort, Dale Lane, Elka Park, New York 12427; 518-589-5197.

BROOKWOOD CAMPS
Route 32
Glen Spey, New York 12737

General Information Gives 300 boys and girls from around the United States and abroad a summer camp experience filled with fun, a healthful environment, and skill development. Established 1938. Owned by Kenro, Inc. Operated by Ken Fielder. Affiliated with American Camping Association, New York State Camp Directors' Association, Association of Private Camps. Located 80 miles northwest of New York City. Features include a majestic 5-mile lake; superior athletics facilities (new complex); beautiful grounds; large, mature staff; location in the tri-state region.

Profile of Summer Employees Total number 120; average age 23. Employees are 50% female. Requires nonsmokers.

Employment Information Openings are from June 22 to August 22. Year-round positions also offered. College credit possible. Jobs available: 65 *general counselors* at $800–$1800 per season; 20 *group leaders* with a minimum age of 25 at $1500–$3000 per season; 10 *tennis instructors* at $800–$2000 per season; 6 *gymnastics instructors* at $800–$2000 per season; 18 *swimming instructors* with WSI, CPR, and lifeguard certification at $1000–$2500 per season; 4 *archery instructors* at $800–$2000 per season; 4 *golf instructors* at $800–$2000 per season; 6 *horseback-riding instructors* at $800–$2000 per season; 12 *sailing/canoeing instructors* with small crafts certificate at $800–$2000 per season; 10 *waterskiing/windsurfing instructors* at $800–$2000 per season; 4 *arts and crafts instructors* at $800–$2000 per season; 3 *nurses* with RN license (minimum age 21) at $800–$2000 per season; 4 *dramatics instructors* at $800–$2000 per season; 4 *dance instructors* at $800–$2000 per season; 4 *photography instructors* at $800–$2000 per season. International students encouraged to apply.

Benefits Preemployment training, on-the-job training, formal ongoing training, on-site room and board, laundry facilities, travel reimbursement, health insurance, tuition reimbursement, full days off.

Contact Applicant should send resume, write for application, call for information, or apply in person by June 20 to Ken Fiedler, Director, Brookwood Camps, Department SED, 3242 Judith Lane, Oceanside, New York 11572; 516-764-2112.

At Brookwood Camps we look for counselors who love children, sports, and the outdoors. We offer pre- and post-season work opportunities, as well as an incentive recruiting program for campers and staff. (Please note that unless otherwise specified, the minimum age for all positions detailed in this listing is 19.)

BUCK'S ROCK CAMP
193 North Detroit Avenue
North Massapequa, New York 11758

General Information A creative arts camp primarily devoted to the development of talents and the potential of boys and girls ages 11–16. Established 1942. Owned by Stanley K. Simon and Ed Budd. Operated by Ron Danzig. Affiliated with American Camping Association, Connecticut Camping Association. Located 75 miles northwest of New York City on 165 acres. Features include glass-blowing; silversmithing; silk screening; photography; horseback riding; theater, dance, and music.

Profile of Summer Employees Total number 170; average age 28. Employees are 50% female, 10% minorities, 76% college students, 10% international, 5% local residents. Prefers nonsmokers.

Employment Information Openings are from June 20 to August 20. Jobs available: *fine arts instructor; woodworking instructor; weaving instructor; photography instructor; ceramics instructor; sewing instructor; silversmithing instructor; creative writing instructor; commercial art instructor; printing instructor; stage design and construction personnel; music instructor; videotaping instructor; sports instructor; farming instructor; waterfront staff; computer science instructor; kitchen staff; dining room personnel; maintenance staff; guidance counselors; registered nurses.* International students encouraged to apply.

Benefits On-the-job training, formal ongoing training, on-site room and board at no charge, laundry facilities, health insurance.

Contact Applicant should write for application or call for information by December to Stan Simon, Director, Buck's Rock Camp, Department SED, 193 North Detroit Avenue, North Massapequa, New York 11758; 516-293-8711.

Buck's Rock is one of the best known private camps in the country, and the educational work we are doing has attracted excellent teachers who have joined our staff. We have openings for 40 graduate artists, teachers, and craft workers (the minimum age is 21).

CAMP BACO FOR BOYS/CAMP CHE–NA–WAH FOR GIRLS
Route 28N
Minerva, New York 12851

General Information Residential camp serving 160 girls and 190 boys in a traditional eight-week program. Located 225 miles north of New York City on 100 acres. Features include location in the beautiful Adirondack Mountains; separate activity programs for boys and girls.

Profile of Summer Employees Total number 110; average age 19. Employees are 20% high school students, 80% college students. Prefers nonsmokers.

Employment Information Openings are from June 27 to August 22. College credit possible. Jobs available: 4 *swimming instructors* with WSI, LGT, and BLS certification at $800–$1500 per season; 3 *tennis instructors* with college team play or coaching experience at $800–$1500 per season; 1 *gymnastics instructor* with college team and teaching experience at $800–$1500 per season; 2 *music instructors* with ability to accompany on piano at $800–$1500 per season; 2 *ceramics instructors* at $800–$1500 per season; 2 *sailing/windsurfing instructors* with LGT, BLS, and American Red Cross small crafts instructor certification at $800–$1500 per season; 2 *canoeing instructors* with LGT, BLS, and American Red Cross small crafts instructor certification at $800–$1500 per season; *basketball instructor* with team play experience at $800–$1500 per season; *soccer instructor* at $800–$1500 per season; *baseball/softball instructor* at $800–$1500 per season; *instructors (various sports)* at $800–$1500 per season; *hiking/pioneering instructor* with first aid or CPR certification at $800–$1500 per season.

Benefits On-the-job training, formal ongoing training, on-site room and board at no charge, laundry facilities.

Contact Applicant should send resume, write for application, or call for information by May 15 to Bob Wortman, Director, Camp Baco for Boys/Camp Che–Na–Wah for Girls, Department SED, 80 Neptune Avenue, Woodmere, New York 11598; 516-374-7757, fax 516-295-1377.

> *Come experience our warm, family atmosphere and the many opportunities we provide for coeducational socialization and friendship.*

CAMP ECHO LAKE
Warrensberg, New York 12885

General Information Coeducational summer program for children ages 7–16 based on one 8-week session. Established 1946. Owned by Morry, Amy, George, and Tony Stein. Affiliated with American Camping Association. Located 200 miles north of New York City on 150 acres. Features include sprawling campus in a completely wooded setting; spring-fed lake; tennis courts (12 hard surface, 4 clay, 9 lighted); numerous high-quality sports fields; excellent on-site trip program; modern cabins.

Profile of Summer Employees Total number 180; average age 21. Employees are 45% female, 5% high school students, 75% college students, 15% international, 5% local residents. Requires nonsmokers.

Employment Information Openings are from June 16 to August 20. College credit possible. Jobs available: 2 *group leaders* with leadership experience at $1100 per season; 20 *cabin specialists* with a love of working with children at $750 per season; 5 *waterfront* *positions* with CPR and lifeguard certificate at $900 per season; 2 *gymnastics instructors* at $900 per season; 8 *tennis instructors* with experience teaching tennis at $1000 per season; 1 *woodshop director* with experience teaching woodshop at $900 per season; 8 *athletics instructors* with experience teaching sports at $900 per season; 2 *video instructors* with teaching experience at $900 per season; *food-service person* with experience at $150–$200 per week. International students encouraged to apply.

Benefits Preemployment training, on-the-job training, on-site room and board at no charge, laundry facilities, travel reimbursement, health insurance, internships.

Contact Applicant should send resume, write for application, or call for information by April 1 to Dawn Ewing, Staff Recruiter, Camp Echo Lake, Department SED, 221 East Hartsdale Avenue, Hartsdale, New York 10530; 914-472-5858, fax 914-472-9142.

Camp Echo Lake is searching for staff members who love to laugh, spend time with kids, are not afraid of a challenge, and want to have a summer like they've never had before.

CAMP HENRY KAUFMANN
Route 292
Holmes, New York 12531

General Information Girl Scout camp in the Catskills serving girls ages 7–15 from the five boroughs of New York City. Established 1953. Owned by Girl Scout Council of Greater New York. Affiliated with American Camping Association. Located 70 miles north of New York City on 425 acres. Features include rolling hills; lake; pool; farm; winding trails; breathtaking surroundings.

Profile of Summer Employees Total number 40; average age 20. Employees are 30% minorities, 20% high school students, 60% college students, 30% international, 10% local residents.

Employment Information Openings are from June 25 to August 27. College credit possible. Jobs available: 1 *waterfront director* with first aid, CPR, and WSI certificates (minimum age 21) at $2500–$3500 per season; 3 *boating/swimming instructors* with lifeguard, advanced lifesaving, and CPR certificates at $1800–$2500 per season; 1 *business manager* with retail or math background and driver's license (minimum age 21) at $1800–$2000 per season; 4 *unit leaders* with camp and child-care experience (minimum age 21) at $1000–$1200 per season; 4 *assistant unit leaders* with camp and child-care experience (minimum age 18) at $900–$1000 per season; 8 *counselors* with camp and child-care experience (minimum age 18) at $800–$1000 per season; 4 *program specialists* with drama, nature, sports, and arts experience at $1000–$1500 per season; 1 *assistant camp director* with camp employment experience (minimum age 21) at $1800–$2000 per season; 2 *cooks* with cafeteria, catering, large group, and cooking experience at $2500–$3800 per season; 3 *kitchen aides* at $700–$900 per season; 1 *counselor-in-training director* with camp employment experience (minimum age 21) at $1000–$1200 per season; 1 *nurse* with EMT, LPN, or RN license plus first aid and CPR certificates at $3000–$3500 per season; 4 *interns* at $700 per season. International students encouraged to apply.

Benefits Preemployment training, on-the-job training, on-site room and board at no charge, laundry facilities, health insurance.

Contact Applicant should send resume, write for application, or call for information by May 15 to Denise DeYonker, Outdoor Program Administrator, Camp Henry Kaufmann, 43 West 23rd Street, New York, New York 10010; 212-645-4000.

Employees at Camp Henry Kaufman have the opportunity to meet people from all over the United States as well as from foreign countries. In addition, staff members have the chance to develop and build transferable skills.

CAMP JEANNE D'ARC
Narrows Road
Merrill, New York 12955

General Information Adirondack camp for 120 girls ages 6–17 on 14-mile, crystal-clear lake. Established 1922. Owned by Fran and Joe McIntyre. Affiliated with American Camping Association, New York State Camp Directors' Association, Camp Directors' Roundtable. Located 30 miles west of Plattsburgh on 230 acres. Features include two-story Swiss chalet-type cabins with fireplace and living room; indoor plumbing and electricity; sailing and waterskiing; riding, tennis; creative activities; optional outdoor camping.

Profile of Summer Employees Total number 50; average age 22. Employees are 100% female, 10% minorities, 10% high school students, 65% college students, 10% international, 15% local residents. Prefers nonsmokers.

Employment Information Openings are from June 25 to August 19. Jobs available: *riding instructor* at $1000–$1200 per season; *waterskiing instructor* at $1000–$1200 per season; *riflery instructor* at $1000–$1200 per season; *tennis instructor* at $1000–$1200 per season; *canoeing instructor* at $1000–$1200 per season; *sailing instructor* at $1000–$1200 per season; *music/guitar instructor* at $1000–$1200 per season; *dance instructor* at $1000–$1200 per season; *drama instructor* at $1000–$1200 per season; *arts and crafts instructor* at $1000–$1200 per season; *outdoor-camping counselor* at $1000–$1200 per season. International students encouraged to apply.

Benefits Preemployment training, on-the-job training, laundry facilities, travel reimbursement.

Contact Applicant should send resume, write for application, call for information, or apply in person by June 15 to Joseph E. McIntyre, Director, Camp Jeanne D'Arc, 422 Peregrine Drive, Indialantic, Florida 32903; 800-969-2532, fax 407-773-9701.

We offer a traditional camp program in a Catholic/Christian environment, emphasizing activities that have life-long values. Campers and counselors have come from forty-eight states and more than thirty foreign countries to take part in the four program areas we offer: aquatics, land sports, creative activities, and/or outdoor camping.

CAMP LOYALTOWN–AHRC
Glen Avenue
Hunter, New York 12442

General Information Summer residential camp for mentally retarded children and adults. Established 1974. Owned by Camp Loyaltown, Inc. Operated by Association for the Help of Retarded Children (Nassau County Chapter). Located 150 miles north of New York City on 240 acres. Features include location in the Catskill Mountains resort area; peaceful, idyllic setting; caring family atmosphere; varied daily activities.

Profile of Summer Employees Total number 125; average age 20. Employees are 50% female, 3% high school students, 90% college students, 30% international. Prefers nonsmokers.

Employment Information Openings are from June to August. College credit possible. Jobs available: 1 *waterfront director* with WSI certificate at $1500–$1900 per season; 4 *lifeguards* with lifeguard certification at $1400–$1600 per season; 80 *cabin counselors* with major in special education or related fields at $1100–$1500 per season; 2 *arts and crafts instructors* with knowledge of skill levels of mentally retarded persons at $1300–$1500 per season; 6 *kitchen assistants* at $1200–$1500 per season; 4 *office staff* with knowledge of office procedures, typing, and clerical duties at $1200–$1600 per season; 4 *cooks* with good experience in ordering plus preparing and serving quantity and quality meals; 1 *dance instructor* with knowledge of skill levels of mentally retarded persons at $1300–$1500 per season; 1 *drama instructor* with knowledge of skill levels of mentally retarded persons at $1300–$1500 per season; 1 *music instructor* with knowledge of skill levels of mentally retarded persons at $1300–$1500 per season; 1 *nature instructor* with knowledge of skill levels of mentally retarded persons at $1300–$1500 per season; 1 *cooking instructor* with knowledge of skill levels of mentally retarded persons at $1300–$1500 per season; 1 *sewing instructor* with knowledge of skill levels of mentally retarded persons at $1300–$1500 per season; 1 *athletics instructor* with knowledge of skill levels of mentally retarded persons at $1300–$1500 per season; 1 *woodshop instructor* with knowledge of skill levels of mentally retarded persons at $1300–$1500 per season; 1 *recreation instructor* with knowledge of skill levels of mentally retarded persons at $1300–$1500 per season; 1 *ceramics instructor* with knowledge of skill levels of mentally retarded persons at $1300–$1500 per season.

Benefits Preemployment training, on-the-job training, formal ongoing training, on-site room and board at no charge, laundry facilities.

Contact Applicant should write for application by May to Paul H. Cullen, Director of Camping, Camp Loyaltown–AHRC, 189 Wheatley Road, Brookville, New York 11545; 516-626-1000, fax 516-626-1493.

Working at Camp Loyaltown gives students an exceptional learning experience and provides the opportunity to decide if they want careers working in service fields for the handicapped. We need staff members who want to work with and share their lives with mentally handicapped campers, both children and adults. (Please note that international students who wish to apply for employment must do so through an agency such as Camp America or Bunacamp.)

CAMP MOGISCA
P.O. Box 209
Glen Spey, New York 12737

General Information Residential camp serving 200 girls ages 6–17 weekly with a general program that includes canoeing and horseback riding. Established 1921. Owned by Morris Area Girl Scout Council. Affiliated with American Camping Association. Located 70 miles northwest of New York City on 900 acres. Features include location that borders the Delaware River; pool and lake; tennis court; stable and 2 riding rings; beautiful wooded setting; modern facilities.

Profile of Summer Employees Total number 35; average age 21. Employees are 92% female, 10% minorities, 80% college students, 2% retirees, 70% international, 30% local residents. Prefers nonsmokers.

Employment Information Openings are from June 19 to August 21. College credit possible. Jobs available: 1 *director* with experience (minimum age 25) at $4000–$4300 per season; 1 *program director* with experience (minimum age 21) at $1800–$2000 per season;

1 *business manager* with a minimum age of 21 at $2200–$2600 per season; 1 *health supervisor* with RN or EMT license at $3200–$3600 per season; 1 *cook* at $3200–$3800 per season; 5 *riding staff* at $1200–$2200 per season; 1 *waterfront director* with WSI, canoe instructor, and lifeguard certification at $2400–$3000 per season; 6 *waterfront staff* with Red Cross certification at $1200–$2400 per season; 1 *environmentalist* at $1200–$2000 per season; 20 *unit staff* at $1000–$1800 per season.

Benefits Preemployment training, on-the-job training, on-site room and board at no charge, laundry facilities, health insurance, three free weekends.

Contact Applicant should send resume, write for application, call for information, or apply in person by May 15 to Janet Thomas, Director of Program and Properties, Camp Mogisca, Department SED, 1579 Sussex Turnpike, Randolph, New Jersey 06789-1811; 201-927-7722, fax 201-927-7683.

International students who wish to apply for employment must do so through Camp America.

CAMP NORTHWOOD
RD 1
Remsen, New York 13438

General Information Residential camp serving highly functional learning disabled (ADD) children ages 8–18 during a seven-week session. Established 1976. Owned by Gordon and Donna Felt. Affiliated with American Camping Association, American Waterskiing Association. Located 220 miles northwest of New York City on 15 acres. Features include highly professional staff; 2:1 camper-counselor ratio; outstanding facilities; noncompetitive environment; waterskiing; location next to Adirondack State Park.

Profile of Summer Employees Total number 70; average age 22. Employees are 45% female, 10% minorities, 20% college students, 20% international, 15% local residents. Prefers nonsmokers.

Employment Information Openings are from June 28 to August 22. College credit possible. Jobs available: 12 *lifeguards* with American Red Cross lifeguard training at $1100–$1700 per season; 5 *swimming instructors* with American Red Cross WSI certification at $1100–$1700 per season; 2 *nurses* with RN or LPN license at $2500–$4000 per season; 2 *tennis instructors* with teaching experience at $1000–$1500 per season.

Benefits Preemployment training, on-the-job training, on-site room and board at no charge, laundry facilities.

Contact Applicant should send resume, write for application, or call for information to Gordon Felt, Director, Camp Northwood, Department SED, 10 West 66th Street, New York, New York 10023; 212-799-4089, fax 212-877-2968.

CAMP OF THE WOODS
Route 30
Speculator, New York 12164

General Information Nondenominational Christian family camp accommodating over 750 people; also Christian girls' camp serving 72 girls ages 8–16. Established 1900. Owned by Gospel Volunteers Inc. Affiliated with Christian Camping International, American

Camping Association. Located 90 miles north of Albany on 120 acres. Features include location in Adirondack Mountains; beautiful lakefront with a quarter-mile natural sand beach; 1,500-seat auditorium; full recreational facilities and program; excellent guest speakers and teachers; full music program, including concert band, chorale, string ensemble, etc.

Profile of Summer Employees   Total number 250; average age 20. Employees are 55% female, 5% minorities, 45% high school students, 45% college students, 2% retirees, 1% international, 1% local residents. Requires nonsmokers.

Employment Information   Openings are from May 11 to September 7. Christmas break, year-round positions also offered. College credit possible. Jobs available: 50 *counselors/ teachers* with ability to provide leadership and programming for children preschool through high school at $500–$1200 per season; 10 *recreation leaders* with tennis, hiking, rafting, and team sports experience at $600–$1500 per season; 10 *waterfront staff* with WSI certificate (director) and CPR training (staff) at $600–$1500 per season; 45 *music instructors (instrumental/vocal; double as waiters/waitresses)* at $600–$1500 per season; 45 *food-service personnel* at $500–$2000 per season; 50 *operational personnel (dishwashers, maintenance, housekeepers)* at $500–$1200 per season; 10 *office/clerical staff* at $600–$1000 per season; *supervisors (all departments); 4 nurses* with RN, LPN, or EMT license at $1000–$2000 per season. International students encouraged to apply.

Benefits   Preemployment training, on-the-job training, on-site room and board at no charge, laundry facilities.

Contact   Applicant should write for application or call for information by March 15 to Ardith Murray, Personnel Director, Camp of the Woods, Department SED, Route 30, Speculator, New York 12164; 518-548-4311, fax 518-548-4324.

Camp of the Woods provides the challenge of serving God through meeting and serving people. We are looking for those willing to grow and be challenged physically, spiritually, and socially in beautiful natural surroundings.

CAMP SEQUOIA
Rock Hill, New York 12775

General Information   Camp providing an environment where children can feel good about themselves and grow in many ways. Established 1932. Owned by Len Shapiro. Affiliated with American Camping Association, American Waterskiing Association, United States Tennis Association. Located 90 miles northwest of New York City on 300 acres. Features include well-rounded program development; camper-counselor ratio of less than 3:1; well-maintained facilities; close proximity to local town; third generation owners and directors.

Profile of Summer Employees   Total number 200; average age 22. Employees are 50% female, 90% college students, 2% retirees, 5% international, 3% local residents. Prefers nonsmokers.

Employment Information   Openings are from June 21 to August 21. College credit possible. Jobs available: 8 *swimming instructors* with WSI/CPR/BLS certification at $800–$1000 per season; 8 *lifeguards* with lifeguard training certification at $800–$1000 per season; 3 *waterskiing instructors* with extensive teaching experience and lifeguard certification at $800–$1000 per season; 8 *outdoor-education instructors* with extensive outdoor experience plus CPR and BLS certification at $700–$1000 per season; 16 *arts instructors (ceramics, fibers, woodworking, photography)* with extensive art background at $800–$1000 per season; 24 *athletics instructors (basketball, softball, volleyball, hockey,* *soccer, tennis)* with extensive playing background at the varsity level plus teaching and coaching experience at $700–$1200 per season; *theater staff (directors, choreographers, technical personnel)* with hands-on stage experience plus strong theater background at $800–$1200 per season; 40 *general counselors* with ability and dedication to helping youngsters grow at $700–$1000 per season; 3 *horseback-riding instructors* with CHA, CPR, and BLS certification at $1000–$1200 per season; 2 *fitness/weight training counselors* with strong background in fitness/weight training and CPR certification at $700–$1000 per season.

Benefits   On-the-job training, on-site room and board at no charge, laundry facilities, travel reimbursement, staff participation in camp activities, opportunities to travel, transportation provided on nights off.

Contact   Applicant should write for application or call for information by April 1 to Mark Zides, Director, Camp Sequoia, Department SED, Box 1045, Woodstock, New York 12498; 914-679-5291.

At Camp Sequoia, children have the freedom to select many of their activities, and staff members can meet new people from different places.

CAMP SEVEN HILLS
Olean Road
Holland, New York 14080

General Information   Residential Girl Scout camp serving 150–200 girls ages 6–17 weekly. Established 1927. Owned by Girl Scout Council of Buffalo/Erie. Affiliated with American Camping Association, Camp Horsemanship Association, Girl Scouts of the United States of America. Located 45 miles south of Buffalo on 571 acres. Features include large, indoor riding arena, 22 horses, and outstanding English riding program; sports complex with tennis courts; 2 small lakes; Olympic-size swimming pool; location close to Niagara Falls and Toronto, Canada; high- and low-ropes course; hills, meadows, and woodlands.

Profile of Summer Employees   Total number 50; average age 21. Employees are 98% female, 1% minorities, 10% high school students, 80% college students, 40% international, 25% local residents. Prefers nonsmokers.

Employment Information   Openings are from June 25 to August 22. College credit possible. Jobs available: 1 *program director* with extensive camping and Girl Scout background at $2400–$2700 per season; 1 *health supervisor* with RN, LPN, or EMT license (New York) at $1800–$2000 per season; 1 *waterfront director* with WSI and lifeguard certificates at $1800–$2000 per season; 5 *waterfront assistants* with WSI and lifeguard certificates at $1100–$1500 per season; 10 *unit leaders* with camp experience (college age and Girl Scout background helpful) at $1300–$1500 per season; 15 *assistant unit leaders* with experience working with children at $950–$1150 per season; 2 *riding instructors* with CHA certification at $1300–$1900 per season; 1 *arts and crafts director* with art background and experience teaching arts and crafts at $1300–$1500 per season; 1 *ropes-course specialist* with Project Adventure/ropes-course training and experience plus group dynamics experience at $1300–$1500 per season; 1 *counselor-in-training director* with extensive Girl Scout camp experience and experience teaching older adolescents at $1300–$1500 per season; 1 *sports director* with experience teaching a variety of sports to children at $1300–$1500 per season; 1 *stable manager* with extensive knowledge of barn management and equine care at $1250–$1400 per season; 1 *handyperson* with valid driver's license, knowledge of basic carpentry, and minimal maintenance skills at $1200–$1300 per season. International students encouraged to apply.

Benefits Preemployment training, on-the-job training, on-site room and board at no charge, laundry facilities, health insurance, tuition reimbursement, worker's compensation, disability insurance, time off.

Contact Applicant should send resume, write for application, call for information, or apply in person by June 1 to Barb Smith, Camping Services Director, Camp Seven Hills, Department SED, 70 Jewett Parkway, Buffalo, New York 14214; 716-837-6400, fax 716-837-6407.

Foreign nationals who wish to be considered for employment must apply through Camp America.

CAROUSEL DAY SCHOOL
9 West Avenue
Hicksville, New York 11801

General Information Summer day camp for children ages 2–13. Affiliated with American Camping Association, Long Island Association of Private Schools and Day Camps. Features include 2 pools and 4 sports fields.

Employment Information Openings are from June 29 to August 21. College credit possible. Jobs available: *lifeguards* with WSI and Red Cross certification; *sports instructors/counselors* with knowledge of basketball coaching and skills in soccer and baseball; *nature instructors* with ability to develop a nature science program; *general counselors; director/instructor for crafts program* with ability to order, supervise, and implement crafts programs.

Contact Applicant should send resume by May 10 (apply early for best choice of jobs) to Carousel Day School, Department SED, 9 West Avenue, Hicksville, New York 11801.

Carousel Day School staff members enjoy good working conditions in a social atmosphere. Salaries range from $800 to $2500 a season.

CENTRAL NEW YORK GIRL SCOUT CAMP NEAR WILDERNESS
Box 486, RD 1
West Monroe, New York 13167

General Information Residential Girl Scout camp offering general camp activities to 900 girls per summer. Established 1961. Owned by Central New York Girl Scouts Inc. Affiliated with American Camping Association. Located 25 miles north of Syracuse on 180 acres. Features include Girl Scout programs; private lake; challenge course; trips; primitive camping.

Profile of Summer Employees Total number 38; average age 22. Employees are 90% female, 8% minorities, 2% high school students, 15% college students, 3% retirees, 10% international, 15% local residents.

Employment Information Openings are from June 21 to August 18. Jobs available: 5 *swimming instructors* with lifeguard training at $1100–$1500 per season; 1 *counselor-in-*

training director with Girl Scout program knowledge at $1300–$1600 per season; 1 *health director* with RN, LPN, or EMT license at $1600–$2000 per season; 1 *business manager* with office skills at $1100–$1500 per season; 1 *project-adventure director* with knowledge of challenge courses at $1200–$1600 per season; 1 *cook* at $1600–$2000 per season; 1 *assistant cook* at $1400–$1800 per season; 3 *kitchen aides* at $800–$1000 per season; 1 *maintenance person* at $800–$1000 per season. International students encouraged to apply.

Benefits   Preemployment training, on-the-job training, on-site room and board at no charge, travel reimbursement, health insurance.

Contact   Applicant should send resume, write for application, or call for information by June 1 to Carol Van Wie, Outdoor Program Director, Central New York Girl Scout Camp Near Wilderness, Department SED, P.O. Box 6505, Syracuse, New York 13217; 315-437-6531.

Come join us and share in the world of out-of-doors in beautiful upstate New York.

CORTLAND REPERTORY THEATRE, INC.
37 Franklin Street
Cortland, New York 13045

General Information   Professional summer theater producing five productions and offering over sixty performances during an eleven-week schedule. Established 1972. Affiliated with Actors' Equity Association, Finger Lakes Association, Cortland Chamber of Commerce. Located 30 miles south of Syracuse on 1 acre. Features include historic Pavilion Theatre; proximity to scenic Little York Lake; location in beautiful Dwyer Memorial County Park; mild summer weather; friendly small-town environment; professional Actors' Equity Association (small professional theater) contract.

Profile of Summer Employees   Total number 50; average age 28. Employees are 45% female, 10% minorities, 5% high school students, 25% college students, 2% retirees, 20% local residents.

Employment Information   Openings are from May 27 to August 24. College credit possible. Jobs available: 1 *box office manager* with customer service orientation, a car, and box office experience at $140–$150 per week; 1 *box office clerk* with strong customer service background, a car, and box office experience (preferred) at $130–$140 per week; 1 *publicity director* with strong interest in theater, a car, and a journalism major (preferred) at $140–$150 per week; *technical interns* with high school experience and a committment to exploring a theater career at $500–$600 per season; *acting interns* with ability to perform in person at spring auditions at $500–$600 per season; 1 *Equity stage manager* with professional experience and AEA membership at $240–$265 per week; 1 *props master/mistress* with professional experience or B.F.A. degree at $175–$185 per week; 1 *costume designer* with professional experience or M.F.A. degree; 1 *scene designer* with professional experience or M.F.A. degree; 1 *lighting designer* with professional experience or M.F.A. degree; 1 *house manager* with customer service background, volunteer coordinator and problem solving skills, plus car required at $100 per week; 1 *technical director* with professional experience or M.F.A. degree at $250–$275 per week; 1 *master carpenter* with professional experience or M.F.A. degree at $200–$225 per week; 1 *master electrician* with professional experience or B.F.A. degree at $185–$195 per week; 1 *production manager/coordinator* with professional experience or M.F.A. degree at $200–$250 per week; 1 *costumer* with experience sewing, cutting, and running a shop or B.F.A. degree at $200–$225 per week.

Benefits   On-the-job training, on-site room and board at no charge.

Contact   Applicant should send resume and submit a list of references (acting interns must audition in person; publicity interns must submit a writing sample) by February 15 to David Colwell, Managing Director, Cortland Repertory Theatre, Inc., Department SED, P.O. Box 783, Cortland, New York 13045; 607-753-6161.

Cortland Repertory Company provides an opportunity for interns and apprentices to earn Actors' Equity Association (AEA) membership points. (Please note that compensation for costume, scene, and lighting designers is paid on a "per production" basis and ranges from $500 to $550, depending on position.)

DRIFTWOOD ON THE OCEAN
Montauk Highway, Route 27
Montauk, New York 11954

General Information   Seasonal oceanfront resort facility. Established 1954. Owned by Driftwood Apartment Corporation. Affiliated with American Hotel and Motel Association, New York State Hotel and Motel Association, East Hampton Chamber of Commerce. Located 120 miles east of New York City on 9 acres.

Profile of Summer Employees   Total number 15; average age 25. Employees are 80% female, 40% minorities, 40% international, 60% local residents.

Employment Information   Openings are from May 15 to October 15. Jobs available: 4 *chamberpersons* with previous experience (preferred) at $225 per week. International students encouraged to apply.

Benefits   On-the-job training, on-site room and board, laundry facilities.

Contact   Applicant should write for application or call for information by June 15 to William Brinkman, Managing Agent, Driftwood On The Ocean, Department SED, Box 5, Montauk, New York 11954; 516-668-5744.

DURHAM TEMPORARIES, INC.
295 Madison Avenue
New York, New York 10017

General Information   A temporary services agency placing personnel in all phases of office work. Established 1967. Owned by Peter, Barry, and Brian Durham. Affiliated with Chamber of Commerce, New York City Convention Bureau. Features include varied client base, including some Fortune 500 companies; varied positions.

Employment Information   Spring break, winter break, Christmas break, year-round positions offered. Jobs available: *temporary personnel such as clerical (with and without typing), receptionists, word processors, data-entry operators, secretaries, telemarketers, hosts/hostesses, light industrial/maintenance personnel, mailroom staff, warehouse persons, and convention personnel* with proper identification. International students encouraged to apply.

Benefits   Preemployment training, on-the-job training.

Contact Applicant should call for information or apply in person to Helene Frost, Branch Manager, Durham Temporaries, Inc., Department SED, 295 Madison Avenue, New York, New York 10017; 212-599-6171, fax 212-599-6176.

This organization offers employees the ability to learn about different industries and fields while still in college so that career decisions are easier to make.

THE FRESH AIR FUND
Sharpe Reservation, Van Wyck Lake Road
Fishkill, New York 12524

General Information Four residential camps serving 2,500 inner-city youngsters each summer. Established 1947. Owned by The Fresh Air Fund. Affiliated with American Camping Association, New York State Outdoor Education Association, Child Welfare League of America. Located 65 miles north of New York City on 3,000 acres. Features include 2 lakes and a swimming pool; model farm, planetarium, and wildlife refuge; location close to New York City; 14 miles of trails through wooded terrain; service to physically disabled children.

Profile of Summer Employees Total number 250; average age 20. Employees are 45% female, 35% minorities, 3% high school students, 90% college students, 15% international, 30% local residents. Prefers nonsmokers.

Employment Information Openings are from June 22 to August 24. College credit possible. Jobs available: 150 *general counselors* with some college and experience with children (minimum age 18) at $1250–$1750 per season; 18 *village leaders* with camp experience at $1650–$2150 per season; 4 *waterfront directors* with WSI certificate and three years experience (minimum age 21) at $2100–$2800 per season; 16 *waterfront assistants* with lifeguard training certificate at $1450–$1850 per season; 28 *program specialists (photography, video, music, sewing, pioneering, nature, arts and craft)* with ability to teach specialty at $1450–$1850 per season; 7 *nurses* with RN license at $3200–$3700 per season.

Benefits Preemployment training, on-the-job training, formal ongoing training, on-site room and board at no charge, laundry facilities, travel reimbursement, three-day breaks between twelve-day camp sessions, transportation provided to nearby town during free time.

Contact Applicant should write for application or call for information by June 1 to Thomas S. Karger, Associate Executive Director, The Fresh Air Fund, 1040 Avenue of the Americas, New York, New York 10018; 800-367-0003, fax 212-302-7875.

Good experience for those considering careers in social work, psychology, special education, or recreation. International students who wish to apply for employment should do so through exchange organizations.

FROST VALLEY YMCA CAMPS
HC Box 55
Claryville, New York 12725

General Information Frost Valley strives to develop self-esteem and healthy lifestyles through traditional camp activities. Established 1886. Operated by Frost Valley Association. Affiliated with American Camping Association, Young Men's Christian Association.

Located 100 miles northwest of New York City on 4,500 acres. Features include wellness philosophy/healthful lifestyles; diverse camper population; beautiful mountain environment; international campers and staff; environmental focus; leadership and self-esteem building.

Profile of Summer Employees   Total number 160; average age 20. Employees are 50% female, 15% minorities, 15% high school students, 65% college students, 2% retirees, 15% international, 5% local residents. Requires nonsmokers.

Employment Information   Openings are from June 22 to August 2. Year-round positions also offered. College credit possible. Jobs available: 10 *unit leaders* with camp experience (minimum age 21) at $1300–$1800 per season; 40 *counselors* with experience with children (minimum age 18) at $900–$1300 per season; 5 *waterfront staff* with lifeguard, CPR, and first aid certification at $1000–$1300 per season; 5 *riding staff* with experience teaching Western riding at $1000–$1300 per season; 2 *nurses* with current nursing license at $2500–$3500 per season; 3 *art instructors* with experience teaching art at $1000–$1300 per month; 10 *trip leaders* with experience in canoeing, biking, and hiking at $140–$180 per week; 3 *sports staff* with experience teaching various team sports at $1000–$1300 per month; 8 *program area directors* with ability to supervise staff in various program areas and develop programs for those areas, including riding, waterfront, art, sports, and health at $1300–$1800 per season.

Benefits   Preemployment training, on-the-job training, on-site room and board at no charge, laundry facilities, travel reimbursement.

Contact   Applicant should send resume, write for application, call for information, or apply in person by March 31 to Peter M. Swain, Director of Camping, Frost Valley YMCA Camps, Department SED, HC Box 55, Claryville, New York 12725; 914-985-2291, fax 914-985-0056.

Frost Valley offers year-round employment in our conference and environmental education centers, including opportunities to work in late spring (starting May 15).

GOLDEN ACRES FARM AND RANCH RESORT
CR 14
Gilboa, New York 12076

General Information   Family farm and ranch resort catering to young professional families with children. Established 1950. Owned by Patricia and Jerry Gauthier. Affiliated with New York State Hospitality and Tourism Association, American Camping Association. Located 60 miles southwest of Albany on 600 acres. Features include family resort; dude ranch with indoor riding arena; farm animals; kosher food; location in central Catskill Mountains; indoor and outdoor pools.

Profile of Summer Employees   Total number 75; average age 21. Employees are 60% female, 10% high school students, 70% college students, 2% retirees, 10% local residents. Prefers nonsmokers.

Employment Information   Openings are from May 20 to September 7. College credit possible. Jobs available: 13 *counselors* with child-care experience at $168 per week; 3 *nursery counselors* with baby-care experience at $168 per week; 1 *sports director* with outgoing and friendly personality at $168–$200 per week; 1 *social director* with driver's license at $175–$250 per week; 4 *front-desk clerks* with computer experience plus cash and credit card experience at $175–$250 per week; 3 *bellhops/maintenance personnel* with driver's license and handyman abilities (minimum age 21) at $175–$250 per week; 1 *head housekeeper* with supervisory skills at $200–$300 per week; 11 *chambermaids* with clean, neat appearance at $168–$180 per week; 1 *bartender* with bartending experience and cash handling references at $150–$175 per week; 20 *food-service assistants* with food preparation or serving experience at $168–$250 per week; 1 *baker* with experience working with yeast products at $250–$350 per week; 1 *camp director* with teaching or comparable experience at $200–$350 per week; 1 *dining room manager* with supervisory and dining room experience at $200–$350 per week; 8 *wranglers* with riding experience at $168–$225 per week; 1 *bookkeeper* with accounting or bookkeeping experience and computer literacy at $200–$350 per week. International students encouraged to apply.

Benefits On-the-job training, on-site room and board at $67 per week, laundry facilities, use of resort facilities, opportunity to meet people from all over the world, staff parties and outings.

Contact Applicant should send resume, write for application, or call for information by May 1 to Patricia Gauthier, Golden Acres Farm and Ranch Resort, Department SED, County Road 14, Gilboa, New York 12076; 607-588-7329.

There is a guaranteed end-of-season bonus of $40–$75 per week. Accommodations available for couples or families with children over the age of 4.

KUTSHER'S SPORTS ACADEMY
Monticello, New York 12701

General Information Residential, coeducational sports camp featuring an elective instructional program for 500 campers. Established 1968. Owned by Kutsher Family. Affiliated with American Camping Association. Located 90 miles northwest of New York City on 100 acres. Features include high-quality staff and instruction; friendly environment; sports facilities; scenic countryside; program (coaches provide help to counselors in their sport).

Profile of Summer Employees Total number 160; average age 21. Employees are 31% female. Prefers nonsmokers.

Employment Information Openings are from June 25 to August 24. College credit possible. Jobs available: *counselors* with a specialty in at least one sport such as basketball, tennis, soccer, baseball, softball, gymnastics, track and field, sailing, waterskiing, wrestling, judo, karate, weight training, field hockey, or swimming; or college students with college or high school athletics experience at $700–$1200 per season; *coaches* with experience in college, high school, or club coaching at $1800 per season; *nurses* at $2000 per season.

Benefits Preemployment training, on-the-job training, formal ongoing training, on-site room and board at no charge, laundry facilities, travel allowance.

Contact Applicant should write for application or call for information to Robert Trupin, Executive Director, Kutsher's Sports Academy, Department SED, 3 Snowflake Lane, Westport, Connecticut 06880; 203-454-4991.

Kutsher's Sports Academy has a traditional camp atmosphere. We are searching for counselors who are very strong in at least one sport and who also enjoy seeing children grow both athletically and socially.

MUSIC THEATRE NORTH
Snell Theater
Potsdam, New York 13676

General Information   Professional summer theater that produces five high-quality Broadway musicals in two- or three-week runs from June to August. Established 1979. Owned by Potsdam College. Affiliated with Association of Performing Arts Presenters, New York Ontario Theater Alliance. Located 150 miles north of Syracuse. Features include air-conditioned, 452-seat, 20 year-old theater with dressing rooms, rehearsal halls, and scene/lighting/costume shops; location at Potsdam College in the foothills of the Adirondack Mountains.

Profile of Summer Employees   Total number 135. Employees are 60% female, 5% high school students, 35% college students, 10% local residents.

Employment Information   Openings are from May 20 to August 25. Jobs available: 3 *stitchers* at $175–$200 per week; 1 *costume shop manager* at $250–$300 per week; 1 *cutter/draper* at $200–$220 per week; 3 *carpenters* at $175–$200 per week; 1 *master carpenter* at $220–$280 per week; 1 *technical director* at $325–$375 per week; 2 *costume designers* at $300–$375 per week; 2 *scenic designers* at $350–$400 per week; 2 *lighting designers* at $275–$300 per week; 1 *master electrician* at $175–$200 per week; 2 *assistant lighting designers* at $225–$250 per week; 1 *properties staff* at $175–$200 per week; 1 *sound designer/technician* at $250–$300 per week; 5 *directors* at $500–$700 per week; 2 *musical directors* at $375–$540 per week. International students encouraged to apply.

Benefits   Preemployment training, on-the-job training, on-site room and board at $80 per week, laundry facilities, excellent contacts for future, employment in other theaters.

Contact   Applicant should send resume and cover letter explaining interest, names, plus phone numbers of three references by February 1 to Kathryn M. Del Guidice, Managing Producer, Music Theatre North, Department SED, P.O. Box 526, Potsdam, New York 13676; 315-265-3070, fax 315-265-3793.

NATIONAL PARK SERVICE

Contact   Applicant should write for application (must be 18 by May 13; U.S. citizenship required) to Regional Office of the National Park Service, North Atlantic Region, National Park Service, 15 State Street, Boston, Massachusetts 02109.

Jobs located in New York at the following facilities: Fire Island, Fort Stanwix, Gateway Breezy Point/Jamaica Bay and Staten Island, Manhattan Sites Unit, Roosevelt-Vanderbilt National Historic Site, Sagamore Hill, Saratoga, Statue of Liberty/Ellis Island, Martin Van Buren National Historic Site, Women's Rights. Also see District of Columbia listing.

NORTH SHORE HOLIDAY HOUSE
74 Huntington Road
Huntington, New York 11743

General Information Residential camp serving girls from low-income homes. Established 1914. Located 25 miles east of New York City on 5 acres. Features include small operation with close-knit, friendly staff and wonderful campers; traditional camp activities.

Profile of Summer Employees Total number 22; average age 19. Employees are 100% female, 50% minorities, 20% high school students, 80% college students, 33% international, 20% local residents. Prefers nonsmokers.

Employment Information Openings are from June 21 to August 17. College credit possible. International students encouraged to apply.

Benefits Preemployment training, on-the-job training, formal ongoing training, on-site room and board at no charge, laundry facilities.

Contact Applicant should send resume or call for information by May 1 to Marty Gordon, Director, North Shore Holiday House, Department SED, 3 Marine Street, Huntington, New York 11743; 516-549-6892.

OFFENSE-DEFENSE FOOTBALL CAMP
State University of New York at Stony Brook
Stony Brook, New York 11794

General Information Residential and day camp offering instruction in full-gear contact football to boys ages 8–18. Established 1969. Owned by Mike Meshken. Affiliated with New England Camping Association. Located 25 miles east of New York City on 200 acres. Features include college campus in country setting; pool; weight room; 60 college coaches each day; 19 NFL pros.

Profile of Summer Employees Total number 80; average age 23. Employees are 12% female, 20% college students, 3% retirees. Prefers nonsmokers.

Employment Information Openings are from June 25 to July 10. Jobs available: 2 *swimming instructors* with WSI certificate; 15 *counselors* with the ability to work well with children at $100–$150 per week; 20 *football coaches* with experience as a high school or college football coach at $200–$300 per week; 3 *student athletics trainers* with some hours completed at $150–$200 per week; 4 *athletics trainers* with trainer certification at $275–$400 per week.

Benefits Preemployment training, on-the-job training, formal ongoing training, on-site room and board, laundry facilities.

Contact Applicant should send resume or call for information by April 1 to Mike Meshken, President, Offense-Defense Football Camp, Department SED, P.O. Box 317, Trumbull, Connecticut 06611; 800-243-4296.

We seek individuals to work with young athletes to improve their football skills. Come and join our staff of college coaches, professional players, and athletic medical personnel at a full-pads, instructional football camp.

PECONIC DUNES CAMP
Soundview Avenue
Southold, New York 11958

General Information   Residential camp stressing recreational activities and serving up to 170 children weekly. Established 1931. Operated by Suffolk County Organization for the Promotion of Education. Affiliated with American Camping Association. Located 75 miles east of New York City on 40 acres. Features include private beach on Long Island Sound; mile-long spring-fed lake; daily swimming instruction; nature program; wide variety of sports; full-time nurse on premises.

Profile of Summer Employees   Total number 40; average age 20. Employees are 60% female, 15% minorities, 35% high school students, 55% college students, 10% local residents. Prefers nonsmokers.

Employment Information   Openings are from June 21 to August 24. Jobs available: 1 *waterfront director* with WSI certificate at $1000–$1200 per month; 3 *waterfront staff* with lifesaving or WSI certificate at $600–$750 per month; 8 *junior counselors* with high school student status and mature attitude at $400–$600 per season; 6 *general counselors* with college student status at $800–$1000 per season; 6 *senior counselors* with college senior or graduate status plus experience at $1200 per season; 1 *nurse* with RN or LPN license at $500–$600 per week; 4 *maintenance personnel* with high school student status and mature attitude at $800–$1000 per season; 1 *chef* with mature, responsible personality (pay commensurate with experience); 4 *kitchen helpers* with high school student status and mature attitude at $800 per season. International students encouraged to apply.

Benefits   On-site room and board at no charge, laundry facilities.

Contact   Applicant should write for application or call for information by April 15 to Thomas Capolongo, Program Specialist, Peconic Dunes Camp, Department SED, 810 Meadow Road, Smithtown, New York 11787; 516-360-0800, fax 516-360-0356.

STAGEDOOR MANOR THEATRE CAMP
Karmel Road
Loch Sheldrake, New York 12759

General Information   Residential, coeducational camp serving 240 campers in performing arts. Established 1975. Owned by Carl Samuelson. Affiliated with American Camping Association. Located 100 miles east of Binghamton on 40 acres. Features include close proximity to town and health club; hotel-style camp; indoor and outdoor pools; nearby lake for boating; 5 theater spaces; location in the Catskill Mountains just 2½ hours from New York City.

Profile of Summer Employees   Total number 100; average age 25. Employees are 50% female, 50% college students, 25% international, 2% local residents. Prefers nonsmokers.

Employment Information   Openings are from June 21 to August 25. College credit possible. Jobs available: 6 *theater directors* with B.A. degree and experience at $1700–$2000 per season; 6 *pianists* with excellent sight reading ability and musical theater experience at $1600–$1800 per season; 3 *choreographers* with musical theater experience at $1600–$1800 per season; 10 *technicians* with theater experience at $1000–$1500 per season; 3 *designers* with theater experience at $1000–$1500 per season; 3 *swimming guards* with American Red Cross lifeguard training at $1400–$2000 per season; 3 *nurses* with RN or LPN license at $1600–$3000 per season; 2 *office managers* with administrative experience at $1600–$2500 per season; 4 *group leaders* with camp management experience at $1600–$1800 per season; 2 *head counselors* with camp management experience at $2000–$2500 per season; 2 *office assistants* with typing and bookkeeping skills at $1000–$1400 per season; 2 *grounds persons* with gardening, painting, and housekeeping skills at $1000–$1200 per season; 30 *counselors* with involvement in theater, sports, etc. and college student status at $850–$1200 per season; 2 *tennis counselors* at $1000–$1200 per season.

Benefits Preemployment training, on-the-job training, formal ongoing training, on-site room and board at no charge, laundry facilities, classes offered during time off, recreational facilities available for use during off hours, including tennis, horseback riding, etc.

Contact Applicant should send resume or call for information by May 15 to Dr. Jason Teran, Camp Director, Stagedoor Manor Theatre Camp, Department SED, 100 Silver Beach, #706, Daytona Beach, Florida 32118; 904-252-9164.

Stagedoor Manor Theatre Camp gives individuals the opportunity to develop portfolios/resumes in theater and performing arts while working with a friendly, international staff.

SURPRISE LAKE CAMP
50 West 17th Street
New York, New York 10011

General Information General, residential camp for Jewish children ages 7–15. Established 1902. Affiliated with United Jewish Appeal Federation, Association of Jewish Sponsored Camps, American Camping Association. Located 60 miles north of New York City on 750 acres. Features include half-mile long private lake; beautifully wooded area and rugged terrain; easy access and great atmosphere.

Profile of Summer Employees Total number 200; average age 19. Employees are 50% female, 15% high school students, 40% college students, 30% international. Prefers nonsmokers.

Employment Information College credit possible. Jobs available: 12 *lifeguards* with Red Cross lifeguard training (minimum) at $500–$1400 per season; 3 *arts and crafts instructors* at $400–$1400 per season; 2 *drama instructors* at $400–$1400 per season; 1 *low-ropes instructor* at $400–$1400 per season; 1 *archery instructor* at $400–$1400 per season; 2 *nature instructors* at $400–$1400 per season; 1 *Israeli dance instructor* at $400–$1400 per season; 1 *physical fitness instructor* at $400–$1400 per season; 1 *photography instructor;* 1 *tennis instructor;* 10 *unit supervisors* with ability to supervise 40–50 kids and 6–8 counselors (camp supervisory experience required) at $1600 per season.

Benefits Preemployment training, on-the-job training, on-site room and board, travel reimbursement.

Contact Applicant should write for application or call for information and send letter with position sought as well as relevant experience to Recruitment Coordinator, Surprise Lake Camp, Department SED, 50 West 17th Street, New York, New York 10011; 212-924-3131, fax 212-924-5112.

Instructors should be specialists who can teach and direct high-quality programs.

VANDERBILT YMCA OF GREATER NEW YORK
224 East 47th Street
New York, New York 10017

General Information   Community center and day camp located in midtown Manhattan, serving children ages 5–15 who live in the five boroughs of New York City. Recreational camp with swimming and sports emphasis. Established 1932. Owned by YMCA of Greater New York. Affiliated with Turtle Bay Association, Community Board 6. Features include 2 pools, gym, and playground; location in New York City, where thousands of cultural and educational activities are available; trained staff; hotel serving out-of-town guests.

Profile of Summer Employees   Total number 40; average age 21. Employees are 50% female, 25% minorities. Prefers nonsmokers.

Employment Information   Openings are from June 29 to September 4. Spring break, winter break, Christmas break, year-round positions also offered. Jobs available: 2 *unit leaders* with first aid and/or CPR certification and six months camp administration experience at $260–$275 per week; 2 *swimming teachers* with WSI and CPR instructor certification at $245–$250 per week; *senior counselor* with first aid and CPR certification, six months experience working with children (minimum age 18) at $200–$225 per week; 1 *art teacher (part-time position, 15 hours/week)* with one year experience teaching art to children at $180 per week; 1 *music teacher (part-time position, 10 hours/week)* with experience working with children and music at $120 per week; 1 *teen unit director* with experience working with teens at $260–$275 per week; 5 *lifeguards* with WSI, first aid, and CPR certification; *nursery teacher* with New York Schools certification, N–6 at $380 per week; *teacher's aide* with high school diploma and experience working with children at $300 per week; 1 *sports unit leader* with CPR and first aid certification and experience teaching a variety of sports to children at $260–$275 per week. International students encouraged to apply.

Benefits   Preemployment training, on-the-job training.

Contact   Applicant should send resume or write for application by May to Suzanne Bent, Camp Director or Julie Gallanty, Director of Youth and Community Services, Vanderbilt YMCA of Greater New York, Department SED, 224 East 47th Street, New York, New York 10017; 212-755-2410 Ext. 214, fax 212-755-7579.

Vanderbilt YMCA day camp is searching for caring, enthusiastic, and creative staff members who enjoy working with children and would thrive in a camp in the heart of New York City. Many cultural and educational opportunities are available.

YMCA CAMP CHINGACHGOOK
Pilot Knob Road
Kattskill Bay, New York 12844

General Information   Residential camp serving 225 campers and offering two-week sessions. Established 1913. Owned by Capital District YMCA. Affiliated with American Camping Association. Located 60 miles north of Albany on 200 acres. Features include location in Adirondack Park on Lake George; extensive high-ropes course; waterfront focus; character development emphasis; sailing and waterskiing; active outdoor lifestyle.

Profile of Summer Employees   Total number 75; average age 20. Employees are 45% female, 5% minorities, 20% high school students, 75% college students, 15% international, 50% local residents. Prefers nonsmokers.

Employment Information Openings are from May 1 to November 1. College credit possible. Jobs available: 75 *camp staff* at $500–$4500 per season. International students encouraged to apply.

Benefits Preemployment training, on-the-job training, formal ongoing training, on-site room and board at no charge.

Contact Applicant should send resume or write for application by March 15 to George W. Painter, Executive Director, YMCA Camp Chingachgook, 13 State Street, Schenectady, New York 12305; 518-374-9136.

YMCA/YWCA CAMPING SERVICES–CAMPS GREENKILL/MCALISTER/TALCOTT
Big Pond Road
Huguenot, New York 12746

General Information Residential camps serving general population. Camps are split into two age groups: 6–10 and 11–15. Established 1906. Owned by YMCA of Greater New York. Located 85 miles northwest of New York City on 1,000 acres. Features include location in the foothills of the Catskill Mountains; high-ropes course; strong aquatics emphasis; international camp; private lakes; specialization in new and young campers.

Profile of Summer Employees Total number 80; average age 21. Employees are 50% female, 20% minorities, 8% high school students, 60% college students, 20% international, 10% local residents. Prefers nonsmokers.

Employment Information Openings are from June 15 to August 25. Jobs available: 30 *general counselors* at $90–$110 per week; 3 *aquatic directors* with WSI, LGT, CPR, BLS, or first aid certification (minimum age 21) at $160–$180 per week; *unit director* with leadership and camp experience at $130–$150 per week; 6 *swimming instructors* with WSI certificate at $120–$140 per week; 10 *kitchen staff* at $125–$135 per week; 2 *high-ropes instructors* at $125–$135 per week; 2 *rock-climbing instructors* at $125–$135 per week; 2 *small craft instructors* with small craft certificate at $125–$135 per week. International students encouraged to apply.

Benefits Preemployment training, on-the-job training, formal ongoing training, on-site room and board at no charge, laundry facilities, travel reimbursement.

Contact Applicant should write for application or call for information by June 1 to Jerry Huncosky, Director of Camping, YMCA/YWCA Camping Services–Camps GreenKill/ McAlister/Talcott, Department SED, P.O. Box B, Huguenot, New York 12746; 914-856-4382, fax 914-858-7823.

We operate traditional YMCA camps emphasizing values in all programs.

North Carolina

CAMP GOLDEN VALLEY
Route 2, Box 766
Bostic, North Carolina 28017

General Information Residential camp for girls ages 6–18 with a Girl Scout program emphasis. Capacity is 160 girls per session. Established 1972. Owned by Pioneer Girl Scout Council. Affiliated with American Camping Association. Located 85 miles northwest of Charlotte on 620 acres. Features include beautiful North Carolina Mountains; rustic but modern facilities (treehouse, platform tents, and cabin units); horses; swimming, tennis, basketball, softball, volleyball, and archery; canoes and paddleboats; 15-acre lake; campcraft skills; sailing, waterskiing, and backpack trips.

Profile of Summer Employees Total number 25. Employees are 100% female, 25% minorities, 25% college students, 4% international, 80% local residents.

Employment Information Jobs available: 1 *assistant director and program director* with broad liberal arts background (minimum age 21) at $175–$205 per week; *camp nurse* with RN license (North Carolina) and a minimum age of 21 at $175–$185 per week; 1 *waterfront director* with WSI certificate (ARC or equivalent) and lifeguard training (minimum age 21) at $135–$165 per week; 4 *waterfront assistants* with lifeguard training (minimum age 18) at $110–$140 per week; 5 *unit leaders* with previous experience as camp counselor, teacher, or youth leader (minimum age 21) at $135–$165 per week; 13 *unit assistants* with previous Girl Scout or youth leader experience (minimum age 18) at $110–$140 per week. International students encouraged to apply.

Benefits Preemployment training, on-site room and board at no charge, laundry facilities, accident insurance, American Red Cross First Aid/CPR certification.

Contact Applicant should write for application or call for information by May 1 to Julie Stockton, Resident Camp Director, Camp Golden Valley, Department SED, 324 North Highland Street, Gastonia, North Carolina 28052-2194; 704-434-0105.

We serve Girl Scouts and non-Girl-Scouts and have a staff committed to providing quality care and programs for girls. Camp Golden Valley enjoys helping children to grow and develop.

CAMP KANATA
13524 Camp Kanata Road
Wake Forest, North Carolina 27587

General Information Coeducational, residential, YMCA camp for children ages 7–14. The individual child is the camp's focus and is given the opportunity to develop initiative, self-esteem, and self-confidence as well as grow in new physical skills. Established 1954. Operated by Durham YMCA. Affiliated with American Camping Association. Located 10 miles north of Raleigh on 188 acres. Features include 188 wooded acres; 2 spring-fed lakes; 17 cabins; barn with 14 stalls; 7,000 square foot gymnasium; ropes course.

Profile of Summer Employees Total number 42; average age 20. Employees are 50% female, 2% minorities, 30% high school students, 70% college students, 4% international, 35% local residents. Prefers nonsmokers.

Employment Information Openings are from June 8 to August 15. Jobs available: 28 *cabin counselors* with past work experience with children at $1000–$1300 per season; 2

nurses with RN license at $2000–$2500 per season; 1 *arts and crafts director* with experience in supervising arts and crafts program at $1250 per season; 1 *program director* with creativity and camp experience (minimum age 20) at $1500–$2000 per season; 1 *staff-trainee director* with camp experience (minimum age 20) at $1500–$1800 per season; 1 *waterfront director* with camp experience and WSI, lifeguard instructor, or YMCA certificates (minimum age 20) at $1800–$2200 per season; 1 *waterskiing coordinator* with camp and maintenance experience (minimum age 21) at $1200–$1400 per season; 1 *ropes-course director* with camp experience and ropes-course training (minimum age 20) at $1200–$1400 per season.

Benefits Preemployment training, on-the-job training, on-site room and board at no charge, laundry facilities.

Contact Applicant should write for application or call for information and call to schedule an interview by April 15 to Richard R. Hamilton, Assistant Director, Camp Kanata, 13524 Camp Kanata Road, Wake Forest, North Carolina 27587; 919- 556-2661.

Camp Kanata is interested in hiring those who want to have a positive impact on children and are willing to put the needs of the camper before their own.

CAMPS MONDAMIN AND GREEN COVE
Tuxedo, North Carolina 28784

General Information Residential camps focusing on noncompetitive, lifetime, and outdoor skills with an emphasis on extended trips. Established 1922. Owned by The Bell Family. Located 10 miles south of Hendersonville on 800 acres. Features include close proximity to the Blue Ridge Mountains, beautiful lakes and rivers, and national forests; rustic but comfortable facilities.

Profile of Summer Employees Total number 100; average age 25. Employees are 50% female, 2% minorities, 60% college students, 5% retirees, 2% international, 5% local residents. Requires nonsmokers.

Employment Information Openings are from June 2 to August 20. Jobs available: 2 *swimming instructors* with WSI certificate at $1200 per season; 2 *tennis instructors* at $1200 per season; 2 *crafts and games instructors* with archery and riflery experience helpful at $1200 per season; 2 *sailing instructors* with small boat experience at $1200 per season; 2 *mountain-biking instructors* with camping experience and mechanical expertise at $1200 per season; 2 *horseback-riding instructors* with hunter-style riding and barn experience at $1200 per season; 2 *mountaineering instructors (hiking, rock-climbing)* with Outward Bound or NOLS experience helpful (other experience considered) at $1200 per season.

Benefits Preemployment training, on-the-job training, on-site room and board at no charge, laundry facilities.

Contact Applicant should send resume, write for application, or call for information by March 31 to Frank or Nancy Bell, Directors, Camps Mondamin and Green Cove, Department SED, Tuxedo, North Carolina 28784; 704-693-7446, fax 704-696-8895.

Our camps focus on helping children grow and mature through contact with a high-quality staff. The program we offer is noncompetitive, intensive but rewarding, and allows children to plan their own time with the guidance and support of a counselor.

FALLING CREEK CAMP FOR BOYS
P.O. Box 98
Tuxedo, North Carolina 28784

General Information   A privately owned camp in the western North Carolina mountains seeking to provide boys ages 6–15 with the maximum opportunity for growth and fun in a mountain setting. Established 1969. Owned by Charles W. McGrady. Located 12 miles south of Hendersonville on 780 acres. Features include many opportunities for backpacking, rock-climbing, and white-water canoe trips; great working conditions and leave time; good fellow workers and campers; beautiful mountain setting, remote yet convenient to highways.

Profile of Summer Employees   Total number 80. Employees are 15% female, 90% college students, 10% international. Prefers nonsmokers.

Employment Information   Openings are from May 30 to August 20. College credit possible. Jobs available: 3 *swimming instructors* with WSI certificate/lifeguard certificate at $1625–$1800 per season; 1 *riflery instructor* with experience with guns and target shooting at $1625–$1800 per season; 1 *archery instructor* with experience with range shooting at $1625–$1800 per season; 2 *arts and crafts instructors* at $1625–$1800 per season; 3 *land sports counselors* at $1625–$1800 per season; 3 *tennis instructors* with experience at $1625–$1800 per season; 2 *camp nurses* with RN license at $1800–$2400 per season; 2 *mountaineering staff* with experience in rock-climbing and backpacking trips at $1625–$1800 per season; 2 *canoeing staff* with experience in white water in closed and open boats at $1625–$1800 per season; 2 *horseback-riding staff* with experience in English-saddle instructing at $1625–$1800 per season. International students encouraged to apply.

Benefits   Preemployment training, on-the-job training, on-site room and board, optional laundry service.

Contact   Applicant should send resume, write for application, or call for information by June 1 (applicants must apply early so an interview can be arranged) to Donnie Bain, Director, Falling Creek Camp for Boys, Department SED, P.O. Box 98, Tuxedo, North Carolina 28784; 704-692-0262.

NATIONAL PARK SERVICE

Contact   Applicant should write for application (must be 18 by May 13; U.S. citizenship required) to Regional Office of the National Park Service, Southeast Region, National Park Service, 75 Spring Street, SW, Atlanta, Georgia 30303.

Jobs located in North Carolina at the following facilities: Blue Ridge Parkway, Cape Hatteras, Cape Lookout, Carl Sandburg Home, Great Smoky Mountains National Park, Guilford Courthouse. Also see District of Columbia listing.

NORTH BEACH SAILING/BARRIER ISLAND SAILING CENTER
Box 8279 Duck Station
Kitty Hawk, North Carolina 27949

General Information Sailing center specializing in the rental and sale of windsurfing, sailing, and jet ski equipment, and the teaching of proper use of equipment. Offers a line of clothing for enthusiasts. Established 1985. Owned by William H. Miles Jr. Affiliated with American Windsurfing Industry Association, Outer Banks Chamber of Commerce. Located 70 miles south of Virginia Beach, Virginia. Features include ocean and beaches; sailing; windsurfing; swimming; jet skis; kayaks.

Profile of Summer Employees Employees are 50% female, 10% high school students, 50% college students, 25% local residents. Prefers nonsmokers.

Employment Information Openings are from May 1 to October 15. Jobs available: 8 *windsurfing instructors* with windsurfing experience and ability to relate to students in a positive manner at $250–$350 per week; 4 *sailing instructors* with sailing experience and ability to relate to students in a positive manner at $250–$350 per week; 8 *rental/desk persons* with ability to deal with customers in an efficient, positive manner and knowledge of sailing and windsurfing at $150–$200 per week; 3 *retail salespersons* with sales experience, sailing/windsurfing experience, and ability to deal with people in a positive manner at $200–$300 per week; 1 *parasailing instructor* with Coast Guard captain's license; 2 *kayaking and canoeing instructors (teaching and renting duties)* with kayaking and canoeing experience. International students encouraged to apply.

Benefits On-the-job training, opportunity to learn to sail and windsurf.

Contact Applicant should send resume or call for information by May 1 to Bill Miles, President, North Beach Sailing/Barrier Island Sailing Center, Box 8279 Duck Station, Kitty Hawk, North Carolina 27949; 919-261-6262, fax 919-261-1494.

ROLLING THUNDER RIVER CO.

General Information Provides white-water rafting trips in North Carolina, Tennessee, and Georgia. Established 1977. Owned by Ken and Dina Miller. Affiliated with America Outdoors, United States Forest Service. Located 60 miles west of Asheville on 7 acres. Features include opportunity to work outdoors; interesting people; boating (rafts, canoes, kayaks); hiking; swimming.

Profile of Summer Employees Total number 15; average age 20. Employees are 50% female, 75% college students, 25% local residents.

Employment Information Openings are from May 15 to September 15. College credit possible. Jobs available: 15 *river guides* with advanced first aid, basic lifesaving, and CPR certification plus training with company; 2 *photographers* with photography experience; *maintenance and repair person*. International students encouraged to apply.

Benefits Preemployment training, on-the-job training, on-site room and board at no charge, kitchen and laundry facilities for staff use.

Contact Applicant should send resume, write for application, call for information, or apply in person by March 31 to Dina Miller, Owner/Manager, Rolling Thunder River Co., Department SED, P.O. Box 88, Almond, North Carolina 28702; 704-488-2030.

Wages for employees are $35 per day.

RUBIN'S OSCEOLA LAKE INN
P.O. Box 2258
Hendersonville, North Carolina 28793

General Information Summer resort hotel with 80 rooms, serving three meals daily. Established 1941. Owned by Stuart Rubin. Affiliated with Hendersonville Chamber of Commerce. Features include entertainment and delicious food; lake, pool, and all sports; informal atmosphere; pleasant climate; scenic attractions.

Profile of Summer Employees Total number 40. Employees are 50% female. Prefers nonsmokers.

Employment Information Openings are from May 22 to November 1.

Benefits On-the-job training, on-site room and board at no charge, bonus payable upon completion of contract.

Contact Applicant should send resume by June 1 to Stuart Rubin, Owner/Manager, Rubin's Osceola Lake Inn, Department SED, 250 Palm Avenue, Palm Island, Miami Beach, Florida 33139; 305-534-8356.

UNITED METHODIST CAMPS
1307 Glenwood Avenue
Raleigh, North Carolina 27605

General Information Three campsites located in eastern North Carolina providing camping and outdoor experiences. Established 1949. Owned by United Methodist Church. Features include sailing and water experiences (featured at Don-Lee Camp, located 33 miles east of New Bern on the Neuse River); horseback riding and rustic camp with tent cabins (featured at Chestnut Ridge Camp, located 15 miles west of Durham); treehouses and canoeing (featured at Rockfish Camp, located 15 miles south of Fayetteville on lake).

Profile of Summer Employees Total number 150; average age 19. Employees are 60% female, 10% high school students, 90% college students. Prefers nonsmokers.

Employment Information Openings are from June 1 to August 15. Jobs available: *cabin counselors* at $115–$140 per week; *nurses* at $115–$140 per week; *lifeguards* at $115–$140 per week; *sailing staff/canoeing instructors* at $115–$140 per week; *naturalists* at $115–$140 per week.

Benefits Preemployment training, on-the-job training, on-site room and board at no charge, laundry facilities, health insurance, accident insurance.

Contact Applicant should write for application or call for information by January 2 to G. Paul Phillips III, Director, Camping Ministries, United Methodist Camps, P.O. Box 10955, Raleigh, North Carolina 27605; 919-832-9560.

United Methodist Camps provide a coeducational learning opportunity for persons with camping/outdoors experience wanting to work with children and teens.

YMCA BLUE RIDGE ASSEMBLY
84 Blue Ridge Circle
Black Mountain, North Carolina 28711

General Information YMCA conference center serving families, teenagers, and adults. Established 1906. Affiliated with Young Men's Christian Association. Located 17 miles east of Asheville on 1,200 acres. Features include location in the Appalachian woodlands; view of the Blue Ridge Mountains; athletics facilities, swimming pool, tennis courts, and hiking.

Profile of Summer Employees Total number 90; average age 18. Employees are 60% female, 11% minorities, 5% high school students, 85% college students, 3% retirees, 14% international, 5% local residents. Prefers nonsmokers.

Employment Information Openings are from June 1 to August 19. College credit possible. Jobs available: *food-service personnel* at $1100 per season; *dining room staff* at $1100 per season; *swimming pool staff* at $1100 per season; *crafts and gift shop personnel* at $1100 per season; *maintenance personnel* at $1100 per season; *switchboard operators* at $1100 per season. International students encouraged to apply.

Benefits Preemployment training, on-the-job training, formal ongoing training, on-site room and board at no charge, laundry facilities, travel reimbursement, health insurance, tuition reimbursement, internships and programs for staff.

Contact Applicant should write for application or call for information by April 1 to Summer Employment Director, YMCA Blue Ridge Assembly, 84 Blue Ridge Circle, Black Mountain, North Carolina 28711; 704-669-8422.

YMCA CAMP CHEERIO
Camp Cheerio Road
Glade Valley, North Carolina 28627

General Information Residential camp serving 200 campers per session during one- and two-week sessions. An adventure camp serving 15 campers weekly is also offered. Established 1959. Owned by High Point YMCA. Affiliated with American Camping Association, Young Men's Christian Association. Located 60 miles east of Winston-Salem on 134 acres. Features include beautiful mountain setting; 2-acre lake; swimming pool; 16 cabins with bathroom facilities; 4 tennis courts; 2 rappelling towers.

Profile of Summer Employees Total number 70; average age 21. Employees are 10% minorities, 40% high school students, 60% college students, 5% international, 10% local residents. Prefers nonsmokers.

Employment Information Openings are from June 1 to August 20. Year-round positions also offered. College credit possible. Jobs available: 16 *senior cabin counselors* with rising college sophomore status at $130–$150 per week; 16 *junior cabin counselors* with rising high school senior status at $95–$105 per week; 1 *aquatic director* with a minimum age of 21 at $165–$238 per week; 1 *rappelling director* with a minimum age of 21 at $130–$150 per week. International students encouraged to apply.

Benefits Preemployment training, on-the-job training, on-site room and board, laundry facilities, health insurance.

Contact Applicant should send resume, write for application, call for information, or apply in person by April 1 to Ron Austin, Camp Director, or Michaux Crocker, Assistant

Camp Director, YMCA Camp Cheerio, Department SED, P.O. Box 6258, High Point, North Carolina 27262; 919-869-0195.

As a branch of the Young Men's Christian Association, we hold to a spiritual emphasis. Through the use of natural surroundings and under Christian auspices and trained leadership, YMCA camping seeks to help the camper achieve his fullest potential in mental development, physical well-being, social growth, and spiritual awareness.

North Dakota

NATIONAL PARK SERVICE

Contact   Applicant should write for application (must be 18 by May 13; U.S. citizenship required) to Regional Office of the National Park Service, Rocky Mountain Region, National Park Service, P.O. Box 25287, Denver, Colorado 80225-0287.

Jobs located in North Dakota at the following facilities: Fort Union Trading Post, Knife River Indian Villages, Theodore Roosevelt National Park. Also see District of Columbia listing.

Ohio

CAMP BUTTERWORTH
8551 Butterworth Road
Maineville, Ohio 45039

General Information   Girls' residential camp providing the opportunity to have fun, try new activities, and live in the outdoors with girls from diverse backgrounds. Owned by Great Rivers Girl Scout Council, Incorporated. Located 20 miles northeast of Cincinnati on 147 acres. Features include location overlooking the Little Miami River; many scenic hiking trails; wide variety of wildlife; close proximity to Cincinnati and expressway; swimming pool; site surrounded by wooded, rolling hills.

Profile of Summer Employees   Total number 35; average age 20. Employees are 95% female, 10% minorities, 1% high school students, 75% college students, 1% retirees, 10% international, 75% local residents. Prefers nonsmokers.

Employment Information   Openings are from June 14 to August 8. Year-round positions also offered. Jobs available: 1 *camp director* with experience and a college degree (minimum age 25) at $3910–$4619 per season; 1 *health supervisor* with RN, EMT, PA, or MD certification at $2600–$3900 per season; 1 *program director* with experience (minimum age 21) at $1800–$2500 per season; 1 *business manager* with business expereince (minimum age 21) at $1800–$2100 per season; 1 *equestrian director* with horseback-riding and teaching experience (minimum age 21) at $1600–$2100 per season; 2 *horseback-riding instructors* with experience (minimum age 18) at $1280–$1600 per season; 1 *pool director* with WSI and lifeguard certification plus canoe experience preferred (minimum age 21) at $1600–$2000 per season; 2 *waterfront assistants* with lifeguard certification (minimum age 18) at $1280–$1600 per season; 2 *naturalists/crafts consultants* with experience (minimum age 18) at $1280–$1800 per season; 4 *unit leaders* with experience (minimum age

21) at $1500–$1800 per season; 10 *unit counselors* with a minimum age of 18 at $1200–$1500 per season; 1 *administrative assistant* with a minimum age of 17 at $1120–$1440 per season; 6 *kitchen staff* at $1120–$3910 per season. International students encouraged to apply.

Benefits Preemployment training, on-the-job training, on-site room and board at no charge, laundry facilities, health insurance.

Contact Applicant should send resume, write for application, or call for information by May 21 to Susan Osborn, Outdoor Program Director, c/o Great Rivers Girl Scout Council, Inc., Camp Butterworth, 4930 Cornell Road, Cincinnati, Ohio 45242; 513-489-1025, fax 513-489-1417.

CAMP STONYBROOK
4491 East State Route 73
Waynesville, Ohio 45068

General Information Residential troop camp providing a diverse population of girls with a rustic, outdoor experience. Owned by Great Rivers Girl Scout Council, Incorporated. Located 35 miles north of Cincinnati on 315 acres. Features include many hiking trails; creek running through property; area rich in fossils; pool; par course and other sports facilities; location near Caesar's Creek State Park.

Profile of Summer Employees Total number 16; average age 20. Employees are 95% female, 12% minorities, 5% high school students, 75% college students, 5% international, 85% local residents. Prefers nonsmokers.

Employment Information Openings are from June 14 to August 8. Jobs available: 1 *director* with experience and a college degree (minimum age 25) at $3910–$4619 per season; 3 *health supervisors* with RN, EMT, or PA license at $3680–$3910 per season; 1 *program director* with camp experience (minimum age 21) at $1800–$2200 per season; 1 *business manager* with business experience (minimum age 21) at $1800–$2100 per season; 1 *pool director* with lifeguard and WSI certification and/or canoe experience (minimum age 21) at $1600–$2000 per season; 2 *waterfront assistants* with lifeguard certification (minimum age 18) at $1280–$1600 per season; 1 *naturalist/crafts consultant* with experience (minimum age 18) at $1280–$1600 per season; 1 *unit leader* with a minimum age of 21 at $1500–$1800 per season; 2 *unit counselors* with a minimum age of 18 at $1200–$1500 per season; 6 *kitchen staff* at $1120–$3910 per season. International students encouraged to apply.

Benefits Preemployment training, on-the-job training, on-site room and board at no charge, laundry facilities, health insurance.

Contact Applicant should send resume, write for application, or call for information by May 15 to Susan Osborn, Outdoor Program Director, c/o Great Rivers Girl Scout Council, Inc., Camp Stonybrook, 4930 Cornell Road, Cincinnati, Ohio 45242; 513-489-1025, fax 513-489-1417.

GEAUGA LAKE
1060 North Aurora Road
Aurora, Ohio 44202

General Information Traditional amusement park with water area serving over 1 million guests annually. Established 1888. Owned by Funtime Incorporated. Affiliated with International Association of Amusement Parks and Attractions. Located 12 miles east of Cleveland on 278 acres.

Profile of Summer Employees Total number 1,600; average age 17. Employees are 60% female, 25% minorities, 60% high school students, 20% college students, 5% retirees, 1% international, 95% local residents.

Employment Information Openings are from May 22 to September 7. College credit possible. Jobs available: *departmental administrative assistant* with typing, filing, and recordkeeping experience and/or ability, familiarity with word processors or personal computers, computation and problem solving skills, and enjoyment of public contact at $180–$220 per week; *internal auditor* with self-discipline, strong computational, organizational, and interpersonal skills, plus knowledge of public accounting helpful (must be accounting major) at $180–$220 per week; *event coordinator* with organizational, problem solving, and written and verbal communications skills at $180–$220 per week; *gift shop person* with sales and inventory control ability plus possession of service, interpersonal relations, and supervisory skills at $180–$220 per week; *food-service person* with ability to perform cost containment and inventory control duties, assess product quality, plus possession of service, interpersonal relations, and supervisory skills at $180–$220 per week; *culinary person* with ability to perform menu planning, pricing, and food preparation plus good interpersonal skills at $180–$220 per week; *volleyball coordinator* with good organizational, interpersonal, and communications skills plus knowledge of or experience in volleyball at $180–$220 per week; *lifeguard* with certification or ability to meet, or be trained to meet, certification requirements plus good interpersonal communication skills and ability to handle stress at $180–$220 per week. International students encouraged to apply.

Benefits Preemployment training, on-the-job training, transportation arranged from off-site housing, merit increases and promotion possibilities, company-sponsored employee events and trips, entertainment and food discounts at area merchants.

Contact Applicant should send resume, write for application, or call for information by March 15 to Employment Coordinator, Geauga Lake, 1060 North Aurora Road, Aurora, Ohio 44202; 216-562-8303, fax 216-562-7020.

We offer an excellent opportunity for hands-on experience. Because we restaff each season, our jobs are positions of real authority and responsibility, not merely "trainee" or "summer help" jobs. Few work opportunities offer the level of leadership development, skill enhancement, or social interaction that ours provide.

NATIONAL PARK SERVICE

Contact Applicant should write for application (must be 18 by May 13; U.S. citizenship required) to Regional Office of the National Park Service, Midwest Region, National Park Service, 1709 Jackson Street, Omaha, Nebraska 68102.

Jobs located in Ohio at the following facilities: Cuyahoga Valley, Mound City Group National Monument, Perry's Victory and International Peace Memorial, William Howard Taft National Historic Site. Also see District of Columbia listing.

Oklahoma

NATIONAL PARK SERVICE

Contact Applicant should write for application (must be 18 by May 13; U.S. citizenship required) to Regional Office of the National Park Service, Southwest Region, National Park Service, P.O. Box 728, Santa Fe, New Mexico 87501.

Jobs located in Oklahoma at the following facility: Chickasaw National Recreation Area. Also see District of Columbia listing.

Oregon

CRATER LAKE LODGE COMPANY
Crater Lake National Park
Crater Lake, Oregon 97604

General Information Operates all concession facilities in Crater Lake National Park. Located 83 miles northeast of Medford. Features include location at the south rim of Crater Lake at a 7,100 foot elevation in the Cascade Range; 40 cabin rooms, service station, 198-site campground, boat tours, food service, gift shop, and grocery store; many foreign visitors; the nation's deepest lake (1,932 feet).

Employment Information Openings are from June 12 to September 15. Year-round positions also offered. College credit possible. Jobs available: 65 *food-service workers;* 4 *maintenance/janitorial/registration personnel* with valid driver's license; 3 *office workers* with experience and accounting skills plus money-counting ability; 4 *boat tour operators* with Red Cross card; 20 *gift shop personnel (retail); front-desk personnel; housekeeping staff; laundry staff; bellhop; rim tour operator.*

Benefits On-site room and board, opportunities for advancement for returning employees.

Contact Applicant should send resume or write for application by April 15 to Teresa Greer, Personnel Manager, Crater Lake Lodge Company, Department SED, P.O. Box 128, Crater Lake, Oregon 97604; 503-594-2511.

Compensation for all positions detailed in this listing is $4.75 per hour.

NATIONAL PARK SERVICE

Contact Applicant should write for application (must be 18 by May 13; U.S. citizenship required) to Regional Office of the National Park Service, Pacific Northwest Region, National Park Service, 83 South King Street, Suite 212, Seattle, Washington 98104.

Jobs located in Oregon at the following facilities: Crater Lake, John Day Fossil Beds, Fort Clatsop, Oregon Caves. Also see District of Columbia listing.

YWCA CAMP WESTWIND
2353 North Three Rocks Road
Otis, Oregon 97368

General Information   Coeducational, residential camp of traditional activities for children ages 7–18 and adults. Established 1936. Owned by YWCA. Affiliated with American Camping Association. Located 90 miles west of Portland on 500 acres. Features include location on Pacific Ocean; environmentally rich site (estuary, rainforest, river, oceanfront, beaches, tidepools); special programs (horseback riding, marine science, teen and family sessions).

Profile of Summer Employees   Total number 35; average age 20. Employees are 70% female, 4% minorities, 2% high school students, 97% college students, 2% international, 70% local residents.

Employment Information   Openings are from June 15 to August 31. College credit possible. International students encouraged to apply.

Benefits   Preemployment training, on-the-job training, on-site room and board at no charge.

Contact   Applicant should write for application or call for information by June 5 to Miriam Callaghan, Camp Administrator, YWCA Camp Westwind, Department SED, 1111 Southwest Tenth Avenue, Portland, Oregon 97205; 503-223-6281.

Camp Westwind is searching for counselors and program staff members who enjoy children, the outdoors, and working with a group of diverse people as part of a team. The YWCA mission, "advancement of women and the elimination of racism and other forms of discrimination," is built into the program by example and focuses on an awareness of nature and the global community.

Pennsylvania

BEACON LODGE CAMP FOR THE BLIND
RD 1, Mount Union
Mount Union, Pennsylvania 17066

General Information   Residential camp serving the blind and visually impaired, deaf and hearing impaired, and special needs/physically disabled adults and children. Established 1948. Operated by Lions/Lioness Clubs of Pennsylvania. Affiliated with Pennsylvania Recreation and Parks, Conference of Lions Camps of the U.S. Located 75 miles west of Harrisburg on 583 acres. Features include location beside the beautiful blue Juniata River; all wooded area (except for 20 acres); modern facilities; program offering canoeing, kayaking, and rowboating on river; pond for fishing.

Profile of Summer Employees   Total number 70; average age 22. Employees are 70% female, 8% high school students, 51% college students, 41% retirees, 49% local residents. Prefers nonsmokers.

Employment Information   Openings are from May 25 to August 21. College credit possible. Jobs available: 1 *outfitter* with experience in hiking and bicycle touring plus valid driver's license (minimum age 21) at $1500 per season; 2 *nurses* with RN license at $3500 per season; 1 *canteen manager* with mature attitude and some fast food restaurant experience at $1500 per season; 1 *lifeguard/pool supervisor* with WSI, CPR, and basic first aid certification plus a minimum age of 18 (21 years of age preferred) at $1600–$1700 per season; 4 *lifeguards* with advanced lifesaving certificate at $1400–$1500 per season; 1 *quartermaster* with previous camping experience at $1400–$1500 per season; 1 *crafts instructor* with demonstrable coursework or experience in woodworking, macrame, pottery, ceramics, weaving, and candlemaking at $1400–$1600 per season; 1 *kayaking instructor* with Red Cross kayaking instructor certification or equivalent at $1500–$1700 per season; 1 *canoeing instructor* with Red Cross canoeing instructor certification or equivalent at $1500–$1700 per season; 1 *archery instructor* with archery instructor certification (target or field) and a minimum age of 18 at $1500–$1700 per season; 1 *air-riflery instructor* with NRA air-riflery instructor certification (minimum age 18) at $1500–$1700 per season; 1 *trip counselor* with demonstrable experience in group trip planning (minimum age 18) at $1400–$1500 per season; 1 *program director* with B.A. degree in therapeutic recreation or related field at $1700–$1900 per season; 2 *unit directors* with minimum two years experience at Beacon Lodge (minimum age 21) at $1700–$1900 per season; 22 *general counselors* with scouting, camping, or similar experience and a genuine interest in working with people at $1300–$1500 per season. International students encouraged to apply.

Benefits   Preemployment training, on-site room and board at no charge, laundry facilities.

Contact   Applicant should send resume, write for application, or call for information by April 15 to Steve Arcona, Camp Director, Beacon Lodge Camp for the Blind, Department SED, RD 1, Box 315, Mount Union, Pennsylvania 17066; 814-542-2511.

BRYN MAWR CAMP
RR 5, Box 410
Honesdale, Pennsylvania 18431

General Information   Girls' camp serving 350 children ages 5–15 for eight weeks. Year-round conference center and mountain retreat. Established 1921. Owned by Herb Kutzen. Operated by Bryn Mawr Camp Inc. Affiliated with American Camping Association, Wayne County Camping Association. Located 105 miles north of New York City on 135 acres. Features include seventy-two years of tradition and family values; home of the 5 Star Basketball Camp; outstanding programs on 18 tennis courts; 2 heated swimming pools; 10,000 square-foot gymnasium; 15,000 square-foot theater arts building seating 1,000.

Profile of Summer Employees   Total number 130. Employees are 85% female, 5% minorities, 2% high school students, 60% college students, 13% retirees, 15% international, 5% local residents. Requires nonsmokers.

Employment Information   Openings are from June 15 to September 5. Spring break positions also offered. College credit possible. Jobs available: 10 *swimming instructors* with WSI certificate at $1000–$1600 per season; 2 *small craft instructors* with American Red Cross small craft license at $1000–$1400 per season; 3 *waterskiing instructors* with experience at $1000–$1500 per season; 16 *tennis instructors* at $800–$1600 per season; 4 *arts and crafts instructors* at $800–$1600 per season; 3 *dance instructors* at $800–$1600 per season; 5 *English-riding instructors* at $800–$1600 per season; 12 *kitchen assistants* at $1000–$1800 per season; 5 *laundry/light-housekeeping personnel* at $1000–$1400 per season; 2 *office staff* at $1000–$1600 per season; 5 *athletics instructors* at $800–$1600 per season; 4 *drama instructors* at $800–$1600 per season; 4 *gymnastics instructors* at $800–

$1600 per season; 3 *piano/technical theater personnel* at $800–$1600 per season; 12 *general counselors* at $800–$1200 per season. International students encouraged to apply.
Benefits Preemployment training, on-the-job training, formal ongoing training, on-site room and board at no charge, laundry facilities, travel reimbursement, staff uniforms furnished, use of staff bicycles, planned staff days off, pre- and post-camp work, year-round employment opportunities, skill bonuses, travel allowances.
Contact Applicant should send resume, write for application, or call for information by May 15 to Herb Kutzen, Director or Brad Finkelstein, Director of Personnel, Bryn Mawr Camp, Department SED, 81 Falmouth Street, Short Hills, New Jersey 07078; 201-467-3518, fax 201-467-3750.

Bryn Mawr Camp is also the home of the Bryn Mawr Conference Center and Mountain Retreat, a year-round facility adapted to the needs of corporations, schools, specialty programs, and other diversified groups.

CAMP AKIBA
Reeders, Pennsylvania 18352

General Information Residential camp offering an eight-week session. Akiba is private, independent, and accredited. Established 1926. Owned by Howard Gordon. Affiliated with American Camping Association, Pocono Mountains Vacation Bureau. Located 50 miles north of Allentown on 350 acres. Features include 21 tennis courts; 2 Olympic-size pools; 40-acre lake; 6 volleyball courts (2 sand); 2 miniature golf courses; 5 softball and 4 basketball courts.
Profile of Summer Employees Total number 225; average age 20. Employees are 100% college students.
Employment Information Openings are from June 20 to August 20. College credit possible. Jobs available: 8 *pool instructors* with ALS and WSI certificate at $1200–$1600 per season; 2 *lakefront personnel* with SCI certificate or experience at $1100–$1500 per season; 10 *tennis instructors* with teaching experience at $1200–$2000 per season; 150 *general counselors* with a desire to work with children at $900–$1700 per season; 2 *riflery instructors* with experience handling .22 caliber rifles at $900–$1300 per season; 2 *archery instructors* with teaching experience at $900–$1300 per season; 2 *mini-bikes/go-cart instructors* with mini-bike and go-cart experience at $900–$1400 per season; *video/photo instructor* with video or photo experience at $900–$1400 per season; *team sport instructor* with experience and skill in sport at $900–$1500 per season; *individual sport instructor* with experience and skill in sport at $900–$1500 per season; *arts and crafts instructor* with ability to teach and construct projects at $1000–$1500 per season; *outdoor-adventure instructor* with experience and ability to teach ropes course, rappelling, and rafting at $900–$1500 per season; *jet-skiing instructor* with experience and ability to teach at $900–$1400 per season; *waterskiing instructor* with experience and ability to teach at $900–$1500 per season; *horseback-riding instructor* with experience and ability to teach at $1000–$1400 per season. International students encouraged to apply.
Benefits Preemployment training, on-the-job training, on-site room and board at no charge, laundry facilities, travel reimbursement, health insurance.
Contact Applicant should send resume, write for application, or call for information by May 1 to Marie B. Ray, Executive Director, Camp Akiba, Department SED, Box 840, Bala–Cynwyd, Pennsylvania 19004; 215-649-7877, fax 215-660-9556.
Come join our Akiba family.

CAMP CAYUGA
RD 1, Box 1180
Honesdale, Pennsylvania 18431

General Information Coeducational camp for children ages 5–15. Established 1956. Owned by Brian and Trish Buynak. Affiliated with American Camping Association, Wayne County Camping Association, American Red Cross. Located 115 miles northwest of New York City on 300 acres. Features include Olympic-size swimming pool; private natural stream-fed lake; 25-horse stable on premises; 45 modern cabins; location in the Pocono Mountain region; over 50 fun activities; camper-staff ratio of 3:1.

Profile of Summer Employees Total number 100; average age 23. Employees are 50% female, 10% minorities, 68% college students, 2% retirees, 15% international, 5% local residents.

Employment Information Openings are from June 19 to August 22. Winter break, Christmas break positions also offered. College credit possible. Jobs available: 10 *swimming instructors* with WSI certification (minimum age 19) at $1100–$1600 per season; 5 *sailing instructors* with lifeguard certification (minimum age 19) at $1100–$1600 per season; 4 *gymnastics instructors* with college experience (minimum age 19) at $1000–$1300 per season; 4 *ceramics instructors* with college experience (minimum age 19) at $1000–$1300 per season; 4 *martial arts instructors* with teaching experience (minimum age 19) at $1100–$1400 per season; 3 *riflery instructors* with NRA certification or equivalent (minimum age 19) at $1100–$1300 per season; 4 *drama instructors* with at least one year of college completed (minimum age 19) at $1000–$1300 per season; 4 *archery instructors* with at least one year of college completed (minimum age 19) at $1000–$1300 per season; 5 *tennis instructors* with coaching experience (minimum age 19) at $1100–$1300 per season; 3 *Yamaha quad-riding instructors* with at least one year of college completed (minimum age 19) at $1100–$1300 per season; 3 *computer instructors* with at least one year of college completed (minimum age 19) at $1000–$1300 per season; 4 *radio broadcasting instructors* with at least one year of college completed (minimum age 19) at $1000–$1300 per season; 3 *wrestling instructors* with coaching/teaching experience (minimum age 19) at $1100–$1300 per season; 3 *windsurfing instructors* with lifeguard certification (minimum age 19) at $1100–$1600 per season; 12 *horseback-riding instructors* with quality experience (minimum age 19) at $1000–$1300 per season; 3 *rocketry instructors* with at least one year of college completed (minimum age 19) at $1000–$1300 per season; 3 *cheerleading instructors* with at least one year of college completed (minimum age 19) at $1000–$1300 per season; 3 *dance instructors* with at least one year of college completed (minimum age 19) at $1000–$1300 per season; 3 *basketball instructors* with coaching experience (minimum age 19) at $1000–$1300 per season; 5 *waterfront directors* with teaching experience (minimum age 24) at $1500–$2800 per season; 4 *program directors* with coaching experience (minimum age 25) at $1500–$2800 per season; 4 *athletics directors* with coaching experience (minimum age 25) at $1500–$2800 per season; 4 *head counselors* with a minimum age of 25 at $1500–$2800 per season; 4 *waterskiing instructors* with lifeguard certification (minimum age 19) at $1200–$1600 per season; 3 *video camera instructors* with at least one year of college completed (minimum age 19) at $1000–$1300 per season; 3 *golf instructors* with at least one year of college completed (minimum age 19) at $1000–$1300 per season; 6 *nurses* with RN, LPN, or EMT license (free tuition for family) at $1500–$3000 per season; 4 *arts and crafts instructors* with at least one year of college completed (minimum age 19) at $1000–$1300 per season; 4 *office personnel* with office experience (minimum age 19) at $1000–$1500 per season; 4 *volleyball instructors* with at least one year of college completed (minimum age 19) at $1000–$1300 per season.

Benefits Preemployment training, on-the-job training, formal ongoing training, on-site room and board at no charge, laundry facilities, travel reimbursement, end-of-season bonus, tipping and gratuities, free Alpine ski reunion.

Contact Applicant should write for application or call for information by June 1 to Brian B. Buynak, Director, Camp Cayuga, Department SED, P.O. Box 452, Washington, New Jersey 07882; 908-689-3339, fax 908-689-8209.

At Camp Cayuga, our specialty is caring. We seek out staff members who can provide warm, mature guidance and relate to each camper individually. We are committed to bringing children of diverse backgrounds together in a healthy camp environment where the youngster will be given the opportunity and the help to develop artistically, athletically, and socially and also be taught the importance of friendship, independence, and cooperation with others. A safe, healthy, and enjoyable summer is promised for all. So come and be part of the Camp Cayuga experience. The memories you make will last a lifetime!

CAMP NETIMUS
RD 1, Box 117
Milford, Pennsylvania 18337

General Information Residential girls' camp offering four- or eight-week sessions. Offers thirty-six activities (girls can choose their own schedule). Help children to develop self-confidence and a positive self-image. Established 1930. Owned by Camp Netimus Inc. Located 110 miles southeast of New York City on 400 acres. Features include family atmosphere; caring, nurturing, supportive atmosphere; cabins; location in northeastern Pennsylvania; waterfalls, lake, and mountains; international staff; individualized programs.

Profile of Summer Employees Total number 75; average age 24. Employees are 90% female, 1% high school students, 4% college students, 5% retirees, 4% international, 5% local residents. Prefers nonsmokers.

Employment Information Openings are from June 10 to August 20. College credit possible. Jobs available: *lifeguard trainers* with WSI certificate at $1000–$3000 per season; *sailing instructor* with lifeguard training at $1000–$3000 per season; *fine arts instructor* at $1000–$3000 per season; *jewelry/metal craft instructor* at $1000–$3000 per season; *waterskiing instructor* with lifeguard training (minimum age 21) at $1000–$3000 per season; *horseback-riding instructor* at $1000–$3000 per season; *nurses* at $1000–$3000 per season; *fencing instructor* at $1000–$3000 per season; *rock-climbing instructor* at $1000–$3000 per season; *stained glass instructor* at $1000–$3000 per season; *woodworking instructor* at $1000–$3000 per season; *canoeing instructor* with lifeguard training at $1000–$3000 per season; *outdoor and environmental instructor* at $1000–$3000 per season. International students encouraged to apply.

Benefits Preemployment training, on-the-job training, formal ongoing training, on-site room and board at no charge, laundry facilities, transportation on day off, skill development (CPR, first aid, lifeguard training), salary bonus for certifications.

Contact Applicant should send resume, write for application, call for information, or apply in person by April 30 to Donna Kistler, Director, Camp Netimus, Department SED, RD 1, Box 117A, Milford, Pennsylvania 18337; 800-225-0604, fax 717-296-6128.

Camp Netimus provides staff members with the opportunity to teach in a "be yourself" atmosphere. Spend a summer in the Poconos and have the opportunity to develop your camp skills.

CAMP NOCK–A–MIXON
Traugers Crossing Road
Kintnersville, Pennsylvania 18930

General Information Residential, coeducational camp serving 340 youngsters ages 7–15 during a 7½-week session. Established 1938. Owned by Mark Glaser. Affiliated with American Camping Association. Located 48 miles north of Philadelphia on 115 acres. Features include 2 pools for instruction and recreation; 2 lakes for boating and sailing; 10 tennis courts; 2 indoor recreation halls; nature areas; creative arts/drama activities.

Profile of Summer Employees Total number 100; average age 19. Employees are 45% female, 10% high school students, 90% college students. Requires nonsmokers.

Employment Information Openings are from June 20 to August 17. Jobs available: 30 *general counselors* at $800–$1100 per season; 30 *specialists and counselors* at $850–$1150 per season; 10 *swimming instructors* with WSI certificate and/or lifeguard training at $1000–$2000 per season; 6 *tennis counselors* at $850–$1150 per season; 2 *drama directors* at $900–$1150 per season; 1 *crafts director* at $1200–$1800 per season.

Benefits Preemployment training, on-the-job training, formal ongoing training, on-site room and board at no charge, laundry facilities, days off to visit nearby Philadelphia, New York City, and Atlantic City (all within 2 hours travel time).

Contact Applicant should write for application or call for information by May 1 to Mark Glaser, Director, Camp Nock–A–Mixon, Department SED, 16 Gum Tree Lane, Lafayette Hill, Pennsylvania 19444; 215-941-0128.

CAMP SUSQUEHANNOCK FOR GIRLS
Friendsville, Pennsylvania 18818

General Information Residential camp for 85 girls ages 7–17. Offers four- or eight-week sessions. Established 1986. Owned by Edwin and George Shafer. Affiliated with American Camping Association, Camp Directors' Roundtable. Located 15 miles south of Binghamton, New York on 750 acres. Features include lake; excellent sports instruction; children and staff from other countries.

Profile of Summer Employees Total number 26; average age 21. Requires nonsmokers.

Employment Information Openings are from June 17 to August 17. College credit possible. Jobs available: 2 *swimming instructors* with lifeguard certificate at $800–$1000 per season; 2 *arts and crafts instructors* at $800–$1000 per season; 1 *nurse* with RN license at $1500–$1650 per season; 2 *horseback riders* at $900–$1200 per season.

Benefits Preemployment training, on-the-job training, on-site room and board at no charge, laundry facilities, travel reimbursement.

Contact Applicant should write for application by March 15 to Mrs. George C. Shafer, Codirector, Camp Susquehannock for Girls, Department SED, 860 Briarwood Road, Newtown Square, Pennsylvania 19073; 215-356-3426.

COLLEGE SETTLEMENT OF PHILADELPHIA
600 Witmer Road
Horsham, Pennsylvania 19044

General Information Residential and day camp serving disadvantaged youths ages 7–14 from the Philadelphia metropolitan area. Established 1922. Affiliated with American Camping Association, United Way. Located 20 miles south of Philadelphia on 235 acres. Features include location in suburbs; outpost facility for trips; interracial, intercultural opportunities provided; ropes course on site; diverse habitat including ponds, woods, fields, and meadows.

Profile of Summer Employees Total number 60; average age 25. Employees are 50% female, 20% minorities, 80% college students, 10% international, 10% local residents. Prefers nonsmokers.

Employment Information Openings are from June 10 to August 25. Year-round positions also offered. College credit possible. Jobs available: 12 *cabin counselors* at $1600 per season; 3 *unit leaders* at $1800 per season; 3 *trip leaders* with first aid/CPR certificate at $1800–$2000 per season; 2 *environmentalists* at $1600–$1800 per season; 3 *swimming instructors* with WSI and LGT certification (preferred) at $1700–$2000 per season; 1 *administrative assistant* at $1600–$1800 per season; 1 *provisions coordinator* at $1600–$1800 per season. International students encouraged to apply.

Benefits Preemployment training, on-the-job training, on-site room and board at no charge, laundry facilities, travel reimbursement.

Contact Applicant should send resume, write for application, call for information, or apply in person by May 1 to Wally Grummun, Director of Resident Programs, College Settlement of Philadelphia, Department SED, 600 Witmer Road, Horsham, Pennsylvania 19044; 215-542-7974.

The camp philosophy encourages extended family-community relationships and stresses care and concern for one another and the surroundings.

THE ENSEMBLE THEATRE COMMUNITY SCHOOL
Box 188
Eagles Mere, Pennsylvania 17731

General Information Summer theater school serving high school students ages 14–18. Established 1984. Located 40 miles north of Williamsport. Features include location in the Allegheny Mountains; intensive training and performances; ensemble-oriented approach; faculty and students live in large residential Victorian house; performances and classes conducted in community arts facility; swimming, tennis courts, basketball facilities, and hiking trails.

Profile of Summer Employees Total number 12; average age 24. Employees are 50% female, 15% minorities, 33% college students. Prefers nonsmokers.

Employment Information Openings are from June 23 to August 9. College credit possible. Jobs available: 1 *acting instructor* with extensive training and experience in teaching and performing at $1200–$1500 per season; 1 *acting instructor/director* with extensive training and experience in teaching and performing at $1200–$1500 per season; 1 *movement instructor* with extensive training and experience in teaching and performing at $1200–$1500 per season; 1 *music instructor* with extensive training and experience in teaching and performing at $1200–$1500 per season; 1 *technical director* with extensive

training and experience in teaching and performing at $1200–$1500 per season; 4 *college interns* with training and experience in theater and related arts at $300–$350 per season.
Benefits Preemployment training, on-the-job training, on-site room and board at no charge, laundry facilities.
Contact Applicant should send resume by February 28 to Seth Orbach, Associate Director, The Ensemble Theatre Community School, 511 East 82nd Street, #4FW, New York, New York 10028; 212-794-0126.

ETC offers a mentor system for college students and new teachers. Teachers are encouraged to develop curricula and are given opportunities to teach independently and in teams.

HARMONY HEART CAMP
RR 2, Box 246
Jermyn, Pennsylvania 18433

General Information Christian outreach to children from New York City ages 7–15 through a well-rounded camping program. Established 1946. Owned by World Impact, Inc. Affiliated with Christian Camping International, Camp Horsemanship Association. Located 15 miles north of Scranton on 30 acres. Features include location on Heart Lake; CHA horsemanship program; high-quality Christian staff; beautiful country setting.
Profile of Summer Employees Total number 25; average age 19. Employees are 5% female, 20% minorities, 40% high school students, 60% college students, 1% international, 30% local residents. Requires nonsmokers.
Employment Information Openings are from June 15 to August 15. Jobs available: 12 *counselors* at $100 per week; 2 *swimming instructors* with WSI certificate or equivalent; 1 *camp nurse* with RN license (preferred) at $100 per week; 1 *program director* with related experience; 1 *crafts instructor* at $100 per week; 1 *head cook* with related experience; 10 *support staff* at $30 per week. International students encouraged to apply.
Benefits Preemployment training, on-the-job training, on-site room and board at no charge.
Contact Applicant should write for application or call for information by June 1 to Larry Bartlett, Camp Director, Harmony Heart Camp, Department SED, RR 2, Box 246, Jermyn, Pennsylvania 18433; 717-254-6272.

Our camp provides the opportunity for Christian evangelism and discipleship as well as cross-cultural evangelism. It also provides a great opportunity to meet fellow Christians and to gain valuable work experience.

HERSHEYPARK
100 West Hersheypark Drive
Hershey, Pennsylvania 17033

General Information Facility produces five residential shows, song and dance revues, and other types of family entertainment. Established 1972. Owned by Hershey Entertainment Resort Company. Located 90 miles southwest of Philadelphia on 87 acres. Features include location in Chocolatetown, USA; professional shows; professional production team; Equity-eligible performers; subsidized housing.

Profile of Summer Employees   Total number 75; average age 21. Employees are 50% female. Prefers nonsmokers.

Employment Information   Openings are from May to September. College credit possible. Jobs available: 60 *singing/dancing performers* with experience (must audition) at $310–$330 per week; 5 *stage managers* with experience at $300–$350 per week; 3 *sound technicians* with experience at $300–$330 per week; 6 *seamstresses/dressers* at $285 per week.

Benefits   On-site room and board at $190 per month, laundry facilities.

Contact   Applicant should send resume by March 31 to Stacy Benson, Assistant Entertainment Manager, Hersheypark, Department SED, 100 West Hersheypark Drive, Hershey, Pennsylvania 17033; 717-534-3349, fax 717-534-3192.

HIDDEN VALLEY CAMP
P.O. Box 98, Wallerville Road
Equinunk, Pennsylvania 18417

General Information   Residential camp serving girls ages 7–17. Established 1971. Owned by Rolling Hills Girl Scout Council. Affiliated with Girl Scouts of the United States of America, American Camping Association. Located 25 miles south of Hancock, New York. Features include 40-acre lake on property; location near Delaware River and Pocono Mountains; nearby stables.

Profile of Summer Employees   Total number 25; average age 20. Employees are 98% female, 20% minorities, 10% high school students, 90% college students, 4% international, 10% local residents.

Employment Information   Openings are from June 20 to August 20. Jobs available: 1 *business manager* with a minimum age of 23 at $1000 per season; 1 *program manager* with a minimum age of 23 at $2000 per season; 15 *unit leaders* with a minimum age of 21 at $1000 per season; 10 *unit assistants* with a minimum age of 18 at $800 per season; 1 *waterfront director* with WSI certificate (minimum age 21) at $1000 per season; 1 *waterfront assistant* with lifeguard certificate (minimum age 18) at $800 per season; 1 *boating director* with WSI and canoe certificates (minimum age 21) at $950 per season; 1 *health supervisor* with RN, LPN, or EMT license (minimum age of 21) at $1200 per season; 1 *cook* with a minimum age of 21 at $1200 per season; 1 *assistant cook* with a minimum age of 18 at $900 per season; 4 *kitchen aides* with a minimum age of 18 at $600 per season; 1 *riding instructor* with riding experience (minimum age 21) at $1000 per season. International students encouraged to apply.

Benefits   Preemployment training, on-the-job training, on-site room and board, laundry facilities, health insurance.

Contact   Applicant should send resume, write for application, or call for information by May 31 to Lani Jeffrey, Camping Services Manager, Hidden Valley Camp, Department SED, P.O. Box 5361, North Branch, New Jersey 08876; 908-725-1226.

NATIONAL PARK SERVICE

Contact   Applicant should write for application (must be 18 by May 13; U.S. citizenship required) to Regional Office of the National Park Service, Mid-Atlantic Region, National Park Service, 143 South Third Street, Philadelphia, Pennsylvania 19106.

Jobs located in Pennsylvania at the following facilities: Allegheny Portage Railroad (includes Johnstown Flood National Memorial), Delaware Water Gap, Edgar Allen Poe National Historic Site, Fort Necessity, Friendship Hill, Gettysburg (includes Eisenhower National Historic Site), Hopewell Furnace, Independence (Gloria Dei, Old Swedes Church, and Thaddeus Kosciuszko National Memorial), Steamtown, Upper Delaware Scenic and Recreational River, Valley Forge. Also see District of Columbia listing.

NEW JERSEY CAMP JAYCEE
Ziegler Road
Effort, Pennsylvania 18330

General Information   Residential camp serving 135 developmentally disabled campers weekly. Established 1975. Owned by New Jersey Jaycee Foundation. Operated by Association for Retarded Citizens of New Jersey. Affiliated with Association for Retarded Citizens of New Jersey, American Camping Association, New Jersey Jaycees. Located 18 miles southwest of Stroudsburg on 185 acres. Features include 2-acre lake; natural setting near Pocono Mountains; excellent meals; high staff-camper ratio; location near resort areas.

Profile of Summer Employees   Total number 76; average age 24. Employees are 50% female, 10% minorities, 95% college students, 65% international, 35% local residents.

Employment Information   Openings are from June 15 to August 20. Jobs available: 2 *swimming instructors* with WSI certificate at $160–$190 per week; 2 *lifeguards* with Red Cross certificate at $150–$170 per week; 6 *specialists* with experience pertaining to developmental disabilities and special campers at $150–$180 per week; 2 *nurses* with RN license at $1800–$2400 per season; 1 *EMT* with EMT license at $170–$220 per week; 1 *maintenance assistant* with driver's license and light maintenance experience at $160–$170 per week; 15 *counselors* with experience pertaining to developmental disabilities at $135–$150 per week. International students encouraged to apply.

Benefits   Preemployment training, on-the-job training, formal ongoing training, on-site room and board at no charge, laundry facilities, travel reimbursement, days off with transportation, beautiful staff hall.

Contact   Applicant should send resume, write for application, call for information, or apply in person by May 15 to Ron Martin, Executive Director, New Jersey Camp Jaycee, Department SED, 985 Livingston Avenue, North Brunswick, New Jersey 08902; 908-247-9670, fax 908-214-1834.

Employees of the camp receive five full days of training and can use the facilities during time off. The camp is located near transportation to New York City and Philadelphia.

PENNSYLVANIA DEPARTMENT OF TRANSPORTATION
Bureau of Personnel, Room 803, Transportation and Safety Building
Harrisburg, Pennsylvania 17120

General Information   State government agency responsible for the planning, design, construction, and maintenance of Pennsylvania's transportation systems. Established 1970.

Profile of Summer Employees   Total number 500. Employees are 10% minorities, 75% college students.

Employment Information   Openings are from March to October. College credit possible. Jobs available: *engineering/scientific/technical interns* with current enrollment as a college student majoring in engineering, math, science, or architecture; *highway maintenance workers; government service interns* with current enrollment as a college student in any major; *transportation/construction inspectors* with two years of construction inspection experience.

Benefits   On-the-job training, travel reimbursement.

Contact   Applicant should write for application to Diana Shreve, College Relations Coordinator, Pennsylvania Department of Transportation, Room 803, Transportation and Safety Building, Harrisburg, Pennsylvania 17120; 717-783-2680.

Many students return for consecutive summers with the department. Wages range from $5 to $10 per hour depending on position and number of years of college completed. (The Pennsylvania Department of Transportation is an equal opportunity employer.)

PENNSYLVANIA EASTER SEAL SOCIETY
P.O. Box 497
Middletown, Pennsylvania 17057

General Information   Three residential camps serving mentally and physically disabled children and adults. Established 1941. Owned by Pennsylvania Easter Seal Society. Affiliated with American Camping Association. Located 10 miles south of Harrisburg on 40 acres. Features include caring staff; mature leadership; locations close to Philadelphia, Pittsburgh, Hersheypark , Washington, D.C., and the Pocono Mountains.

Profile of Summer Employees   Total number 150; average age 21. Employees are 60% female, 5% minorities, 10% high school students, 75% college students, 15% international, 20% local residents.

Employment Information   Openings are from June 15 to August 15. Jobs available: 40 *counselors* with education or human services major at $130–$150 per week; 2 *nurses* with LPN or RN license at $300–$400 per week; 3 *arts and crafts directors* with degree or major in art at $140–$175 per week; 3 *waterfront directors* with Red Cross lifesaving/WSI certificate at $140–$150 per week.

Benefits   Preemployment training, on-the-job training, on-site room and board.

Contact   Applicant should write for application or call for information by May 15 to Richard C. Lewis, Jr., Director of Recreation and Camping, Pennsylvania Easter Seal Society, Department SED, P.O. Box 497, Middletown, Pennsylvania 17057; 717-939-7801, fax 717-986-8324.

Pennsylvania Easter Seals operates three camps at different sites in the state: Camp Harmony Hall, near Harrisburg, Pennsylvania; Camp Dandy Allen, near Whitehaven in the Pocono Mountains; and Camp Lend-A-Hand in Conneaut Lake, Pennsylvania, near Erie.

PINE FOREST CAMPS
Box 242
Greeley, Pennsylvania 18425

General Information Residential camps serving children ages 6–16 and offering four- and eight-week sessions. Established 1931. Owned by Marvin and Mickey Black and Ted S. Halpern. Affiliated with American Camping Association. Located 88 miles north of New York City on 1,000 acres. Features include private lakes and lands; location 1,800 feet above sea level in the forests of the Pocono Mountains; only one owner in 60 years.
Profile of Summer Employees Total number 260; average age 20. Prefers nonsmokers.
Employment Information Openings are from June 24 to August 20. College credit possible. Jobs available: 16 *tennis instructors* with high school or college varsity player status at $1000–$2000 per season; 16 *athletics instructors (general)* with high school or college varsity player status at $1000–$1500 per season; 6 *arts and crafts instructors* with major in art at $800–$1200 per season; 4 *drama/theater instructors* with major in theater at $800–$1200 per season; 8 *canoe/boating instructors* with certification at $800–$1200 per season; 4 *sailing/windsurfing instructors* with certification at $800–$1500 per season; 4 *archery instructors* with experience at $800–$1000 per season; 3 *drivers* with good driving record (minimum age 21) at $1000 per season; *overnight hikers* with scouting experience at $1000–$1200 per season; 2 *athletics directors* with college degree in physical education at $1500–$2000 per season; 6 *head counselors* with college graduate status at $1500–$2400 per season; 2 *lake directors* with college graduate status and WSI certificate at $2000–$2500 per season; 2 *pool directors* with college graduate status and WSI certificate at $2000–$2500 per season; 12 *swimming instructors* with WSI certificate at $600–$1200 per season. International students encouraged to apply.
Benefits Preemployment training, on-the-job training, on-site room and board, laundry facilities, travel reimbursement.
Contact Applicant should send resume, write for application, call for information, or apply in person by June 15 to Marvin and Mickey Black, Directors, Pine Forest Camps, 407 Benson East, Jenkintown, Pennsylvania 19046; 215-887-9700, fax 215-887-3901.

PINEMERE CAMP ASSOCIATION
RD 8, Box 8001
Stroudsburg, Pennsylvania 18360

General Information Residential camp serving 205 children; affiliated with the Jewish centers throughout the mid-Atlantic region. Established 1943. Located 45 miles north of Allentown on 180 acres. Features include 8¾ acre private lake; Olympic-size pool; 130x80-foot enclosed field house; athletics field; 3 Adirondack shelters.
Employment Information College credit possible. Jobs available: 2 *swimming instructors* with WSI certificate at $800–$1200 per season; 1 *lifeguard instructor* with lifeguard instructor certificate at $800–$1200 per season; 6 *general counselors* with experience at $800–$1000 per season; 1 *ropes-course instructor* with experience at $800–$1100 per season; 1 *CPR instructor* with CPR instructor certificate at $800–$1100 per season; 1 *first aid instructor* with first aid instructor certificate at $800–$1100 per season; 1 *ceramics instructor* with experience and working knowledge of kilns at $800–$1100 per season; 1 *archery instructor* with experience at $800–$1100 per season; 2 *riflery instructors* with

NRA instructor certificate at $800–$1100 per season; 1 *music instructor* with guitar or other portable instrument playing ability at $800–$1100 per season; 1 *drama instructor* with experience at $800–$1100 per season; 1 *gymnastics instructor* with beam and mat experience at $800–$1100 per season; 1 *canoe trip leader* with lifeguard certification (minimum age 21) at $800–$1200 per season; 1 *head waiter* with supervisory ability at $800–$1200 per season.

Benefits   On-site room and board, end-of-season bonus possible.

Contact   Applicant should write for application to Robert H. Miner, Executive Director, Pinemere Camp Association, Department SED, 438 West Tabor Road, Philadelphia, Pennsylvania 19120; 215-924-0402.

SHAVER'S CREEK ENVIRONMENTAL CENTER, PENNSYLVANIA STATE UNIVERSITY
Department of Leisure Studies, 203 South Henderson Building
University Park, Pennsylvania 16802

General Information   Environmental educational day camp is for ages 6–11. Adventure program is for ages 12–14. Environmental programs are for general public, fairs, and festivals within the community. Established 1972. Owned by Pennsylvania State University. Affiliated with National Wildlife Federation, Alliance for Environmental Education, Pennsylvania Alliance for Environmental Education. Located 120 miles west of Harrisburg on 750 acres. Features include 72-acre lake; boating and aquatic study; Raptor Rehabilitation Center; hands-on environmental museum/exhibit room; use of Pennsylvania State facilities; trails, herb gardens, and flower gardens.

Profile of Summer Employees   Total number 5; average age 21. Employees are 50% female, 10% minorities, 60% college students, 10% international, 5% local residents.

Employment Information   Openings are from June 1 to August 25. Year-round positions also offered. College credit possible. Jobs available: 5 *environmental education interns* with first aid and CPR certificates at $100 per week. International students encouraged to apply.

Benefits   Preemployment training, on-the-job training, formal ongoing training, on-site room and board at no charge, use of Pennsylvania State Health Clinic.

Contact   Applicant should write for application or call for information by March 1 to Judy B. Elson, Intern Coordinator, Shaver's Creek Environmental Center, Pennsylvania State University, Department SED, 203 South Henderson Building, University Park, Pennsylvania 16802; 814-863-2000.

An internship at Shaver's Creek offers a wide variety of opportunities for individuals to get hands-on experience in the environmental education field. Interns work with both children and adults, get extensive training in areas of natural history, and learn to work with live animals (snakes, turtles, amphibians, and birds of prey).

THREE RIVERS SHAKESPEARE FESTIVAL
University of Pittsburgh, 1617 CL
Pittsburgh, Pennsylvania 15260

General Information   Offers professional classical theater. Established 1980.

Profile of Summer Employees   Total number 50; average age 25. Employees are 30% female, 75% college students, 15% local residents. Prefers nonsmokers.

Employment Information   Openings are from April 30 to August 20. College credit possible. Jobs available: *actors* with experience and training at $150–$200 per week; *technical crew* with experience and training at $150–$200 per week; *costume crew* with experience and training at $150–$200 per week; *assistant stage managers* with experience and training at $150–$200 per week.

Benefits   Access to facilities of the city.

Contact   Applicant should send resume by January to Dr. Attilio Favorini, Producing Director, Three Rivers Shakespeare Festival, Department SED, University of Pittsburgh, 1617 CL, Pittsburgh, Pennsylvania 15260; 412-624-1953, fax 412-687-8929.

Staff members have the opportunity to work in a professional atmosphere and gain valuable experience within an urban, academic setting.

Rhode Island

BALLARD'S INN
Block Island, Rhode Island 02865

General Information   Seafood restaurant catering to boating clientele. Established 1954. Owned by Paul Filippi. Affiliated with Block Island Chamber of Commerce. Located 50 miles south of Providence. Features include location on island accessible by ferry; busy summer resort; unspoiled beaches; youthful environment.

Profile of Summer Employees   Total number 100; average age 25. Employees are 50% female, 20% minorities, 5% high school students, 75% college students, 5% local residents.

Employment Information   Openings are from May 15 to October 15. Jobs available: 2 *lifeguards* with CPR and Red Cross water safety certificates at $200–$300 per week; 25 *waiters/waitresses* with experience at $75 per week; 20 *kitchen helpers* at $250–$300 per week; 20 *cocktail servers* at $75 per week; 6 *office staff* at $200–$250 per week; 6 *cashiers* at $200–$250 per week; 10 *bartenders* at $150 per week; 6 *maintenance persons* at $250–$350 per week; 2 *busboys* at $95 per week.

Benefits   On-the-job training, formal ongoing training, on-site room and board at $75 per week.

Contact   Applicant should send resume by March 15 to Paul Filippi, President, Ballard's Inn, Department SED, 1092 Great Road, Lincoln, Rhode Island 02865; 401-334-2667.

NATIONAL PARK SERVICE

Contact   Applicant should write for application (must be 18 by May 13; U.S. citizenship required) to Regional Office of the National Park Service, North Atlantic Region, National Park Service, 15 State Street, Boston, Massachusetts 02109.

Jobs located in Rhode Island at the following facility: Roger Williams National Historic Site. Also see District of Columbia listing.

ROCKY POINT AMUSEMENTS, INC.
1 Rocky Point Avenue
Warwick, Rhode Island 02889

General Information Family-oriented amusement park situated along the Narragansett Bay. Established 1847. Located 10 miles south of Providence. Features include beautiful and scenic location; world's largest shore dinner hall; freefall ride (one of eight in the United States); only corkscrew roller coaster in New England.

Profile of Summer Employees Total number 600; average age 20. Employees are 40% female.

Employment Information Openings are from May to September. Jobs available: 150 *ride operators* with a minimum age of 18; 100 *cashiers; gate attendants;* 200 *food-service personnel; assistant ride operators; office personnel; carpenters/mechanics/maintenance personnel; barmaids/bartenders.* International students encouraged to apply.

Benefits Preemployment training, on-the-job training, formal ongoing training.

Contact Applicant should write for application, call for information, or apply in person by April 15 to Albert Albino, Operations Manager, Rocky Point Amusements, Inc., Department SED, 1 Rocky Point Avenue, Warwick, Rhode Island 02889; 401-737-8000, fax 401-738-3690.

We offer excellent working conditions, interesting work, a warm social atmosphere, and more. (Please note that wages for jobs detailed in this listing vary by position and qualifications. On-site lodging may also be available on a very limited basis. Applicants must be able to speak English clearly.)

South Carolina

FRIPP ISLAND CLUB
201 Tarpon Boulevard
Fripp Island, South Carolina 29920

General Information Private coastal resort island offering clientele a full range of recreational facilities. Owned by The Fripp Company, Inc. Located 17 miles east of Beaufort. Features include 8 pools and a beach club; championship golf course; 10-court racquet club; full-service marina; private ownership; very peaceful atmosphere.

Profile of Summer Employees Total number 45; average age 20. Employees are 50% female, 33% high school students, 33% college students, 33% local residents. Prefers nonsmokers.

Employment Information Openings are from April 1 to September 30. Year-round positions also offered. College credit possible. International students encouraged to apply.

Benefits On-the-job training, on-site room and board at $150 per month, use of club facilities.

Contact Applicant should send resume, write for application, call for information, or apply in person by April 30 to Logan Crowther, Recreation Director, Fripp Island Club, 201 Tarpon Boulevard, Fripp Island, South Carolina 29920; 803-838-2131, fax 803-838-2733.

NATIONAL PARK SERVICE

Contact Applicant should write for application (must be 18 by May 13; U.S. citizenship required) to Regional Office of the National Park Service, Southeast Region, National Park Service, 75 Spring Street, SW, Atlanta, Georgia 30303.

Jobs located in South Carolina at the following facilities: Fort Sumter, Kings Mountain. Also see District of Columbia listing.

SUN BEACH SERVICE
North Myrtle Beach, South Carolina 29582

General Information Coordinator of ocean lifeguard services and beach vendors for the City of North Myrtle Beach. Located 10 miles north of Myrtle Beach.

Employment Information Openings are from May 30 to September. Jobs available: 50 *lifeguards (also responsible for rental of floats, umbrellas, and beach chairs)* with Red Cross Advanced Lifeguard and CPR certification (minimum age 17); 10 *sailboat operators* with experience handling Hobie sailboats (ocean sailing experience preferred); 30 *beach vendors* with lifesaving and CPR certification (minimum age 17).

Benefits On-site room and board, outdoor work, end of season bonus for those able to stay through Labor Day.

Contact Applicant should write for application by March 31 to David Hatley, Director, Sun Beach Service, 525 Sixth Avenue South, North Myrtle Beach, South Carolina 29582; 803-272-4170.

We're looking for mature, responsible, and honest young men and women who realize the seriousness of their jobs. Applicants must have pleasant personalities and be able to get along well with people. Salary for lifeguards and sailboat operators is based on rental commission, experience level, and merit. Vendors receive a percentage of their sales.

THUNDERBIRD YMCA
1 Thunderbird Lane
Lake Wylie, South Carolina 29710

General Information Coeducational, residential camp serving ages 8–16 with seventeen-day sessions. Established 1937. Owned by YMCA of Greater Charlotte. Affiliated with American Camping Association, Young Men's Christian Association. Located 12 miles south of Charlotte on 108 acres. Features include value-based program with emphasis on interpersonal skills; 1 mile of shoreline; nature preserve on 110 acres at additional site; 1:4 counselor-camper ratio; beautifully maintained facilities; environmental education and conferences from September to May.

Profile of Summer Employees Total number 130; average age 20. Employees are 45% female, 10% minorities, 25% high school students, 75% college students, 5% international, 15% local residents. Prefers nonsmokers.

Employment Information Openings are from June 30 to August 14. Year-round positions also offered. Jobs available: 2 *outpost instructors* with CPR or first aid training at $100 per week; 3 *outdoor-living skills personnel* at $100 per week; 4 *waterskiing instructors* with boat driving experience and CPR or first aid training at $85–$100 per week; 4 *challenge-course instructors* with CPR or first aid training at $85–$100 per week; 5

horseback-riding instructors with English riding experience at $85–$100 per week; 1 *horseback-riding chief* with CHA certification and experience at $150–$250 per week; 2 *riflery instructors* at $85–$100 per week; 2 *archery instructors* at $85–$100 per week; 4 *swimming instructors* with lifeguard training (YMCA or ARC) and YMCA progressive instructor or WSI certificate at $85–$100 per week; 4 *canoeing instructors* with experience and American Red Cross certificate at $85–$100 per week; 5 *sailing instructors* with experience at $85–$100 per week; 2 *golf instructors* at $85–$100 per week; 4 *gymnastics instructors* with experience at $85–$100 per week; 3 *dance/aerobics/cheerleading/roller-blade instructors* at $85–$100 per week; 6 *general athletics instructors* at $85–$100 per week. International students encouraged to apply.

Benefits   Preemployment training, on-the-job training, on-site room and board at no charge.

Contact   Applicant should send resume, write for application, call for information, or apply in person by February 28 to Georgia D. Harris, Assistant Director, Thunderbird YMCA, Department SED, 1 Thunderbird Lane, Lake Wylie, South Carolina 29710; 803-831-2121, fax 803-831-2977.

We have a high return rate of staff members from junior counselors to administrative staff. Campers and staff members come from all over the United States and the world. We're looking for committed, motivated, and dedicated employees who are willing to place the needs of campers before their own. All positions are dual positions as instructors and cabin counselors. Salaries listed are base pay for first-year staff.

South Dakota

CUSTER STATE PARK RESORT COMPANY
HC 83, Box 74
Custer, South Dakota 57730

General Information   Operates 4 resorts and offers services such as lodging, dining, groceries, gas, and souvenirs and gifts, as well as activities that include trail rides, jeep tours, and cookouts. Established 1919. Owned by Wild Phil's, Inc. Affiliated with South Dakota Restaurant Association, South Dakota Innkeepers' Association, National Tour Association. Located 30 miles south of Rapid City on 73,000 acres. Features include world's largest public buffalo herd; scenic mountain and plains area site; only 20 miles from Mount Rushmore; location in the beautiful Black Hills; numerous outdoor activities.

Profile of Summer Employees   Total number 250; average age 28. Employees are 65% female, 15% minorities, 10% high school students, 50% college students, 20% retirees, 1% international, 20% local residents.

Employment Information   Openings are from April 15 to October 30. College credit possible. Jobs available: 35 *sales clerks* at $515–$650 per month; 45 *wait persons* at $515 per month; 10 *cooks/chefs* at $800–$1400 per month; 15 *cook's assistants* at $515–$650 per month; 8 *kitchen/food preparation staff* at $515–$750 per month; 50 *housekeeping staff* at $515–$750 per month; 17 *front-desk/reservations persons* at $515–$750 per month; 5 *hosts/hostesses* at $600–$800 per month; 6 *maintenance personnel* at $515–$1000 per month; 5 *jeep drivers* with a clean driver's license (minimum age 21) at $515–$800 per month; 8 *wranglers* at $515–$750 per month; 4 *bookkeepers* at $515–$800 per month; 5 *bartenders* with a minimum age of 21 at $515–$800 per month; 3 *manager trainees* with a desire to learn the resort business at $515–$800 per month; 18 *dishwashers/buspersons* at $515–$650 per month. International students encouraged to apply.

Benefits On-the-job training, formal ongoing training, on-site room and board, laundry facilities, tuition reimbursement, internships, scholarship bonuses.

Contact Applicant should send resume, write for application, call for information, or apply in person by May 1 to Phil Lampert, President, Custer State Park Resort Company, Department SED, HC 83, Box 74, Custer, South Dakota 57730; 605-255-4541, fax 605-255-4706.

NATIONAL PARK SERVICE

Contact Applicant should write for application (must be 18 by May 13; U.S. citizenship required) to Regional Office of the National Park Service, Rocky Mountain Region, National Park Service, P.O. Box 25287, Denver, Colorado 80225-0287.

Jobs located in South Dakota at the following facilities: Badlands, Jewel Cave, Mt. Rushmore, Wind Cave. Also see District of Columbia listing.

PALMER GULCH LODGE/MT. RUSHMORE KOA
Hill City, South Dakota 57745

General Information Tourist resort serving visitors to nearby wilderness area. Established 1972. Owned by Satellite Cable Services, Inc. Affiliated with South Dakota Campground Owners' Association, South Dakota Innkeepers' Association, Black Hills, Badlands, and Lakes Association. Located 25 miles south of Rapid City on 125 acres. Features include family environment; campsites, cabins, horses, pools, miniature golf, waterslide, fishing, hiking, movies, and activities for kids; close proximity to Black Elk Wilderness Area, Mount Rushmore National Park, Crazy Horse Memorial, and Custer State Park (site used in "Dances With Wolves").

Profile of Summer Employees Total number 50. Employees are 50% female, 5% minorities, 33% high school students, 33% college students, 33% retirees, 40% local residents.

Employment Information Openings are from May 1 to September 30. Jobs available: 10 *registration office/store personnel* at $180–$200 per week; 10 *maintenance personnel* at $180–$225 per week; 3 *reservations staff* at $180–$200 per week; 10 *housekeeping staff* at $180–$200 per week; 4 *waterslide staff* with lifesaving, CPR, or first aid certification at $180–$200 per week.

Benefits On-the-job training, formal ongoing training, on-site room and board at $75 per month, laundry facilities, free admission to Black Hills attractions, free use of resort recreation facilities, special employee activities.

Contact Applicant should write for application or call for information by May 1 to Al Johnson, Vice President, Palmer Gulch Lodge/Mt. Rushmore KOA, Department SED, Box 295, Hill City, South Dakota 57745; 605-574-2525, fax 605-574-2574.

RUBY HOUSE RESTAURANT
Main Street
Keystone, South Dakota 57751

General Information A very busy restaurant and saloon that offers a full menu. Established 1963. Owned by Leo H. Toskin. Affiliated with National Tour Association, American Automobile Association, Keystone Chamber of Commerce. Located 22 miles south of Rapid City. Features include close proximity to Mount Rushmore; location in the Black Hills.

Profile of Summer Employees Total number 80; average age 19. Employees are 50% female, 30% minorities, 65% college students, 5% local residents.

Employment Information Openings are from April 15 to October 15. College credit possible. Jobs available: *waiter/waitress* with six months experience; *host/hostess* with ability to count change; *bartender* with six months experience (minimum age 21); *cocktail waitress* with ability to count change (minimum age 21); *cook; prep cook; dishwasher; janitor; office personnel* with good math skills and 10-key experience; *BBQ/deli person.*

Benefits On-the-job training, on-site room and board at no charge, laundry facilities, amusement and attraction pass card.

Contact Applicant should write for application or call for information by May 20 to LaCinda Paxton, Office Manager, Ruby House Restaurant, P.O. Box 163, Keystone, South Dakota 57751; 605-666-4404, fax 605-666-4405.

Compensation for staff members ranges from $2.35 to $4.25 an hour depending on position.

Tennessee

CHEROKEE ADVENTURES WHITEWATER RAFTING
Route 1, Box 605
Erwin, Tennessee 37650-9524

General Information Guided rafting trips, camping, and open-air adventure/bonfire. Established 1979. Owned by Dennis I. Nedelman. Affiliated with America Outdoors. Located 18 miles north of Johnson City on 50 acres. Features include location 1¼ hours from Asheville and adjacent to Cherokee National Forest; interesting clientele; camping on property.

Profile of Summer Employees Total number 20; average age 25. Employees are 40% female, 40% college students, 2% international, 58% local residents. Prefers nonsmokers.

Employment Information Openings are from June 1 to August 31. Jobs available: 6 *raft guides* with sense of responsibility and an outgoing personality plus Red Cross standard first aid and CPR certification; 1 *grounds/maintenance person* with willingness to work and ability to perform maintenance and patching duties; 2 *cooks/cleaning staff* with ability to prepare lunches and perform general cleaning; *reservationist/general office person* with adaptability and good phone manner plus ability to type 50 wpm. International students encouraged to apply.

Benefits On-the-job training, free boat training provided if desired, bonus available for certain positions.

Contact Applicant should send resume, write for application, or call for information by April 30 to Dennis I. Nedelman, President, Cherokee Adventures Whitewater Rafting, Department SED, Route 1, Box 605, Erwin, Tennessee 37650; 615-743-7733.

GIRL SCOUT CAMP SYCAMORE HILLS
Box 40466
Nashville, Tennessee 37204

General Information Residential camp serving 180 girls per session for general and specialized programs. Established 1959. Owned by Cumberland Valley Girl Scout Council. Affiliated with American Camping Association. Located 35 miles northwest of Nashville on 742 acres. Features include beautiful, wooded rolling hills; new covered riding arena; unique dining barn; rappelling cliffs and hiking trails; new team challenge course.

Profile of Summer Employees Total number 60; average age 20. Employees are 99% female, 2% minorities, 90% college students, 10% local residents. Prefers nonsmokers.

Employment Information Openings are from June 1 to July 31. Jobs available: 1 *assistant camp director* with Girl Scout resident camp experience at $180–$275 per week; 1 *unit coordinator* with Girl Scout resident camp experience at $130–$200 per week; 1 *business manager* with accounting training at $130–$200 per week; 1 *health supervisor* with RN, EMT, or paramedic certification at $130–$275 per week; 3 *high-adventure staff* with lifeguard training at $110–$275 per week; 8 *equestrian counselors* with horseback-riding experience at $100–$135 per week; 1 *waterfront director* with lifeguard and WSI certification at $130–$200 per week; 4 *waterfront counselors* with lifeguard training at $100–$135 per week; 2 *rappelling staff* with at least two years experience at $100–$200 per week; 2 *arts and crafts staff* with training and experience at $100–$200 per week; 1 *canoeing director* with canoeing instructor certification at $110–$160 per week; 1 *nature director* with background in the field at $110–$160 per week; 9 *unit leaders* at $110–$160 per week; 18 *unit counselors* at $100–$135 per week; 1 *counselor-in-training director* with Girl Scout resident camp experience at $110–$160 per week.

Benefits Preemployment training, on-the-job training, on-site room and board, laundry facilities, health insurance, free certification in some areas.

Contact Applicant should write for application or call for information by May 27 to Charlotte S. Palmer, Camp Director, Girl Scout Camp Sycamore Hills, Box 40466, Nashville, Tennessee 37204; 615-383-0490.

We offer a week of special courses, clinics, and workshops free to Camp Sycamore Hills staff members the week prior to the regular staff training week.

NATIONAL PARK SERVICE

Contact Applicant should write for application (must be 18 by May 13; U.S. citizenship required) to Regional Office of the National Park Service, Southeast Region, National Park Service, 75 Spring Street, SW, Atlanta, Georgia 30303.

Jobs located in Tennessee at the following facilities: Big South Fork, Fort Donelson,

Great Smoky Mountains, Obed Wild and Scenic River, Shiloh, Stones River National Battlefield. Also see District of Columbia listing.

Texas

ASTROWORLD/WATERWORLD
9001 Kirby Drive
Houston, Texas 77054

General Information   Family entertainment center serving approximately 2 million guests each year. Owned by Six Flags Corporation. Features include over 100 rides, shows, and attractions; local daily bus service; abundant eating facilities; location near Galveston beach; both an amusement and water park; close proximity to the Astrodome and a medical center.

Profile of Summer Employees   Total number 3,000; average age 17. Employees are 50% female, 65% minorities, 75% high school students, 20% college students, 5% retirees, 1% international, 95% local residents.

Employment Information   Openings are from March 1 to December 31. Jobs available: *food-service personnel; ride operators; merchandise hosts/hostesses; parking lot attendants; game hosts/hostesses; show hosts/hostesses; custodians; security personnel; lifeguards; cash control agents; front-gate hosts/hostesses; show technicians; wardrobe attendants; warehouse positions.* International students encouraged to apply.

Benefits   On-the-job training, formal ongoing training, special events, including movie nights, cookouts, softball leagues, etc.

Contact   Applicant should apply in person by December 15 to Andrew Grisdale, Staffing Specialist, AstroWorld/WaterWorld, 9001 Kirby Drive, Houston, Texas 77054; 713-794-3217, fax 713-799-1491.

   AstroWorld opens in March for weekend operation; WaterWorld in April. Both parks are also open weekends beginning in September. AstroWorld closes in December; WaterWorld in late September. Staff members who join us have the opportunity to meet new people and make new friends. Compensation ranges from $4.25 to $5.00 an hour, depending on position.

CAMP STEWART FOR BOYS
Route 1, Box 110
Hunt, Texas 78024-9714

General Information   Traditional camp offering a fun, challenging program to 250 boys for twenty-eight day or eighteen-day programs. Established 1924. Owned by Mr. Silas B. Ragsdale Jr. Affiliated with Christian Camping International, Camp Association Mutual Progress, American Horse Show Association, American Tennis Association. Located 80 miles northwest of San Antonio on 522 acres. Features include location on headwaters of the Guadalupe River; role-model staff members and peer associations; the chance to learn the skill of teaching and to learn more about one's self; worldwide enrollment; Christian atmosphere; outstanding food.

Profile of Summer Employees Total number 80; average age 24. Employees are 10% female, 10% minorities, 86% college students, 2% international, 2% local residents. Requires nonsmokers.

Employment Information Openings are from June 1 to August 25. College credit possible. Jobs available: 10 *riding instructors* with ability to take CHA clinic at Stewart (required) at $1000–$2000 per season; 8 *swimming instructors* with WSI certificate at $1000–$2000 per season; 2 *tennis instructors* at $1000–$2000 per season; 2 *crafts instructors* at $1000–$2000 per season; 4 *sports personnel* at $1000–$2000 per season; 2 *riflery instructors* with NRA certificate at $1000–$2000 per season; 2 *archery instructors* at $1000–$2000 per season; 3 *rock-climbing instructors* at $1000–$2000 per season; 2 *challenge-course instructors* at $1000–$2000 per season; 1 *band leader* at $1000–$2000 per season; 2 *secretaries* at $1000–$2000 per season; 12 *kitchen personnel* with knowledge of kitchen skills at $1000–$3000 per season; 24 *general counselors* with ability to lead and good moral character at $1000–$2000 per season. International students encouraged to apply.

Benefits Preemployment training, on-the-job training, on-site room and board at no charge, health insurance.

Contact Applicant should write for application or call for information by April 1 to Kathy C. Ragsdale, Codirector, Camp Stewart for Boys, Department SED, Route 1, Box 110, Hunt, Texas 78024-9714; 512-238-4670, fax 512-238-4737.

NATIONAL PARK SERVICE

Contact Applicant should write for application (must be 18 by May 13; U.S. citizenship required) to Regional Office of the National Park Service, Southwest Region, National Park Service, P.O. Box 728, Santa Fe, New Mexico 87501.

Jobs located in Texas at the following facilities: Alibates Flint Quarries, Amistad, Arkansas Post Big Bend, Big Thicket National Preserve, Chamizal, Fort Davis, Guadalupe Mountains, Lyndon B. Johnson National Historic Site, Lake Meredith, Padre Island, San Antonio Missions. Also see District of Columbia listing.

TEJAS GIRL SCOUT COUNCIL CAMPS
4411 Skillman, P.O. Box 64815
Dallas, Texas 75206

General Information Tejas Girl Scout Council serves a diverse population of girls each summer at its three camp properties: Camp Bette Perot, Camp Whispering Cedars, and Camp Rocky Point. Owned by Tejas Girl Scout Council. Affiliated with United Way, American Camping Association. Features include wide variety of equestrian programs; swimming; canoeing; wind-surfing; tubing; specialized programs.

Profile of Summer Employees Employees are 100% female, 8% minorities, 80% college students, 5% international, 90% local residents. Prefers nonsmokers.

Employment Information Openings are from June 1 to August 20. Spring break positions also offered. Jobs available: *director* with experience in hiring, training, and supervision—administrative skills a must (minimum age 25) at $275–$325 per week; *program director* with leadership and outdoor training plus background training in a variety of program skills, and work experience with children as a teacher or counselor (minimum age 20) at $120–$175 per week; *assistant director* with experience in planning and implementing outdoor living and activity experiences in camps (minimum age 21) at $125–$175 per week; *business manager* with training in business and office practices and sound judgement in purchasing and coordinating various business activities in a camp situation (minimum age 21) at $100–$140 per week; *health supervisor* with RN, LVN, PA, EMT, or Nurse Practioner certification and Standard First Aid and CPR certification, plus ability to adapt to camp work situation and knowledge of typical child and physical needs of campers (minimum age 21) at $175–$300 per week; *waterfront director* with ALS certification or equivalent, WSI (preferred), and at least six weeks pool-area experience (minimum age 21) at $120–$175 per week; *lifesaver/guard* with current ALS certification and lifeguard training or the equivalent (minimum age 18) at $90–$135 per week; *assistant equestrian director* with documented endorsement of previous successful experience in general horseback-riding instruction or certification from an organization with an instructor training program (minimum age 25) at $125–$175 per week; *equestrian riding instructor* with previous experience teaching beginning to intermediate riding skills (minimum age 18) at $90–$140 per week; *equestrian staff* with experience in working with horses and tack, working knowledge of stable care (minimum age 18) at $90–$120 per week; *unit leader* with training in group leadership and staff supervision, and the ability to teach and guide girls (minimum age 21) at $105–$140 per week; *unit counselors* with leadership ability, ability to work with children, and experience as a group leader, camper, or teacher (minimum age 18) at $90–$120 per week. International students encouraged to apply.

Benefits Preemployment training, on-the-job training, formal ongoing training, on-site room and board at no charge, laundry facilities, travel reimbursement, health insurance, 24-hour leave each week.

Contact Applicant should send resume, write for application, or call for information by March 30 to Kimberly Draskovic, Outdoor Program Manager, Tejas Girl Scout Council Camps, Department SED, P.O. Box 64815, Dallas, Texas 75206; 214-823-1342, fax 214-824-3324.

Utah

NATIONAL PARK SERVICE

Contact Applicant should write for application (must be 18 by May 13; U.S. citizenship required) to Regional Office of the National Park Service, Rocky Mountain Region, National Park Service, P.O. Box 25287, Denver, Colorado 80225-0287.

Jobs located in Utah at the following facilities: Arches, Bryce Canyon, Canyonlands, Capitol Reef, Cedar Breaks, Dinosaur, Glen Canyon, Golden Spike National Historic Site, Hovensweep, Natural Bridges, Timpanogos Cave, Zion. Also see District of Columbia listing.

Vermont

ALOHA CAMPS
Fairlee, Vermont 05045

General Information   Residential camp serving 350–400 campers for three- or seven-week sessions. Established 1905. Owned by The Aloha Foundation, Inc. Affiliated with American Camping Association, Vermont Camping Association. Located 150 miles northwest of Boston on 1,000 acres. Features include beautiful lakes; close proximity to Hanover, New Hampshire, and the Green and White Mountains; tents or cabins available; rustic but complete facilities; friendly environment.

Profile of Summer Employees   Total number 200; average age 30. Employees are 60% female, 3% minorities, 5% high school students, 65% college students, 2% retirees, 5% international, 5% local residents. Prefers nonsmokers.

Employment Information   Openings are from June 20 to August 15. College credit possible. Jobs available: *waterfront personnel (swimming, canoeing, sailing)* with lifeguard training at $1000 per season; *tennis, gymnastics, or land sports staff* at $1000 per season; 3 *nurses* at $1800 per season; 2 *riding instructors* at $1200 per season. International students encouraged to apply.

Benefits   Preemployment training, on-site room and board at no charge.

Contact   Applicant should send resume, write for application, or call for information to Posie Merritt Taylor, Managing Director, Aloha Camps, Department SED, RR 1, Box 91A, Fairlee, Vermont 05045; 802-333-9113.

Camper-counselor ratio of nearly 2:1 assures ideal teaching environment. We offer a warm family atmosphere and excellent staff training.

CAMP FARNSWORTH
Route 113
Thetford, Vermont 05074

General Information   Residential Girl Scout camp for ages 6–16 offering four 2-week sessions. Established 1909. Owned by Swift Water Girl Scout Council. Affiliated with American Camping Association, Vermont Camping Association, Certified Horsemanship Association. Located 150 miles north of Boston on 300 acres. Features include location in the Green Mountains of Vermont; private 50-acre lake; 50-foot waterslide; low-ropes course and lake zip line; decision making in small groups.

Profile of Summer Employees   Total number 100; average age 20. Employees are 99% female, 5% minorities, 50% college students, 30% international, 20% local residents. Prefers nonsmokers.

Employment Information   Openings are from June 15 to August 22. Jobs available: 2 *health directors* with RN, LPN, or EMT license at $1600–$2800 per season; 1 *waterfront director* with WSI and LGT certificates plus supervisory experience at $1600–$2800 per season; 8 *waterfront assistants* with WSI and LGT certificates at $1200–$1600 per season; 12 *unit leaders* with supervisory experience at $1600–$2100 per season; 30 *unit assistants* with experience with children at $1200–$1600 per season; 1 *counselor-in-training director* with camp experience in supervisory role at $1700–$2100 per season; 1 *horseback-riding director* with CHA certificate at $1600–$2600 per season; 4 *riding assistants* with instructor experience at $1200–$1600 per season; 1 *adventure director* with experience instructing low-ropes course at $1600–$2600 per season; 1 *ecology director* with experience pertaining to ecology programs at $1600–$2600 per season; 1 *arts director* with experience in arts programs at $1600–$2600 per season; 3 *arts assistants* with teaching experience in arts at $1600–$2600 per season; 1 *food supervisor* with experience in menu planning and quantity cooking at $2300–$3700 per season.

Benefits   Preemployment training, on-the-job training, on-site room and board at no charge, laundry facilities, health insurance.

Contact   Applicant should send resume, write for application, or call for information by June 15 to Nancy Frankel, Director of Outdoor Education, Camp Farnsworth, Department SED, 88 Harvey Road, #4, Manchester, New Hampshire 03103; 603-627-4158.

The program emphasis is on decision making in small groups. Trip units include backpacking, white-water canoeing, sailing, biking, and high adventure.

CAMP THOREAU-IN-VERMONT
RR 1, Box 88, Miller Pond Road
Thetford Center, Vermont 05075-9601

General Information   Coeducational, democratic community living for 150 campers and 60 staff members. Owned by An Experience In People, Inc. Affiliated with American Camping Association, Vermont Camping Association, Camp Horsemanship Association. Located 30 miles north of White River Junction on 280 acres. Features include rural environment; the only camp on a 64-acre lake; hiking in nearby White and Green Mountains; small camp (150 campers) with a large staff (44 counselors and 17 support staff); diverse group of campers (interracial and mixed socio-economic backgrounds) and staff.

Profile of Summer Employees   Total number 60; average age 25. Employees are 50% female, 15% minorities, 8% high school students, 60% college students, 20% international, 10% local residents. Prefers nonsmokers.

Employment Information   Openings are from June 15 to August 22. College credit possible. Jobs available: 8 *counselors/swimming instructors* with WSI and LGT certificates or first aid and CPR certificates at $1200–$1900 per season; 12 *counselors/lifeguards* with LGT, CPR/BLS, and first aid certification at $1200–$1900 per season; 6 *counselors/ small craft instructors* with LGT and canoeing/sailing/kayaking instructor certification at $1200–$1900 per season; 3 *counselors/riding instructors* with CHA and CPR/first aid certificates at $1200–$1900 per season; 2 *counselors/woodshop instructors* with experience plus CPR/first aid certification at $1200–$1900 per season; 3 *counselors/arts and crafts instructors* with experience plus CPR/first aid certification at $1200–$1900 per season; 2 *counselors/photography instructors* with experience plus CPR/first aid certification at $1200–$1900 per season; 4 *counselors/sports instructors (soccer, tennis, volleyball, softball, archery, basketball, frisbee, etc.)* with experience plus CPR/first aid certification at $1200–$1900 per season; 2 *counselors/martial arts and fencing instructors* with experience (belt certified) and CPR/first aid certification at $1200–$1900 per season; 1 *counselor/newspaper person* with experience at $1200–$1900 per season; 2 *counselors/drama instructors* with experience at $1200–$1900 per season; 2 *counselors/nature (small animals) instructors* with experience plus CPR/first aid certification at $1200–$1900 per season; 2 *counselors/hiking and outdoor living instructors* with experience and familiarity with area plus CPR and first aid certification at $1200–$1900 per season; 2 *counselors/ low-ropes instructors* with experience plus CPR/first aid certification at $1200–$1900 per season; 2 *counselors/evening programs instructors* with experience and creativity to design activities for the entire camp at $1200–$1900 per season. International students encouraged to apply.

Benefits Preemployment training, on-the-job training, on-site room and board at no charge, laundry facilities, travel reimbursement, health insurance.

Contact Applicant should send resume, write for application, or call for information by February 15 to Gregory H. Finger, Director, Camp Thoreau-In-Vermont, Department SED, RR 1, Box 105, Tillson Lake Road, Wallkill, New York 12589-9720; 914-895-2974.

Campers have the opportunity to choose much of their own program, and staff members have the chance to participate in camp program planning and to work in at least two different program areas. Youngsters hear about us by word-of-mouth, and since we do not advertise, our staff finds that they are working with children who truly want to be at Thoreau-In-Vermont. Additionally, employees are afforded the experience of working with people from throughout the United States and other parts of the world.

CAMP THORPE, INC.
RR 3, Box 3314
Goshen, Vermont 05733

General Information Provides summer camp experiences for mentally and physically disabled children and adults. Established 1927. Affiliated with Goshen Chamber of Commerce. Located 60 miles south of Burlington on 200 acres. Features include location in the Green Mountains; trout pond; playground; 43 camp buildings; modern cabins; overnight sites; multi-purpose tennis court; 100x50-foot pool.

Profile of Summer Employees Total number 30; average age 22. Employees are 60% female, 90% college students, 30% international, 70% local residents.

Employment Information Openings are from June 15 to August 20. College credit possible. Jobs available: 1 *program director* with B.S. degree at $2000 per season; 2 *head counselors* with two years of college completed at $1500 per season; 5 *specialists (art, nature, music, pool, sports)* with a year of college completed at $1300 per season; 12 *general counselors* with a minimum age of 18 at $1100 per season; 1 *camp nurse* with RN, LPN, or EMT license at $2400 per season. International students encouraged to apply.

Benefits Preemployment training, on-the-job training, on-site room and board, laundry facilities.

Contact Applicant should write for application or call for information by May 30 to Jeffrey J. Heath, Director, Camp Thorpe, Inc., RR 3, Box 3314, Goshen, Vermont 05733; 802-247-6611.

CHALLENGE WILDERNESS CAMP
Bradford, Vermont 05033

General Information Residential camp serving 60 healthy boys ages 9–16 with outdoor skills and wilderness trips. Established 1965. Owned by Dr. J. Thayer and Dr. Candice L. Raines. Affiliated with American Camping Association. Located 26 miles north of Hanover, New Hampshire on 542 acres. Features include exemplary wilderness programming; rugged, primitive setting; 15-acre private lake; backpacking and canoe trips; extensive outdoor skills program.

Profile of Summer Employees   Total number 12; average age 21. Employees are 60% college students, 40% international. Requires nonsmokers.

Employment Information   Openings are from June 15 to August 25. Jobs available: 1 *director of waterfront* with WSI certificate/lifeguard training at $1200–$2000 per season; 1 *kayak instructor* with ACA, ARC, or BCU certificate at $1200–$2000 per season; 3 *rock-climbing instructors* with one 5.10 lead plus two 5.9 seconds at $1200–$2000 per season; 1 *woodworking instructor* with experience with hand tools at $1200–$2000 per season; 1 *marksmanship instructor* with .22 caliber military experience at $1200–$2000 per season; 1 *blacksmithing instructor* with ability to be trained at $1200–$2000 per season; 1 *food-services director* with outdoorsman skills (must also be chef) at $1200–$2000 per season; 1 *kitchen assistant* with outdoorsman skills at $1200–$2000 per season. International students encouraged to apply.

Benefits   On-the-job training, on-site room and board at no charge, laundry facilities.

Contact   Applicant should send resume or write for application to Dr. J. Thayer and Dr. Candice L. Raines, Directors, Challenge Wilderness Camp, 4347 Stow Road, Stow, Ohio 44224; 216-688-7257.

We provide outdoor skills instruction and wilderness trips with activities that include rock-climbing, a ropes course, survival training, orienteering, physical fitness, woodworking, leatherwork, blacksmithing, canoeing, kayaking, fly-tying, fishing, marksmanship, and archery.

HEART'S BEND WORLD CHILDREN'S CENTER
South Wardsboro and Grout Pond Roads
Newfane, Vermont 05345

General Information   Coeducational, residential programs for boys and girls ages 4–15. Sessions are two to six weeks and limited to 60 campers. Established 1970. Owned by Dr. Nina Meyerhof-Lynn. Affiliated with American Camping Association. Located 14 miles north of Brattleboro on 100 acres. Features include location on a beautiful old Vermont farm; holistic eco-community.

Profile of Summer Employees   Total number 20; average age 21. Employees are 60% female, 10% high school students, 70% college students, 10% international, 10% local residents. Prefers nonsmokers.

Employment Information   Openings are from June 20 to August 22. Jobs available: 1 *horse director* with CHA certification (minimum age 21) at $1000–$1300 per season; 1 *head chef* with experience at $1200–$1600 per season; 2 *outdoor-living counselors* with CPR/first aid certificate at $350–$750 per season; 1 *swimming instructor* with lifeguard and WSI certificates (minimum age 21) at $600–$750 per season; 1 *drama counselor* at $350–$750 per season; 1 *visual arts/pottery instructor* at $350–$750 per season; 1 *tennis instructor* at $350–$750 per season; 1 *nurse* with RN license; 4 *bank counselors* with some activity area skill at $350–$750 per season; 1 *farm manager* at $750–$1000 per season. International students encouraged to apply.

Benefits   Preemployment training, on-the-job training, on-site room and board at no charge, laundry facilities.

Contact   Applicant should send resume, write for application, or call for information by April 15 to Margaret Stearns, Camp Coordinator, Heart's Bend World Children's Center,

Department SED, P.O. Box 217, Newfane, Vermont 05345; 802-365-7797, fax 802-365-7798.

At Heart's Bend World Children's Center, we place an emphasis on personal growth, fun, and friendships. Those who join us will find a supportive, caring atmosphere in which each individual's worth is respected.

NORTH HERO HOUSE
Route 2, P.O. Box 106
North Hero, Vermont 05474

General Information Small, 23-room country inn, restaurant, and gift shop located on the shores of Lake Champlain. Owned by John C. Apgar. Located 35 miles north of Burlington. Features include location on Lake Champlain; waterfront area and boat rentals; family-owned and operated; beautiful environment; full use of facilities for staff; excellent job experience for hospitality majors; possible relocation for full-time work in winter ski industry.

Profile of Summer Employees Total number 25; average age 19. Employees are 60% female, 60% college students, 40% local residents. Prefers nonsmokers.

Employment Information Openings are from May 15 to October 15. Year-round positions also offered. College credit possible. Jobs available: 1 *waterfront director* with knowledge of sailing, boating, and general water skills at $1000–$1400 per season; 3 *chambermaids* at $1000–$1400 per season; 3 *waiters/waitresses* at $1000–$1400 per season; 1 *groundskeeper* at $1000–$1400 per season; 4 *cooks* at $1000–$1400 per season; 3 *front-desk personnel* at $1000–$1400 per season; 1 *host* at $1000–$1400 per season. International students encouraged to apply.

Benefits Preemployment training, on-the-job training, on-site room and board at $50 per week, full use of all facilities.

Contact Applicant should send resume or apply in person by June 30 to John C. Apgar, Innkeeper, North Hero House, Department SED, P.O. Box 106, North Hero, Vermont 05474; 802-372-8237.

The North Hero House is an intimate island inn long famous for its fine food, gracious accommodations, and old fashioned hospitality. Many staff members relocate and make Vermont a permanent home.

SKY ACRES GIRL SCOUT CAMP
Washington, Vermont 05675

General Information Residential summer youth camp for girls ages 6–17 who attend one-, two-, or three-week sessions. Small-group activities with 24 girls or less, centered around Girl Scouting. Girl-adult partnership is stressed. Established 1954. Owned by Vermont Girl Scout Council. Affiliated with American Camping Association, Girl Scouts of the United States of America, Vermont Camping Association. Located 50 miles southeast of Burlington on 431 acres. Features include natural resources and terrain such as rolling meadows, coniferous and hardwood forests, a pond for swimming, brooks, and wetland areas; simple and functional buildings; accommodations for campers and most staff members consisting of 4–5 person tents on wooden platforms (cots and mattresses are provided); beautiful views with an elevation of approximately 1,700 feet; opportunities for relaxation and entertainment within 60 miles of the camp, including fairs, flea markets, granite quarries, old woods, roads and trails, shops in Barre and Montpelier, summer theater, an Alpine slide, the Trapp Family Lodge in Stowe, concerts in Burlington, and beaches on the shores of Lake Champlain.

Profile of Summer Employees   Total number 30; average age 21.

Employment Information   Openings are from June 21 to August 16. College credit possible. Jobs available: 1 *camp director* with abilities in administration/supervision and resident camp experience required plus a minimum age of 25 (knowledge of Girl Scout program preferred) at $2500–$4000 per season; 1 *assistant camp director* with abilities in administration, supervision, program planning, Girl Scout program, and camp experience preferred (minimum age of 21) at $1500–$2500 per season; 1 *business manager* with business training (typing, bookkeeping, office practices), accuracy to detail, and a current driver's license (minimum age of 21) at $900–$1400 per season; 1 *health supervisor* with RN, LPN, or EMT license or physician and recent first aid training (minimum age 21) at $1500–$2500 per season; 1 *waterfront director* with current WSI certificate, CPR training, and experience as an aquatics instructor (minimum age 21) at $1500–$2500 per season; 2 *waterfront counselors* with current ALS or WSI certificate and/or SCI certificate (minimum age of 18) at $900–$1400 per season; 4 *unit leaders* with experience with children in groups, supervisory background, plus experience with Girl Scout and outdoor programs (minimum age 21) at $1000–$1600 per season; 12 *unit counselors* with ability to work with children, experience in Girl Scout programs, and outdoor skills (minimum age of 18) at $700–$1100 per season; 1 *trip leader/director of counselors-in-training* with experience with children in groups, current ALS and SCI certificates plus canoe trip experience (minimum age of 21) at $900–$1400 per season; 1 *program director* with previous camp experience in a supervisory capacity plus experience working with groups and teaching in specialized program areas (minimum age 21) at $1000–$1600 per season; 1 *cook* with menu-planning, purchasing, and quality food preparation experience plus ability to supervise kitchen personnel (minimum age 21) at $2200–$3500 per season; 1 *assistant cook* with ability to assist with quantity food preparation and experience in camp or school cooking (minimum age 18) at $1000–$1600 per season; 2 *kitchen helpers* with ability to work with people and a willingness to fulfill responsibilities as directed (minimum age 16) at $600–$1000 per season; 1 *maintenance person* with experience in making minor repairs to buildings, grounds, and equipment (minimum age 18) at $1100–$1700 per season; *program specialists* with training and teaching experience in specialized program areas plus experience working with groups and/or previous camp experience (minimum age 18). International students encouraged to apply.

Benefits   Preemployment training, on-the-job training, formal ongoing training, on-site room and board at no charge, laundry facilities, travel reimbursement, health insurance, tuition reimbursement, first aid and CPR training possible.

Contact   Applicant should send resume, write for application, call for information, or apply in person by May 1 to Carolyn M. Montgomery, Outdoor Program Specialist, Sky Acres Girl Scout Camp, Department SED, 79 Allen Martin Drive, Essex Junction, Vermont 05452; 802-878-7131, fax 802-878-3943.

Energetic, youthful-thinking staff members are vital to a good camp program. We are seeking that special individual—one who is versatile and mature; who genuinely enjoys children; who wishes to help children enjoy simple (sometimes rustic) outdoor living; who believes in the Girl Scout program; who possesses camping and other skills; and who has imaginative ideas and lots of enthusiasm.

Virginia

CAMP FRIENDSHIP
P.O. Box 145
Palmyra, Virginia 22963

General Information Residential camp with a traditional program, specialized equestrian program, and adventure trips for teens in one- and two-week sessions. Established 1967. Owned by Charles R. Ackenbom. Affiliated with American Camping Association, National Rifle Association. Located 25 miles southeast of Charlottesville on 460 acres. Features include a warm, caring environment; pre-season and post-season work opportunities; strong staff training program; diversity in programs, clientele, and staff; beautiful location in Blue Ridge foothills; outstanding facilities.

Profile of Summer Employees Total number 110; average age 25. Employees are 50% female, 5% minorities, 10% high school students, 50% college students, 15% international, 10% local residents. Requires nonsmokers.

Employment Information Openings are from June 6 to August 18. Year-round positions also offered. Jobs available: 28 *cabin counselors/trip leaders* with one or more teaching skills at $1000–$1300 per season; 1 *waterfront director* with WSI certificate at $1200–$1400 per season; 1 *tennis specialist* with tennis teaching experience at $1200–$1400 per season; 1 *ropes-course director* with ropes-course teaching experience at $1200–$1400 per season; 1 *creative arts director* with crafts and drama skills at $1200–$1400 per season; 8 *riding counselors/instructors* with riding teaching experience at $1000–$1200 per season; 4 *village directors* with college degree and supervisory experience at $1300–$1600 per season; 11 *kitchen staff* at $1000–$2000 per season; 3 *drivers/maintenance staff* with driver's license (minimum age 21) at $1200–$1400 per season; 2 *nurses* with RN license; 2 *laundry staff* with willingness to perform night work at $1200–$1400 per season.

Benefits Preemployment training, on-the-job training, on-site room and board at no charge, tuition reimbursement.

Contact Applicant should write for application or call for information by April 1 to Linda Grier, Director, Camp Friendship, Department SED, P.O. Box 145, Palmyra, Virginia 22963; 804-589-8950, fax 804-589-3925.

CAMP MAWAVI
Prince William Forest Park
Triangle, Virginia 22072

General Information Residential, coeducational camp offering a youth-oriented program to 50–70 campers per session. Established 1946. Operated by Camp Fire Potomac Area Council. Located 45 miles south of Washington, D.C. on 150 acres. Features include location in national park; wildlife and woods; ideal area for sightseeing.

Profile of Summer Employees Total number 20; average age 20. Employees are 50% female, 10% minorities, 60% college students, 20% international, 10% local residents. Requires nonsmokers.

Employment Information Openings are from June 24 to August 12. Jobs available: 1 *swimming instructor* with WSI and lifeguard certificates at $1200–$1500 per season; 1 *boating specialist* with lifeguard and Red Cross boating certificate at $1000–$1200 per season; 10 *counselors* at $700–$1000 per season; 1 *office manager* with a car and some knowledge of office routine at $800–$1000 per season; 1 *nurse* with RN license at $1200–$1500 per season. International students encouraged to apply.

Benefits   Preemployment training, on-the-job training, on-site room and board at no charge, health insurance.

Contact   Applicant should write for application, call for information, or apply in person by April 1 to Hille Blackshaw, Council Services Director, Camp Mawavi, Department SED, 8737 Colesville Road, Suite 300, Silver Spring, Maryland 20910; 301-495-7833.

Camp offers backpacking and wilderness camping plus beach trips for teens and is located close to many historical sites such as Jamestown and Williamsburg.

LEGACY INTERNATIONAL'S SUMMER PROGRAM
Route 4, Box 265–D
Bedford, Virginia 24523

General Information   Residential, coeducational leadership training program for youths from all over the world, offering training and workshops in conflict resolution, environmental leadership, global issues, cross-cultural relations, media technology, and English as a foreign language. Established 1979. Operated by Legacy International. Affiliated with American Camping Association. Located 15 miles northeast of Lynchburg on 126 acres. Features include rural setting; location in the foothills of the Blue Ridge Mountains, close to lakes, hiking trails, and mountains; dynamic, multicultural setting with youths representing over twenty-five different countries and cultures; hiking trails, ropes course, pool, basketball and volleyball courts, and soccer field.

Profile of Summer Employees   Total number 50; average age 25. Employees are 50% female, 5% minorities, 10% college students, 30% international, 1% local residents. Prefers nonsmokers.

Employment Information   Openings are from June 15 to August 25. College credit possible. Jobs available: 1 *waterfront director* with first aid, CPR, and WSI certification; 5 *lead counselors (male)* with professional level experience working with youth, preferably in a setting with 24-hour responsibility; 7 *lead counselors (female)* with professional level experience working with youth, preferably in a setting with 24-hour responsibility; 3 *art instructors* with pottery, general arts and crafts, and previous teaching experience; 1 *evening and special program coordinator* with experience planning events (preference given to those with theater and music experience); 1 *program office manager* with typing/word processing (50 wpm) and organizational skills plus an interest in working with people; 1 *program assistant* with organizational and word processing skills; 7 *kitchen staff;* 1 *maintenance person;* 2 *program support/set-up personnel;* 1 *computer instructor* with previous experience teaching computers plus knowledge of Logo and Pascal; 3 *leadership instructors* with demonstrated leadership skills and the ability to teach in a classroom setting; 3 *environmental educators;* 1 *bookkeeper* with previous bookkeeping experience and knowledge of LOTUS; 2 *English as a Foreign Language instructors* with experience and certification in teaching EFL; 1 *evening and special program coordinator* with experience in program planning (theater experience helpful); 1 *photography instructor* with experience teaching photography and black and white darkroom techniques; 1 *video instructor* with teaching and editing/production experience; 1 *Japanese language and culture instructor* with fluency in Japanese, experience teaching, and time spent living in Japan. International students encouraged to apply.

Benefits   Preemployment training, on-the-job training, on-site room and board at no charge, laundry facilities, health insurance.

Contact   Applicant should send resume, write for application, or call for information by June 1 (the sooner we receive applications, the better the applicant's chance for consideration) to Leila Baz, Assistant Director, Legacy International's Summer Program, Department SED, Route 4, Box 265–D, Bedford, Virginia 24523; 703-297-5982, fax 703-297-1860.

For those applicants with little or no experience with youth and a professional level skill, Legacy offers a program and staff placement. Legacy provides pre-placement training and supervised field experience. It's designed for college students or recent graduates who wish to develop skills, gain practical experience for international careers, teaching, and work in the field of human services. A work-exchange program is also available (no salary provided).

NATIONAL PARK SERVICE

Contact   Applicant should write for application (must be 18 by May 13; U.S. citizenship required) to Regional Office of the National Park Service, Mid-Atlantic Region, National Park Service, 143 South Third Street, Philadelphia, Pennsylvania 19106.

Jobs located in Virginia at the following facilities: Appomattox Courthouse, Blue Ridge Parkway, Booker T. Washington National Monument, Colonial National Historical Park, Fredericksburg and Spotsylvania, George Washington Birthplace, George Washington Memorial Parkway/Arlington House/Great Falls Park/Virginia District, Manassas, Petersburg, Prince William Forest Park, Richmond National Battlefield Park (includes Maggie Walker National Historic site), Shenandoah, U.S. Park Police, Wolf Trap Farm Park. Also see District of Columbia listing.

ST. MARGARET'S SCHOOL
444 Water Lane
Tappahannock, Virginia 22560

General Information   Episcopal college-preparatory boarding and day school enrolling girls in grades 8–12. Offers a five-week summer session stressing academic enrichment and remediation enhanced by a multitude of activities. Established 1921. Affiliated with National Association of Independent Schools, Secondary School Admissions Test Board, Coalition of Girls' Boarding Schools. Located 45 miles east of Richmond on 10 acres. Features include location that combines the atmosphere of historic Tidewater, Virginia, with convenient access to the educational and cultural resources of Richmond, Charlottesville, Baltimore, and Washington, D.C.

Profile of Summer Employees   Total number 20; average age 28. Employees are 60% female, 10% minorities, 10% college students. Requires nonsmokers.

Employment Information   Openings are from June 25 to August 5. Year-round positions also offered. Jobs available: 3 *English teachers* at $1600–$2200 per season; 1 *computer teacher* at $1600–$2200 per season; 3 *mathematics teachers* at $1600–$2200 per season; 1 *ESL teacher* at $1600–$2200 per season; 1 *studio art teacher* at $1600–$2200 per season; 2 *dormitory counselors* at $1300–$1800 per season. International students encouraged to apply.

Benefits   On-site room and board at no charge, laundry facilities.

Contact Applicant should send resume and cover letter by May to Thomas W. Price, Assistant Headmaster, St. Margaret's School, Department SED, 444 Water Lane, Tappahannock, Virginia 22560; 804-443-3357, fax 804-443-1832.

St. Margaret's stimulating program provides students with an excellent away-from-home experience.

Washington

CAMP BERACHAH
19830 Southeast 328th Place
Auburn, Washington 98002

General Information Offers ten-day camps (60 campers each), seven horse camps (20 campers each), junior and teen camps (200 campers each), plus football, wrestling, and gymnastics camps (200 campers each). Established 1975. Owned by Philadelphia Church/Multi-Church Board. Affiliated with Christian Camping International. Located 30 miles south of Seattle on 140 acres. Features include indoor Olympic-size pool; gymnasium; beautiful woods; mountain bikes; horses.

Profile of Summer Employees Total number 60; average age 20. Employees are 70% female, 5% minorities, 50% high school students, 20% college students, 25% local residents. Requires nonsmokers.

Employment Information Openings are from June to August. Year-round positions also offered. College credit possible. Jobs available: *counselors* at $75–$100 per week; 1 *recreation director* at $75–$100 per week; 1 *nurse* at $75–$100 per week; 1 *crafts director* at $75–$100 per week. International students encouraged to apply.

Benefits Preemployment training, on-the-job training, on-site room and board at no charge, laundry facilities.

Contact Applicant should send resume, write for application, call for information, or apply in person by May 15 to James Richey, Program Director, Camp Berachah, Department SED, 19830 Southeast 328th Place, Auburn, Washington 98002; 206-854-3765, fax 206-833-7027.

CAMP NOR'WESTER
Route 1, Box 1700
Lopez, Washington 98261

General Information Coeducational, residential camp serving 185 children ages 9–16 during two 4-week sessions. Established 1935. Owned by Charles Curran. Affiliated with American Camping Association. Located 70 miles north of Seattle on 385 acres. Features include location on Lopez Island in Washington State's San Juan Islands; noncompetitive outdoor experience; unique tradition of Northwest Coast Indian art and culture; live-in tents and teepees; mature and diverse staff; 4 miles of waterfront.

Profile of Summer Employees Total number 85; average age 21. Employees are 50% female, 10% high school students, 90% college students. Prefers nonsmokers.

Employment Information   Openings are from June 13 to August 21. Jobs available: 7 *waterfront instructors* with lifeguard training, advanced lifesaving, or emergency water safety certificate at $710–$870 per season; 12 *unit counselors* with lifeguard training certificate (preferred) at $870 per season; 12 *assistant unit counselors* with lifeguard training certificate (preferred) at $790 per season; 3 *activity directors (waterfront, riding, craft)* at $870–$910 per season; 5 *riding instructors* at $690–$870 per season; 6 *crafts instructors* at $690–$870 per season; 2 *cooks* with food handler's card at $1500–$1800 per season; 1 *kitchen manager* with food handler's card at $1500–$1800 per season; 1 *registered nurse* at $2000–$2500 per season; 1 *program director* at $1500 per season; 1 *head counselor* at $1500 per season; 3 *rock-climbing/ropes-course instructors* at $690–$870 per season; 1 *naturalist* at $690–$870 per season; 2 *bike trip leaders* at $690–$870 per season; 1 *archery instructor* at $690–$750 per season; 1 *drama instructor* at $690–$820 per season; 2 *music leaders* at $710–$750 per season; 1 *pool director* with WSI and LGT certificate at $690–$870 per season; 1 *store manager* at $710–$750 per season; 2 *camp operations personnel* with experience with a chainsaw (preferred) at $690–$800 per season; 1 *film maker* with resume and tape/film at $2000–$2500 per season; 1 *photographer (black and white)* with portfolio (preferred) at $750–$870 per season; 4 *dishwashers* with food handler's card at $690–$710 per season; 4 *cook's assistants* with food handler's card at $690–$710 per season. International students encouraged to apply.

Benefits   On-site room and board, laundry facilities, health insurance, full week of staff training.

Contact   Applicant should write for application or call for information by March 15 to Paul Henriksen or Christa Campbell, Directors, Camp Nor'Wester, Route 1, Box 1700, Lopez, Washington 98261; 206-468-2225, fax 206-468-2472.

Camp Nor'Wester emphasizes the development of group living skills through various outdoor-living and challenge-oriented activities. Staff and campers experience a caring and supportive atmosphere. We offer flexible time off with the opportunity to explore and travel the San Juan Islands.

CAMP SEALTH
Vashon Island, Washington

General Information   Residential camp with a capacity of 300 campers offering ten summer sessions. Group living and informal education programs provided. Established 1921. Owned by Central Puget Sound Council of Camp Fire. Affiliated with American Camping Association. Located 20 miles south of Seattle on 400 acres. Features include location on Vashon Island (between Seattle and Tacoma); 1½ miles of Puget Sound beach; beautiful, Pacific Northwest forest setting; extensive trip program for older campers; special programs for asthmatics, diabetics, the visually impaired, the hearing impaired, and epileptics.

Profile of Summer Employees   Total number 95. Requires nonsmokers.

Employment Information   Openings are from June 15 to August 25. College credit possible. Jobs available: 45 *cabin counselors* at $1000 per season; 12 *unit leaders* at $1100 per season; 1 *riding director* at $1250 per season; 1 *assistant riding director* at $1100 per season; 1 *arts and crafts director* at $1100 per season; 1 *waterfront director* at $1250 per season; 1 *assistant waterfront director* at $1100 per season; 8 *program specialists* with experience in waterfront, arts and crafts, archery, and nature activities at $920 per season; 2 *nurses* with RN license at $2100 per season; 2 *paramedics/EMTs* at $1800 per season;

1 *cook* at $1700 per season; 2 *assistant cooks* at $1500 per season; 10 *kitchen assistants* at $920 per season; 1 *office manager* at $1100 per season; 1 *driver* at $1000 per season. **Benefits** Preemployment training, on-site room and board, laundry facilities, health insurance.

Contact Applicant should write for application or call for information by May 15 to David and Shauna Kamenz, Directors, Camp Sealth, 8511 15th Avenue, NE, Seattle, Washington 98115; 206-461-8550.

In-camp activities include a low-element challenge course, rowing, canoeing, swimming, archery, arts and crafts, sports, overnight camping, and special events. The transportation of campers from Seattle to camp is via chartered boat. Specialty programs include baseball, volleyball, horseback riding, sailing (19-foot Lightnings), bike trips, windsurfing, counselors-in-training, river rafting, leadership program, photography, and animal nature programs.

THE FIRS CONFERENCE CENTER AND DAY CAMP
4605 Cable Street
Bellingham, Washington 98226

General Information Residential family camp and weekly day camp for 100–200 participants. Established 1921. Located 90 miles south of Seattle on 32 acres. Features include scenic northwest surroundings; location nestled among tall fir trees and above the shores of Lake Whatcom; waterfront recreation, skiing, and swimming.

Profile of Summer Employees Total number 35; average age 19. Employees are 50% female, 60% high school students, 40% college students, 10% international, 10% local residents. Requires nonsmokers.

Employment Information Openings are from June 14 to August 31. Spring break positions also offered.

Benefits Preemployment training, on-the-job training, formal ongoing training, on-site room and board at no charge.

Contact Applicant should write for application, call for information, or apply in person by June 14 to Darell Smith, Program Director–Children and Youth, The Firs Conference Center and Day Camp, Department SED, 4605 Cable Street, Bellingham, Washington 98226; 206-733-6840, fax 206-733-6926.

Canadian students who wish to apply for employment are encouraged to do so.

MT. RAINIER GUEST SERVICES
P.O. Box 108
Ashford, Washington 98304

General Information Operates 2 inns serving visitors to the Mt. Rainier area. Closest major city is Tacoma. Features include location in central Washington State; the historic, 126-room Paradise Inn (elevation of 5,400 feet); The National Park Inn at Longmire (newly renovated with 26 rooms and location at an elevation of 2,700 feet); rustic atmosphere (rooms do not have televisions); a pristine environment with Alpine meadows, streams, canyons, lakes, rivers, old-growth forests, and glaciers.

Employment Information   Openings are from May 25 to October 1. Jobs available: 20 *housekeeping staff* with ability to clean guest rooms and hotel at $216 per week; 10 *desk clerks* with ability to register guests and handle cash at $216 per week; 20 *cook's helpers/ pantry persons* with ability to perform prep work plus make salads and sandwiches at $216 per week; 30 *kitchen/utility personnel* at $216 per week; 30 *fast food attendants* with ability to take/fill orders, bus tables, and operate cash register at $216 per week; 5 *janitors (night and day)* with ability to clean halls, restrooms, windows, carpets, and empty garbage at $216 per week; 5 *kitchen porters (night and day)* with ability to clean hoods, ovens, floors, and assist in dishwashing at $216 per week; 20 *retail clerks* with ability to perform retail sales, stocking, and cleaning duties at $216 per week; 10 *cooks* with ability to work in a fast food and fine dining restaurant.

Benefits   On-site room and board at $40 per week, bonuses available to those who finish employment agreement, discounts to employees in dining room and gift shops.

Contact   Applicant should write for application (applications are accepted year-round) to Personnel Department, Mt. Rainier Guest Services, Department SED, P.O. Box 108, Ashford, Washington 98304.

Guests and employees come from all over the United States and other parts of the world to visit America's mountain glacier wonderland. (Please note that compensation for cooks ranges from $4.50 to $8 an hour.)

NATIONAL PARK SERVICE

Contact   Applicant should write for application (must be 18 by May 13; U.S. citizenship required) to Regional Office of the National Park Service, Pacific Northwest Region, National Park Service, 83 South King Street, Suite 212, Seattle, Washington 98104.

Jobs located in Washington at the following facilities: Coulee Dam, Fort Vancouver, North Cascades (Stehekin, Skagit Districts), Mt. Rainier, Olympic, San Juan Island, Whitman Mission. Also see District of Columbia Listing.

ROSARIO RESORT
1 Rosario Way
Eastsound, Washington 98245

General Information   Resort with a variety of facilities. Established 1960. Owned by Rosario Hotel, Inc. Located 90 miles north of Seattle. Features include location amidst Washington State's San Juan Islands; beautiful natural environment; Moran Mansion (on National register); spa facilities; close proximity to Moran State Park.

Profile of Summer Employees   Total number 75. Employees are 50% female, 10% minorities, 10% high school students, 50% college students, 10% retirees, 20% local residents. Prefers nonsmokers.

Employment Information   Openings are from May to October. Spring break, Christmas break, year-round positions also offered. College credit possible. Jobs available: 30 *room attendants, laundry workers, and laundry drivers* with physical stamina, attention to detail, and a commitment to stay the entire season at $200 per week; 25 *wait persons (bus, cocktails, bartenders)* with experience required in most positions plus physical stamina, neat appearance, and pleasant personality needed; 10 *cooks (breakfast, dinner)* with pantry prep and boiler experience at $240–$280 per week; 10 *dishwashers* with stamina, attention to detail, willingness to work, and commitment at $200 per week; 12 *clerks (desk, reservations, accounting, cashiers)* with clerical, computer, and some typing skills plus phone experience and an interest in working with people at $200 per week.

Benefits   On-the-job training, on-site room and board at $35 per week, laundry facilities, health insurance, one free meal while on duty, employee cafeteria for off-duty hours.

Contact   Applicant should send resume or call for information by June 1 to S. E. Anthony, Personnel Director, Rosario Resort, Department SED, 1 Rosario Way, Eastsound, Washington 98245; 206-376-2222.

Rosario Resort staff members have the opportunity to learn and gain valuable experience in the resort/hotel industry.

YMCA CAMP SEYMOOR
9725 Cramer Road KPN
Gig Harbor, Washington 98329

General Information   Residential camp serving 140 campers weekly and bi-weekly. Shorter mini-camps of four days are also available. Established 1906. Owned by Tacoma-Pierce County YMCA. Affiliated with Young Men's Christian Association, American Camping Association. Located 18 miles northwest of Tacoma on 150 acres. Features include one-half mile of shoreline on Puget Sound; outdoor swimming pool; environmental education; building with touch tanks for hands-on marine study; outpost trips for individuals of high-school age.

Profile of Summer Employees   Total number 50; average age 21. Employees are 45% female, 10% minorities, 10% high school students, 50% college students, 10% international, 50% local residents. Prefers nonsmokers.

Employment Information   Openings are from June 14 to August 25. Christmas break, year-round positions also offered. College credit possible.

Benefits   Preemployment training, on-the-job training, formal ongoing training, on-site room and board at no charge, laundry facilities, internships possible.

Contact   Applicant should send resume, write for application, call for information, or apply in person by May 31 to Kent W. Sampson, Executive Director, YMCA Camp Seymoor, Department SED, 1002 South Pearl Street, Tacoma, Washington 98465; 206-564-9622, fax 206-564-1211.

West Virginia

CAMP RIM ROCK
Box 69
Yellow Spring, West Virginia 26865

General Information   Residential camp serving 160 girls and offering both a strong general program and an excellent horseback-riding program. Established 1952. Owned by James L. Matheson. Affiliated with American Camping Association, Camp Horsemanship Association. Located 100 miles west of Washington, D.C. on 500 acres. Features include beautiful mountain country; traditional activities and riding programs; 2 pools and Cacapon River; well-balanced sports program; good dance and drama facilities.

Profile of Summer Employees   Total number 50; average age 25. Employees are 95% female, 10% minorities, 75% college students, 40% international. Requires nonsmokers.

Employment Information   Openings are from June 10 to August 31. College credit possible. Jobs available: 5 *swimming counselors* with WSI certificate and ability to teach; 2 *tennis counselors* with teaching experience; 7 *riding staff* with teacher certification; 20 *sports and general counselors* with ability to work with children and skill in sports; 2 *archery instructors* with certification; 2 *canoeing instructors* with certification. International students encouraged to apply.

Benefits   Preemployment training, on-the-job training, on-site room and board at no charge, laundry facilities, travel reimbursement, workers' compensation.

Contact   Applicant should send resume, write for application, call for information, or apply in person by May 1 to Jim Matheson, Director, Camp Rim Rock, Box 69, Yellow Spring, West Virginia 26865; 304-856-2869.

Compensation for jobs detailed in this listing is $1200 and up per season depending on position, experience, and certification.

NATIONAL PARK SERVICE

Contact   Applicant should write for application (must be 18 by May 13; U.S. citizenship required) to Regional Office of the National Park Service, Mid-Atlantic Region, National Park Service, 143 South Third Street, Philadelphia, Pennsylvania 19106.

Jobs located in West Virginia at the following facilities: Harpers Ferry, New River Gorge. Also see District of Columbia listing.

Wisconsin

BOYD'S MASON LAKE RESORT
Fifield, Wisconsin 54524

General Information   American-plan family resort that rents 17 cabins, serves three meals daily, and performs daily maid service for up to 100 guests. Established 1895. Owned by Richard Simon. Affiliated with Park Falls Area Chamber of Commerce, Wisconsin Innkeepers' Association. Located 400 miles north of Chicago, Illinois on 2,600 acres. Features include 4 private lakes; friendly and varied mix of guests and staff; secluded Northwoods environment; deer, eagles, bear, and other animals often sighted; miles of maintained hiking trails.

Profile of Summer Employees   Total number 22; average age 26. Employees are 70% female, 15% college students, 25% local residents.

Employment Information   Openings are from May 10 to October 10. Jobs available: 5 *dining room attendants* at $170 per week; 1 *children's recreation supervisor* with background in the elementary education field at $165 per week; 1 *dishwasher* at $170 per week; 1 *pots and pans washer* at $170 per week; 1 *swing cook* at $176 per week.

Benefits   On-the-job training, on-site room and board at no charge, laundry facilities.

Contact   Applicant should send resume or write for application by May 1 to Richard Simon, Manager/Owner, Boyd's Mason Lake Resort, Department SED, Fifield, Wisconsin 54524; 715-762-3469.

Boyd's Mason Lake Resort offers employees a staff dining room and lounge. Additionally, the staff has the opportunity to utilize guest facilities and the chance to meet a wide variety of people.

CAMP ALGONQUIN
4151 Bryn Afon Road
Rhinelander, Wisconsin 54501

General Information   Residential camp for 150 boys and girls ages 7–17 (gifted, A and B students, those falling behind in school, and learning disabled). Located 285 miles north of Chicago, Illinois on 160 acres. Features include waterskiing, sailing, canoeing, and fishing; 60 buildings; location on lake.

Employment Information   Openings are from June to August. College credit possible. Jobs available: *teachers* with certification (minimum age 21); *general counselors* with knowledge of a variety of activities and games (minimum age 19); *waterfront director* with experience as a waterfront director or pool manager plus current WSI certificate (minimum age 19); *food-service manager (head cook)* with experience in mass food preparation and menu planning, purchasing, inventory and budget control plus the ability to supervise 8 dining hall and kitchen staff members; 2 *assistant cooks* with experience in mass food preparation and dining hall procedures plus ability to work closely with food service manager, prepare meals, and supervise dining hall and/or dishwashing staffs.

Benefits   On-site room and board, use of camp facilities during time off.

Contact   Applicant should write for application or call for information by March 1 to Don McKinnon, Owner/Director, Camp Algonquin, 4151 Bryn Afon Road, Rhinelander, Wisconsin 54501; 715-369-1277.

Camp Algonquin is a unique combination of individualized learning and outdoor recreation designed to develop a child's skills in reading, creative writing, and self-expression while strengthening self-concept and independent thinking. Staff members must have a genuine love for children and a desire to participate in an excellent learning environment that provides an opportunity to work with youngsters from all over the world.

CAMP INTERLAKEN JCC
7050 Old Highway 70
Eagle River, Wisconsin 54521

General Information   Residential, coeducational camp serving 400 campers ages 8–16. Established 1966. Owned by Milwaukee Jewish Community Center. Affiliated with Jewish Community Centers of America, American Camping Association. Located 250 miles north of Milwaukee on 110 acres. Features include complete water and land sports programs; ropes/adventure course; special Judaic program; location in the magnificent Northwoods; family accommodations.

Profile of Summer Employees   Total number 60; average age 20. Employees are 50% female, 5% minorities, 90% college students, 5% international. Prefers nonsmokers.

Employment Information Openings are from June 1 to August 25. Jobs available: 4 *kitchen stewards* with previous kitchen experience at $1500 per season; 1 *gymnastics instructor* with instructor-level expertise and previous teaching experience at $1000 per season; 1 *trip director* with LGT, CPR, and first aid certification at $1700 per season; 1 *sailing instructor* with LGT certificate plus previous teaching experience at $1200 per season; 2 *crafts instructors* with knowledge of ceramics, tie-dyeing, crafts, and painting desirable at $1200 per season; 1 *tennis instructor* with USTA certificate at $1200 per season. International students encouraged to apply.

Benefits Preemployment training, on-the-job training, on-site room and board at $250 per month, travel reimbursement.

Contact Applicant should send resume, write for application, or call for information by March 1 to Kevin Bukatman, Director, Camp Interlaken JCC, Department SED, 6255 North Santa Monica, Milwaukee, Wisconsin 53217; 414-964-4444, fax 414-964-0922.

Camp Interlaken JCC places an emphasis on fun and friendship.

CAMP LUCERNE
Route 1, Box 3150, County YY
Neshkoro, Wisconsin 54960-9329

General Information Residential camp serving 150 campers weekly. Established 1948. Owned by United Methodist Church. Affiliated with American Camping Association. Located 40 miles west of Oshkosh on 450 acres. Features include clear, 50-acre lake; woods and meadow; climate conducive for general camp activity; comfortable sleeping cabins; serene, woodsy area.

Profile of Summer Employees Total number 50; average age 20. Employees are 50% female, 10% minorities, 70% college students, 10% international, 10% local residents. Requires nonsmokers.

Employment Information Openings are from June 4 to August 17. Jobs available: 12 *counselors* at $105–$120 per week; 1 *relief worker* with ability to assist in kitchen (primary responsibility) at $120 per week; 1 *maintenance person* with valid driver's license at $120–$140 per week; *truck driver* with valid driver's license at $105–$125 per week; 2 *waterfront personnel* with lifeguard training at $105–$125 per week; 1 *waterfront director* with lifeguard training and WSI certificate at $125–$140 per week; 1 *dishwasher* at $105–$120 per week; 1 *health supervisor* with first aid/CPR certificate or RN license (preferred) at $160–$185 per week; 1 *dining room coordinator* with ability to assist with food preparation at $110–$125 per week; 1 *assistant cook* with ability to assist with food preparation at $115–$130 per week. International students encouraged to apply.

Benefits Preemployment training, on-site room and board at no charge, laundry facilities.

Contact Applicant should send resume, write for application, or call for information by May 1 to Joel Jarvis, Director, Camp Lucerne, Department SED, Route 1, Box 3150, County YY, Neshkoro, Wisconsin 54960-9329; 414-293-4488.

Qualified, caring staff members primarily serve campers associated with the United Methodist Church, but interdenominational groups also attend. We offer diversified activities including swimming, sailing, canoeing, hiking, cookouts, and biking.

CAMP NEBAGAMON FOR BOYS
P.O. Box 429
Lake Nebagamon, Wisconsin 54849

General Information   Residential boys' camp of 220 campers from forty different communities and several foreign countries. Established 1929. Owned by Roger and Judy Wallenstein. Affiliated with American Camping Association, Midwest Association of Private Camps, American Camping Association–Illinois Section. Located 35 miles southeast of Duluth, Minnesota on 70 acres. Features include beautiful setting in heart of the Northwoods; excellent opportunity to work with professional staff; extensive wilderness trips; outstanding programs in water sports and tennis; caring, nurturing, family-type environment; many options for time off.

Profile of Summer Employees   Total number 125; average age 20. Employees are 20% female, 5% minorities, 27% high school students, 40% college students, 10% international, 18% local residents.

Employment Information   Jobs available: 2 *waterfront directors* with WSI or Red Cross lifeguard certificate at $1400–$2200 per season; 25 *senior cabin counselors* with skills in water and land sports, tennis, target skills, art, campcraft, and photography (college-age) at $900–$1050 per season; 1 *nurse* with RN license at $200–$225 per week; 2 *cooks* with experience cooking for large groups at $200–$225 per week; 2 *drivers* with clean driving record (minimum age 21) at $1400–$1700 per season; 25 *junior cabin counselors* with skills in water and land sports, tennis, target skills, art, campcraft, and photography (11th and 12th graders sought) at $700–$800 per season. International students encouraged to apply.

Benefits   Preemployment training, on-the-job training, formal ongoing training, on-site room and board at no charge, laundry facilities, travel reimbursement, health insurance.

Contact   Applicant should write for application or call for information by March 15 to Roger and Judy Wallenstein, Directors, Camp Nebagamon for Boys, 5237 North Lakewood, Chicago, Illinois 60640; 312-271-9500, fax 000-.

Positions are available for older staff (married and family housing available). An outstanding opportunity to assume responsibility and to practice organizational, interpersonal, and problem-solving skills.

CAMP TIMBERLANE FOR BOYS
AV 11400 Airport Road
Woodruff, Wisconsin 54568

General Information   Noncompetitive, residential camp serving 150 boys from across the country. Four- and eight-week sessions are offered. Established 1960. Owned by Mike Cohen. Affiliated with American Camping Association, Midwest Association of Private Camps, International Camping Fellowship. Located 250 miles north of Milwaukee on 250 acres. Features include 2,000 feet of secluded lake shoreline; location 5 miles from small but active town; easy access by bus or plane; fantastic recreation in the Northwoods.

Profile of Summer Employees   Total number 65; average age 22. Employees are 20% female, 10% minorities, 25% high school students, 60% college students, 5% local residents. Prefers nonsmokers.

Employment Information   Openings are from June 11 to August 14. College credit possible. Jobs available: 2 *counselors/swimming instructors* with lifeguard or WSI certificate at $1000–$1200 per season; 1 *counselor/sailing instructor* at $1000–$1200 per season; 2 *counselors/scuba diving instructors* with PADI advanced open water or divemaster certification at $1000–$1500 per season; 2 *counselors/waterskiing instructors* with teaching and boat-driving experience at $1000–$1500 per season; 2 *counselors/tennis instructors* at $1000–$1500 per season; 1 *counselor/photography instructor* with experience developing black and white film at $1000–$1500 per season; 1 *counselor/pottery instructor* with experience in wheel and kiln use at $1000–$1200 per season; 2 *counselors/horseback riding instructors* with significant English saddle experience at $1000–$1500 per season; 1 *counselor/guitar instructor* at $1000–$1500 per season; 1 *counselor/golf instructor* at $1000–$1500 per season; 6 *trip leaders* with canoeing background and standard first aid certification at $1000–$1500 per season; 2 *nurses* with RN, GN, or LPN license at $1200–$2500 per season; 1 *assistant cook* with commercial experience at $1000–$2000 per season; 2 *maintenance persons* with carpentry experience at $1000–$2000 per season; 1 *driver* with a good driving record at $1000–$1500 per season. International students encouraged to apply.

Benefits   Preemployment training, on-the-job training, formal ongoing training, on-site room and board at no charge, travel reimbursement, accommodates special dietary needs.

Contact   Applicant should write for application or call for information by May 31 to Mike Cohen, Director, Camp Timberlane for Boys, Department SED, 2105 West Marne Avenue, Milwaukee, Wisconsin 53209; 414-228-9111.

Timberlane is a family. Our emphasis is on developing the campers' self-confidence and self-esteem while building social skills in a fun, safe, and adventurous environment. We are noncompetitive, stressing friends, fun, and environmental stewardship. Join us!

CAMP WINDEGO
Route 2, Box 786
Wild Rose, Wisconsin 54984

General Information   Residential Girl Scout camp serving 100 girls per session. Established 1949. Owned by Illinois Shore Girl Scout Council. Affiliated with American Camping Association. Located 40 miles west of Oshkosh on 116 acres. Features include waterfront on Hills Lake; platform tents; English horseback riding; waterskiing and board sailing; sailing and canoeing.

Profile of Summer Employees   Total number 32; average age 20. Employees are 95% female, 5% minorities, 95% college students, 2% international. Prefers nonsmokers.

Employment Information   Openings are from June to August. College credit possible.

Benefits   Preemployment training, on-the-job training, on-site room and board at no charge, laundry facilities, health insurance, aquatic school reimbursement (50%) for waterfront staff.

Contact   Applicant should send resume, write for application, call for information, or apply in person by May 15 to Leslie Wilson, Camp Director, Camp Windego, Department SED, Box 544, 1010 Central, Wilmette, Illinois 60091; 708-251-7301.

CLEARWATER CAMP FOR GIRLS
7490 Clearwater Road
Minocqua, Wisconsin 54548

General Information   Residential camp providing traditional, high-quality camping experiences by caring staff for girls ages 8–16. Established 1933. Owned by Clearwater Camp, Inc. Affiliated with American Camping Association. Located 25 miles southeast of Rhinelander on 80 acres. Features include 3,600-acre Headwaters Lake; 5-acre island with 25 cabins for campers and staff; location surrounded by nature conservancy; sailing and waterfront area; location within 5 miles of a charming resort community; hiking, biking, and canoeing opportunities.

Profile of Summer Employees   Total number 40; average age 20. Employees are 90% female, 2% high school students, 87% college students, 1% international, 1% local residents. Prefers nonsmokers.

Employment Information   Openings are from June to August. College credit possible. Jobs available: 4 *sailing instructors* with experience handling C scows, Red Cross sailing USRA rating, and CPR certification at $1100–$1400 per season; 5 *swimming instructors* with CPR, WSI, and lifeguard certification at $1100–$1400 per season; 1 *archery instructor* with any archery experience at $1100–$1200 per season; 2 *crafts instructors* with varied skills in weaving, pottery, and leather—should possess creativity at $1100–$1300 per season; 2 *tennis instructors* with ability to teach with enthusiasm and CPR certification at $1100–$1400 per season; 2 *riding instructors (English style)* with experience, CHA and HSA certificates, plus certification in first aid and CPR at $1100–$1500 per season; 4 *canoeing instructors* with any canoeing experience plus lifeguard, emergency water safety, and CPR certification at $1100–$1200 per season; 2 *trip leaders* with experience in campcraft, canoeing, and backpacking plus first aid and CPR certification at $1100–$1300 per season; 1 *drama instructor* with talent, ability to direct, and creativity at $1100–$1200 per season; 1 *windsurfing instructor* with lifeguard and EWS certification plus windsurfing instructor rating (if possible) at $1100–$1200 per season; 2 *waterskiing instructors* with boat-driving experience and WSI, EWS, or lifeguard certification at $1100–$1400 per season; *cook and assistant cook* with cooking experience at $1200–$3000 per season; 4 *kitchen girls* with willingness to work; 5 *general counselors* with love for children, willingness and ability to assist youngsters, plus EWS and lifeguard certification at $1100–$1200 per season. International students encouraged to apply.

Benefits   Preemployment training, on-the-job training, on-site room and board at no charge, health insurance, tuition reimbursement.

Contact   Applicant should send resume, write for application, call for information, or apply in person by April 15 to Sunny Moore, Director, Clearwater Camp for Girls, Department SED, 7490 Clearwater Road, Minocqua, Wisconsin 54548; 715-356-5030.

NATIONAL PARK SERVICE

Contact   Applicant should write for application (must be 18 by May 13; U.S. citizenship required) to Regional Office of the National Park Service, Midwest Region, National Park Service, 1709 Jackson Street, Omaha, Nebraska 68102.

Jobs located in Wisconsin at the following facilities: Apostle Islands, St. Croix National Scenic River. Also see District of Columbia listing.

SALVATION ARMY WONDERLAND CAMP AND CONFERENCE CENTER
Camp Lake, Wisconsin 53109

General Information Residential camp serving 100 inner-city children with eight-day sessions. Established 1924. Owned by The Salvation Army. Located 7 miles south of Antioch, Illinois on 140 acres. Features include location between Chicago and Milwaukee; rural area; lake; pool.

Profile of Summer Employees Total number 54; average age 20. Employees are 50% female. Prefers nonsmokers.

Employment Information Openings are from June 16 to August 16. College credit possible. Jobs available: 1 *aquatics director* with WSI certificate and lifeguard training at $130 per week; 1 *aquatics assistant* with WSI certificate and lifeguard training at $120 per week; 6 *counselors (male)* with a year of college training completed (minimum age 19) at $120 per week; 6 *counselors (female)* with a year of college training completed (minimum age 19) at $120 per week; 4 *program unit directors* with two years of college completed (minimum age 21) at $130 per week; 1 *nature director* with two years of college completed (minimum age 21) at $130 per week; 1 *pioneer director* with two years of college completed (minimum age 21) at $130 per week; 1 *arts and crafts director* with two years of college completed (minimum age 21) at $130 per week; 1 *nurse* with RN and EMT/CPR licenses at $250 per week; 1 *nurse's assistant* with student nurse status or experience in nursing at $120 per week; 2 *cooks* with experience in quantity cooking at $150 per week. International students encouraged to apply.

Benefits Preemployment training, on-the-job training, on-site room and board, laundry facilities, Christian staff fellowship.

Contact Applicant should send resume or write for application by April 15 to Personnel Director, Salvation Army Wonderland Camp and Conference Center, Department SED, P.O. Box 222, Camp Lake, Wisconsin 53109; 414-889-4305, fax 414-889-4307.

All applicants should be ministry-minded, willing to serve inner-city children, possess role-model Christian lifestyle, and share personal experience of spiritual values.

TIWAUSHARA PROGRAM CENTER
2967 Brown Deer Court
Redgranite, Wisconsin 54970

General Information Girl Scout residential camp serving ages 7–17. Established 1955. Owned by Fond du Lac Exchange Club. Operated by Wau-Bun Girl Scout Council. Located 30 miles west of Oshkosh on 180 acres. Features include wooded terrain; spring-fed lake; swimming pool; shower house; dining hall; orienteering course.

Profile of Summer Employees Total number 25; average age 22. Employees are 90% female, 15% minorities, 15% high school students, 70% college students, 5% international, 10% local residents. Prefers nonsmokers.

Employment Information Openings are from June 12 to August 14. College credit possible. Jobs available: 1 *assistant camp director* with previous Girl Scout camp experience at $1255–$1430 per season; 1 *business manager* with bookkeeping experience at $995–$1170 per season; 1 *program director* with experience in organized camping at $1170–$1345 per season; 2 *program specialists* with skills in arts and crafts plus ecology at $910–$1040 per season; 3 *lifeguards* with current Red Cross lifeguard certification at $800–

$1200 per season; 1 *nurse* with RN or EMT license at $1300–$1475 per season; 8 *counselors* with experience as youth leader at $860–$1125 per season; 1 *food supervisor* with experience with large quantity cooking at $1380–$1560 per season; 1 *assistant cook* with experience with large quantity cooking at $995–$1215 per season; 2 *kitchen aides* with willingness to learn at $690–$780 per season. International students encouraged to apply.

Benefits On-the-job training, on-site room and board at no charge, laundry facilities, health insurance, worker's compensation.

Contact Applicant should write for application or call for information by May 15 to Kit Bogenschneider, Field Executive/Program Services, Tiwaushara Program Center, Department SED, 307 North Main Street, Fond du Lac, Wisconsin 54935; 414-921-8540, fax 414-921-5892.

Tiwaushara Program Center offers experience working with young people in an extraordinary outdoor setting. The schedule is ideal for teachers or college students seeking to share a summer of adventure with girls.

WISCONSIN BADGER CAMP
Route 2, Box 351
Prairie du Chien, Wisconsin 53821

General Information Residential camp serving 75 developmentally challenged children and adults weekly. Established 1966. Affiliated with American Camping Association, Platteville Chamber of Commerce, Prairie du Chien Chamber of Commerce. Located 80 miles west of Madison on 620 acres. Features include petting farm; inground swimming pool with ramp; caring, conscientious, well-trained staff; beautiful vistas of Mississippi River Valley; 20 miles of trails; special primitive camp.

Profile of Summer Employees Total number 50; average age 20. Employees are 50% female, 5% minorities, 5% high school students, 90% college students, 10% international, 20% local residents. Prefers nonsmokers.

Employment Information Openings are from May 30 to August 15. College credit possible. Jobs available: 17 *male counselors* at $1100–$1300 per season; 17 *female counselors* at $1100–$1300 per season; 2 *swimming directors* with lifesaving certification at $1100–$1300 per season; 1 *recreation director* at $1100–$1300 per season; 1 *arts and crafts director* at $1100–$1300 per season; 1 *nature/farm director* at $1100–$1300 per season; 1 *camping/fishing director* at $1100–$1300 per season; 2 *health-care staff* with RN/GN/LPN/EMT license or status as third year nursing student at $160–$300 per week; 1 *dietary technician* with nutrition or dietetics student status at $1265–$1400 per season; 1 *head cook* with food-service degree or student status at $1300–$1500 per season; 3 *kitchen assistants* at $1100 per season; 2 *coordinators* with degree in special education at $1485–$1700 per season; 1 *program coordinator* with experience or degree in therapeutic recreation at $1485–$1700 per season; 1 *horseback-riding director* with experience or HSA certification at $100–$150 per week; 1 *secretary* at $1100 per season. International students encouraged to apply.

Benefits Preemployment training, on-the-job training, on-site room and board at no charge, scholarships available.

Contact by April 30 to Donald Douglas, Executive Camp Director, Wisconsin Badger Camp, Department SED, P.O. Box 240, Platteville, Wisconsin 53818; 608-348-9689.

Wisconsin Badger Camp accepts any developmentally challenged individual regardless of age, severity of disability, or financial situation. We also offer trips for highly function-

al developmentally disabled individuals to all parts of the United States. Only caring, conscientious, hardworking applicants need apply.

WOODSIDE RANCH RESORT
Highway 82
Mauston, Wisconsin 53948

General Information Full-service American plan dude ranch offering log cabins with fireplaces. Established 1926. Owned by Feldmann Family. Affiliated with Wisconsin Innkeepers' Association, Central Wisconsin River Country. Located 65 miles northwest of Madison on 1,000 acres. Features include three meals a day (all you can eat); all activities including free horesback riding; new pool; buffalo cookouts; breakfast rides (horses and covered wagon); guest rodeos.

Profile of Summer Employees Total number 60. Employees are 60% female, 25% high school students, 25% college students, 50% local residents.

Employment Information Openings are from June 1 to September 7. Christmas break positions also offered. Jobs available: 6 *horse-trail guides* with horse background at $180–$200 per week; 6 *food-service personnel* at $180–$200 per week; 6 *bartenders/country store clerks* with previous bartending experience (preferred) at $200–$220 per week; 1 *recreation director* with recreation background at $250 per week; 1 *yard- and pool-maintenance person* with maintenance background at $200–$250 per week; 2 *housekeepers* at $180–$200 per week; 1 *teamster (horse-drawn wagons)* with past team experience at $200–$250 per week. International students encouraged to apply.

Benefits On-the-job training, on-site room and board at no charge, laundry facilities.

Contact Applicant should write for application to Woodside Ranch Resort, Highway 82, Mauston, Wisconsin 53948.

During off-duty hours, employees can use the pool, tennis courts, mini-golf, and paddle boats and can join in playing volleyball and softball with guests. The staff can also participate in barn dances and other social functions.

Wyoming

ABSAROKA MOUNTAIN LODGE
1231 East Yellowstone Highway
Wapiti, Wyoming 82450

General Information Guest ranch on the eastern edge of Yellowstone National Park with lodging, meals, horseback riding, fishing, and other activities available. Established 1910. Owned by David and Cathy Sweet. Affiliated with American Automobile Association, Mobil Travel Guide, Fodors Travel. Located 40 miles west of Cody on 7 acres. Features include location adjacent to Yellowstone National Park; historical mountain lodge; small, family-run operation; strong service orientation; horseback-riding paradise; unlimited outdoor recreation.

Profile of Summer Employees   Total number 10; average age 22. Employees are 50% female, 10% high school students, 80% college students, 10% retirees, 25% local residents.

Employment Information   Openings are from May 1 to November 1. Jobs available: 2 *cooks* with cooking experience (preferred) at $350–$450 per month; 4 *waitresses/cabin maids* at $350 per month; 2 *wranglers* with extensive horse experience (required) at $350–$450 per month; 1 *maintenance person* with some yard/building maintenance experience (preferred) at $350 per month; 1 *front-desk person* at $350–$400 per month. International students encouraged to apply.

Benefits   On-the-job training, on-site room and board at no charge, laundry facilities, all employee salaries supplemented by gratuities, end-of-season bonus possible.

Contact   Applicant should send resume or write for application and include three employment references by June 1 (preferably by April 1) to David Sweet, Owner, Absaroka Mountain Lodge, 1231 East Yellowstone Highway, Wapiti, Wyoming 82450; 307-587-3963.

Employees can participate in outdoor recreation activities and have the chance to meet people from all over the world. In addition, our close proximity to Yellowstone National Park gives staff members the opportunity to easily visit and enjoy this interesting site.

ALPENHOF LODGE
Box 288, 3255 West McCollister Avenue
Teton Village, Wyoming 83025

General Information   Alpine-style resort lodge with 40 luxury rooms providing clientele with personalized service. Established 1965. Affiliated with Wyoming Restaurant Association. Located 250 miles northeast of Salt Lake City on 1 acre. Features include location at the base of Jackson Hole ski area, 8 miles from Grand Teton National Park and 45 miles from Yellowstone National Park; easy access to rafting, fishing, hiking, etc.; 100-seat, four-star restaurant; bar and bistro with sundeck.

Profile of Summer Employees   Total number 90; average age 22. Employees are 50% female, 1% high school students, 70% college students, 10% international. Prefers nonsmokers.

Employment Information   Openings are from May 20 to October 1. Winter break positions also offered. Jobs available: 5 *housekeeping staff* with ability to clean rooms and willingness to do hard work at $750–$785 per month; 3 *bellmen* with aptitude for greeting guests in a friendly manner, ability to assist with luggage, run errands, and do light maintenance work at $720 per month; 3 *dishwashers* with ability to work hard and quickly at $880 per month; *cocktail waitstaff* with interest in working with public, ability to serve drinks, and cocktail experience at $370 per month; 8 *food waitstaff* with interest in working with public and the ability to serve at $370 per month; 8 *dining room staff (buspersons and wait staff)* with tableside experience and wine knowledge at $275–$420 per month. International students encouraged to apply.

Benefits   Preemployment training, on-the-job training, formal ongoing training, employee rewards/special recognition, some jobs have housing at a nominal charge, excellent working conditions with a five-day work week.

Contact   Applicant should apply in person (a personal interview is required for all positions) to Personnel Manager, Alpenhof Lodge, Box 288, Teton Village, Wyoming 83025; 307-733-3242, fax 307-739-1516.

The Alpenhof Lodge will consider starting dates for all positions as late as June 15, but employees must commit to remain at least until the end of August. Our staff MUST honor their contracted dates. In addition, housing is at a premium in the area, so we suggest that potential employees arrange for housing before applying for a position.

BILL CODY'S RANCH RESORT
2604 Yellowstone Highway
Cody, Wyoming 82414

General Information   Horseback-riding resort catering to families. Established 1925. Owned by Bill Cody's Ranch Inn. Affiliated with American Automobile Association, United States Chamber of Commerce, Cody Country Chamber of Commerce. Located 100 miles south of Billings, Montana. Features include wilderness horseback riding; close proximity to Yellowstone and Teton National Parks.

Profile of Summer Employees   Total number 20; average age 25. Employees are 60% female, 90% college students, 2% local residents. Prefers nonsmokers.

Employment Information   Openings are from April 15 to November 15. Year-round positions also offered. Jobs available: 5 *horse wranglers* with physical abilities to perform required duties and valid driver's license at $300–$500 per month; 2 *cooks* at $300–$500 per month; 6 *housekeepers* at $250–$400 per month; 5 *waiters/waitresses* at $250–$400 per month.

Benefits   On-the-job training, on-site room and board at no charge, laundry facilities, free horseback riding, end-of-season/contract bonus.

Contact   Applicant should write for application to Mrs. William Cody, Manager, Bill Cody's Ranch Resort, 2604 Yellowstone Highway, Cody, Wyoming 82414; 307-587-2097.

Staff members are encouraged to mingle with guests and are afforded the opportunity to meet people from many countries.

HATCHET MOTEL AND RESTAURANT
Moran, Wyoming 83013

General Information   Motel with 22 logged units, housekeeping unit, suite, restaurant, gift shop, and gas station. Established 1953. Owned by Don Albrecht. Affiliated with Jackson Chamber of Commerce, Wyoming Hotel/Motel Association, Wyoming Restaurant Association, American Automobile Association. Located 35 miles east of Jackson on 5 acres. Features include location close to the Grand Tetons and Yellowstone; quiet surroundings; referral for float trips; horseback riding; hiking and fishing nearby.

Profile of Summer Employees   Total number 18; average age 23. Employees are 60% female, 15% high school students, 50% college students, 25% retirees, 10% local residents. Prefers nonsmokers.

Employment Information   Openings are from May 21 to September 10. College credit possible. Jobs available: 2 *station attendants (morning and evening shift)* at $500 per month; 2 *desk attendants (morning and evening shift)* at $500 per month; 2 *cooks (morning and evening shift)* at $500 per month; 5 *kitchen helpers (morning and evening shift)* at $500 per month; 5 *waiters/waitresses (morning and evening shift)* at $375 per month; 2

maids at $500 per month; 1 *yard-maintenance person* at $500 per month; 2 *relief position personnel* at $500 per month. International students encouraged to apply.

Benefits Preemployment training, on-the-job training, formal ongoing training, on-site room and board at no charge, laundry facilities.

Contact Applicant should send resume, write for application, call for information, or apply in person by May 15 to Phil and Diane Mehlhaff, Managers, Hatchet Motel and Restaurant, Department SED, P.O. Box 316, Moran, Wyoming 83013; 307-543-2565.

Hatchet is privately owned and has a family atmosphere. We provide training for all positions and are friendly, fair-minded employers. First consideration is given to those with the longest available time to work. Men and women have separate living quarters.

NATIONAL PARK SERVICE

Contact Applicant should write for application (must be 18 by May 13; U.S. citizenship required) to Regional Office of the National Park Service, Rocky Mountain Region, National Park Service, P.O. Box 25287, Denver, Colorado 80225-0287.

Jobs located in Wyoming at the following facilities: Devil's Tower National Monument, Fort Laramie, Fossil Butte National Monument, Grand Teton, Yellowstone. Also see District of Columbia listing.

RAFTER Y RANCH
Banner, Wyoming 82832

General Information Traditional dude ranch offering a variety of activities for families and others in a warm Western atmosphere. Established 1979. Owned by Ralph I. Goodwin Jr. Affiliated with Sheridan Chamber of Commerce. Located 23 miles north of Sheridan on 950 acres. Features include beautiful ranch in rolling foothills of mountains; guests and crew interact as one big family; log cabins, tennis, swimming hole, riding, hiking, and photography; magnificent meals served in new dining hall; families return year after year.

Profile of Summer Employees Total number 8; average age 19. Employees are 66% female, 20% high school students, 80% college students, 25% local residents.

Employment Information Openings are from June 15 to August 31. Jobs available: 1 *corral boss* at $375–$500 per month; 1 *wrangler* at $300–$350 per month; 1 *first cook* at $375–$500 per month; 1 *assistant cook* at $325–$375 per month; 2 *dining room/cabin persons* at $325–$375 per month; 2 *groundskeepers/men friday* at $325–$375 per month.

Benefits On-the-job training, on-site room and board, laundry facilities, sharing of gratuities pool, time off, participation in all guest activities.

Contact Applicant should send resume and include letter with references by March 31 to Ralph I. Goodwin, Jr., Rafter Y Ranch, Department SED, Banner, Wyoming 82832; 307-683-2221.

Crew members are housed in safe, comfortable quarters and are encouraged to socialize with guests in order to maximize their tips. Our staff members also have the opportunity to learn about the area's history and points of interest. An employee's wage level is dependent upon such factors as his or her knowledge and experience.

SIGNAL MOUNTAIN LODGE
Grand Teton National Park, P.O. Box 50
Moran, Wyoming 83013

General Information Summer resort providing national park visitors with services such as lodging, food, marinas, gifts, guided fishing, groceries, and gas. Owned by Rex Maughan. Affiliated with Jackson Hole Chamber of Commerce. Located 30 miles north of Jackson Hole on 30 acres. Features include location on Jackson Lake at the foot of the Grand Tetons, just 30 miles south of Yellowstone National Park; new, top-rate dormitories for employees; endless outdoor recreational opportunities in the area, including hiking, climbing, fishing, backpacking, camping, and photography; scenic or white-water rafting and canoeing; congenial atmosphere with good food and friends.

Profile of Summer Employees Total number 120; average age 21. Employees are 50% female, 5% minorities, 85% college students, 8% retirees, 3% international, 5% local residents. Prefers nonsmokers.

Employment Information Openings are from May 1 to October 15. College credit possible. Jobs available: 5 *front-desk and reservations persons* with typing skills and the ability to work well with the public; 3 *accounting personnel (day and night audit)* with accounting education and experience; 6 *marina attendants* with the ability to perform boat rentals, shuttle guests to and from boats, and pump gas; 20 *lodging helpers* with the ability to make beds, clean lodging units, launder linens, and clean public areas; 5 *cooks* with cooking experience (fine-dining menus as well as coffee shop); 5 *pantry personnel* with the ability to prepare food, including salads and desserts; 4 *employee dining room staff* with the ability to prepare and serve food plus perform clean up; 15 *waiters/waitresses* with some serving experience; 2 *bartenders* with bartending experience (full-service bar); 2 *cocktail wait persons* with the ability to serve all levels of cocktails and wine; 4 *hosts/ hostesses* with the ability to seat guests and operate a cash register; 9 *buspersons/dishwashers;* 5 *gift store sales clerks* with the ability to operate a cash register, stock shelves, and dust plus retail sales experience; *convenience store attendants* with the ability to operate a cash register, stock grocery shelves, help with operation of gas pumps, and maintain cleanliness; 10 *management and staff positions* with previous supervisory experience and full-season availability. International students encouraged to apply.

Benefits Preemployment training, on-the-job training, on-site room and board at $200 per month, laundry facilities, discounts in the restaurants, gift stores, and marinas, free river rafting trips, bonuses on some positions, close proximity to religious services.

Contact Applicant should write for application or call for information and send letters of reference by May 1 (it is best to apply in January and February) to Roxanne Bierman, Personnel Manager, Signal Mountain Lodge, Department SED, P.O. Box 50, Moran, Wyoming 83013; 307-543-2831, fax 307-543-2569.

We support and encourage various off-duty recreational activities, including the bicycle race up Signal Mountain, the canoe race around Donoho Island, basketball, softball, volleyball, a Christmas-in-August celebration, the annual "We've made it half-way through" party and dance, poetry readings, and an employee newsletter. We promote from within so there is almost always the opportunity to move up in successive seasons. About one third of our employees return each season, and there is a very low rate of turnover throughout the season. (Please note that preference in hiring is given to applicants with the longest work availability. Compensation for hourly positions is $4.35 and up depending on the job, the skills, and the experience level of the each individual. All salaried positions are paid on a monthly basis and include free room and board.)

TOGWOTEE MOUNTAIN LODGE
P.O. Box 91
Moran, Wyoming 83013

General Information   Mountain lodge with horses, fishing, and hiking in the summer; snowmobiling and cross-country skiing in the winter. Established 1925. Owned by Dave and Judie Helgeson. Affiliated with American Hotel and Motel Association, National Federation of Independent Businesses, National Forest Recreation Association. Located 48 miles north of Jackson Hole on 67 acres. Features include remote location; fishing in mountain streams; location near Yellowstone and Grand Teton National Parks with hiking and backpacking in wilderness areas; friendly, helpful staff; horses on premises; abundant snow in winter.

Profile of Summer Employees   Total number 40; average age 25. Employees are 40% female, 5% high school students, 50% college students. Prefers nonsmokers.

Employment Information   Openings are from June 6 to September 29. Christmas break, year-round positions also offered. Jobs available: 3 *front-desk/reservations persons* with good math aptitude and an outgoing personality at $900–$1100 per month; 5 *housekeepers/laundry personnel* with neat appearance and efficient work habits at $800–$900 per month; 7 *wait staff (food servers)* with an outgoing personality and desire to perform a thorough job at $500–$600 per month; 2 *bartenders* with bartending experience at $800–$900 per month; 3 *dishwashers* with ability to accomplish tasks neatly and quickly at $800–$900 per month; 4 *cooks* with cooking experience plus neat and efficient work habits at $1100–$1300 per month; 2 *gas attendants (clerks)* with good math skills and an outgoing personality at $800–$900 per month; 1 *night auditor* with good math aptitude (should enjoy working nights) at $900–$1100 per month; 2 *general laborers* with efficient work habits at $800–$900 per month.

Benefits   On-the-job training, on-site room and board at $300 per month, laundry facilities, health insurance, end-of-season bonus available.

Contact   Applicant should write for application or call for information to Dave Helgeson, Owner, Togwotee Mountain Lodge, Department SED, P.O. Box 91, Moran, Wyoming 83013; 307-543-2847.

   Togwotee Mountain Lodge offers staff members the opportunity to gain hospitality business experience. We seek "people-oriented" individuals with outgoing, friendly personalities. We are well-known for our friendly, courteous staff. (Please note that room and board are deducted from monthly wages.)

YELLOWSTONE PARK SERVICE STATIONS
Yellowstone National Park
Wyoming

General Information   YPSS operates automotive service facilities in Yellowstone National Park. Established 1947. Affiliated with Montana Chamber of Commerce, Gardiner Chamber of Commerce, National Park Conference of Concessioners. Features include opportunity to work outdoors in one of the world's premier parks; world's greatest concentration of geysers; spectacular waterfalls, mountains, and canyons; Yellowstone Lake, the largest Alpine lake in the United States; proximity to Teton National Park and several national forests.

Profile of Summer Employees   Total number 95; average age 23. Employees are 29% female, 2% minorities, 63% college students, 4% retirees, 1% international, 10% local residents. Prefers nonsmokers.

Employment Information   Openings are from May 1 to October 15. College credit possible. Jobs available: 50 *service station attendants* with good people and communication skills at $178 per week; 18 *automobile mechanics* with ASE certification or current enrollment in an ASE program at $240 per week; 3 *accounting clerks* with ability to operate 10-key adding machine by touch plus computer and communication skills at $182 per week; 1 *warehouse helper* with good driving record and communication skills at $182 per week.

Benefits   Preemployment training, on-the-job training, on-site room and board at $58 per week, laundry facilities, health insurance, recreation program, accident insurance, advancement potential.

Contact   Applicant should write for application or call for information by May 1 to Yellowstone Park Service Stations, P.O. Box 11–Department WDM, Gardiner, Montana 59030-0011; 406-848-7333.

We operate 11 retail establishments throughout the 2.2 million acres of Yellowstone National Park. We present our employees with opportunities for advancement since all of our management is promoted from within. In addition, staff members have the chance to meet and work with people from across the United States and the world.

Indexes

Throughout *Summer Employment Directory 1992,* listings are arranged geographically. To further ease your search for the right job opportunity, this section includes two indexes. The first index, the Category Index, assigns each employer to a general field or specialty. For example, if you would like to spend the summer working for an employer whose main concern is the environment, check the listings under Conservation and Environmental Programs. Because of the diversity of programs offered by summer camps, however, we have subdivided camps by program type. These subcategories indicate camps that are specialized (e.g., for campers with physical or mental disabilities or those that focus primarily on a single activity such as horseback riding or the performing arts) as well as camps that offer a broad range of activities.

The second index, the Employer Index, is an alphabetical listing of all employers featured in *SED.*

Category Index

Business and Industry
American Camping Association 154
American Camping Association/
New Jersey Section 144
Blue Bell Ice Cream Inc. 119
Crater Lake Lodge Company 185
Durham Temporaries, Inc. 166
Hamilton Stores, Inc. 131
North Beach Sailing/Barrier
Island Sailing Center 179
Sun Beach Service 201

Camps–Academic
Camp Algonquin 224
Camp Buckskin 120
Maine Teen Camp 94
SuperCamp 26
Wa-Klo 143
YMCA Camp Oakes 44

Camps–Behavioral Problems
Camp Buckskin 120
Camp Thorpe, Inc. 211

Camps–Developmental Disabilities
Camp Friendship (MN) 121

Camp Hemlocks 64
Camp Loyaltown–AHRC 159
Camp Thorpe, Inc. 211
Camp Thunderbird (FL) 70
Eden Wood Camping and
Retreat Center 124
New Jersey Camp Jaycee 195
Rocky Mountain Village–Home
of the Easter Seal Handicamp 55
Wisconsin Badger Camp 230

Camps–General Activities
Adirondack Woodcraft Camps 154
Alford Lake Camp, Inc. 84
Aloha Camps 209
American Youth Foundation–
Camp Miniwanca 109
Awosting and Chinqueka Camps 63
Brookwood Camps 155
Brush Ranch Camps for Girls
and Boys 150
Bryn Mawr Camp 187
Buck's Rock Camp 156
Camps Airy and Louise 96
Camp Akiba 188
Camp Albany 137

Camp Androscoggin	84
Camp Arcadia	85
Camp Baco for Boys/Camp Che–Na–Wah for Girls	157
Camp Berachah	218
Camp Butterworth	182
Camp Cayuga	189
Camp Cody for Boys	138
Camp Echo Lake	157
Camp Emerson	100
Camp Farnsworth	209
Camp Friendship (VA)	215
Camp Golden Valley	176
Camp Good News	101
Camp Hantesa	80
Camp Henry Kaufmann	158
Camp Interlaken JCC	224
Camp JCA Sholom	33
Camp Jeanne D'Arc	159
Camp Jewell YMCA	64
Camp Kanata	176
Camp Kenwood–Evergreen	138
Camp Lakota	34
Camp Laurel	86
Camp Low	73
Camp Lucerne	225
Camp Mary White	151
Camp Matoaka for Girls	87
Camp Mawavi	215
Camp Medill McCormick	76
Camp Merrimac	139
Camp Mishawaka for Boys/Girls	122
Camp Mogisca	160
Camp Mokuleia	74
Camps Mondamin and Green Cove	177
Camp Mountain Meadows	35
Camp Nashoba North	87
Camp Nebagamon for Boys	226
Camp Netimus	190
Camp Nock–A–Mixon	191
Camp Nor'Wester	218
Camp Pembroke	102
Camp Pinecliffe	88
Camp Rim Rock	222
Camp Runoia	89
Camp Sancta Maria	110
Camp Scherman	35
Camp Sealth	219
Camp Sequoia	162
Camp Seven Hills	163
Camp Sherwood	111
Camp Skylemar	89
Camp Stewart for Boys	206
Camp Stonybrook	183
Camp Takajo	90
Camp Tapawingo (IL)	76
Camp Tapawingo (ME)	91
Camp Tel Noar	140
Camp Tevya	140
Camp Thoreau-In-Vermont	210
Camp Thorpe, Inc.	211
Camp Thunderbird for Boys/ Camp Thunderbird for Girls (MN)	123
Camp Timberlane for Boys	226
Camp Vacamas	146
Camp Walden	111
Camp Walt Whitman	141
Camp Wapi-Kamigi	78
Camp Washington	65
Camp Watitoh	102
Camp Waziyatah	92
Camp Wekeela	92
Camp Windego	227
Cape Cod Sea Camps	103
Cedar Lodge	112
Central New York Girl Scout Camp Near Wilderness	164
Channel 3 Country Camp	65
Cheley Colorado Camps	46
Chesapeake Bay Girl Scout Council	69
Circle Pines	113
College Settlement of Philadelphia	192
Colorado Mountain Ranch, Trojan Summer Camp	48
Crystalaire Camp	113
Dudley Gallahue Valley Camps	79
Elks Camp Barrett	97
Elliott P. Joslin Camp	105
Falling Creek Camp for Boys	178
The Firs Conference Center and Day Camp	220
Flying G Ranch, Tomahawk Ranch	50
The Fresh Air Fund	167
Frost Valley YMCA Camps	167
Girl Scout Camp Sycamore Hills	205
Heart's Bend World Children's Center	212

Hidden Valley Camp (ME)	93
Hidden Valley Camp (PA)	194
Interlocken Center for Experiential Learning	141
Jameson Ranch Camp	39
Kennolyn Camps	39
Lake of the Woods and Greenwoods Camps	115
Laurel Resident Camp	66
Maine Teen Camp	94
Marydale Resident Camp	82
McGaw YMCA Camp Echo	116
New Jersey Camp Jaycee	195
New Jersey 4–H Camps	148
Noark Girl Scout Camp	33
North Shore Holiday House	171
Pine Forest Camps	197
Pinemere Camp Association	197
Sanborn Western Camps	56
Santa Catalina School Summer Camp	42
Sky Acres Girl Scout Camp	213
Sky High Ranch	57
Surprise Lake Camp	173
Tejas Girl Scout Council Camps	207
Thunderbird YMCA	201
Tiwaushara Program Center	229
United Methodist Camps	180
Vanderbilt YMCA of Greater New York	174
Wa-Klo	143
The Whiteman Colorado Camps	60
Wild Goose...for Boys	95
Wyonegonic Camps	95
YMCA Camp Cheerio	181
YMCA Camp Ihduhpi	128
YMCA Camp Letts	99
YMCA Camp Lyndon	108
YMCA Camp Oakes	44
YMCA Camp Seymoor	222
YMCA of the Rockies, Camp Chief Ouray	61
YMCA/YWCA Camping Services–Camps GreenKill/McAlister/Talcott	175
YWCA Camp Westwind	186

Camps–Horsemanship
Alford Lake Camp, Inc.	84
Bonnie Castle Riding Camp	100
Brush Ranch Camps for Girls and Boys	150
Buck's Rock Camp	156
Camp Berachah	218
Camp Butterworth	182
Camp Cayuga	189
Camp Friendship (VA)	215
Camp Jewell YMCA	64
Camp Lakota	34
Camp Laurel	86
Camp Mary White	151
Camp Matoaka for Girls	87
Camp Mishawaka for Boys/Girls	122
Camp Mogisca	160
Camps Mondamin and Green Cove	177
Camp Mountain Meadows	35
Camp Netimus	190
Camp Pinecliffe	88
Camp Rim Rock	222
Camp Sancta Maria	110
Camp Sealth	219
Camp Sequoia	162
Camp Seven Hills	163
Camp Walden	111
Camp Waziyatah	92
Cedar Lodge	112
Cheley Colorado Camps	46
Colorado Mountain Ranch, Trojan Summer Camp	48
Dudley Gallahue Valley Camps	79
Flying G Ranch, Tomahawk Ranch	50
4–H Farley Outdoor Education Center	106
Frost Valley YMCA Camps	167
Harmony Heart Camp	193
Heart's Bend World Children's Center	212
Hidden Valley Camp (ME)	93
Hidden Valley Camp (PA)	194
Jameson Ranch Camp	39
Kennolyn Camps	39
Laurel Resident Camp	66
Marydale Resident Camp	82
McGaw YMCA Camp Echo	116
New Jersey 4–H Camps	148
Sanborn Western Camps	56
Santa Catalina School Summer Camp	42
Sky Acres Girl Scout Camp	213

Sky High Ranch 57
Thunderbird YMCA 201
United Methodist Camps 180
Wa-Klo 143
YMCA Camp Oakes 44

Camps–Learning Disabilities
Camp Algonquin 224
Camp Buckskin 120
Camp Courage 121
Camp Northwood 161
Camp Thorpe, Inc. 211

Camps–Outdoor Adventure and Travel
Actionquest Programs 70
Adirondack Woodcraft Camps 154
Alford Lake Camp, Inc. 84
American Youth Foundation–
  Camp Miniwanca 109
Camp Algonquin 224
Camp Androscoggin 84
Camp Butterworth 182
Camp Cody for Boys 138
Camp Echo Lake 157
Camp Friendship (VA) 215
Camp Golden Valley 176
Camp Good News 101
Camp Hemlocks 64
Camp Jewell YMCA 64
Camp Laurel 86
Camp Mary White 151
Camp Mishawaka for Boys/Girls 122
Camps Mondamin and Green
  Cove 177
Camp Mountain Meadows 35
Camp Netimus 190
Camp Sealth 219
Camp Sequoia 162
Camp Seven Hills 163
Camp Takajo 90
Camp Thorpe, Inc. 211
Camp Thunderbird for Boys/
  Camp Thunderbird for Girls
  (MN) 123
Camp Timberlane for Boys 226
Camp Walden 111
Camp Walt Whitman 141
Camp Washington 65
Camp Waziyatah 92
Camp Wekeela 92
Challenge Wilderness Camp 211

Channel 3 Country Camp 65
Cheley Colorado Camps 46
Clearwater Camp for Girls 228
Colorado Mountain Ranch,
  Trojan Summer Camp 48
4–H Farley Outdoor Education
  Center 106
Frost Valley YMCA Camps 167
Heart's Bend World Children's
  Center 212
Interlocken Center for
  Experiential Learning 141
Laurel Resident Camp 66
Maine Teen Camp 94
Marydale Resident Camp 82
McGaw YMCA Camp Echo 116
Menogyn–YMCA Wilderness
  Adventures 125
New Jersey 4–H Camps 148
Noark Girl Scout Camp 33
Philmont Scout Ranch 152
Sanborn Western Camps 56
Shaver's Creek Environmental
  Center, Pennsylvania State
  University 198
Sky Acres Girl Scout Camp 213
Tejas Girl Scout Council Camps 207
Thunderbird YMCA 201
The Timbers Girl Scout Camp 119
The Whiteman Colorado Camps 60
Widjiwagan–YMCA Wilderness
  Adventures 127
Wildlife Camps 26
YMCA Camp Cheerio 181
YMCA Camp Chingachgook 174
YMCA Camp Oakes 44
YMCA Camp Seymoor 222

Camps–Performing and Fine Arts
Appel Farm Arts and Music
  Center 144
Belvoir Terrace 99
Brush Ranch Camps for Girls
  and Boys 150
Buck's Rock Camp 156
Camps Airy and Louise 96
Camp Baco for Boys/Camp
  Che–Na–Wah for Girls 157
Camp Butterworth 182
Camp Echo Lake 157
Camp Emerson 100

Camp Laurel	86
Camp Mountain Meadows	35
Camp Netimus	190
Camp Pinecliffe	88
Camp Rim Rock	222
Camp Sequoia	162
Camp Seven Hills	163
Camp Thorpe, Inc.	211
Camp Vacamas	146
Camp Walden	111
Camp Waziyatah	92
Camp Wekeela	92
Dudley Gallahue Valley Camps	79
The Ensemble Theatre Community School	192
4-H Farley Outdoor Education Center	106
Heart's Bend World Children's Center	212
Hidden Valley Camp (ME)	93
Idyllwild School of Music and the Arts	38
Interlocken Center for Experiential Learning	141
Laurel Resident Camp	66
Maine Teen Camp	94
Sanborn Western Camps	56
Santa Catalina School Summer Camp	42
Sky Acres Girl Scout Camp	213
Stagedoor Manor Theatre Camp	172
Tejas Girl Scout Council Camps	207
Wa-Klo	143

Camps–Physical Disabilities

Bay Cliff Health Camp	109
Beacon Lodge Camp for the Blind	186
Camp Courage	121
Camp Hemlocks	64
Camp Merry Heart/Easter Seals	145
Camp Thorpe, Inc.	211
Peacock Camp for Crippled Children	77
Rocky Mountain Village–Home of the Easter Seal Handicamp	55
Shady Oaks Cerebral Palsy Camp	78
United Cerebral Palsy Association of Greater Hartford	68

Camps–Religious

American Youth Foundation– Camp Miniwanca	109
Camp Good News	101
Camp Interlaken JCC	224
Camp JCA Sholom	33
Camp of the Woods	161
Camp Sancta Maria	110
Camp Washington	65
Cross Bar X Youth Ranch	48
Fellowship Deaconry, Inc. (Day Camp Sunshine and Fellowship Conference Center)	147
The Firs Conference Center and Day Camp	220
Harmony Heart Camp	193
Manidokan Outdoor Ministry Center	97
Salvation Army Wonderland Camp and Conference Center	229
Sky Mountain Christian Camp	43
Surprise Lake Camp	173
Thunderbird YMCA	201
United Methodist Camps	180
West River United Methodist Center	98

Camps–Special Needs

Beacon Lodge Camp for the Blind	186
Camp Buckskin	120
Camp Courage	121
Camp Hemlocks	64
Camp Loyaltown–AHRC	159
Camp Merry Heart/Easter Seals	145
Camp Nejeda	145
Camp Thorpe, Inc.	211
Channel 3 Country Camp	65
Elliott P. Joslin Camp	105
Frost Valley YMCA Camps	167
Pennsylvania Easter Seal Society	196
United Methodist Camps	180

Camps–Sports

Actionquest Programs	70
Alford Lake Camp, Inc.	84
American Youth Foundation– Camp Miniwanca	109
Belvoir Terrace	99
Brookwood Camps	155
Buck's Rock Camp	156

Camp Akiba   188
Camp Androscoggin   84
Camp Baco for Boys/Camp
   Che–Na–Wah for Girls   157
Camp Berachah   218
Camp Cayuga   189
Camp Cody for Boys   138
Camp Echo Lake   157
Camp Emerson   100
Camp Golden Valley   176
Camp Good News   101
Camp Laurel   86
Camp Mary White   151
Camp Matoaka for Girls   87
Camp Mishawaka for Boys/Girls   122
Camp Netimus   190
Camp Nock–A–Mixon   191
Camp Pinecliffe   88
Camp Sancta Maria   110
Camp Sequoia   162
Camp Skylemar   89
Camp Susquehannock for Girls   191
Camp Takajo   90
Camp Thorpe, Inc.   211
Camp Thunderbird for Boys/
   Camp Thunderbird for Girls
   (MN)   123
Camp Timberlane for Boys   226
Camp Walden   111
Camp Walt Whitman   141
Camp Waziyatah   92
Camp Wekeela   92
Clearwater Camp for Girls   228
Crane Lake Camp   104
The Firs Conference Center and
   Day Camp   220
4–H Farley Outdoor Education
   Center   106
Heart's Bend World Children's
   Center   212
Interlocken Center for
   Experiential Learning   141
Kutsher's Sports Academy   169
Laurel Resident Camp   66
Maine Teen Camp   94
McGaw YMCA Camp Echo   116
Offense-Defense Football Camp
   (CA)   41
Offense-Defense Football Camp
   (NY)   171
Offense-Defense Tennis Camp   107

Peconic Dunes Camp   172
Sanborn Western Camps   56
Santa Catalina School Summer
   Camp   42
Sky Acres Girl Scout Camp   213
Tejas Girl Scout Council Camps   207
Thunderbird YMCA   201
Vanderbilt YMCA of Greater
   New York   174
Wa-Klo   143
Wild Goose...for Boys   95
YMCA Camp Chingachgook   174
YMCA Camp Letts   99

Camps–Visual Impairments

Beacon Lodge Camp for the
   Blind   186
Camp Hemlocks   64
Camp Sealth   219
Camp Thorpe, Inc.   211
Foundation for the Junior Blind   36

Conference Centers

American Youth Foundation–
   Camp Miniwanca   109
Aspen Lodge Ranch Resort   45
Bryn Mawr Camp   187
Camp Berachah   218
Camp Hemlocks   64
Camp of the Woods   161
Camp Washington   65
Cheley Colorado Camps   46
Fellowship Deaconry, Inc. (Day
   Camp Sunshine and Fellowship
   Conference Center)   147
The Firs Conference Center and
   Day Camp   220
Glorieta Baptist Conference
   Center   151
Holiday Inn Resort and
   Conference Center of Estes
   Park   51
Ocean Reef Club   72
Philmont Scout Ranch   152
Rockywold–Deephaven Camps
   Inc. (RDC)   142
Salvation Army Wonderland
   Camp and Conference Center   229
Sky Mountain Christian Camp   43
Thunderbird YMCA   201
YMCA Blue Ridge Assembly   181

YMCA of the Rockies, Estes
  Park Center   61
YMCA of the Rockies, Snow
  Mountain Ranch   62

**Conservation and Environmental
Programs**
Adirondack Woodcraft Camps   154
Camp Jewell YMCA   64
Channel 3 Country Camp   65
College Settlement of
  Philadelphia   192
4–H Farley Outdoor Education
  Center   106
Philmont Scout Ranch   152
Rockywold–Deephaven Camps
  Inc. (RDC)   142
Shaver's Creek Environmental
  Center, Pennsylvania State
  University   198
Somerset County Park
  Commission Environmental
  Education Center   149
Thunderbird YMCA   201
Widjiwagan–YMCA Wilderness
  Adventures   127
Wildlife Camps   26

Expeditions, Guide Trips, and Tours
*(Includes guided tours, hiking, canoe
trips, white water rafting, and outdoor
adventure.)*
American & Pacific Tours, Inc.
  (A&P)   29
Camp Jewell YMCA   64
Cherokee Adventures Whitewater
  Rafting   204
Interlocken Center for
  Experiential Learning   141
Menogyn–YMCA Wilderness
  Adventures   125
Philmont Scout Ranch   152
Rolling Thunder River Co.   179
Tikchik Narrows Lodge   31
YMCA Camp Cheerio   181

Government Agencies and Departments
National Park Service (AL)   29
National Park Service (AK)   30
National Park Service (AZ)   32
National Park Service (AR)   32

National Park Service (CA)   41
National Park Service (CO)   53
National Park Service (DC)   69
National Park Service (FL)   72
National Park Service (GA)   74
National Park Service (HI)   75
National Park Service (ID)   75
National Park Service (IL)   77
National Park Service (IN)   80
National Park Service (IA)   81
National Park Service (KS)   81
National Park Service (KY)   81
National Park Service (KY)   82
National Park Service (ME)   95
National Park Service (MD)   98
National Park Service (MA)   107
National Park Service (MI)   117
National Park Service (MN)   126
National Park Service (MS)   129
National Park Service (MO)   129
National Park Service (MT)   132
National Park Service (NE)   136
National Park Service (NV)   136
National Park Service (NH)   142
National Park Service (NJ)   148
National Park Service (NM)   152
National Park Service (NY)   170
National Park Service (NC)   178
National Park Service (ND)   182
National Park Service (OH)   184
National Park Service (OK)   185
National Park Service (OR)   185
National Park Service (PA)   194
National Park Service (RI)   199
National Park Service (SC)   201
National Park Service (SD)   203
National Park Service (TN)   205
National Park Service (TX)   207
National Park Service (UT)   208
National Park Service (VA)   217
National Park Service (WA)   221
National Park Service (WV)   223
National Park Service (WI)   228
National Park Service (WY)   234
Pennsylvania Department of
  Transportation   195
City of Wildwood   150

Hotels and Motels *(Also see **Resorts**)*
Alpenhof Lodge   232
Ballard's Inn   199

The Balsams Grand Resort Hotel 136
Bristol Bay Lodge 30
Furnace Creek Inn and Ranch 37
Hatchet Motel and Restaurant 233
Hopp–Inn Guest House 71
Imperial Hotel 52
Mt. Rainier Guest Services 220
North Hero House 213
Stage Coach Inn 134
Yosemite Park & Curry Co. 45

Ranches *(Includes working dude ranches and resort ranches.)*
Aspen Lodge Ranch Resort 45
Bar Lazy J Guest Ranch 46
Bill Cody's Ranch Resort 233
Double JJ Resort Ranch 114
Drowsy Water Ranch 49
Elk Mountain Ranch 49
El Rancho Stevens 115
The Home Ranch 52
Hunewill Guest Ranch 37
Jameson Ranch Camp 39
Klick's K Bar L Ranch 131
Lazy K Bar Ranch 132
Longs Peak Inn Guest Ranch 53
North Fork Guest Ranch 54
Peaceful Valley Lodge and
   Ranch Resort 54
Rafter Y Ranch 234
63 Ranch 133
Sweet Grass Ranch 134
Tumbling River Ranch 58
Wilderness Trails Ranch 60

Resorts *(Also see **State and National Parks** and **Ranches**.)*
Absaroka Mountain Lodge 231
Alaskan Wilderness Outfitting
   Company, Inc. 29
Antonio's Resort 155
Aspen Lodge Ranch Resort 45
The Balsams Grand Resort Hotel 136
Big Sky of Montana Ski and
   Summer Resort 129
Bill Cody's Ranch Resort 233
Boyd's Mason Lake Resort 223
Custer State Park Resort
   Company 202
Double JJ Resort Ranch 114
Driftwood On The Ocean 166

El Rancho Stevens 115
Emandal–A Farm on A River 36
Fripp Island Club 200
Furnace Creek Inn and Ranch 37
Golden Acres Farm and Ranch
   Resort 168
Grand View Lodge Golf and
   Tennis Club 125
Harmel's Ranch Resort 51
Holiday Inn Resort and
   Conference Center of Estes
   Park 51
Idlease Great Resort 93
Klick's K Bar L Ranch 131
Lawrence Welk Resort 40
Longs Peak Inn Guest Ranch 53
Michillinda Beach Lodge 117
Nelson's Resort 126
Ocean Reef Club 72
Palmer Gulch Lodge/Mt.
   Rushmore KOA 203
Peaceful Valley Lodge and
   Ranch Resort 54
Rainbow King Lodge 31
Redfish Lake Lodge 75
Rockywold–Deephaven Camps
   Inc. (RDC) 142
Rosario Resort 221
Rubin's Osceola Lake Inn 180
St. Mary Lodge & Resort 133
Scanticon Denver 57
Sunny Brook Farm Resort 118
Sunrise Resort 67
Togwotee Mountain Lodge 236
Vail Associates, Inc. 58
Village at Breckenridge Resort 59
Woodside Ranch Resort 231
YMCA of the Rockies, Estes
   Park Center 61

Restaurants *(Includes food service and concessions. Also see **Camps, Hotels and Motels, Ranches, Resorts, State and National Parks,** and **Theme and Amusement Parks/Attractions**.)*
Ballard's Inn 199
Coffee Bar Cafe 47
Hamilton Stores, Inc. 131
Hatchet Motel and Restaurant 233
Klick's K Bar L Ranch 131
Pancake Chef Restaurant 118

Ruby House Restaurant 204
Yosemite Park & Curry Co. 45

State and National Parks
*(Commercially operated visitor services
in State and National Parks including
resorts, restaurants, concessions,
transportation, etc. Also see entries for
the National Park Service in
Government Agencies and
Departments.)*
Acadia Corporation 83
Crater Lake Lodge Company 185
Georgia State Parks and Historic
  Sites 73
Glacier Park, Inc. 130
Grand Canyon National Park
  Lodges 32
Granite Park and Sperry Chalets 130
Rocky Mountain Park Company
  (The Trail Ridge Store) 55
St. Mary Lodge & Resort 133
Signal Mountain Lodge 235
Yellowstone Park Service
  Stations (MT) 135
Yellowstone Park Service
  Stations (WY) 236
Yosemite Park & Curry Co. 45

Summer Schools *(Academic and
general activity programs. Also see
Camps–Academic.)*
Belvoir Terrace 99
The Ensemble Theatre
  Community School 192
Focus Educational Programs 25

Idyllwild School of Music and
  the Arts 38
St. Margaret's School 217

Theaters/Summer Theaters *(Includes
acting and technical/auxillary staff
opportunities.)*
College Light Opera Company 104
Cortland Repertory Theatre, Inc. 165
The Ensemble Theatre
  Community School 192
Los Angeles Designers' Theatre 40
Mount Holyoke College Summer
  Theatre 106
Music Theatre North 170
Straw Hat Auditions 25
Three Rivers Shakespeare
  Festival 198
Westport Country Playhouse 68
Williamstown Theater Festival 108

**Theme and Amusement Parks/
Attractions** *(Includes local historic sites
and attractions.)*
AstroWorld/WaterWorld 206
Geauga Lake 184
The Great Gorge Resort/Action
  Park 147
Hersheypark 193
Rocky Point Amusements, Inc. 200
Santa Cruz Seaside Company/
  Santa Cruz Beach Boardwalk 42
Sea World of Florida 72
Valleyfair Family Amusement
  Park 127
Whiting's Foods 44

Employer Index

Absaroka Mountain Lodge 231
Acadia Corporation 83
Actionquest Programs 70
Adirondack Woodcraft Camps 154
Alaskan Wilderness Outfitting
    Company, Inc. 29
Alford Lake Camp, Inc. 84
Aloha Camps 209
Alpenhof Lodge 232
American & Pacific Tours, Inc.
    (A&P) 29
American Camping Association 154
American Camping Association/
    New Jersey Section 144
American Youth Foundation–
    Camp Miniwanca 109
Antonio's Resort 155
Appel Farm Arts and Music
    Center 144
Aspen Lodge Ranch Resort 45
AstroWorld/WaterWorld 206
Awosting and Chinqueka Camps 63
Ballard's Inn 199
The Balsams Grand Resort Hotel 136
Bar Lazy J Guest Ranch 46
Bay Cliff Health Camp 109
Beacon Lodge Camp for the
    Blind 186
Belvoir Terrace 99
Big Sky of Montana Ski and
    Summer Resort 129
Bill Cody's Ranch Resort 233
Blue Bell Ice Cream Inc. 119
Bonnie Castle Riding Camp 100
Boyd's Mason Lake Resort 223
Bristol Bay Lodge 30
Brookwood Camps 155
Brush Ranch Camps for Girls
    and Boys 150
Bryn Mawr Camp 187
Buck's Rock Camp 156
Camps Airy and Louise 96
Camp Akiba 188
Camp Albany 137
Camp Algonquin 224
Camp Androscoggin 84
Camp Arcadia 85

Camp Baco for Boys/Camp
    Che–Na–Wah for Girls 157
Camp Berachah 218
Camp Buckskin 120
Camp Butterworth 182
Camp Cayuga 189
Camp Cody for Boys 138
Camp Courage 121
Camp Echo Lake 157
Camp Emerson 100
Camp Farnsworth 209
Camp Friendship (MN) 121
Camp Friendship (VA) 215
Camp Golden Valley 176
Camp Good News 101
Camp Hantesa 80
Camp Hemlocks 64
Camp Henry Kaufmann 158
Camp Interlaken JCC 224
Camp JCA Sholom 33
Camp Jeanne D'Arc 159
Camp Jewell YMCA 64
Camp Kanata 176
Camp Kenwood–Evergreen 138
Camp Lakota 34
Camp Laurel 86
Camp Low 73
Camp Loyaltown–AHRC 159
Camp Lucerne 225
Camp Mary White 151
Camp Matoaka for Girls 87
Camp Mawavi 215
Camp Medill McCormick 76
Camp Merrimac 139
Camp Merry Heart/Easter Seals 145
Camp Mishawaka for Boys/Girls 122
Camp Mogisca 160
Camp Mokuleia 74
Camps Mondamin and Green
    Cove 177
Camp Mountain Meadows 35
Camp Nashoba North 87
Camp Nebagamon for Boys 226
Camp Nejeda 145
Camp Netimus 190
Camp Nock–A–Mixon 191
Camp Northwood 161
Camp Nor'Wester 218

Camp of the Woods	161
Camp Pembroke	102
Camp Pinecliffe	88
Camp Rim Rock	222
Camp Runoia	89
Camp Sancta Maria	110
Camp Scherman	35
Camp Sealth	219
Camp Sequoia	162
Camp Seven Hills	163
Camp Sherwood	111
Camp Skylemar	89
Camp Stewart for Boys	206
Camp Stonybrook	183
Camp Susquehannock for Girls	191
Camp Takajo	90
Camp Tapawingo (IL)	76
Camp Tapawingo (ME)	91
Camp Tel Noar	140
Camp Tevya	140
Camp Thoreau-In-Vermont	210
Camp Thorpe, Inc.	211
Camp Thunderbird (FL)	70
Camp Thunderbird for Boys/ Camp Thunderbird for Girls (MN)	123
Camp Timberlane for Boys	226
Camp Vacamas	146
Camp Walden	111
Camp Walt Whitman	141
Camp Wapi-Kamigi	78
Camp Washington	65
Camp Watitoh	102
Camp Waziyatah	92
Camp Wekeela	92
Camp Windego	227
Cape Cod Sea Camps	103
Carousel Day School	164
Cedar Lodge	112
Central New York Girl Scout Camp Near Wilderness	164
Challenge Wilderness Camp	211
Channel 3 Country Camp	65
Cheley Colorado Camps	46
Cherokee Adventures Whitewater Rafting	204
Chesapeake Bay Girl Scout Council	69
Circle Pines	113
Clearwater Camp for Girls	228
Coffee Bar Cafe	47
College Light Opera Company	104
College Settlement of Philadelphia	192
Colorado Mountain Ranch, Trojan Summer Camp	48
Cortland Repertory Theatre, Inc.	165
Crane Lake Camp	104
Crater Lake Lodge Company	185
Cross Bar X Youth Ranch	48
Crystalaire Camp	113
Custer State Park Resort Company	202
Double JJ Resort Ranch	114
Driftwood On The Ocean	166
Drowsy Water Ranch	49
Dudley Gallahue Valley Camps	79
Durham Temporaries, Inc.	166
Eden Wood Camping and Retreat Center	124
Elk Mountain Ranch	49
Elks Camp Barrett	97
Elliott P. Joslin Camp	105
El Rancho Stevens	115
Emandal–A Farm on A River	36
The Ensemble Theatre Community School	192
Falling Creek Camp for Boys	178
Fellowship Deaconry, Inc. (Day Camp Sunshine and Fellowship Conference Center)	147
The Firs Conference Center and Day Camp	220
Flying G Ranch, Tomahawk Ranch	50
Focus Educational Programs	25
Foundation for the Junior Blind	36
4–H Farley Outdoor Education Center	106
The Fresh Air Fund	167
Fripp Island Club	200
Frost Valley YMCA Camps	167
Furnace Creek Inn and Ranch	37
Geauga Lake	184
Georgia State Parks and Historic Sites	73
Girl Scout Camp Sycamore Hills	205
Glacier Park, Inc.	130
Glorieta Baptist Conference Center	151
Golden Acres Farm and Ranch Resort	168

Grand Canyon National Park Lodges	32
Grand View Lodge Golf and Tennis Club	125
Granite Park and Sperry Chalets	130
The Great Gorge Resort/Action Park	147
Hamilton Stores, Inc.	131
Harmel's Ranch Resort	51
Harmony Heart Camp	193
Hatchet Motel and Restaurant	233
Heart's Bend World Children's Center	212
Hersheypark	193
Hidden Valley Camp (ME)	93
Hidden Valley Camp (PA)	194
Holiday Inn Resort and Conference Center of Estes Park	51
The Home Ranch	52
Hopp–Inn Guest House	71
Hunewill Guest Ranch	37
Idlease Great Resort	93
Idyllwild School of Music and the Arts	38
Imperial Hotel	52
Interlocken Center for Experiential Learning	141
Jameson Ranch Camp	39
Kennolyn Camps	39
Klick's K Bar L Ranch	131
Kutsher's Sports Academy	169
Lake of the Woods and Greenwoods Camps	115
Laurel Resident Camp	66
Lawrence Welk Resort	40
Lazy K Bar Ranch	132
Legacy International's Summer Program	216
Longs Peak Inn Guest Ranch	53
Los Angeles Designers' Theatre	40
Maine Teen Camp	94
Manidokan Outdoor Ministry Center	97
Marydale Resident Camp	82
McGaw YMCA Camp Echo	116
Menogyn–YMCA Wilderness Adventures	125
Michillinda Beach Lodge	117
Mount Holyoke College Summer Theatre	106
Mt. Rainier Guest Services	220
Music Theatre North	170
National Park Service (AL)	29
National Park Service (AK)	30
National Park Service (AZ)	32
National Park Service (AR)	32
National Park Service (CA)	41
National Park Service (CO)	53
National Park Service (DC)	69
National Park Service (FL)	72
National Park Service (GA)	74
National Park Service (HI)	75
National Park Service (ID)	75
National Park Service (IL)	77
National Park Service (IN)	80
National Park Service (IA)	81
National Park Service (KS)	81
National Park Service (KY)	81
National Park Service (KY)	82
National Park Service (ME)	95
National Park Service (MD)	98
National Park Service (MA)	107
National Park Service (MI)	117
National Park Service (MN)	126
National Park Service (MS)	129
National Park Service (MO)	129
National Park Service (MT)	132
National Park Service (NE)	136
National Park Service (NV)	136
National Park Service (NH)	142
National Park Service (NJ)	148
National Park Service (NM)	152
National Park Service (NY)	170
National Park Service (NC)	178
National Park Service (ND)	182
National Park Service (OH)	184
National Park Service (OK)	185
National Park Service (OR)	185
National Park Service (PA)	194
National Park Service (RI)	199
National Park Service (SC)	201
National Park Service (SD)	203
National Park Service (TN)	205
National Park Service (TX)	207
National Park Service (UT)	208
National Park Service (VA)	217
National Park Service (WA)	221
National Park Service (WV)	223
National Park Service (WI)	228
National Park Service (WY)	234
Nelson's Resort	126

New Jersey Camp Jaycee 195
New Jersey 4–H Camps 148
Noark Girl Scout Camp 33
North Beach Sailing/Barrier
  Island Sailing Center 179
North Fork Guest Ranch 54
North Hero House 213
North Shore Holiday House 171
Ocean Reef Club 72
Offense-Defense Football Camp
  (CA) 41
Offense-Defense Football Camp
  (NY) 171
Offense-Defense Tennis Camp 107
Palmer Gulch Lodge/Mt.
  Rushmore KOA 203
Pancake Chef Restaurant 118
Peaceful Valley Lodge and
  Ranch Resort 54
Peacock Camp for Crippled
  Children 77
Peconic Dunes Camp 172
Pennsylvania Department of
  Transportation 195
Pennsylvania Easter Seal Society 196
Philmont Scout Ranch 152
Pine Forest Camps 197
Pinemere Camp Association 197
Rafter Y Ranch 234
Rainbow King Lodge 31
Redfish Lake Lodge 75
Rocky Mountain Park Company
  (The Trail Ridge Store) 55
Rocky Mountain Village–Home
  of the Easter Seal Handicamp 55
Rocky Point Amusements, Inc. 200
Rockywold–Deephaven Camps
  Inc. (RDC) 142
Rolling Thunder River Co. 179
Rosario Resort 221
Rubin's Osceola Lake Inn 180
Ruby House Restaurant 204
St. Margaret's School 217
St. Mary Lodge & Resort 133
Salvation Army Wonderland
  Camp and Conference Center 229
Sanborn Western Camps 56
Santa Catalina School Summer
  Camp 42
Santa Cruz Seaside Company/
  Santa Cruz Beach Boardwalk 42

Scanticon Denver 57
Sea World of Florida 72
Shady Oaks Cerebral Palsy
  Camp 78
Shaver's Creek Environmental
  Center, Pennsylvania State
  University 198
Signal Mountain Lodge 235
63 Ranch 133
Sky Acres Girl Scout Camp 213
Sky High Ranch 57
Sky Mountain Christian Camp 43
Somerset County Park
  Commission Environmental
  Education Center 149
Stage Coach Inn 134
Stagedoor Manor Theatre Camp 172
Straw Hat Auditions 25
Sun Beach Service 201
Sunny Brook Farm Resort 118
Sunrise Resort 67
SuperCamp 26
Surprise Lake Camp 173
Sweet Grass Ranch 134
Tejas Girl Scout Council Camps 207
Three Rivers Shakespeare
  Festival 198
Thunderbird YMCA 201
Tikchik Narrows Lodge 31
The Timbers Girl Scout Camp 119
Tiwaushara Program Center 229
Togwotee Mountain Lodge 236
Tumbling River Ranch 58
United Cerebral Palsy
  Association of Greater
  Hartford 68
United Methodist Camps 180
Vail Associates, Inc. 58
Valleyfair Family Amusement
  Park 127
Vanderbilt YMCA of Greater
  New York 174
Village at Breckenridge Resort 59
Wa-Klo 143
Westport Country Playhouse 68
West River United Methodist
  Center 98
The Whiteman Colorado Camps 60
Whiting's Foods 44
Widjiwagan–YMCA Wilderness
  Adventures 127

Wilderness Trails Ranch	60
Wild Goose...for Boys	95
Wildlife Camps	26
City of Wildwood	150
Williamstown Theater Festival	108
Wisconsin Badger Camp	230
Woodside Ranch Resort	231
Wyonegonic Camps	95
Yellowstone Park Service Stations (MT)	135
Yellowstone Park Service Stations (WY)	236
YMCA Blue Ridge Assembly	181
YMCA Camp Cheerio	181
YMCA Camp Chingachgook	174
YMCA Camp Ihduhpi	128
YMCA Camp Letts	99
YMCA Camp Lyndon	108
YMCA Camp Oakes	44
YMCA Camp Seymoor	222
YMCA of the Rockies, Camp Chief Ouray	61
YMCA of the Rockies, Estes Park Center	61
YMCA of the Rockies, Snow Mountain Ranch	62
YMCA/YWCA Camping Services–Camps GreenKill/ McAlister/Talcott	175
Yosemite Park & Curry Co.	45
YWCA Camp Westwind	186

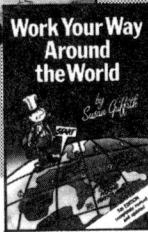

THE 90-MINUTE RESUME

Peggy Schmidt

With a new approach that teams the resume writer with a friend or family member who acts as an "interviewer," this book shows how to:

- Communicate your skills and experience effectively on paper—even if you're not a good writer
- Sell yourself as a terrific job candidate with unique skills
- Come alive on paper so you get that interview

The 90-Minute Resume turns resume writing into an enjoyable project that gets the job done and gets results.

The author: Peggy Schmidt writes "Your New Job," a weekly newspaper column, and is the author of *Making It on Your First Job* and *Making It Big in the City* (McGraw-Hill, 1984).

$5.95 paperback

INTERNSHIPS 1992

Describing over 50,000 opportunities, this is the most complete annual directory available for college students and career-changers seeking on-the-job training positions.

Thousands of college students and adults changing careers or reentering the work force turn to *Internships* every year to find temporary jobs that will open doors to full-time work. This edition lists over 50,000 positions in some two dozen career fields in:

- Communications
- Creative arts
- Human services
- International business
- Public affairs
- Science/industry

There's even a section that covers thousands of opportunities and living arrangements in Washington, D.C., America's internship hub. Features in the 1992 edition of this popular annual include:

- More internships offered in engineering, computer science, and business
- A separate section focusing on internship opportunities for minorities

- An index that allows you to identify opportunities in specific industries
- An index that helps you pinpoint internships that fit your major

Complete details on the position, desired qualifications, compensation, and whom to contact are included.

$27.95 paperback

1992 DIRECTORY OF OVERSEAS SUMMER JOBS

Over 50,000 job opportunities for summer 1992 in over 40 countries, from archaeological digs in France to teaching English in Spain to working in a Norwegian hotel. Important facts about visas, work permits, and health insurance.

$14.95 paperback

1992 DIRECTORY OF SUMMER JOBS IN BRITAIN

Over 30,000 summer positions for 1992 in the British Isles. Includes details on wages and hours, work conditions, and required qualifications.

$13.95 paperback

ADVENTURE HOLIDAYS 1992

Ballooning in England, horseback riding in Israel, and camel caravanning in Africa are just a few of the hundreds of beyond-the-ordinary vacations detailed in this book.

$12.95 paperback

WORK YOUR WAY AROUND THE WORLD

How to pay for travel expenses by finding work abroad, from ski instructor to prawn fisherman to sheep shearer. Profiles of countries include job opportunities, local customs, and regulations.

$16.95 paperback